Roots of Rebellion

Roots of Rebellion

The Evolution of Black Politics
and Protest Since World War II

edited by
Richard P. Young
Stanford University

Harper & Row, Publishers
New York, Evanston, and London

Cover photograph: Michel Craig

301. 451
4 75 λ

To Nancy and Tommy, and John Maurer

Contents

This book has grown out of a number of black studies courses which I have taught in the past few years. In class discussions, I learned that many of my students, particularly those who were white, had little comprehension of the underlying reasons for contemporary black militancy. This was partly the result of their lack of knowledge of the massive social changes of the past generation which led to the black urban rebellions of the 1960s and the present appeal of ideologies of black revolution. In response to what was considered a real need, this book of readings was organized to give the student, or the general reader, a broad view of the factors responsible for the growth of black frustration and militancy since World War II.

The selections in this reader trace the development of black protest from the 1940s, when Jim Crow practices were the rule even in the North and most Negroes played roles of accommodation, to the present period of black pride and rebellion against the status quo. The writings of sociologists, political scientists, psychologists, and psychiatrists, black and white, have been included to explain this development. However, the perspective of this reader is not exclusively that of the social sciences. The writings and speeches of leading figures of both the "Negro Revolution" and the contemporary black revolutionary movement have been included to provide a balance between the views of those who observe social phenomena and those who are political actors.

While the prime purpose of this reader is the explanation of the growth of black radicalism during the past generation, the readings also serve a number of other functions: Part One outlines recent changes in white attitudes and behavior toward black Americans; Part Two provides a socio-

economic profile of black America; Part Three explains the development of black pride; and Parts Four and Five trace the development of conventional black politics and protest since World War II. The assumption underlying this reader is that only by understanding the broad currents of change in American race relations since World War II can one begin to understand contemporary black militancy.

Many people have helped me with this book. I wish particularly to thank Maryann Kofoed and Lee Nourse for their editorial assistance; Brenda McLean, Lois Renner, and Elizabeth Rafferty for their help with the typing; and finally, my editor, Walter Lippincott, and Madeline Anderson, for their patience and assistance.

Richard Young

On July 2, 1964, when the most comprehensive civil rights legislation passed in this century was signed into law by President Lyndon Johnson, it seemed to many observers that the nation had finally entered a more just, and probably more serene, era of race relations. Although riots broke out in Harlem two weeks after the signing of the 1964 Civil Rights Act, the belief persisted that the basic problems of Negro Americans had been confronted and were on their way to solution. This optimism was dampened by riots in other northern cities that summer and by the Republican nomination of a candidate for the presidency who had opposed the civil rights bill. Nevertheless, Johnson's triumphant victory in the fall seemed to mean, in respect to racial policies, that the nation had a President with strong public and Congressional support who was prepared to attack the broad problems facing black Americans. The President's War on Poverty had nothing less than the total elimination of American poverty as its goal, and his civil rights programs were equally ambitious. When the Voting Rights Act of 1965 was signed into law on August 6, President Johnson stated that the act would "strike away the last major shackle" of the Negro's "ancient bonds." But one week later Watts was in flames, and the course of race relations for the rest of the decade became apparent.

Since Watts, the nation has not only witnessed summers of civil disorder, but it has seen the development of black power ideologies, the radicalization of black college students, and the formal organization of local black revolutionary groups. Arguments that blacks have been reacting to intolerable economic conditions and constant humiliation have not led to massive public and private programs to remedy these social ills. Instead, in growing numbers,

white Americans have demanded "law and order," and in the elections of 1968 and 1969 they gave strong support to candidates who
pledged that they would greet civil turmoil with firmness. This reaction was not simply an expression of white racism. While it is true
that many whites are either overtly racist or are completely indifferent to the problems of black people, a large number of white Americans oppose racial discrimination. What has happened in recent
years is that a sizable number of reasonably liberal whites have
become convinced that black gains have led to rising expectations
which have in turn created insatiable demands for power and
wealth. With some reluctance, these people have decided that
firmness is necessary to preserve civil order and that Afro-Ameri-
cans must learn that progress in America is incremental and can
only occur through conventional political channels. A majority of
whites appear to believe that massive public expenditures on anti-
poverty programs will only reward black militancy and encourage
blacks to riot and make unreasonable demands.

　　　This hostility to contemporary black protest stems, in part,
from white ignorance of both the realities of black history and the
true nature of black advances in recent years. Current black radicalism becomes more understandable once two central facts of
Afro-American history are grasped. The first is that black unrest
is not new; during most of our nation's past, black violence was
contained only through systems of ruthless repression. The second
fact is that current black protest is not the result of black gains,
but is instead an expression of anger over the fact that despite a
generation of symbolic advances, virtually no progress has been
made toward the elimination of black poverty or powerlessness.
Both of these points require some elaboration.

I.

　　　It would clearly be beyond the scope of an introductory
essay to review systematically the history of white oppression of
blacks in America; to tell that story would be to write the history
of the Afro-American. Nevertheless, a few general remarks must
be made about the history of American race relations for the current racial crisis to be understood. One element of this history
which must be stressed is that until recently the United States was
an overtly racist society.[1] In other words, at least until the 1940s,

　　　[1] For a recent review of a number of historical studies of American racism, see C. Vann Woodward, "White Racism and Black 'Emancipation,'" *The New York Review of Books,* 12, no. 4 (February 27, 1969), pp.

the bulk of white Americans and their leaders regarded Negroes as racially inferior. Even the great debate over slavery which preceded the Civil War took place in the context of white racism. Opposition to the spread of slavery was fed more by northern fears of competition from slave labor and the presence of blacks in the North and West than any moral concern for the welfare of black slaves. Those whites who did profess to oppose slavery on moral grounds rarely accepted the principle of racial equality. Much abolitionist sentiment reflected paternalistic concern for a "child-like" race rather than indignation over the treatment of fellow men. In a speech in Charleston, Illinois, in 1858, Abraham Lincoln, who was no abolitionist, made it clear that opposition to slavery in the federal territories did not mean the acceptance of blacks as equals:

> I will say, then, that I am not, nor ever have been,
> in favor of bringing about in any way the social
> and political equality of the white and black races:
> that I am not, nor ever have been, in favor of
> making voters or jurors of negroes, nor of qualifying
> them to hold office, nor to intermarry with white
> people. . . .
> And inasmuch as they cannot so live, while they
> do remain together there must be the position of
> superior and inferior, and I as much as any other
> man am in favor of having the superior position
> assigned to the white race.[2]

Until recently, the relationship of "superior and inferior" described by Lincoln was maintained by two social institutions, slavery and Jim Crow. Slavery was abolished by the events of the Civil War, but a caste system remained which hardened by the late nineteenth century into a rigid system of oppression known as Jim Crow. Slavery and Jim Crow were not merely means by which blacks were exploited. They were also systems of social control and socialization. This point is of extreme importance, because it means that during the period of more than three centuries when black labor was ruthlessly exploited by white Americans, social institutions existed which prevented the outbreak of

5–11. Also of relevance are Thomas F. Gosset, *Race: The History of an Idea in America,* Dallas: Southern Methodist University Press, 1963; and I. A. Newby, *Jim Crow's Defense: Anti-Negro Thought in America, 1900–1930,* Baton Rouge: Louisiana State University Press, 1965.

[2] Quoted in Richard Hofstadter, *The American Political Tradition,* Vintage edition, New York: Knopf, 1948, p. 116.

black violence on a large scale and conditioned black people to acquiesce in their own subjugation. The existence of these institutions could only be justified by racist thought in a nation which called itself a democracy.

During the slavery period, slave insurrections were prevented by the denial of all rights to slaves and the constant policing of their activities. As one southern planter wrote, "Slavery and Tyranny must go together and there is no such thing as having an obedient and useful Slave, without the painful exercise of undue and tyrannical authority."[3] Whippings, mutilations, and hangings were accepted managerial practices in the southern economy. As Stanley Elkins has poignantly shown, this treatment prevented the development of the slave's individual autonomy and kept him in a state of complete dependence on his master.[4] The maintenance of this dependency required the debasement of the slave. A North Carolina judge aptly described the nature of this system of social control in an 1852 decision:

> *What acts in a slave towards a white person will amount to insolence, it is manifestly impossible to define—it may consist in a look, the pointing of a finger, a refusal or neglect to step out of the way when a white person is seen to approach. But each of such acts violates the rules of propriety, and if tolerated, would destroy the subordination, upon which our social system rests.*[5]

Most slaves were denied any education or responsibility. Bred like animals, forced to live in squalor, and denied even basic family rights, slaves seemed to verify their masters' belief that Negroes were unfit for freedom. Slave owners complained of the laziness and stupidity of their bondsmen. Yet if planters allowed their slaves the education and freedom required for labors more intellectually demanding than field work, they faced the threat of insurrection. The actions of Nat Turner, Denmark Vesey, and the countless other blacks who took part in slave revolts demonstrated that, in truth, black men were not inherently passive.[6] The black

[3] Quoted in Kenneth M. Stampp, *The Peculiar Institution: Slavery in the Ante-Bellum South,* Vintage edition, New York: Knopf, 1956, p. 141.

[4] *Slavery: A Problem in American Institutional and Intellectual Life,* Chicago: University of Chicago Press, 1959.

[5] Quoted in Herbert Aptheker, *Essays in the History of the American Negro,* New York: International, 1964, p. 14.

[6] Herbert Aptheker, *American Negro Slave Revolts,* New York: Columbia University Press, 1943.

man acquiesced in his own subjugation only as long as he remained under absolute physical and psychological control.

The effects of slavery were only slightly mitigated by the federal measures which were taken after the Civil War on behalf of southern freedmen. Reconstruction was a short-lived and totally inadequate attempt by the victorious North to prepare the liberated slaves for first-class citizenship.[7] Although postwar policies protected black voting and civil rights, the federal government failed to launch a comprehensive program of economic and educational aid to the freedmen. Lacking even rudimentary education and having no land, most blacks soon returned to a state of economic dependence on the same planters who had held them in bondage a few years earlier. Given the fact that northern whites had never viewed Negroes as their equals, it is not surprising that federal protection of black civil rights ended within a dozen years of the North's victory. In 1877, the disputed presidential election of the previous year was finally resolved by an involved compromise which, among other things, ended federal tampering with white southern "home rule" in return for southern acceptance of the election of the Republican candidate, Rutherford B. Hayes.

In the decades which followed, southern white supremacy was restored. Soon after the reestablishment of home rule, laws were passed which required racial segregation in schools and public places and prohibited interracial marriages. This pattern of rigid segregation which was erected in the late nineteenth century was designed as much to keep Negroes "in their place" as to separate the races physically. Jim Crow encompassed far more than the social relations between the two races. It also meant the denial of political and legal rights to black people. From 1890 to 1910, blacks were barred from voting in every southern state by means of state constitutional amendments.[8] This assertion of white supremacy was not confined to conventional political channels; blacks who opposed Jim Crow were subjected to beatings, burnings, and lynchings. During the transitional period of the 1890s, hundreds of Negroes were lynched. Lynchings were public, almost festive occasions, which "taught" black people that challenging white power meant possible death.

The perpetuation of Jim Crow required that blacks be kept submissive and ignorant. As Ray Stannard Baker observed in the first decade of this century, white southerners wanted "Negroes

[7] See John Hope Franklin, *Reconstruction after the Civil War*, Chicago: University of Chicago Press, 1961.

[8] C. Vann Woodward, *The Strange Career of Jim Crow*, second revised edition, New York: Oxford, 1966.

who are really inferior and who *feel* inferior."[9] Like slavery, Jim
Crow socialized black people into accepting their inferior status.
Facing constant humiliation and powerlessness, it is not surprising
that blacks often viewed themselves as inferior to whites. Thus, to
a large degree, the role of accommodation was internalized. During the
first half of the twentieth century, only intermittent violence was
needed to maintain white supremacy. This pattern of black accommodation to white power existed in the South until the 1950s. It
was perhaps best described by John Dollard in his study, *Caste
and Class in a Southern Town:*

> *Accommodation involves the renunciation of pro-
> test or aggression against undesirable conditions
> of life and the organization of the character so
> that protest does not appear, but acceptance does.
> It may come to pass in the end that the unwelcome
> force is idealized, that one identifies with it and
> takes it into the personality; it sometimes even
> happens that what is at first resented and feared
> is finally loved. In this case a unique alteration of
> the character occurs in the direction of masochism.
> Each Negro as he is added to the group must learn
> to accommodate himself to the caste situation,
> regardless of whether he lives in the South or the
> North. He must renounce the theoretical equality
> of opportunity and accept the actual social situation
> as it is defined by the regional culture. He must
> learn to devalue his personal physical character-
> istics; he must "remember his place." If resentment
> is produced by these renunciations, it must be
> squelched and the facade, at least, of a smooth
> acceptance must appear in its place.[10]*

As Dollard suggested, black accommodation was the rule
in the North as well as in the South, at least until World War II.
Black people were barred from many northern public places and
were socially segregated; theories of Negro inferiority were part
of the conventional wisdom on both sides of the Mason-Dixon
line. For example, in a study of Chicago Negroes published in
1941, W. Lloyd Warner and his associates found that

[9] *Following the Color Line,* Torchbook edition, New York: Harper
& Row, 1964, p. 241.
[10] Anchor edition, Garden City: Doubleday, 1957, p. 255.

> *. . . the Chicago system of race relations is*
> *becoming more like that of the Deep South.*
> *Although the position of the Negro is certainly*
> *different in Chicago from that below the Mason-*
> *Dixon line, a study of the city's entire community*
> *life, including the white world, indicates that if*
> *caste . . . is not present in Chicago, then something*
> *very close to it definitely is. The situation must be*
> *described as at least a castelike system.*[11]

On the eve of American entry into World War II, black Americans were imprisoned in a rigid caste system. Blacks could migrate north of the Mason-Dixon line, but they could not escape racist stereotypes personified by entertainers like Amos 'n Andy and Stepin Fetchit, nor could their children escape schools which eulogized the achievements of the Anglo-Saxon race. Even in the "free" North, Negroes were marked by the effects of a racist culture. Many blacks internalized white values and covertly regarded themselves as objects of loathing. As two psychiatrists concluded after an extensive study of Negro personality in the 1940s, "identification with the white oppressor has been the bane of Negro cohesion from the very beginning of slavery, when it took the form of pride in being a house slave, rather than a field slave. This sop of an illusory identification with the master did incalculable harm to Negro cohesion, because it formed one base for class distinction between Negroes."[12] As a result of black identification with the white man, black anger was directed against other blacks rather than whites.

II.

Since World War II, black people, in growing numbers, have rejected the role of accommodation and have protested against the inequalities of socioeconomic conditions which exist between the two races. In recent years, thousands of blacks have taken part in outright rebellions against the status quo, and an ideology of black revolution has found many adherents in America's urban

[11] W. Lloyd Warner, Buford H. Junker, and Walter A. Adams, *Color and Human Nature: Negro Personality Development in a Northern City*, Washington: American Council on Education, 1941, p. 12.

[12] Abram Kardiner and Lionel Ovesey, *The Mark of Oppression: Explorations in the Personality of the American Negro*, Meridian edition, Cleveland: World, 1962, p. 365.

ghettos. The story of these developments is told in detail in the selections which comprise this reader. Although these readings represent a variety of views, it is my opinion that some general conclusions can be drawn from these diverse selections about the growth of black radicalism in the past generation.

Part One deals with the massive changes which have occurred in the status of the Afro-American since World War II. Writing in 1942, Gunnar Myrdal, in his monumental study of American race relations, *An American Dilemma,* foresaw that the struggle against Nazi Germany had intensified the pressures for changes in the relations between white and black Americans. As Myrdal observed, the coexistence of white democracy with the oppression of black Americans depended upon white acceptance of theories of Negro inferiority. Yet during the 1930s, American social science had discredited racist theories. The ideological struggle against Nazism made the conflict between the American Creed and American racial practices even more glaring. On the one hand, Germany was being attacked for its racist, antidemocratic ideology; yet in America, most Negroes were denied the vote and were treated as second-class citizens. Myrdal predicted, with some confidence, that this contradiction would be resolved in favor of the Negro's entrance into the mainstream of American society.

In a sense, Myrdal's confidence has been justified. Since the publication of his book, racist stereotypes have been purged from most of the nation's media and educational systems. White attitudes have changed so dramatically that by the late 1950s, if opinion surveys are to be believed, even a majority of *southern* whites accepted the principle of racial equality.[13] Legal barriers to black participation in the social, economic, and political life of America have been virtually eliminated. This process began with President Truman's decision to desegregate the armed forces. It was spurred by the school desegregation decision of the Supreme Court in 1954, and culminated with the 1964 and 1965 Civil Rights Acts which gave the federal government the power to attack frontally white southern institutions of segregation and black political disfranchisement. But despite these advances, Myrdal's optimism was unfounded. As the readings in Part Two show, the symbolic gains of black people have not been matched by similar improvements in their socioeconomic conditions.

The gap between black and white America has not narrowed since World War II. In other words, black relative deprivation has remained constant for the past twenty-five years in spite

13 Herbert Hyman and Paul Sheatsley, "Attitudes toward Desegregation," *Scientific American,* July, 1964, pp. 16–23.

of the massive social changes which have occurred. For example, black family income has been consistently only slightly more than half of white family income since 1945; the rate of black unemployment has been double that for whites. The *quality* of living may even have worsened for most black people. The urban ghettos continue to deteriorate both physically and socially. In the rural South, black labor is being displaced by farm machinery. Many of the young leave in search of work; those who remain face unemployment and, in many cases, even starvation.

The socioeconomic realities of black America have puzzled those who look merely to economic indicators to predict social disorder. If the relative deprivation of blacks has been constant for a generation, why didn't this deprivation cause rebellions to break out in the 1950s or 1940s, or, for that matter, the 1930s? Ironically, it is this very lack of socioeconomic progress, *relative to white Americans,* which explains why large numbers of blacks turned to violence in the 1960s. For although the socioeconomic relationship between the races has changed only slightly, the expectations of black Americans have changed dramatically—partly because of the symbolic advances made by blacks in the past generation. (It is my belief that if this rise in the level of black expectation had been matched by a significant improvement in the socioeconomic conditions of black Americans, there would not be a crisis in race relations today.)

This rise in black expectations resulted from black abandonment of the role of accommodation and the development of black pride; the articles in Part Three describe this process. Postwar changes in white thinking and the symbolic victories of the civil rights movement brought about a radical change in the socialization of American Negroes. Just as blacks had been conditioned by the earlier racism of the dominant culture to perceive themselves as less than equal to whites, the purging of racist sentiments from mass media and schools created a climate in which blacks could grow up freed from "the mark of oppression." Older Negroes developed more pride in themselves. Thus, while white acceptance of the principle of racial equality may have been hypocritical, as many blacks have charged, black abandonment of racist dogma has been sincere and far-reaching in its implications. In this sense, the much publicized "Negro Revolution" of the 1950s and 1960s was truly revolutionary, because it created a new-found pride on the part of black people. As blacks became more confident that they were as good as white people, the disparity between black and white social and economic conditions became more galling.

The growing insistence of blacks in the postwar period for real equality with whites did not need to lead to rebellion or movements for separatism. As the selections in Parts Four and Five demonstrate, blacks have attempted to utilize the channels of conventional politics and protest to better their lot; only in recent years have blacks rioted or supported revolutionary movements in sizable numbers. However, as James Q. Wilson has observed, black political activity "can only marginally affect the income, housing, occupation, or life chances of Negro electorates."[14] For a time, protest seemed the means for achieving the goals which conventional politics had failed to obtain. Yet the victories of the civil rights movement, including the legislation of 1964 and 1965, served ultimately to show that the goals of that movement were irrelevant to the problems of most black people. Guaranteeing blacks the right to vote did little to increase the power of a minority, particularly as white politicians came to view black support as a liability. Of more basic importance, legal guarantees of equality of opportunity did nothing to help the majority of black people who are poor and ill-equipped to compete in an advanced industrial society. The rise of expectations and the failure of conventional politics and protest to lead to better conditions for blacks has proved to be an explosive combination.

Most of the readings in Part Six illustrate the total disenchantment of many black militants with American society. At present, only a minority of America's black people support the black revolutionaries. A study made in 1968 for the National Advisory Commission on Civil Disorders found that only six percent of the black respondents favored a "separate nation here."[15] Nevertheless, a far larger number of blacks are deeply alienated and are sympathetic to many aspects of the black nationalist movement. Support for a black revolution is growing. Whether this growth will continue and whether this country is heading toward a racial civil war depends far more on how white Americans will react to the problems facing black America than on the activities of black militants. Four views of the future of American race relations are presented in Part Seven. My own view can be expressed succinctly. Unless our society makes a major commitment to eliminate black poverty and powerlessness within the next decade, we face the likelihood of civil war. I think the readings which follow support this somber conclusion.

[14] James Q. Wilson, "The Negro in American Politics: The Present," in John P. Davis, ed., *The American Negro Reference Book,* Englewood Cliffs, N.J.: Prentice-Hall, 1966, p. 456.
[15] Angus Campbell and Howard Schuman, "Racial Attitudes in Fifteen American Cities," in *Supplemental Studies for the National Advisory Commission on Civil Disorders,* Washington, D.C.: U. S. Government Printing Office, June, 1968, p. 16.

In 1942, the Swedish sociologist, Gunnar Myrdal, wrote that *"not since Reconstruction has there been more reason to anticipate fundamental changes in American race relations, changes which will involve a development toward the American ideals."*[1] Myrdal felt that this was the major conclusion which could be drawn from his classic study of the Negro in America, *An American Dilemma.* The reasons for Myrdal's optimism are presented in the concluding chapter of his work which is reprinted here. If Myrdal's optimism appears unrealistic from our perspective, his prediction that American race relations would undergo basic change seems prophetic almost three decades later. Although Myrdal wrote in a period when race relations were relatively static, he foresaw that white abandonment of theories of white superiority would lead to massive social change.

Focusing on white attitudes, Myrdal concluded that by the early 1940s it had become difficult, if not impossible, for white Americans to continue to be comfortable with the contradiction between their adherence to the "American Creed of liberty, equality, justice, and fair opportunity for everybody" and the Negro's status in America.[2] Myrdal argued that the discrediting of racist theories by American social scientists in the 1930s and the ideological conflict with Nazi Germany made the scandal of American racist practice impossible to ignore. In addition, growing black militancy would make it even more difficult to minimize the injustices suffered by blacks. Myrdal believed that white acceptance of the American

[1] Gunnar Myrdal, *An American Dilemma: The Negro Problem and Modern Democracy,* New York: Harper & Row, 1944, p. xix.
[2]*Ibid.,* pp. xlvii–xlviii.

Creed would lead to the abandonment of racist practices and the eventual assimilation of Negroes into American society.

As the next selection by Arnold Rose indicates, much of Myrdal's optimism was justified. Writing in 1964, twenty years after the publication of *An American Dilemma,* Rose, who was Myrdal's research associate, reviewed the changes in American race relations from the 1940s to 1964. He concluded that "there could be no doubt that the races were moving rapidly toward equality and desegregation. . . ." Rose attributed these changes to such underlying factors as industrialization, urbanization, and technological progress as well as to the changing role of America in the world and the expansion of the power of the federal government. His article lists the political and legal gains made by black people in the two decades following World War II, gains which culminated in the passage of the 1964 Civil Rights Act. Rose's selection emphasizes the changes which have taken place in white attitudes toward blacks; according to opinion surveys, by the 1960s the majority of whites rejected racism and accepted integration. Rose was confident that this progress would continue.

Critics of Myrdal and Rose argue that white acceptance of the principle of racial equality has been hypocritical and that black gains during the postwar period have been largely symbolic. This charge is supported by the assertion that blacks have made little *real* socioeconomic progress since World War II, nor have they gained any real power. Another line of criticism is that Myrdal and Rose gave too much attention to white attitudes toward the Negro and erroneously assumed that blacks would respond to white abandonment of the caste system by seeking entrance into white society. Parts Two, Three, and Four deal with these arguments in detail.

America
Again
at the
Crossroads

Gunnar Myrdal

1. THE NEGRO PROBLEM AND THE WAR

The three great wars of this country have been fought for
the ideals of liberty and equality to which the nation was pledged.
As a consequence of all of them, the American Negro made great
strides toward freedom and opportunity.[1] The Revolutionary War
started a development which ultimately ended slavery in all Northern
states, made new import of slaves illegal and nearly accomplished
abolition even in the South—though there the tide soon turned in
a reaction toward fortification of the plantation system and of Negro
slavery. The Civil War gave the Negro Emancipation and Reconstruction in the South—though it was soon followed by Restoration
of white supremacy. The First World War provided the Negro his
first real opportunity as a worker in Northern industry, started the
Great Migration out of the South, and began the "New Negro" movement—though the end of the War saw numerous race riots and
the beginning of a serious decline in employment opportunities.
After the advances on all three occasions there were reactions, but
not as much ground was lost as had been won. Even taking the
subsequent reactions into account, each of the three great wars
in the history of America helped the Negro take a permanent step
forward.

Now America is again in a life-and-death struggle for liberty
and equality, and the American Negro is again watching for signs
of what war and victory will mean in terms of opportunity and

Reprinted by permission of Harper & Row, from Gunnar Myrdal,
"America Again at the Crossroads" and pp. 1438–1439 in *An American
Dilemma*. Copyright, 1944, 1962 by Harper & Row, Publishers, Inc.

rights for him in his native land. To the white American, too, the Negro problem has taken on a significance greater than it has ever had since the Civil War. This War is crucial for the future of the Negro, and the Negro problem is crucial in the War. There is bound to be a redefinition of the Negro's status in America as a result of this War.

The exact nature of this structural change in American society cannot yet be foreseen. History is not the result of a predetermined Fate. Nothing is irredeemable until it is past. The outcome will depend upon decisions and actions yet to be taken by whites and Negroes. What we can know definitely, however, are the trends as they developed up to the War and the changes so far during the War. On the basis of this knowledge, we can discern the gamut of possibilities for the future. If, in addition, we have some insight into the temper and inclination of the people who are both the actors and the spectators of the drama being staged, we can estimate which are the most probable developments.

2. SOCIAL TRENDS

Looking back over the ground we have mapped in our inquiry, we can make two general observations. One is the following: *What we usually call "social trends" have their main significance for the Negro's status because of what is in white people's minds.* It is true, for instance, that the decreasing relative demand for unskilled work, compared with skilled and semi-skilled work, and the change of much dirty and heavy labor to clean and easy labor, have dangerous implications for the Negro's employment opportunities. But if these technological and economic trends have disastrous effects on the Negro, the cause of this is the persistency with which white people want to keep him out of skilled and pleasant work. It is also true that the trend toward mass unemployment in America tends to turn Negro labor into a relief burden. But, again, the concentration of unemployment upon the Negro people is explainable only as the direct and indirect effects of discrimination. The restricted immigration of white Europeans to America and other population changes are reversing the century-old trend, in which the Negro was becoming a smaller portion of the total population of the United States, into a trend in which the Negro is becoming a slightly increasing proportion of the population. But if this change of trend will disappoint some white Americans and perhaps tend to increase racial friction, the cause is again race discrimination.

The second observation is this: *The important changes in the Negro problem do not consist of, or have close relations with, "social trends" in the narrower meaning of the term but are made up of changes in people's beliefs and valuations.* We started by stating the hypothesis that the Negro problem has its existence in the American's mind. There the decisive struggle goes on. It is there that the changes occur. Our investigation has amply confirmed our basic assumption, as an abbreviated summary of some of our main findings regarding recent trends will demonstrate.

In the field of *"social"* relations we traced a slow but visible decrease of discrimination in the South during recent decades up until the outbreak of the present War. The racial etiquette was gradually loosening. White people were beginning to take cognizance of distinctions in education and class within the Negro community and becoming prepared to treat Negroes somewhat differently according to their individual worth. The "no social equality" theory was not quite so rigid as in earlier generations. The entire Jim Crow apparatus was maintained, but its motivation was no longer so self-evident. Southern liberals were demanding with increasing courage and determination that the doctrine "separate, but equal" should be followed out in its "equality" aspect as well as in its "separateness" aspect—that segregation should not be utilized as a means of discrimination.

The separation of the two groups in the South was, meanwhile, becoming more and more perfected as the frequency of personal master-servant relations was decreasing and as the segregated Negro institutions and Negro professions were being built up. There even seemed to be a growing mental isolation between whites and Negroes. Behind this potentially most dangerous development was not only the exclusionist policy of the whites, but also the sullen dissatisfaction and bitter race pride of the Negroes themselves. They were "withdrawing" themselves as a reaction to the segregation and discrimination enforced by the whites.

In the North the sudden influx of Southern Negroes during the Great Migration caused a temporary rise in social discrimination. Since, in spite of this, there was much less of it in the North than in the South, the migration meant a decrease of social segregation and discrimination for the Negro people as a whole. It also seemed that, despite the sharp temporary rise on account of the migration, the trend in the North, too, was toward decreasing race prejudice.

In the administration of *justice* there was a definite improvement in the South, even if Negroes in that region are still far from enjoying equality before the law. There was a slow rise in the quality of the police and the courts. Lynching, peonage, and other conspicuous aberrations of justice were becoming stamped out. This development was spurred by the increasing interest and interference in the judicial order of the region, shown by the federal courts and other federal agencies, and also by the state governments. The activity of such private organizations as the N.A.A.C.P. and the Interracial Commission were also of paramount importance for this development. More fundamentally the prestige of law was rising in the South and people were becoming more law-abiding. These changes were related to a general rise in education of the Southerners and to their fuller participation in the larger American culture.

In the North the Negro continued to enjoy full equality before the law. There was some strain in the North during the Great Migration, sometimes mounting to race riots during which the arm of the law was not always just and impartial. But on the whole the judicial order of the region was upheld, and equality in justice was not a major problem.

In the *political* sphere, the South continued to disfranchise the Negro, contrary to the clear precept of the American Creed and the Constitution. The masses of whites were also kept from political participation. Real issues were kept out of politics and there was a great amount of corruption. But these things proved increasingly difficult to keep up. Economic and ideological changes, related to the region's rapid industrialization, urbanization, and labor unionization, stepped up by the Great Depression and the New Deal, caused political splits in the Southern Democratic party machines. The splits usually remained latent, but here and there, now and then, they forced themselves into the open. The "Solid South" seemed definitely endangered. The poll tax was under fierce attack in all Southern states, and some had already abolished it.

Meanwhile such things as the rise of the price level since the 'nineties and the improved educational level of Southern Negroes made the statutory devices to keep Negroes from the polls—by property and literacy requirements as well as by the poll tax— less and less effective. Negro disfranchisement came increasingly to depend upon extra-legal and illegal sanctions. We viewed this situation as extremely unstable for several reasons: the legal culture of the South was rising; there were no more loopholes left for legalizing Negro disfranchisement; the Solid South was showing signs of breaking up; the liberal forces in the North were getting increasingly exasperated with the South; and the Supreme Court was starting to enforce the Constitution as it applied to voting in the South. Southern liberals were standing up, not only against the poll tax, but often also against the one-party system and the exclusion of Negro voters from the primaries. Even conservative Southerners were occasionally found to hold the opinion that some-time in the future the Negro was going to vote in the South. While the Negro was almost as effectively disfranchised in the South in the years before the outbreak of the present War as he has ever been, our judgment, when taking all these changes into account, thus was that his political position was potentially much stronger and that his gradual enfranchisement was bound to come.

In the North the Negro enjoyed uninfringed his right to vote, and the steadily continuing migration to the North meant that the Negro vote was growing.

In the enjoyment of *public services* the Negro was dis-criminated against severely in the South in blunt repudiation of the Constitution and the state laws. But even in this sphere we saw a slow improvement of his status as a result of the rising legal cul-ture of the region; the pressures from the Negroes, from public opinion in the North, from the federal courts and administration as well as from the white Southerners' own better conscience. It was becoming somewhat less unusual that a playground or even a little park was arranged for Negroes in some cities. The Negro schools were greatly improved even if they usually still remained inferior. Without question the New Deal was of tremendous importance for the Negro in respect to the share he received of public services. It is true that the Washington administration did not dare and, in any case, did not succeed in stamping out discrimination in relief, agricultural policies, or anything else in the South, but it definitely decreased it. It also brought a new kind of public servant to the South, educated and zealous officials who were not primarily interested in "keeping the Negro in his place" but in encouraging and advancing him. This introduced a new and wholesome type of public contact for the Negro people in the South, and Negroes got a feeling that public authority could be other than arbitrary and suppressive.

In the North public services were, on the whole, granted to Negroes as to other citizens in similar circumstances.

While in all these spheres the trends at the outbreak of the present War were definitely in the direction of a rise in the status of the Negro in America,* the same cannot be said about

---

* Coming back to South Carolina after an absence of twenty years, John Andrew Rice noted as one of the outstanding changes: "The South-erner's attitude toward the Negro is incredibly more humane than it was in the South I knew as a child." *(I Came Out of the Eighteenth Century* [1942], p. 195.)

those relating to his occupational status. In Southern agriculture the Negro's plight had been becoming continually worse and showed no prospects for a brighter future. His low place on the occupational ladder usually as a plantation tenant—the increase of Negro landownership had stopped 40 years earlier—his dependence on cotton, his lack of education, and the intense race prejudice in the blighted rural regions of the South made him the main sufferer of the boll weevil, of Southern over-population and "white infiltration," of mechanization and, during the 'thirties, of the collapsing world market and the contractionist national agricultural policy. Yet there were no wholehearted attempts on a mass scale, either by the federal government or by any other agency, to reeducate rural Southern Negroes to take up new occupations in other areas. America was under the spell of economic defeatism so far as a belief in continued rapid industrialization was concerned, and there was no hope of placing the dislocated Negro sharecropper in the industrial cities.

Some rural Negroes moved to Northern and Southern cities, increasing unemployment there. Monopoly of jobs by the whites increased during the Great Depression, and Negroes did not find any new employment openings. Various national policies, such as the Wages and Hours Law, instituted to stamp out sweatshop conditions, could not avoid hurting the employment opportunities of Negroes since they were marginal workers. Under these conditions it is a wonder that Negroes were able to retain as many of their jobs as they did. But Negro unemployment mounted in all cities, particularly in the North, and the Negro workers increasingly became a relief burden. The whole country, and particularly the North, was much more generous toward the Negro in doling out relief to him than in allowing him to work and earn his bread by his own labor.

Meanwhile, the new unions in the mass production industries gave Negro workers hope by organizing them together with whites in fields in which Negroes were already working. But, with few exceptions, they did not open up new industries for Negro employment during the 'thirties, neither did they pave the way for Negroes to rise by promotion from the level of unskilled workers to that of the semi-skilled and skilled. Negro business did not flourish either, and the small gains made in a few professions were quantitatively insignificant. There is no question but that the development in the economic sphere was grave. But as discrimination was slowly decreasing in all other spheres, as there were good prospects that national politics would remain liberal and progressive, as Negro defense organizations and the Negro advisors in the federal administration were hammering on the inequalities, and as the new unions were pledged to nondiscrimination, there seemed to be good prospects that even the threatening trends respecting the Negro's economic status could have been turned, if the country had got out of the long stagnation in a normal way and had entered a new era of continued industrialization. Some of the economic policies of the New Deal were poorly thought out and badly integrated; in some respects they were damaging to the Negro. But administrators and experts were eager to learn from their mistakes and could be expected to accomplish better economic planning and direction when they were relieved of the pressure of emergency and improvisation.

3. THE DECAY OF THE CASTE THEORY

The problem of what would have occurred if there had been no war is now purely academic. The Second World War is bound to change all trends. But before we analyze the implications of the War for the Negro problem, we need to take a still broader perspective and ask: what has happened to white opinions on the Negro problem in the span of three generations since Emancipation?

In the South three generations ago white people had for their defense a consistent and respectable theory, endorsed by the church and by all sciences, printed in learned books and periodicals, and expounded by the South's great statesmen in the Capitol at Washington. The Negro's subordinate status was a principle integrated into a whole philosophy of society and of human life. The Negro was a completely different species of mankind: undeveloped, "child like," amoral, and much less endowed with intellectual capacities than the white man; he was meant by the Creator to be a servant forever; if kept in his "place" he was useful or at least tolerable, and there he was also happy; "social equality" was unthinkable as it implied intermarriage which would destroy the white race and Anglo-Saxon civilization. Much of this theory—which acquired an elaborate structure to satisfy the specific needs to justify discrimination in various spheres of life—remained through Reconstruction, and it was again hailed in the Restoration of white supremacy. Indeed, much of it remained until a couple of decades ago. But now it is almost destroyed for upper class and educated people. Its maintenance among lower class and uneducated people meets increasing difficulties. *The gradual destruction of the popular theory behind race prejudice is the most important of all social trends in the field of interracial relations.*

It is significant that today even the white man who defends

discrimination frequently describes his motive as "prejudice" and says that it is "irrational." The popular beliefs rationalizing caste in America are no longer intellectually respectable. They can no longer, therefore, be found in current books, newspapers or public speeches. They live a surreptitious life in thoughts and private remarks. There we have had to hunt them when studying the matter in this inquiry. When they were thus drawn out into the open they looked shabby and ashamed of themselves. Everybody who has acquired a higher education knows that they are wrong. Most white people with a little education also have a hunch that they are wrong. There is today a queer feeling of *credo quia absurdum* hovering over the whole complex of popular beliefs sustaining racial discrimination. This makes the prejudiced white man nearly as pathetic as his Negro victim.

The white man is thus in the process of losing confidence in the theory which gave reason and meaning to his way of life. And since he has not changed his life much, he is in a dilemma. This change is probably irreversible and cumulative. It is backed by the American Creed. The trend of psychology, education, anthropology, and social science is toward environmentalism in the explanation of group differences, which means that the racial beliefs which defended caste are being torn away. It also means, by implication, that the white majority group in power is accused of being the cause of the Negro's deficiencies and unhappiness. Authority and respectability are no longer supporting the popular beliefs. The beliefs are no longer nourished from above. Instead they are increasingly fought. There is a considerable time-lag between what is thought in the higher and in the lower social classes. But as time passes the lower social strata also will change their beliefs. These ideas are spread by the advance of education.

All of this is important. People want to be rational, and they want to feel that they are good and righteous. They want to have the society they live in, and their behavior in this society, explained and justified to their conscience. And now their theory is being torn to pieces; its expression is becoming recognized as a mark of ignorance.

On the other side of the caste gulf the development leads to increased bitterness. To the Negro the white man's trouble with his conscience cannot but seem to be insincerity or something worse. The Negro protest is rising, spurred by the improvement in education. The Negro group is being permeated by the democratic and equalitarian values of the American culture. Since at the same time there has been increasing separation between the two groups, Negroes are beginning to form a self-conscious "nation within the nation," defining ever more clearly their fundamental grievances against white America.

America can never more regard its Negroes as a patient, submissive minority. Negroes will continually become less well "accommodated." They will organize for defense and offense. They will be more and more vociferous. They will watch their opportunities ever more keenly. They will have a powerful tool in the caste struggle against white America: the glorious American ideals of democracy, liberty, and equality to which America is pledged not only by its political Constitution but also by the sincere devotion of its citizens. The Negroes are a minority, and they are poor and suppressed, but they have the advantage that they can fight whole-heartedly. The whites have all the power, but they are split in their moral personality. Their better selves are with the insurgents. The Negroes do not need any other allies.

This moral process had proceeded far when the Second World War broke out.

4. NEGROES IN THE WAR CRISIS

This War is an ideological war fought in defense of democracy. The totalitarian dictatorships in the enemy countries had even made the ideological issue much sharper in this War than it was in the First World War. Moreover, in this War the principle of democracy had to be applied more explicitly to race. Fascism and nazism are based on a racial superiority dogma—not unlike the old hackneyed American caste theory—and they came to power by means of racial persecution and oppression. In fighting fascism and nazism, America had to stand before the whole world in favor of racial tolerance and cooperation and of racial equality. It had to denounce German racialism as a reversion to barbarism. It had to proclaim universal brotherhood and the inalienable human freedoms. The fact that the Japanese utilize anti-white feelings in Asia and elsewhere made it even more necessary to stress the racial equality principle.

In the internal political struggle before America became involved in the War, the isolationists had worked up the idea that there was much to improve at home without trying to improve the rest of the world. They did not disdain even to point to the injustices inflicted upon the Negro; many isolationists to the left put the Negro cause to the forefront. A Georgia senator who had made a lengthy talk about the danger to democracy abroad was challenged by an isolationist co-senator with the question whether the fight for democracy should not begin in Georgia. The plight of the Negro sharecropper and the presence of peonage and lynching were brought up to stress the unsolved tasks at home and to win Negro sympathies for the isolationist cause.[2] One permanent result of this pre-war discussion was that, in this War, the promises to establish the full democratic liberties, not only abroad but also in America, played an even more prominent role than in the First World War.

For the Negroes this new War carried unpleasant reminiscences of the earlier one. The situation looked bitterly ironical. This time, too, the Negro had to fight desperately to get the right to fight for his country. In the armed forces Negroes were discriminated against in the usual ways and to almost the same extent. Mobs had attacked Negro soldiers and war workers, and a Southern senator had requested the Army to keep Negro soldiers out of the South. Negroes also had to fight to get into the war industries and had only partial success. In the First World War they actually made considerable advances in industrial employment, and the Great Migration was a welcome consequence. But this time the nation was well stocked with unemployed whites at the beginning of the defense boom. A technological development had also intervened, decreasing the industrial demand for unskilled labor—the type of jobs for which Negroes are least unwelcome. Up to the time when this is being written (August, 1942), the Negro has been almost excluded from the great bulk of the war industries. Discrimination is the rule practically everywhere.

Under the threat of a Negro march on Washington, skillfully staged by A. Philip Randolph, the President made a solemn proclamation against discrimination in the defense industries and government agencies and appointed a committee, having both Negro and white members, to see that it was observed. Other branches of the Administration made declarations and issued orders against discrimination: some of these statements were apparently sincere in their intention, some were face-saving moves, and most had their locus somewhere in the wide range between. The Republican National Committee resolved that racial discriminations are "wrongs under the Constitution" and pledged the opposition party to work to correct them. The national labor unions also lined up for non-discrimination. The Negroes heard and read the kindly promises. They again noted the public acceptance of their own reading of the Constitution and the American Creed. But they knew the grim reality.

In the twenty years between the two World Wars the general level of education of the American Negroes had become considerably higher, and so had their capacity for democracy. The

Negro press had become better equipped, and it reached farther. The Negro organizations had grown in strength. The national Negro leaders had become firmer, and they were more resentful. This time they were not willing cheerfully to postpone their complaints until the War was over. The elderly Du Bois renounced with bitterness the credulous advice he once gave his people in the First World War to "close ranks." In this new War the Negro leaders advertised freely—and sometimes provocatively—the danger of a low morale among Negroes.

In this War there was a "colored" nation on the other side—Japan. And that nation started out by beating the white Anglo-Saxons on their own ground. The smoldering revolt in India against British rule had significance for the American Negroes, and so had other "color" incidents in the world conflict: the wavering sympathies of several native populations in the Dutch and British possessions in the Pacific, the mistrust against Great Britain among the Arab peoples, the first abandonment of Ethiopia, and the ambiguity of the plans for the colonial chessboard of Africa. Even unsophisticated Negroes began to see vaguely a color scheme in world events, although their thoughts are usually not yet organized in a definite pattern.[3] In a "letter to the editor" by a Negro, which crept into a liberal white paper in the Upper South, the concluding sentences read:

> The Negro races on earth are very suspicious of
> the white man's good intentions. This is very likely
> to be the last war that the white man will be able to
> lead humanity to wage for plausible platitudes.[4]

And this low-toned threat from a single Southern Negro became occasionally more shrill in the North: all colored people should be united in their interests against the whites, and the aim should not be "national unity" but a real color war which would definitely end white imperialism and exploitation.

But this was exceptional. World politics and the color issue are, in the final analysis, of secondary importance to American Negroes, except as avenues for the expression of dissatisfaction. The American Negro is thoroughly Americanized; his complaint is merely that he is not accepted. What really matters to him is his treatment at home, in his own country. A Negro journalist, explaining the feeling of the Negro to the white public, has this to say:

> Because he must fight discrimination to fight for
> his country and to earn a living, the Negro to-day

is angry, resentful, and utterly apathetic about the war. "Fight for what?" he is asking. "This war doesn't mean a thing to me. If we win I lose, so what?"[5]

Reading the Negro press and hearing all the reports from observers who have been out among common Negroes in the South and the North convince me that there is much sullen skepticism, and even cynicism, and vague, tired, angry dissatisfaction among American Negroes today. The general bitterness is reflected in the stories that are circulating in the Negro communities: A young Negro, about to be inducted into the Army, said, "Just carve on my tombstone, 'Here lies a black man killed fighting a yellow man for the protection of a white man.'" Another Negro boy expressed the same feeling when he said he was going to get his eyes slanted so that the next time a white man shoved him around he could fight back.[6] Their caste status being what it is in America, Negroes would, indeed, not be ordinary human beings if such dissatisfaction and bitterness were not their reaction to all the morale talk about democracy, the four freedoms, the American way of life, all the violent denunciations of Nazi race hatred and the lack of freedom under totalitarian rule. We should also remember, however, that, even if Negroes are still mainly excluded from work in the manufacturing industries and from employment offering much future prospect, the war boom has created a lot of secondary employment for Negroes, too. There is more money in circulation and some trickles down to the Negroes. With a little money in his pocket even the poor Negro day laborer or domestic worker feels that he can afford to stiffen himself. Many white housewives notice strange thoughts and behavior on the part of their Negro servants these days.

The loyalty of the American Negro in war and peace is, however, proverbial. The only thing Negroes ask for is to be accepted as Americans. The American Constitution is even dearer to them than to their white compatriots. They are more unreservedly antifascist. Few American Negroes want the Axis powers to win the War. But this is not much of an issue to Negroes, as they, about as much as white Americans, are convinced of the invincibility of their country. Negroes have never doubted the strength and resourcefulness of the whites. Even more, they know that America offers more possibility of democracy, even for themselves, than do the Axis nations. In one of the most thoughtful statements on the question of Negro loyalties since the beginning of the war crisis, Ralph Bunche, says:

There should be no illusions about the nature of this struggle. . . . The fight now is not to save democracy, for that which does not exist cannot be saved. But the fight is to maintain those conditions under which people may continue to strive for realization of the democratic ideals. This is the inexorable logic of the nation's position as dictated by the world anti-democratic revolution and Hitler's projected new world order.[7]

But it is quite common that Negroes feel a satisfaction in the temporary adversities and want the War to become as serious a matter as possible to the white people in power. There have been reports that poor Negro sharecroppers in the South sometimes indulge in dreams of a Japanese army marching through the South and killing off a number of "crackers." They do not want them to land in the North, though, and they certainly do not want them to stay. But much more common is a glowing ill-concealed satisfaction over the war adversities on various fronts. Practically every issue of any Negro newspaper gives proof of this attitude. It must be conceded that Negroes have also some good rational reasons for this feeling. They know, of course, that, as a Northern Negro social scientist explains:

. . . the graver the outside danger to the safety of this country, the more abundant the gains will be likely to be [for the Negroes]. But until such time as this country is actually in grave danger most of the attention given to the problem of [Negro] morale will be that of conjuring up the right type of propaganda to allay their discontent.[8]

A white commenator complained some months ago that the Negro press is something of a fifth column. He received the unanimous and angry answer in all Negro papers that this is exactly contrary to the truth. Negroes are standing only for the democratic principles, to defend which America is waging war. They are dissatisfied because these principles are ignored in America itself. They are just the opposite of war dodgers and traitors: they pray to have the right to fight and die for their country and to work in the war industries, but they are excluded. They can, with new reason, point to the inconsistency between American ideals and practices, as does one of their wisest editors, Elmer A. Carter: ". . . this strange and curious picture, this spectacle of America at war to preserve the ideal of government by free men, yet clinging to the social vestiges of the slave system."[9] This ideological attack is so clear-cut and simple and so obviously to the point that it appeals even to the least educated Negro. The cause of the American Negro has supreme logical strength. And the Negro is better prepared than ever before in his history to fight for it.

5. THE WAR AND THE WHITES

This simple logic is, of course, apparent to white Americans, too. And the whites were on the way, even before the War, to lose their caste theory and their complacency in the face of obvious abuses of the American Creed. They are also stirred up by the War and the great cause of human liberties at stake. In the North the question can be publicly approached in only one spirit, that of the American Creed. A newspaper editorial reads like this:

> If the United Nations win this war the principle of the world-wide legal equality of races will have to be recognized. Since this is largely a war of ideas, and since racial equality before the law has become one of the central ideas on the democratic side, we can almost say that this principle, in itself, may be the deciding factor. The Chinese, the East Indians, the numerous African peoples and many other groups are on our side, or would be so if they were completely convinced that we mean what we say by equality just as unreservedly as the Nazis mean what they say by inequality. But we Americans cannot very well talk convincingly in these terms unless we prove our sincerity in our own country. Our largest recognizable racial minority is the Negro.[10]

The titular leader of the Republican party, Wendell Willkie, speaking in July, 1942, at the annual conference of the N.A.A.C.P. in Los Angeles, California, had this to say:

> Today it is becoming increasingly apparent to thoughtful Americans that we cannot fight the forces and ideas of imperialism abroad and maintain a form of imperialism at home. The war has done

this to our thinking. . . . So we are finding under
the pressures of this present conflict that long-
standing barriers and prejudices are breaking down.
The defense of our democracy against the forces
that threaten it from without has made some of its
failures to function at home glaringly apparent. Our
very proclamation of what we are fighting for have
rendered our own inequities self-evident. When we
talk of freedom and opportunity for all nations the
mocking paradoxes in our own society become so
clear they can no longer be ignored.[11]

The world conflict and America's exposed position as the
defender of the democratic faith is thus accelerating an ideological
process which was well under way. In this dramatic stage of the
American caste struggle a strategic fact of utmost importance is
this, that the entire caste order is extra-legal if not actually illegal
and unconstitutional. The legal order of the land does not sanction
caste but, on the contrary, is framed to guarantee equality and to
suppress caste. The only important exceptions are the Jim Crow
laws in the Southern states. But even they are written upon the
fiction of equality, although, if equality were enforced, they would
not only lose in efficacy as means of expressing caste subordination, but also become tremendously burdensome economically for
society and, consequently, the whites would be robbed of one of
their main interests in upholding them.

The whites are aware of the tremendous social costs of
keeping up the present irrational and illegal caste system. Among
other things, this anomaly is one of the main factors keeping the
respect for law and order and the administration of laws at such
a low level in America. The whites investigate these irrationalities
and the consequent social wastage; they build scientific systems to
explain their social causation, in fact, they know all about it and
deplore it. They have the political power to make caste legal and
orderly, whether with Negro consent or without it. But practically
never will whites be heard making such proposals, and still less
will they seriously discuss and plan for such a change. They cannot afford to compromise the American Creed.

Caste may exist, but it cannot be recognized. Instead, the
stamp of public disapproval is set upon it, and this undermines
still more the caste theory by which the whites have to try to
explain and justify their behavior. And *the Negroes are awarded
the law as a weapon in the caste struggle.* Here we see in high

relief how the Negroes in their fight for equality have their allies in the white man's own conscience. The white man can humiliate the Negro; he can thwart his ambitions; he can starve him; he can press him down into vice and crime; he can occasionally beat him and even kill him; but he does not have the moral stamina to make the Negro's subjugation legal and approved by society. Against that stands not only the Constitution and the laws which could be changed, but also the American Creed which is firmly rooted in the Americans' hearts.

6. THE NORTH MOVES TOWARD EQUALITY

In the North the Creed was strong enough long before the War to secure for the Negro practically unabridged civic equality in all his relations with public authority, whether it was in voting, before the courts, in the school system or as a relief recipient. But he is discriminated against ruthlessly in private relations, as when looking for a job or seeking a home to live in. The white Northerner, in his private dealings with people to whom he does not feel akin, has dangerous traditions derived from the exploitation of new immigrants. But even in those nonpublic spheres, and particularly in the problem of breadwinning, the white Northerner is becoming prepared, as a citizen, to give the Negro his just opportunity. But apparently, as a private individual, he is less prepared to feel that he himself is the man to give the Negro a better chance: in his own occupation, trade union, office or workshop, in his own residential neighborhood or in his church. The social paradox in the North is exactly this, that almost everybody is against discrimination in general but, at the same time, almost everybody practices discrimination in his own personal affairs.

It is the cumulation of all these personal discriminations which creates the color bar in the North and for the Negro causes unusually severe unemployment, crowded housing conditions, crime and vice. About this social process the ordinary white Northerner keeps sublimely ignorant and unconcerned. This aloofness is, of course, partly opportunistic but it can be fought by education. When now, in the war emergency, the Negro is increasingly given sympathetic publicity by newspapers, periodicals, and the radio, and by administrators and public personalities of all kinds, one result is that the white Northerner is gradually waking up and seeing what he is doing to the Negro and is seeing also the consequences of his democratic Creed for his relations with Negroes.

We have become convinced in the course of this inquiry that the North is getting prepared for a fundamental redefinition of the Negro's status in America. The North will accept it if the change is pushed by courageous leadership. And the North has much more power than the South. The white South is itself a minority and a national problem.

Also working in favor of the Negro is another trend, namely, the concentration of responsibility. Particularly in the crucial economic sphere this trend is rapid. Labor relations are coming increasingly to be planned and regulated by broad union policies and by national legislation and administration. The War will force this change forward step by step. After the War, in the great crisis of demobilization and liquidation, mass unemployment will be a main problem. Large-scale public intervention will be a necessity. In this endeavor no national administration will dare to allow unemployment to be too much concentrated upon the Negro.

The average white Northerner will probably agree with a policy which holds open employment opportunities for Negroes, because, as we said, he is against economic discrimination as a general proposition. There is also—together with all opportunistic ignorance and unconcernedness—a bit of rational defense for the distance he preserves between his political and his private opinion. In the individual shop where he works or the residential section where he lives, he sees the danger in admitting a few Negroes, since this will bring an avalanche of Negroes on his shop or his neighborhood. This danger is, of course, due to the fact of the Negro's general exclusion. It is part of the vicious circle holding the Negro down.

If government policy prevents general discrimination, however, there will be no avalanche of Negroes on any one white employer or group of employers. The Negroes, who comprise less than 10 per cent of the population, must be given their chance in private enterprise or be supported by public funds. "Buck-passing" is no longer possible when the problem comes to be viewed nationally. And the planning and directing agencies will be compelled to make the white public see the problem nationally in order to get public support for the policy they must pursue. As private relations are increasingly becoming public relations, the white Northerner will be willing to give the Negro equality.

These are the reasons why we foresee that the trend of unionization, social legislation, and national planning will tend to break down economic discrimination, the only type of discrimination which is both important and strong in the North. Other types of discrimination will then tend to decrease according to the law of cumulative causation which has been frequently referred to in this book.

7. TENSION IN THE SOUTH

The situation in the South is different. Unlike the white Northerner, who is most inclined to give the Negro equality in public relations and least inclined to do so in private relations, the white Southerner does not differentiate between public and private relations—the former as well as the latter have significance for prestige and social equality. Moreover, he is traditionally and consistently opposed to Negro equality for its own sake, which the Northerner is not. He may be privately indulgent much more than the white Northerner, but he is not as willing to give the Negro equal treatment by public authority. This is one of the romantic principles behind the legal inequity in the South. But the Southerner is a good American, too, and the region has been becoming rapidly "Americanized" during the last generation.

The ordinary conservative white Southerner has, therefore, a deeper split in his moral personality than does the white Northerner. The War is stirring up the conflict in his soul. The air is filled with reminders of the great cause of democracy and the equality of peoples, which is the main issue in the War America is waging against nazism, fascism, and Japanese imperialism. His "own Negroes" are making some money, reading the Negro press and getting restless. The N.A.A.C.P. and other protest organizations are fighting ever more daringly in his own cities. In his newspapers he reads how the national leaders, from the President down, come out with blunt denunciations of racial discrimination. He is finding that Northern leaders are increasingly getting interested in the poll tax, the white primary, Negro disfranchisement, injustices against Negroes, and other peculiar institutions of the South which he guards behind the doctrine of "states' rights."

What is he supposed to do? Give up Jim Crow and so perhaps allow a Negro to marry his daughters; build good schools for Negroes, though the schools are not too good for his own children; punish white invaders of Negro rights, though they otherwise may be perfectly good and upright citizens; relinquish white supremacy? Is he supposed to retreat from all "Southern traditions"? He sees "outside aggression" wherever he turns.

This is an old story and a phase of a mental cycle through

which the unfortunate South has often passed before. The fact that this time the white Southerner's caste theory is weaker than ever and does not inspire much of his own intellectual confidence makes his dilemma worse. His emotions on the color issue are less stable also because his personal ties to the Negro group have been decreasing, and racial isolation has been intensified during the last generation. He "knows the Negro" less well than did his father and grandfather, though he continues to pretend that he knows him well, because to "know the Negro" is also a Southern tradition. Having fewer personal contacts with Negroes he is likely to exaggerate the signs of opposition from the Negroes, for he feels that the Negroes have good reason to develop opposition. The presence in Southern communities of Negro soldiers, many from the North, increases his uneasiness. Du Bois, writing about the First World War, talks about:

> . . . the deep resentment mixed with the pale ghost of fear which Negro soldiers call up in the breast of the white South. It is not so much that they fear that the Negro will strike if he gets a chance, but rather that they assume with curious unanimity that he has *reason* to strike, that any other persons in his circumstances, or treated as he is would rebel. Instead of seeking to relieve the cause of such a possible feeling, most of them strain every effort to bottle up the black man's resentment.[12]

In the present crisis, Guion G. Johnson, a liberal Southern white historian, could already in July, 1941, report from the South that

> . . . there has been some uneasiness that "our Negroes" are being tampered with, and white advocates of racial goodwill have occasionally found it more difficult within the last year to speak out boldly. White persons who have for decades been working toward interracial cooperation may now find themselves charged with fifth column activity and Negro leaders may be denounced as communists or nazis.[13]

Another prominent white Southern liberal describes in a letter to the author the mental state of the white South as of summer, 1942:

> . . . we are in the midst of a situation in the South
> where we seem to have been thrown back with
> great losses where we had expected great gains:
> and . . . the situation in the South may be of the
> proportions of a crisis greater than we have had in
> many years. For the first time in my experience
> the situation is so complex that we do not know
> how to proceed to next steps. Just a few years ago
> we almost had unanimity in plans for cooperative
> arrangements, in which Negroes and whites were
> enthusiastic and in which representatives of nearly
> all phases of the South were participants. We had
> worked into entirely new patterns of fellowship
> and participation, and there were many evidences
> that the South was beginning to be proud of this
> progress. Today, as far as I know, there is prac-
> tically none of this left. The South is becoming
> almost unanimous in a pattern of unity that refers
> to white unity. The thousands of incidents and acci-
> dents in the South are being integrated into the old
> pattern of Southern determination against an out-
> side aggression.[14]

In the approaching conflict between the Negro and the
South, this writer sees that

> . . . a South which was just coming into its own,
> getting ready for an enriched agriculture, a more
> balanced economy, a more liberal viewpoint will
> sacrifice all this in a pathetic blood and sweat epi-
> sode reminiscent of the Civil War and Reconstruc-
> tion.

Similar to this deeply concerned statement of a liberal
white Southerner, we may cite the equally troubled view of a Negro
clergyman, Dr. J. S. Nathaniel Tross:

> I am afraid for my people. They have grown rest-
> less. They are not happy. They no longer laugh.
> There is a new policy among them—something
> strange, perhaps terrible.[15]

The situation is so critical in the South today that fifty Southern
Negro leaders have seen fit to gather together, deliberately exclud-

ing Northern Negroes, and to plead for racial amity. They accept social segregation, but request the elimination of all other inequalities. This development was made necessary by the fearful backing away of some Southern liberals—notably Mark Ethridge, John Temple Graves, and Virginius Dabney—from the social segregation issue. The meeting of the Southern Negroes serves both as an attempt to prevent the racial lines from being drawn more sharply and as a disclaimer of responsibility for future violence.

An important element in the situation is that the Southern Negroes, if they are attacked, are more prepared to fight this time than they have ever been before. A competent Negro social scientist, who has recently been studying conditions in the Upper South, confirms this view and, in May, 1943, confides that he expects the outbreak of serious race riots in the South within the next year.

The situation is grave, and the years to come will provide a serious test of the political resourcefulness of white public authorities and of other white and Negro leaders. But regardless of what happens, we do not believe that this is a turn for the worse in race relations in the South. Even if there are going to be serious clashes and even if their short-run effects will be devastating to the Negroes involved and, perhaps, to Negroes in the whole region, we believe that the long-run effect of the present opinion crisis in the South, because it is a catharsis for the whites, will be a change toward increased equality for the Negro. When we make this judgment, we recall a remark once made in a conversation by a prominent and conservative Negro social scientist in the South. He stated as his considered opinion that tensions are not necessarily bad and that under certain conditions even race riots may have wholesome effects in the long run. He continued in about the following way: "They stir up people's conscience. People will have to think matters over. They prevent things from becoming settled. If the race situation should ever become fixed, if the Negro were really accommodated, then, and only then, would I despair about a continued great improvement for Negroes. As long as there is friction and fighting, there is hope."

At this juncture the white North is moving in a direction contrary to the South. The white South is becoming increasingly isolated. There has not been such a great distance in the views of the Negro problem between the white majority groups in the two regions since Reconstruction. Though it is seldom expressed clearly, the outside observer feels convinced that an increasing number of white Northerners mean business this time. It is true, as James Weldon Johnson once observed, that "essentially the status of the Negro in all other sections will depend upon what it is in the South,"[16] but the North will find it increasingly necessary to have its say about the Negroes' status in the South. The North cannot well afford any longer to let the white Southerners have their own way with the Negroes as completely as they have had.

The national compromise has lasted for two generations; it may now be approaching its end, at least, relatively. Ten years from now this period in the history of interracial relations in America may come to look as a temporary *interregnum*. The compromise was not a stable power equilibrium. Signs of its end have been frequent during the 'thirties: a whole set of Supreme Court decisions, the New Deal in the South, the increasing activity of federal agencies to stamp out peonage, the agitation for a federal lynching law and for an abolition of the poll tax by Congress, the repeal of the two-thirds majority rule for the nomination of the Democratic candidate for the Presidency, and so on.

The Negro problem is becoming national in scope in a different sense than was meant when white Southerners expressed a belief that the Negro migration to the North would give the North more of a share in the trouble of having Negroes as neighbors and that then the North would understand the racial philosophy of the South better. The Negro vote and the labor vote in the North also have considerable weight in checking Southern conservatism and have increasing power to do so. But aside from all that, national planning cannot leave out the South or humor too much its irrationality. As a matter of fact the South, particularly its agriculture and its population pressure, will continue to remain one of the main national worries.

Because of this development, spurred by the war crisis and the coming peace crisis, it seems justifiable to predict a growing tension between the two regions, one which will not be restricted to the Negro issue. There is not going to be a civil war, of course. The South is this time relatively much weaker in all respects. The North will probably not become more considerate if the interracial tension in the South gets out of hand and results in bloody clashes. As recourse to civil war is out of the question and as things thus have to be settled by political means, the fact becomes of importance that the white South is not united against a redefinition of the Negro's status. The South has been, and is, changing rapidly, and Southern liberalism has been coming to be a force though it was practically nowhere in political power and today is fearfully timid on the Negro issue. Even the ordinary conservative white Southerner has a deeply split personality. In the short run this can be suppressed, and the tension can lead to violent reactions. But in the long run it means that the conservative white Southerner himself can be won over to equalitarian reforms in line with the American Creed.

8. INTERNATIONAL ASPECTS

What has actually happened within the last few years is not only that the Negro problem has become national in scope after having been mainly a Southern worry. It has also acquired tremendous international implications, and this is another and decisive reason why the white North is prevented from compromising with the white South regarding the Negro. The situation is actually such that any and all concessions to Negro rights in this phase of the history of the world will repay the nation many times, while any and all injustices inflicted upon him will be extremely costly. This is not yet seen clearly by most Americans, but it will become increasingly apparent as the War goes on.

We mentioned in passing that the American Negro cannot help observing the color angle to this War. He is obviously getting vicarious satisfaction out of this perspective, and he is also testing some vague feelings of solidarity and allegiance to the cause of other colored peoples involved in the world conflagration. But this is a minor part of the international implications. The American Negro is thoroughly American in his culture and whole outlook on the world. He is also loyal to America, and there is no danger that he will betray it. This is at least certain in the short-range view, which covers this War and the coming peace. How the Negro would react if he were left dissatisfied and if later a new war were to be fought more definitely along color lines is more difficult to predict.

The main international implication is, instead, that America, for its international prestige, power, and future security, needs to demonstrate to the world that American Negroes can be satisfactorily integrated into its democracy. In a sense, this War marks the end of American isolation. America has had security behind the two protecting oceans. When now this isolation has been definitely broken, the historians will begin to see how it has always greatly determined the development of America. Statesmen will have to take cognizance of the changed geopolitical situation of the nation and carry out important adaptations of the American way of life to new necessities. A main adaptation is bound to be a redefinition of the Negro's status in American democracy.

It is commonly observed that the mistrust of, or open hostility against, the white man by colored people everywhere in the world has greatly increased the difficulties for the United Nations to win this War.* Many old sins and stupidities are today staring back upon the white man, and he continues to commit them, though he now knows better. The treatment of the Negro in America has not made good propaganda for America abroad and particularly not among colored nations. That good American who has acquired such a rare understanding for the Asiatic people's mind, Pearl S. Buck, comments:

> Japan . . . is declaring in the Philippines, in China, in India, Malaya, and even Russia that there is no basis for hope that colored peoples can expect any justice from the people who rule in the United States, namely, the white people. For specific proof the Japanese point to our treatment of our own colored people, citizens of generations in the United States. Every lynching, every race riot, gives joy to Japan. The discriminations of the American army and navy and the air forces against colored soldiers and sailors, the exclusion of colored labor in our defense industries and trade unions, all our social discriminations, are of the greatest aid today to our enemy in Asia, Japan. "Look at America," Japan is saying to millions of listening ears. "Will white Americans give you equality?"[17]

And she assures her compatriots:

> We cannot . . . win this war without convincing our colored allies—who are most of our allies—that we are not fighting for ourselves as continuing superior over colored peoples. The deep patience of colored peoples is at an end. Everywhere among them there is the same resolve for freedom and equality that white Americans and British have, but it is a grimmer resolve, for it includes the determination to be rid of white rule and exploitation and white race prejudice, and nothing will weaken this will.[18]

* Not only colored peoples have been disturbed by America's treatment of her Negroes. The German radio often mentions America's harsh treatment of Negroes in its propaganda broadcasts to European peoples. (New York *Times* [September 2, 1942], p. 3.)

This is perhaps an exaggeration. Perhaps the War can this time be won even without the colored people's confidence. But the absence of their full cooperation, and still more their obstructive activities, will be tremendously costly in time, men and materials. Caste is becoming an expensive luxury of white men.

It seems more definitely certain that it will be impossible to make and preserve a good peace without having built up the fullest trust and goodwill among the colored peoples. They will be strong after the War, and they are bound to become even stronger as time passes. For one thing, this is certain in so far as numbers are concerned. During the short span of the last three centuries, which include almost the entire epoch of white power expansion, the peoples of European stock increased sevenfold, while the others increased only threefold. The whites grew from a bare 100 millions, or a fifth of the globe's total, to over 700 millions, or a third of all mankind. The increase for the whites was fastest during the last century when they gradually became able to control deaths but had not as yet brought births under control. The whites are, however, now in the second phase of this dynamic sequence: the white birth rate is falling so fast that it is catching up with the relatively stable death rate. The population expansion of the whites is now slowing down, absolutely and relatively. Many of the Western nations, including America and all those other peoples on the highest level of industrial civilization, will probably start to shrink in population numbers within a few decades. The colored nations, on the other hand, are just entering the first stage where expansion is likely to be pushed by an increasingly improved control over death, and it is unlikely that the increase in birth control will keep pace with the improvement of the control over death. The whites will, therefore, from now on become a progressively smaller portion of the total world population. If we except the Russian peoples, who are still rapidly increasing, the rapid change in proportion stands out still more dramatically.

Another broad trend is almost as certain, namely, that the "backward" countries, where most colored people live, are going to become somewhat industrialized. The examples of Japan and, more recently, of Russia and China give support to the view that in the future we shall see many backward countries industrialized at a tremendously more rapid rate than were the pioneer Western countries, who had to find out everything for themselves. The same examples illustrate also how such backward nations can advantageously use the newly created industrial apparatus for producing war materials, and they illustrate, too, how they can fight with them.

Particularly as Russia cannot be reckoned on to adhere to

white supremacy, it is evident from these facts—though nobody in our countries seems to take it seriously—that within a short period the shrinking minority of white people in our Western lands will either have to succumb or to find ways of living on peaceful terms with colored people. If white people, for their own preservation, attempt to reach a state in which they will be tolerated by their colored neighbors, equality will be the most they will be strong enough to demand.

History is never irredeemable, and there is still time to come to good terms with colored peoples. Their race pride and race prejudice is still mostly a defensive mental device, a secondary reaction built up to meet the humiliations of white supremacy. This is apparent in the case of the American Negro. It probably holds true even for other colored people who have not yet had a taste of power. A Chinese propaganda leaflet assures the Americans:

> Chinese nationalism or race-consciousness is essentially defensive in character. It has developed out of continuous fight for freedom, and has never been offensive.[19]

It should be apparent that the time to come to an understanding on the basis of equality is rapidly running out. When colored nations have once acquired power but still sense the scorn of white superiority and racial discrimination, they are likely to become indoctrinated by a race prejudice much more akin to that of the whites—a race prejudice which can be satisfied only by the whites' humiliation and subjugation.

9. MAKING THE PEACE

Americans in general are concerned with the task of making a constructive peace after the War. It is commonly understood that this task is fraught with immense and unprecedented difficulties and, particularly, that the flagrant mismanagement of international affairs by the great democracies in the period between the two World Wars, the devastation caused by the Second World War, the breaking up of the state structures of Europe, and the approaching liquidation of colonial imperialism in the Far East have created a psychological state in mankind which, aside from all physical and economic deficiencies, raises almost insurmountable obstacles for the peacemakers. Americans generally recognize also that the protection of the two oceans is gone forever, that American isolationism will never more be possible, that America is in world politics for better or for worse, and that this time it has to stick to the making and upholding of the peace which is yet to be written.

Americans also recognize that America has to take world leadership. The coming difficult decades will be America's turn in the endless sequence of main actors on the world stage. America then will have the major responsibility for the manner in which humanity approaches the long era during which the white peoples will have to adjust to shrinkage while the colored are bound to expand in numbers, in level of industrial civilization and in political power. For perhaps several decades, the whites will still hold the lead, and America will be the most powerful white nation.

America goes to this task with the best of intentions. Declarations of inalienable human rights for people all over the world are now emanating from America. Wilson's fourteen points were a rehearsal; Roosevelt's four freedoms are more general and more focused on the rights of the individual. The national leaders proclaim that the coming peace will open an age of human liberty and equality everywhere. This was so in the First World War, too. This time something must be done to give reality to the glittering generalities, because otherwise the world will become entirely demoralized. It will probably be impossible to excite people with empty promises a third time. It is commonly agreed, and taken as proved by the coming of this War, that peace cannot be preserved if the development of a democratic life in every nation is not internationally guaranteed and the possibility of oppression is not checked. It is anticipated that international agencies will be created to sanction such a development.

In view of the clarity and unanimity in America on these fundamental points, few white Americans fully realize all the obvious implications. I have, for instance, met few white Americans who have ever thought of the fact that, if America had joined the League of Nations, American Negroes could, and certainly would, have taken their cases before international tribunal back in the 'twenties. Some versatile Negro protest leaders are, however, familiar with the thought. After this War there is bound to be an international apparatus for appeal by oppressed minority groups. In America, Negro organizations like the N.A.A.C.P. are excellently equipped for such conspicuous litigation. It is, indeed, possible that such implications of the coming democratic peace, when they become better seen and publicly discussed, will act as deterrents and as a motive for isolationism in some American circles. But there is no way back. America is irredeemably in world politics.

Behind her two protecting oceans America has until now

lived an exuberant and carefree life without having to bother much about its international reputation. Probably no other modern people has cared less about what impression it makes on other nations. The ordinary American might have been interested to know, but has not bothered much about, the fact that lynchings and race riots are headlines in Bombay; that Huey Long and Father Coughlin, the wave of organized crime during and after Prohibition, the fiscal bankruptcy of Chicago some years ago, the corrupt political machines in Philadelphia, the Dayton trial of Darwinism, provided stories for the Sunday papers in Oslo; that many men and women in democratic countries around the entire world have had their first and decisive impression of American public life from the defense of Sacco and Vanzetti and the Scottsboro boys. Friends of America abroad have tried to make the picture of American life more balanced and more accurate by fixing public attention on the numerous good sides, on American accomplishments, on all the good intentions and on the favorable trends. But they have been only partly successful, and America itself has—until this War— never cared to advertise America abroad.

This—like America's openness to criticism, which is the positive side of this unconcernedness—is a sign of great strength, but it was the strength of a departed isolation. There was also ignorance behind the attitude. Aware of all the good things in his country and rightly convinced that, on the whole, they greatly out- weigh all the imperfections, the ordinary American takes it for granted that America is liked and trusted abroad.

The loss of American isolation makes all this most serious. America has now joined the world and is tremendously dependent upon the support and good-will of other countries. Its rise to leadership brings this to a climax. None is watched so suspiciously as the one who is rising. None has so little license, none needs all his virtue so much as the leader. And America, for its own security, cannot retreat from leadership.

There is, of course, another possible solution besides good- will, and that is power. In some quarters in America the observer finds exaggerated notions about the power which America's financial strength after the War will allow her. Americans have not commonly taken to heart what was conclusively proved by experience in the period between the two World Wars, namely, that, after the loans are given, the power belongs to the debtor and not to the creditor.

Military power, however, can be substituted for good-will. But America does not have the will or stamina for real imperialism. The farmer, the laborer, the merchant, the intellectual, in one word, the common man who ultimately makes political decisions is against suppression abroad. In the international field the Southerner is not unlike his Northern compatriot. All American adventures in imperialism give abundant proofs of half-heartedness and show again the power over the Americans of the American Creed. If America does not go fascist, American militarism will not be an adequate substitute for good-will.

The treatment of the Negro is America's greatest and most conspicuous scandal. It is tremendously publicized, and democratic America will continue to publicize it itself. For the colored peoples all over the world, whose rising influence is axiomatic, this scandal is salt in their wounds. In all white nations which, because of the accident of ethnic homogeneity or for other causes, have not been inculcated with race prejudice, the color of the victim does not provide any excuse for white solidarity. That this is so in Russia is well known and advertised. It holds true also in many other white nations.

10. AMERICA'S OPPORTUNITY

But these consequences of the present course of America's and the world's history should not be recorded only in terms of compelling forces. The bright side is that the conquering of color caste in America is America's own innermost desire. This nation early laid down as the moral basis for its existence the principles of equality and liberty. However much Americans have dodged this conviction, they have refused to adjust their laws to their own license. Today, more than ever, they refuse to discuss systematizing their caste order to mutual advantage, apparently because they most seriously mean that caste is wrong and should not be given recognition. They stand warmheartedly against oppression in all the world. When they are reluctantly forced into war, they are compelled to justify their participation to their own conscience by insisting that they are fighting against aggression and for liberty and equality.

America feels itself to be humanity in miniature. When in this crucial time the international leadership passes to America, the great reason for hope is that this country has a national experience of uniting racial and cultural diversities and a national theory, if not a consistent practice, of freedom and equality for all. What America is constantly reaching for is democracy at home and abroad. The main trend in its history is the gradual realization of the American Creed.

In this sense, the Negro problem is not only America's greatest failure but also America's incomparably great opportunity for the future. If America should follow its own deepest convictions, its well-being at home would be increased directly. At the same time America's prestige and power abroad would rise immensely. The century-old dream of American patriots, that America should give to the entire world its own freedoms and its own faith, would come true. America can demonstrate that justice, equality and cooperation are possible between white and colored people.

In the present phase of history this is what the world needs to believe. Mankind is sick of fear and disbelief, of pessimism and cynicism. It needs the youthful moralistic optimism of America. But empty declarations only deepen cynicism. Deeds are called for. If America in actual practice could show the world a progressive trend by which the Negro became finally integrated into modern democracy, all mankind would be given faith again—it would have reason to believe that peace, progress and order are feasible. And America would have a spiritual power many times stronger than all her financial and military resources—the power of the trust and support of all good people on earth. *America is free to choose whether the Negro shall remain her liability or become her opportunity.*

The development of the American Negro problem during the years to come is, therefore, fateful not only for America itself but for all mankind. If America wants to make the second choice, she cannot wait and see. She has to do something big and do it soon. For two generations after the national compromise of the 1870's between the North and the South on the Negro problem, the caste status of the Negro was allowed to remain almost unchanged. It was believed by most well-meaning people that self-healing would work, that the Negro problem would come to solve itself by the lapse of time. George Washington Cable wrote in the 'eighties:

> There is a vague hope, much commoner in the North than in the South, that somehow, if everybody will sit still, *"time"* will bring these changes.[20]

Two decades later, Ray Stannard Baker reported from the South:

> All such relationships will work themselves out gradually, naturally, quietly, in the long course of the years: and the less they are talked about the better.[21]

Most of the literature on the Negro problem continues to this day to be written upon this same static assumption.

We have given the reasons why we believe that the *interreg-*

num, during which the forces balanced each other fairly well, is now at an end. The equilibrium, contrary to common belief, was unstable and temporary. As American Negroes became educated and culturally assimilated, but still found themselves excluded, they grew bitter. Meanwhile the whites were in the process of losing their caste theory. The international upheavals connected with the two World Wars and the world depression brought these developments to a crisis. American isolation was lost. Technical developments brought all nations to be close neighbors even though they were not trained to live together.

We are now in a deeply unbalanced world situation. Many human relations will be readjusted in the present world revolution, and among them race relations are bound to change considerably. As always in a revolutionary situation when society's moorings are temporarily loosened, there is, on the one hand, an opportunity to direct the changes into organized reforms and, on the other hand, a corresponding risk involved in letting the changes remain uncontrolled and lead into disorganization. To do nothing is to accept defeat.

From the point of view of social science, this means, among other things, that social engineering will increasingly be demanded. Many things that for a long period have been predominantly a matter of individual adjustment will become more and more determined by political decision and public regulation. We are entering an era where fact-finding and scientific theories of causal relations will be seen as instrumental in planning controlled social change. The peace will bring nothing but problems, one mounting upon another, and consequently, new urgent tasks for social engineering. The American social scientist, because of the New Deal and the War, is already acquiring familiarity with planning and practical action. He will never again be given the opportunity to build up so "disinterested" a social science.

The social sciences in America are equipped to meet the demands of the post-war world. In social engineering they will retain the old American faith in human beings which is all the time becoming fortified by research as the trend continues toward environmentalism in the search for social causation. In a sense, the social engineering of the coming epoch will be nothing but the drawing of practical conclusions from the teaching of social science that "human nature" is changeable and that human deficiencies and unhappiness are, in large degree, preventable.

In this spirit, so intrinsically in harmony with the great tradition of the Enlightenment and the American Revolution, the author may be allowed to close with a personal note. Studying human beings and their behavior is not discouraging. When the author recalls the long gallery of persons whom, in the course of this inquiry, he has come to know with the impetuous but temporary intimacy of the stranger—sharecroppers and plantation owners, workers and employers, merchants and bankers, intellectuals, preachers, organization leaders, political bosses, gangsters, black and white, men and women, young and old, Southerners and Northerners—the general observation retained is the following: Behind all outward dissimilarities, behind their contradictory valuations, rationalizations, vested interests, group allegiances and animosities, behind fears and defense constructions, behind the role they play in life and the mask they wear, people are all much alike on a fundamental level. And they are all good people. They want to be rational and just. They all plead to their conscience that they meant well even when things went wrong.

Social study is concerned with explaining why all these potentially and intentionally good people so often make life a hell for themselves and each other when they live together, whether in a family, a community, a nation or a world. The fault is certainly not with becoming organized *per se*. In their formal organizations, as we have seen, people invest their highest ideals. These institutions regularly direct the individual toward more cooperation and justice than he would be inclined to observe as an isolated private person. The fault is, rather, that our structures of organizations are too imperfect, each, by itself, and badly integrated into a social whole.

The rationalism and moralism which is the driving force behind social study, whether we admit it or not, is the faith that institutions can be improved and strengthened and that people are good enough to live a happier life. With all we know today, there should be the possibility to build a nation and a world where people's great propensities for sympathy and cooperation would not be so thwarted.

To find the practical formulas for this never-ending reconstruction of society is the supreme task of social science. The world catastrophe places tremendous difficulties in our way and may shake our confidence to the depths. Yet we have today in social science a greater trust in the improvability of man and society than we have ever had since the Enlightenment.

Footnotes

[1] A parallel analysis of the relationship between war and improvement in the status of Negroes may be found in Guion G. Johnson, "The Impact of War Upon the Negro," *Journal of Negro Education* (July, 1941), pp. 596–611.

[2] Horace R. Cayton, "The Morale of the Negro in the Defense

Crisis," unpublished manuscript of paper read to the 20th Annual Institute of the Society for Social Research, The University of Chicago (August 15, 1941), p. 11.

Cayton reflected pessimistically:

"It is not that any of these men or groups are really interested in changing in any fundamental way, the position of the Negro in the United States. This would prove, in most instances, just as embarrassing to them as it would to those leaders who are interested in an immediate declaration of war. But the Negro presents a 'pat' argument for those who want to say that democracy should be built at home. Nevertheless, the Negro was thrilled to at last have national figures speak about this plight on the radio, from the platform and in the newspapers. Neglected, for the most part, by the pro-war groups, the anti-war crowd has made a deep impression on the Negro public." *(Idem.)*

[3] There is a question whether Negroes have identified themselves with other colored peoples as much as Southern whites have identified American Negroes with Japan. A confidential public opinion poll taken before Pearl Harbor showed that the South, with no Japanese population, was more anti-Japanese than Americans on the West Coast, who had a definite Japanese problem. Also symbolic is the following AP dispatch from Atlanta, Georgia (from the New York *Herald Tribune* [April 5, 1942], p. 3).

"Atlanta children were heard reciting this wartime rhyme:
'Eenie, meenie, minie, moe,
Catch the emperor by the toe,
If he hollers make him say:
"I surrender to the U.S.A." ' "

This, of course, is a paraphrase of the doggerel containing an anti-Negro sentiment, known to every American child (in two versions):

"Eenie, meenie, minie, moe,
Catch a nigger by the toe
If he hollers, let him go
Eenie, meenie, minie, moe."

"Eenie, meenie, minie, moe,
Catch a nigger by the toe
If he hollers, make him pay
Fifty dollars every day."

[4] Raleigh *News and Observer* (May 3, 1942).

[5] Earl Brown, "American Negroes and the War," in *Harper's Magazine* (April, 1942), p. 546.

[6] Horace R. Cayton, "Fighting for White Folks?," *Nation* (September 26, 1942), p. 268.

[7] "The Negro in the Political Life of the United States," *Journal of Negro Education* (July, 1941), p. 583.

[8] Cayton, "The Morale of the Negro in the Defense Crisis," p. 14.

[9] "Shadows of the Slave Tradition," *Survey Graphic* (November, 1942), p. 467.

[10] New York *Times,* April 3, 1942.

[11] Cited in New York *Times,* July 20, 1942.

[12] W. E. B. Du Bois, *Darkwater* (1920), p. 236.

[13] Guion G. Johnson, *op. cit.,* pp. 609–610.

[14] Letter (August 13, 1942).

[15] Cited from *PM* (August 16, 1942), p. 17.

[16] *Along This Way* (1934), p. 411.

[17] *American Unity and Asia* (1942), p. 29.

[18] *Ibid.,* p. 25.

[19] *Contemporary China. A Reference Digest,* published by Chinese News Service, Inc. (August 10, 1942).

[20] *The Negro Question* (1890), p. 48.

[21] *Following the Color Line* (1908), p. 305.

2

The American Negro Problem in the Context of Social Change

Arnold M. Rose

The "Negro protest" must be seen in the context of the Negro problem in the United States and of the forces of social change operating throughout the society. The protest movement is directed against a situation in American society, and it finds its strengths and its obstacles in that situation, which itself is in a condition of rapid flux. To describe this context systematically would require a lengthy book. In this article I propose merely to paint the situation, and the major changes occurring within it, in crude broad strokes . . .

MAJOR CAUSES OF CHANGE

An analysis of the dynamic forces operating in the present situation inevitably involves the selection of what is most significant in the complexity of current affairs. I give greatest emphasis to forces involving social power, both economic and political, sometimes wielded deliberately but more often impersonally in the form of great trends affecting the whole society. I give smaller stress to changes in public ideologies and least weight to factors usually singled out as "psychological"—although it seems to me that a

This article is a revision of the preface to the 1964 paper-bound edition of Arnold M. Rose, *The Negro in America,* New York, Harper & Row, Publishers, 1964. Reprinted by permission of Harper & Row, and the American Academy of Political and Social Science from Arnold M. Rose, "The American Negro Problem in the Context of Social Change," *Annals* of the American Academy of Political and Social Science, 357 (January, 1965), pp. 1–17.

better sociopsychological analysis than is dominant today in academic circles would not separate the individual psychological factors from those involving social power and ideologies.

The major forces causing the rapid change in race relations since 1940 seem to have been continuing industrialization and technological advance, the high level of mobility among the American people, economic prosperity, the organization and political education of minority groups, an increased American awareness of world opinion, consistent support for civil rights on the part of the Supreme Court and a lesser support from the other branches of the federal government and the Northern state governments, and the propaganda and educational efforts for more equal implementation of civil rights. Some of these forces are likely to continue to exert the same pressure as in the recent past; others are likely to change in their influence, and new forces are likely to have increasing influence.

Industrialization and Technological Progress

Industrialization has created changes in race relations in several ways. First, it has eliminated cotton agriculture as the dominant source of Southern wealth. Racism grew up as an American ideology partly in response to the need to maintain a reliable and permanent work force in the difficult job of growing cotton. While American Negro slavery was older than extensive cotton agriculture, it took on major economic and political significance in connection with the rise of "King Cotton" after 1793, and the patterns of discrimination and prejudice that have persisted to the present day took their form originally in the cotton-growing areas. Cotton agriculture remained a dominant element in the economy of the Southern states until the 1930's, but then it lost its pre-eminence because of the diversification of agriculture and the rise of manufacturing. The continuation of racism after the displacement of cotton as "king" is an example of the sociological principle that ideologies continue after the conditions that gave rise to them cease to exist. Nevertheless, the decline of cotton agriculture permitted other forces to weaken racism.

Industrialization prompted a sizable move of people from rural areas into the cities, where they found factory jobs and entered service occupations. Urbanization has always been associated with the weakening of traditional social structures. The caste system governing the relations between whites and Negroes in the South had its birth in the rural areas and imposed its structure upon a relatively static rural society. When Negroes moved into the cities—and even in the South the majority of them now live in cities—the elaborate requirements of the caste system could hardly be maintained. Relationships in the city are too casual and too functional to require the constant manifestations of subordination on the part of Negroes that characterized the rural caste system. Segregation became more physical than symbolic, and behind the walls of segregated isolation, Negroes were better able to build resistance to subordination.

Industrialization also brought about emigration from the South. While the great migration of Negroes was to the Northern cities until about 1940, it became increasingly a westward migration after that. The migration was, of course, partly due to the lag in Southern industrialization, but even with that now being overcome, the especially strong discrimination against Negroes in the South has motivated their continued migration out of the region. The majority of Negroes, however, no longer live in the Deep and Upper South—the old Border states have realigned themselves largely with Northern states—and the outward migration must necessarily slow down. The main significance of the northward and westward migration for the Negroes was that it separated them from the fullblown caste system of the South, even though they met other forms of discrimination and prejudice in the other regions of the country. In the North—which, for this purpose, includes the West also—they vote freely and have the almost full protection of the laws and the law-enforcement machinery. They, as well as the whites, get a better education in the North, and this has been a major factor in improving their status. Thus, Negroes have been much better able to improve their condition in the North, and they have used their improved condition—especially their vote—to help Negroes still living in the South.

Technological progress has been an important—though not the sole—factor which has contributed to the high level of prosperity since 1940. The prosperity and the almost full employment associated with it during the period 1940–1954 have been especially beneficial to Negroes. Measurements vary, but it has been estimated that the rise of average real income among Negroes since 1940 has been two to three times that among whites, though practically all of that improvement occurred before the economic recession of 1955. As the average income of Negroes is still significantly below that of the whites, the rapid improvement of their economic condition must be seen against the backdrop of great economic discrimination and poverty in the pre-1940 period. The prospects for further automation and the industrial use of nuclear energy will involve still higher productivity and a higher standard of living for employed workers in the future—and Negroes are no longer excluded from the general economic improvement, especially in the North. The rise in average family income among Negroes since 1935 has meant not only a fuller participation in the material benefits of the modern economy, but also a greater opportunity to obtain more education and other cultural benefits. It should also be remembered that continuing general prosperity among whites has tended to reduce one major source of frustration among whites, which sometimes contributes to scapegoating and race-baiting.

Technological change—especially in the form of automation —is having another effect—partly negative—on the position of Negroes in the United States. As a relatively unskilled element in the work population, the Negro is often the most rapidly displaced worker when changing technology requires an upgrading of skills. This process is aggravated by the fact that many Negroes are relative newcomers to the ranks of Northern industrial workers, and therefore have the lowest seniority and least protection from unionization. Hence, Negroes are the hardest hit by technological unemployment. Technological change and low seniority have, for all practical purposes, replaced discrimination as the main force in excluding Negroes from factory jobs in the North and West. Thus Negroes constitute a disproportionately large number of the "permanently unemployed," and their rate of becoming unemployed was about double that of white workers during the several recessions that have occurred since 1955. In July 1963, 11.2 per cent of the Negroes in the labor force were unemployed, compared to 5.1 per cent among whites. Occupational training for Negroes is crucial. If minority workers get new job training, they will cease to be subject to special handicaps and will substantially close the gap between them and the already skilled workers of the majority group, who now also need retraining.

Protest and Pressure Associations

The development of an educated elite and of a lively sense of group identification among Negroes has significantly impelled American race relations into a more equalitarian direction since the turn of the century. A wide range of protest and pressure associations have exerted their influence, sometimes with and sometimes without collaboration of liberal whites. Although this movement was quite highly developed by 1940, it has taken on some significant additional elements since then. The nonviolent resistance technique —as a means of achieving desegregation borrowed from Gandhi, who was himself influenced by Thoreau—was apparently first used in the United States in 1942, by the then newly organized Congress on Racial Equality (CORE) in Chicago. Applied first in selected Northern cities, it was gradually tried in the Border states and did not begin work in the South until about 1954. The technique caught nationwide attention in 1955 with the spontaneous and independent development of the Montgomery (Alabama) bus strike, led by the Reverend Martin Luther King. After the successful conclusion of this effort, King organized the Southern Christian Leadership Conference (SCLC) which worked for desegregation in other Southern cities. In 1960, the CORE technique of "sit-ins," used for years on an inter-racial basis, was adopted spontaneously by groups of Southern Negro college students and employed all over the South with considerable success. These students formed the Student Nonviolent Co-ordinating Committee (SNCC), and a sympathetic group of Northern students—both white and Negro—formed the Students for Integration (SFI) and the Northern Student Movement (NSM) to provide moral and physical aid to the Southern SNCC and to CORE. The NSM also conducts an educational program for culturally deprived Negro children in certain Northern cities.

The significance of all these organizations was not simply that the Gandhian technique of nonviolent resistance was successfully added to the repertory of those seeking equal rights for Negroes, but also that large sections of the Negro masses were now directly participating in the efforts for the improvement of their status. The new organizations, rivals to some extent among themselves, placed themselves in partial opposition to the older NAACP and Urban League because their more traditional techniques of legal action in the courts and negotiation with whites in positions of power did not lend themselves to direct, local participation. The competition was healthy, however, for while the Negro youth and some lower income persons joined the newer organizations, the growing Negro adult middle class was stimulated to give increasing support to the older organizations. In the summer of 1963, all these organizations—supported by significant segments of organized religion and labor—joined forces to promote a dramatic "March on Washington."

Violence as a technique for changing the pattern of race relations was also developed in the post-World War II period. Some of this was a purely spontaneous response to white violence and did not take an organized form, as in the case of the Jacksonville, Florida, Negroes in March 1964, who rioted and destroyed white property when a Negro woman was killed by a white man. But of greater significance was the acceptance of a philosophy of violence by a small number of fairly well-educated Negroes, such as the group led by James Lawson of the United African Nationalist Movement, and by small numbers of poorly educated Negroes in the Muslim Brotherhood, the African Nationalist Pioneer Movement, and other nationalist organizations.

While cold conflict with white America had been found among the Negro lower class ever since the Garvey movement of the 1920's, it was never so well organized as in the Black Muslim movement ("Temple of Islam") of the 1950's and 1960's. This disciplined organization, probably reaching a membership of 100,000 by 1960, had as its stated goal a segregated territory within the United States, and it espoused—vaguely, in order not to violate the law—future violence to attain this goal. In 1964, one of its leaders, Malcolm X of New York, broke off from the parent movement headed by Prophet Elijah Muhammed to head a movement promising more immediate violence.

These were the new organized power currents that developed among Negroes in the post-World War II era. While not all of them sought integration, all of them did seek equality. They suggested a heightened group identification and impatience among Negroes,[1] and since they occurred at a time when desegregation was becoming a reality, they suggested that Negroes themselves—while hastening the demise of discrimination—might delay integration in its final stages. That is, group identification may become so strong that Negroes, like American Jews, may not want full integration.

Effects of World War II

As the Negro population was becoming more politically alert to the possibilities of changing race relations, the white population was becoming more aware of the need to change its traditional ways of associating with and thinking about Negroes. Perhaps the most important force here was the Second World War itself. It transformed the United States from an isolated and isolationist nation into a leading power with responsibilities in every part of the world. The American people had to see themselves as other people saw them, and they found the world's major criticism to be America's handling of its racial violence. Newspapers in every country reported on American discrimination and racial violence. A significant number of Americans became aware of this criticism, and it had a profound effect on their consciences. World reaction gained even

[1] The crescendo of Negro opposition to discrimination during the 1950's and 1960's, which reached the proportions of what was called a "Negro Revolt" by the summer of 1963, surprised many white Americans. Increased group identification, resulting in protest on the part of Negroes, was predicted in my book, *The Negro's Morale,* published in 1949.

greater significance as the colored nations of Asia and Africa, formerly under colonial rule, gained their independence. As the United States government partly realigned its foreign policy toward these new nations, it was obliged to encourage a more equalitarian treatment of nonwhite minorities at home. The formation of newly independent African nations after 1957 increased race-pride among American Negroes and strengthened their drive toward equality.

The Second World War and its aftermath brought unprecedented numbers of Americans in touch with other peoples. The Armed Services transported millions of Americans to Europe and Asia, and the tourist trade sent millions more to all parts of the world. Asiatics and Africans, especially students, began to visit the United States in significant numbers. A colored man on the downtown streets of New York City and Washington, D.C., was almost as likely to be a foreign as a native one, and even Southerners could no longer be sure whether the Negroes they saw in their cities were Americans or Africans. Perhaps more far-reaching was the change in the nation's mass media. Before 1940, newspapers, movies, and radio either ignored the Negro or stereotyped him unfavorably; after 1950, these media paid the Negro—foreign and native—a great deal of objective or favorable attention. Some social science research and certain novels made the Negro almost popular in some mainly intellectual white circles. With the rising living standards of the American Negro and his efforts to integrate himself into American life, white Americans generally were also much more likely to have direct contact with middle-class Negroes.

Federal Government Assistance

The more educated white Americans and those in closest contact with foreign opinion were most involved in the effort to eliminate discrimination and prejudice. This included the chief federal government officials. The United States Supreme Court led the way, perhaps because it was closer to the Constitution, which had been a thoroughly equalitarian document since 1868, and perhaps because it weighted foreign opinion along with domestic white opinion. The Supreme Court had generally sought to guarantee Negroes some legal protection, but it had equivocated until 1944 about the right to vote and about the equal use of public facilities. That year, a unanimous Court—in the case of Smith *v.* Allwright—declared unequivocally that the "white primary" was illegal, and that other such subterfuges to prevent Negroes from voting in the South were unconstitutional. Since then, the Court has consistently decided, with undivided opinions, that no branch of any government in the

United States could practice any discrimination whatsoever on grounds of race or religion.

Perhaps the most important of these decisions was the one handed down on May 17, 1954, which held that it was unconstitutional for the public schools to segregate the races. This decision withdrew the last legal support from the Southern states' effort to segregate public facilities, such as parks, playgrounds, libraries, and bathing beaches, as well as schools. The "separate but equal" doctrine was dead. The decision also applied to privately owned transportation facilities directly engaged in interstate commerce, including rail and bus terminal waiting rooms and restaurants. Only a small proportion of the local governments affected took immediate steps to desegregate, but through various pressures, the elaborate caste system of the South began to be dismantled. After 1954, the federal courts adjudicated many cases that were brought in order to implement the historic decision wiping out "separate but equal" facilities, but it could go no further in principle, for it was now operating in complete accord with the Constitutional provisions for full equality.

The Executive branch of the federal government began to fulfill its responsibilities for enforcing equality during the 1930's. The Roosevelt administration (1933–1945) practiced equality in the administration of some of its programs and for the first time hired Negroes in other than custodial or honorary capacities. The main innovation of the Roosevelt era, however, was forced on the President by the combined pressure of all the Negro organizations during the war, namely, the establishment of a Fair Employment Practices Commission (FEPC) which had the task of preventing discrimination in employment by industries holding contracts with the federal government. The Truman administration (1945–1953) went further in eliminating discrimination in federal employment and in the operation of federal programs, although it lost the FEPC in 1946 through Congressional action. Its main achievements along these lines were the virtual abolition of discrimination and segregation in the armed services and the support and publicity given to the President's Civil Rights Commission. The Eisenhower administration (1953–1961) continued the existing nondiscriminatory policies and gave administrative support to the courts' rulings on school desegregation—even to the point of calling out federal troops to enforce school desegregation in Little Rock, Arkansas, in 1957. The Kennedy administration (1961–1963) pumped life into the government committee to enforce nondiscrimination in employment by industries with government contracts—thereby reviving in effect the FEPC for major manufacturing companies—and extended administrative support to the courts' rulings on nondiscrimination by the states and by agencies of interstate transportation. Most important was the 1961 ruling by the Interstate Commerce Commission that rail and bus terminals might not segregate passengers. Further Executive action was taken in late 1962: President Kennedy signed a long delayed Executive Order to restrict government guarantees on loans to builders who insisted on excluding Negroes, and the Attorney General began a policy of calling on the National Guard and federal troops to assist in enforcing court orders for school desegregation. In June 1963, the President responded to the crescendo of Negro protests against discrimination —stimulated by growing unemployment and by the observance of the centennial anniversary of the Emancipation Proclamation—by setting before Congress a comprehensive program of proposed legislation guaranteeing voting rights and desegregation of public schools and prohibiting private enterprises involved in interstate commerce to refuse to do business with Negroes. While the last-mentioned feature had been in the statutes of twenty-eight Northern states since shortly after the Supreme Court (1883) had declared unconstitutional the Civil Rights Act of 1875, Congress regarded it as a drastic innovation and showed a strong inclination to cut down a portion of the President's proposal. After the death of President Kennedy in November 1963, President Johnson gave even more effective support to the civil rights bill then before Congress, and the bill became law on July 2, 1964.

The Legislative branch has the greatest power but the least achievement, largely because of the presence within it of Southern congressmen. These are a minority but hold the balance of power between the conservatives and liberals—a position they exploit in order to prevent enactment of civil rights legislation—and they have a disproportionate share of congressional leadership positions because of their seniority. Until 1964, the Congress' main contribution to the equalization of the races was a negative one: it has not sought to reverse the actions of the Judicial and Executive branches —except for killing the FEPC in 1946. In 1957, Congress passed its first statute since the 1870's to enforce civil rights; it was a weak law, which gave federal authorities some power to restrain local polling officials from preventing voting by Negroes. In 1960 it passed a second statute which slightly strengthened this law. It is doubtful that these statutes helped the position of Negroes enough to offset the damage inflicted on other liberal legislation, such as the bill to provide federal aid for education, by the political bargaining that was required. Negroes would be among those helped by the enactment of many bills which Southern congressmen block by deals with the conservatives: scarcely a bill comes before Congress these days—except occasionally in the fields of defense and foreign policy—which does not have a "race angle." Pending legislation that enhances the civil rights of Negroes has usually been killed by the Southern congressional bloc, who extend support to non-Southern conservatives in their opposition to other socially progressive measures, in exchange for help in preventing the passage of civil rights bills. Until the mass civil rights' demonstration of mid-1963, there did not seem to be much hope for significant legislation from Congress.

Some of what Negro leaders want from the federal government can be provided by the Executive branch, and the votes of Negroes are more effective in the Presidential elections than in the Congressional races. It is doubtful, however, that civil rights groups will diminish their efforts to get federal legislation. The main effort in 1960–1961 was to modify certain procedural rules in the Congress so that substantive civil rights legislation would be easier to pass. By 1963, however, the pressure from an awakening Negro populace —aided by many whites—forced Negro leaders to seek more substantive legislation to outlaw discrimination in voting, education, employment, and business relations.

The Civil Rights Act of 1964, which passed both houses of Congress with overwhelming majorities, despite a Southern filibuster in the Senate and the opposition of the leading contender for the Republican nomination for President, was the most comprehensive legislation to be enacted since post-Civil War days. Its success was due to the active support of President Lyndon Johnson, to demonstrations by civil rights and religious organizations, and to recognition by the congressional leadership of both parties of the facts of social change and of the moral and international issues involved. The main provisions of the eleven titles of the Act were: Title 1 prohibits voting registrars from applying different standards to white and Negro voting applicants and permits the Attorney General to sue in federal courts to enforce this. Title 2 prohibits refusal of service on account of race in hotels, restaurants, gasoline stations, and places of amusement if their operations affect interstate commerce, and it permits the Attorney General to sue in federal courts to enforce this. Title 3 requires that Negroes have equal access to, and treatment in, publicly owned or operated facilities and permits the offended citizen or the Attorney General to sue to enforce this. Title 6 provides that no person shall be subjected to racial discrimination in any program receiving federal aid. Title 7 bars discrimination by employers or unions with twenty-five or more employees or members and places enforcement powers in the hands of both a new Commission and the Attorney General. Title 9 permits the federal courts and the Attorney General to intervene in any state suit in which racial discrimination may be involved. If these provisions of the law are enforced, they will wipe out the remnants of the American caste system insofar as law can do so.

State Government Assistance

The Northern state governments and some local governments have been effective sources of change in American race relations. After the federal FEPC was killed by Congress in 1946, New York led the states in passing legislation setting up FEPC's within their jurisdictions. By the late 1950's, many Northern and Western states and cities with a sizeable Negro population had such legislation, designed to prevent discrimination in employment: the count in 1963 was twenty states and forty cities with some kind of FEPC law—covering 60 per cent of the total population and about 50 per cent of the minorities. A more difficult problem for the North was discrimination in housing, but in 1958 New York again led the way by making it illegal to discriminate against a person on grounds of race, religion, or nationality in the sale or rental of most categories of housing. By 1963, seventeen states and cities had passed legislation of this sort. It is as yet too early to ascertain the effectiveness of these statutes in eliminating housing discrimination and segregation.

FORCES MAINTAINING SEGREGATION

Such have been the main forces promoting the equalization of Negroes in American society since 1940. The main forces maintaining the subordination and segregation of Negroes have been those of tradition and the *status quo*. In 1954, however, a new factor entered which has undoubtedly prevented change from being more rapid than it might otherwise have been. This was the organization of Southern white opposition, mainly in the White Citizens' Councils. There had been no significant organization aiming to hold the Negro in a subordinate position since the decline of the Ku Klux Klan in the late 1920's. Minor and local organizations had made sporadic efforts, but the leading reactionary movements of the period between 1930 and 1954 avoided attacking the position of Negroes. The reaction to the rapid changes of the post-1940 period did not gain organized expression until 1954. Racists did not organize their resistance to changes in the caste system effectively until the very keystone of that system was endangered by the Supreme Court decision to desegregate the public schools. But the economic, political, and legal aspects of the caste system had already changed materially, and the pattern of social segregation had long been threatened before the proponents of the caste system organized themselves to protect it. For twenty-five years, the old racist ideology had found only occasional—and little heeded—spokesmen, and it was only after 1954 that it was again vigorously reasserted—and this at a time when the original source for this thinking had disappeared together with most of its material benefits. The ideology of racism was now no longer the response to a conflict between economic and political forces on the one hand and the idealism of the American creed and Constitution on the other, but merely an expression of a traditional psychology.

The South

The Southern resistance movement drew strength from all social classes, but there were also defectors from all classes. Many of the leaders of the White Citizens' Councils were upper class, and they used their economic power to hurt Negroes who sought a greater measure of civic equality. But some of the economic leaders of the South took the position that resistance to the Supreme Court decision disturbed the social peace and was bad for business. They concluded that the South should stop "fighting the War Between the States" and should become forward-looking and efficient. Political and other organizational leaders were similarly divided; while few whites admitted being pro-Negro or in favor of equality, many influential people of the South felt that the Negro could no longer be simply subordinated. It is difficult to know how the less articulate whites of the South divided, but they did divide. While many participated in violent actions to prevent desegregation, a majority of the voters of Little Rock, Arkansas, for example, voted for a school board that had announced its intention to desegregate the public schools in accord with the federal court order. There was similar evidence in other parts of the South that significant numbers of whites were quietly resigned to desegregation. The articulate and organized group, however, was the one that favored the maintenance of the caste system, and it used boycotts, influence on the Southern legislatures, violence, and other means to resist the changes. In general, this group is larger and more effective in the Deep South than in the Upper South; it is of little consequence in the Border states. With some exceptions, the only ones to benefit from the caste system today are those, mainly in the lower classes, who get psychological satisfaction out of a sense of racial superiority. There is also a small, and decreasing, number who benefit economically from the caste system by keeping the Negroes handicapped in job competition.

Some of the leaders of the resistance to change are those who believe that leaders should follow the wishes of the led. But there are also other types of leaders; a few have sought to make money by exploiting the fears of the white South. Another minor type seems to have a psychological need to lead violent movements. Still another rare type hoped to build a full-scale fascist movement out of the Southern resistance to desegregation, and they have had some success in attracting support from extreme right-wing radicals all over the country. But all of them together have not succeeded in stemming the changes in the system of discrimination and segregation. On occasions, a spontaneous leader will lead a day or two of violence, but most of the continuing leaders of the Southern resistance are persons with some traditional and legitimate authority. Imbued with a strong racist ideology, and a strong personal desire to keep the Negro subordinate, they also have a vested interest in keeping things on an even keel, and generally tend to hold their followers back from unplanned violence. Violence directed against Negroes might easily spread to white-owned property and other institutions, and so the traditional leaders try to keep racial agitation in check.

The North

In the North, there is little organized resistance to change in race relations, though there are small property-owners' associations that oppose the movement of Negroes into certain neighborhoods and oppose the passage of "fair-housing" or "open-occupancy" legislation. There are a great number of unorganized white Northerners who resist personal association with Negroes, particularly as neighbors and as social club members. Few Northern whites try to keep Negroes out of coemployment or out of the large, impersonal, voluntary associations, churches, or trade unions, but they still resist intimate association. For a few years following the development of the Southern resistance, there was an unorganized but articulate movement among some Northern leaders to put brakes on the trend toward equalization, particularly as it affected the South. Taking up the Southern theme of "leaving the South alone to work out its own problems," they argued that "both kinds of extremists are dangerous." But the majority of Northern leaders seem to have been persuaded that the South has always moved more rapidly toward better race relations when prodded by the North. The Northern proponents of "moderation" were most articulate in the period 1955–

1958, but they probably will be heard again if widespread violence occurs in the South. In 1964, right-wing extremist whites in California and Washington organized to curtail the Fair Housing statutes; they may be the forerunners of larger movements of resistance in the North.

The race relations crisis presents a continuing dilemma for those segments of Northern opinion that have strong ties with the South. This is true not merely for those who have family and personal connections with Southerners, but for Northern businessmen and trade union leaders with Southern branches. The national labor movement, for example, has not moved as forthrightly on integration within its own ranks as might have been expected because of pressures from Southern—and some Northern—locals and because of its hopes of organizing more white Southern workers. In 1959, Negro labor leaders formed the Negro American Labor Council to pressure the AFL-CIO into a position of complete integration. For a period, the leadership of the national labor movement refused to recognize the Negro group except in the critical terms of "dual unionism." By the end of 1961, however, the president of the AFL-CIO, George Meany, verbally capitulated and created organizational machinery to eliminate discrimination and segregation in the member unions. Organized labor remains, however, a divided force on the race issue, not only because of its Southern elements but also because the craft unions in the North refuse to modify their work rules to allow "new elements" into their crafts.

SUMMARY OF PROGRESS TO 1964

In the dynamic situation created by all these forces, any description of the position of Negroes written at any one moment is bound to be dated before it can be printed. The picture at the beginning of 1964 is here painted in broad strokes, necessarily superficial and incomplete. In 1940 Negroes were excluded from most occupations outside of agriculture and service; by 1960 some Negroes were to be found in nearly every occupation. Between 1940 and 1960 the proportion of white males in the labor force who had "white-collar jobs" rose from 30.3 to 41.2 per cent, while among nonwhite males the corresponding rise was from 5.0 to 16.0 per cent. At the same time the rise in skilled and semiskilled "blue-collar jobs" was from 34.3 to 38.6 per cent among white males and from 16.6 to 32.7 per cent among nonwhite males. Considerable employment discrimination remained in the South and even in the Border states, but it was greatly diminished in the Northern and

Western states. This did not mean that Negroes were approaching occupational equality, for there was the heritage of inadequate training, low-skill orientations, poor general education, and low seniority. The training lag was the most serious, because union and company seniority rules often made it impossible for Negroes to obtain training for better jobs.

Discrimination in economic benefits provided by the government—poor-relief, unemployment compensation, old-age assistance, public housing, and others—had been all but wiped out, except where there was local control in some Southern communities. A notable exception arose in Louisiana in 1960 where the "Aid to Dependent Children" program was curtailed for mothers who had illegitimate children while receiving ADC aid for their older children. This was applied almost exclusively to Negroes.

Politics

Negroes were voting without restriction in most areas of the Upper South, and in some cities of the Deep South. Between 1956 and 1960, while the increase in the total population voting was 8 per cent, the estimated increase in the number of Negroes voting was 16 per cent. The only state that almost systematically excluded Negroes from the polls—as they had been throughout the South in 1940—was Mississippi. Here, and in many rural areas of the other Deep Southern states, they were illegally prevented from voting by the whim of local polling officials and by threats of violence. The poll tax still existed in five states as a requirement for voting, although by the beginning of 1964 a Constitutional amendment was passed to make it illegal for federal elections. Several Southern states had literacy and "understanding" tests for all voting, but they were given to Negroes with discriminatory severity. Negroes occasionally ran for the minor local offices. In Atlanta a Negro was elected to the Georgia state legislature with the aid of white voters. The main changes in Southern politics resulting from Negro voting were the election of liberal Democrats in several states and the breaking of the barriers which hitherto had prevented conservatives from voting Republican.

Hence, the two-party system began to develop in the South—especially in Texas and Florida. In the 1948 and 1960 presidential elections, Negro votes in several Southern as well as Northern states provided the margin of victory for the Democratic candidates. In 1963 there were five Negro congressmen and many local public officials, mainly in Northern cities, and Negroes were thoroughly integrated into the local political parties of the Northern states. In

Massachusetts in 1962, a Negro was elected to a major state office —attorney general—for the first time since Reconstruction days. Many Negroes were in significant appointive posts, including federal judgeships. The great majority of Negroes were voting Democratic, although there was some evidence of their flexibility in switching party affiliation when a local Republican candidate seemed more pro-Negro than his Democratic counterpart.

In 1964, 90 per cent of the Negroes voted Democratic, and their votes carried a number of "liberal" legislators into office.

Law Enforcement

In 1940, law enforcement in the South was virtually non-existent when Negroes were the victims—whether whites or other Negroes were the criminals—and brutally severe when whites were the victims and Negroes the law violators. By the 1950's there were many cases, even in the Deep South, of white persons who committed crimes against Negroes being prosecuted and punished, although this was by no means general. Negro criminals whose victims were other Negroes were much more likely to be dealt with properly by law enforcement officials. Practically all Southern cities employed Negro policemen after 1945 to maintain law and order in their Negro communities, and Southern judges were no longer likely to release Negro criminals on the word of a white man. There was still considerable "overenforcement" of the law when Negroes were apprehended for crimes against whites, but civil suits between a white and a Negro were handled much more equitably. Despite the mass violence which attended many instances of desegregation, extralegal violence of the everyday, person-to-person basis which was characteristic of the pre-1940 period was now greatly reduced. Lynching was a rare event after 1950, and even murders of Negro prisoners by white policemen and jailers became infrequent.

Thus, even while tension between the races in the South mounted, and the mass violence attending some desegregation got great publicity, total violence declined. This seemed to be due to the fact that potential white perpetrators of violence were aware that they were in some danger of retribution from the law or from retaliating Negroes. In the North, police brutality remained sporadic and individual—it had never been a matter of policy—and there was no evidence of discrimination by judges. While the Second World War years saw some major race riots in the North and West, the formation of interracial citizens' committees in many Northern cities practically eliminated them from 1944 on. The major exception was Chicago and some of its suburbs, where there were numerous small riots all through the 1940's and 1950's when Negroes moved into new residential neighborhoods or attempted to swim at the "white" public bathing beaches.

Social Relations

These changes in the economic, political, and legal spheres were occurring regularly and generally with little public attention or controversy. Changes in the area of social relations, however, were coming about in some areas but not in others, and at times received a great deal of notice. The movement of rural Negroes into the Northern and Southern cities was associated with housing segregation, and housing segregation brought the inevitable segregation of neighborhood facilities, over-crowding, high rents, run-down buildings, slums, and expansion into new neighborhoods attended by conflict with whites. This became the most serious aspect of the race problem, certainly in the North. The chief legal buttress for housing segregation had been the "restrictive covenant," a clause written into a deed for property preventing its resale to members of specified groups, mainly Negroes. In 1948, the United States Supreme Court decided that the racial restrictive covenant was unenforceable in the courts, thus wiping out the legal support for housing segregation and allowing it to rest on voluntary action.

The decision eased the situation for Negroes somewhat, and it was followed by various organized efforts to develop integrated housing in the North. Publicly subsidized housing was no longer segregated, and some privately sponsored integrated housing projects were developed. But the great masses of urban Negroes remained segregated, and there was some evidence that housing segregation was increasing in the South. Negroes themselves fought the housing restrictions generally only when there was insufficient space to live; only a few of them sought to break the pattern of segregation itself. By the end of the 1950's some Northern states passed statutes making it illegal to refuse to rent or sell housing to Negroes, and generally in the North the space pressures on Negroes eased considerably.

Late in 1962 the President issued an executive order which restricts the lending of money with government guarantees if the housing affected is not available for lease or purchase by minority groups. Political considerations limited the coverage of this order to only about a third of the 90 per cent of all housing units covered by such loans. A full withholding of government credit and guarantees would remove the strongest barrier to housing integration. Whether Negroes would move in large numbers to take advantage of it is more questionable. At this time, residential segregation is one of the most serious and least soluble aspects of the race problem, particularly in the Northern states.

Segregation of other public and privately owned but essentially public facilities remained the effect of housing segregation in the North. This has become known as "de facto" segregation, and there were several local efforts to mix children in the public schools despite the fact that their residences were largely segregated. Forced segregation of schools, playgrounds, restaurants, hotels, and other public and commercial establishments became exceptional in the North as the climate of opinion changed and the old "public accommodations" statutes of the Northern states once again became operative. Some cities began movements to upgrade Negro education—to compensate for cultural deprivation in the family and community—preparatory to initiating programs to end de facto school segregation. In the South, desegregation of these kinds of facilities began as a result of the court decisions and the organized movements already examined.

By 1961, school systems were formally desegregated in all the border states; in many scattered areas of the Upper South and in a few cities of the Deep South there was token desegregation. Violence had attended school desegregation in Dover, Delaware; Clinton and Nashville, Tennessee; Little Rock, Arkansas; and New Orleans, Louisiana. But it was accomplished peacefully and more thoroughly in the larger school systems of Washington, D.C.; St. Louis, Missouri; Dallas and Houston, Texas; and Atlanta, Georgia. By 1961 only Mississippi, Alabama, and South Carolina had none of their schools desegregated, and by 1963 even these had token desegregation in a few schools. There was only spotty and token desegregation in all of the Deep Southern states and some of the Upper South states, but over one-third of all Negro children living in school districts segregated by statute before 1955 were in desegregated schools by 1963.

Desegregation of the other public and the privately owned commercial establishments took roughly the same pattern, though with a few years of delay. In the two years of 1960 and 1961, the sit-in movement opened some restaurants to Negroes in about two hundred cities of the South, and there was continuing desegregation after that. But the majority of restaurants in many of these cities remained segregated, and Negro patronage of the nonsegregated restaurants was rare. Some hotels in the larger Southern cities, such as Houston and Atlanta, quietly desegregated. An issue arose over the exclusion of dark-skinned representatives of foreign nations from the highway restaurants of Maryland, a Border state, and the federal government intervened with partial success. Hotels, theaters, and recreational facilities were opened to Negroes on approximately the same basis as restaurants: in every state but Mississippi and Alabama there were at least some desegregated, but the majority in the Deep South and even some areas of the Upper South remained segregated, and Negro patronage of the desegregated facilities was rare. Interstate transportation was effectively desegregated, and—after the Montgomery, Alabama, bus boycott of 1957—so was the local transportation within many Southern cities.

One of the major gains in the North was the desegregation of most of the major voluntary associations. The major professional associations were desegregated in the South also. Except for weak, formal associations—such as the PTA's—most other Southern voluntary associations remained segregated. Social clubs and informal groups remained segregated throughout the country, with a few exceptions in the North. College fraternities and sororities remained mainly segregated in fact, although a campaign in the North to remove formal barriers was largely successful. Almost the same could be said of the churches, although in mixed neighborhoods, churches sometimes served members of both races.

Interracial marriages were probably on the increase in the North, although they were still not frequent. In the South, interracial marriage continued to be illegal: this was the one type of law discriminating among the races still on the statute books of the Southern states; not even the Negro organizations have sought to challenge it, and hence the courts had no occasion to declare it unconstitutional. The probability is that the courts would declare it unconstitutional, for they had nullified a California statute barring marriage between whites and Orientals. But apparently the Negro leadership thought it unwise to challenge this last formal barrier of the caste system, at least until other forms of desegregation should be accomplished in greater degree. At the present writing (winter, 1964), there are two cases in the state courts challenging the constitutionality of the laws forbidding interracial marriage.

The formerly elaborate "etiquette of race relations" was crumbling in the South, and it became common to hear Negroes addressed by whites by their formal titles of "Mr.," "Mrs.," and "Miss." The self-demeaning manner of Negroes in the presence of whites disappeared except in the rural areas. With the improvement in occupational opportunities, Negroes were much less likely to be domestic servants. The barriers to serious conversations between the races broke down in the North, but remained in the South. The results of these changes were that Northern whites could perceive Negroes as human beings for the first time, while relations between the races in the South grew cold as they became increasingly restricted to matters of common economic interest. The white Southerners were no longer sure they understood "their" Negroes, and Negroes could no longer be relied on to maintain their "place" in the presence of whites. A Gallup poll taken in July 1963 showed that 83 per cent of white Southerners expected that there would soon be complete integration of the races in public accommodations, although six years earlier this proportion was only 45 per cent. What is more, 49 per cent expected this integration to be achieved within the coming five years, and only 9 per cent expected it would take longer than twenty years. The same poll showed that 56 per cent of the total population believed that Negroes were treated the "same as whites" in their community, with Negroes in every region outside the South sharing this majority view.

A National Opinion Research Center poll, conducted in December 1963, showed that 30 per cent of white Southerners accepted *school* integration, as compared to only 2 per cent in 1942 and 14 per cent in 1956. Among white Northerners, the proportions accepting the principle of *school* integration was 75 per cent in 1963, 61 per cent in 1956, and 40 per cent in 1942. Acceptance of *residential* integration among Southern whites rose from 12 per cent in 1942 to 51 per cent in 1963; among Northern whites, it rose from 42 per cent to 70 per cent. Estimates of Negroes' intelligence—as measured by answers to the question, "Can Negroes learn things just as well as whites if they are given the same education and training?"—likewise rose, thus indicating the decline in racism. Among Southern whites, the proportion agreeing rose from 21 per cent in 1942 to 60 per cent in 1963; among Northern whites, the rise was from 50 per cent to 80 per cent.

FUTURE DEVELOPMENT

There could be no doubt that the races were moving rapidly toward equality and desegregation by 1964. In retrospect, the change of the preceding twenty years appeared as one of the most rapid in the history of human relations. Much of the old segregation and discrimination remained in the Deep South, and housing segregation with its concomitants was still found throughout the country, but the all-encompassing caste system had been broken everywhere. Prejudice as an attitude was still common, but racism as a comprehensive ideology was maintained by only a few. The change had been so rapid, and caste and racism so debilitated, that this author ventures to predict—if the present trends continue—the end of all legal segregation and discrimination within a decade, and the decline of informal segregation and discrimination to a mere shadow in two decades. The attitude of prejudice might remain indefinitely, but it will be on the minor order of Catholic-Protestant prejudice within three decades. These changes would not mean that there would be equality between the races within this time, for the heritage of past discriminations would still operate to give Negroes lower "life chances." But the dynamic social forces creating inequality will, if the present trends continue, be practically eliminated in three decades. As far as separation of the races without overt discrimination is concerned, this will come for a while to be more associated with Negro group identification than with white exclusionism. It would only be appropriate to guess that most sociologists would find these predictions "optimistic," but then, most sociologists found the predictions contained in *An American Dilemma* of twenty years ago optimistic, and most of these predictions have since come true.

The student of society, who must have historical perspective and be aware of continuities and rigidities in the social structure, may consider the development in American race relations from 1942 to 1964 among the most rapid and dramatic of social changes to have ever been achieved without violent revolution. To the participants themselves the changes did not appear to be so rapid. People generally live from day to day, and from month to month, without historical perspective, and hence tend not to perceive changes that occur over a period of years. The "social present" usually means much more to people than does social change. Young people who have come to awareness of the world around them during the latter part of the period under consideration see only the conditions of the last few years; for them the conditions of the pre-1940 period are "ancient history," and hence the changes of twenty years are not part of their image of the modern world.

These things are true for all social change. But of particular significance for our analysis is the fact that Negroes *still* experience discrimination, insult, segregation, and the threat of violence, and in a sense have become more sensitive and less "adjusted" to these things. To them the current problems and current conflicts have much more significance than those of ten or twenty years ago. Schooled as they are by the American Creed, their standard of comparison for the present situation is not what existed in 1940, but what the Constitution and "the principles of democracy" say should be. Further, most American Negroes are aware of great changes going on in Africa, and in fact are inclined to exaggerate the "improvements" there resulting from the demise of old-fashioned colonialism. From their perspective, the changes occurring in the United States are much too slow; they want "freedom *now*," as the slogan goes. White Americans, who have in mind the United States Constitution and their country's role in a world whose population is two-thirds colored, might agree with them.

Part
Two
The Reality
of the Ghetto

   Although black Americans made significant economic progress during World War II, the postwar period has been marked by
a lack of black advances, relative to those made by whites, in the
areas of income and employment. As Leonard Broom and Norval
Glenn show in their study of black occupational mobility and
income change from 1940 to the mid-1960s, the relative deprivation
of blacks has remained depressingly constant. Although Negroes
did make some progress in gaining entrance into higher-status
occupations in the postwar period, blacks as a group made virtually
no gains on whites in respect to income. Between 1945 and 1965,
black income fluctuated between fifty-one and fifty-seven percent of
white income. The rate of black unemployment has been twice that
for white Americans. Thus, Broom and Glenn argue that despite the
fact that the *absolute* economic position of blacks is better than
it was in the 1940s, because of improvements in Negro education
and the general prosperity of white Americans, blacks are angered
over the lack of improvement in their *relative* socioeconomic status.
In addition, the absolute economic *gap* between white and black
America is widening.
   But economic statistics tell only part of the story of black
poverty. In the second selection, Kenneth Clark describes the "culture of poverty" which flourishes in America's urban ghettos. This
selection is a chapter from Clark's book, *Dark Ghetto,* which grew
out of his two years as a consultant to Harlem Youth Opportunities
Unlimited (Haryou). As Clark shows, the realities of Harlem—unemployment, poor housing, crime, and family instability—create a
climate of despair and hopelessness which makes it virtually impossible for lower-class blacks to escape their poverty. Although Clark's
focus is Harlem, he emphasizes the fact that the realities of Harlem
are representative of conditions in all of America's black ghettos.

3
Occupation
and
Income

Leonard Broom
Norval Glenn

During recent decades there have been improvements of
the greatest consequences in the occupational and economic standing of Negro Americans. Viewed in absolute terms, these gains are
impressive. For instance, in 1940 only 8.5 percent of employed
Negro workers had white-collar or skilled manual occupations,
whereas by 1960 almost 20 percent were employed in such work.
The percentage employed as laborers and domestic service workers
fell from 54 percent in 1940 to 33 percent in 1960. Unemployment
in the nonwhite labor force fell during this period from 16.8 percent
to 8.7 percent. The median wage and salary income of gainfully
employed nonwhite males rose from $460 in 1939 to $3,023 in 1962.
In actual buying power, in constant (1962) dollars, the increase was
threefold—from $995 in 1939 to $3,023 in 1962.

However, these substantial occupational and income gains
have not been sufficient to forestall Negro restiveness. Advancement may bring not satiation of ambition but desire for even greater
advancement. Success is companion to a discovery of the possible
and an increase in aspiration. But this is not the full story. Men
evaluate their achievements not only in absolute but in relative
terms, not only in dollars earned but also in relation to the earnings
of co-workers and competitors. Many Negroes lack precise knowledge of the gap between Negro and white economic status, but
they are nevertheless aware that the gap has not narrowed greatly.
The satisfaction derived from increased prosperity has been diluted

Reprinted by permission of Harper & Row, Publishers, from Leonard
Broom and Norval D. Glenn, *Transformation of the Negro American,* Col-
ophon Edition, pp. 105–122. Copyright © 1965 by Leonard Broom and
Norval D. Glenn.

by the observation that whites are also more prosperous and that Negroes are nearly the same distance behind. Furthermore, the rate of Negro advancement, which was very rapid during World War II, declined during the postwar period and therefore fell far short of the hopes, kindled by wartime experience, that Negroes were at last catching up.

Improved occupational and educational status has made keener the Negro's perception of his relative disadvantage. For the first time, many Negroes have a vantage point from which to estimate with some accuracy their relative condition. A semiliterate agricultural laborer can easily tell that his economic status is far below that of most whites, but he is unlikely to be able to make a meaningful comparison. In contrast, an industrial worker knows where he stands in the labor hierarchy and can guess how far he would have to go to be on a par with white workers. A Negro college professor in a predominantly Negro college knows reasonably well what his degree is worth compared with the same degree (perhaps from the same institution) held by a white professor teaching in a neighboring university. Negroes now are not only more able but also more inclined to gauge their standing relative to whites because more of them have contacts with whites on an equal footing. Where Negro social isolation has decreased and egalitarian social contacts have increased, one effect undoubtedly has been a rise in aspirations and a heightened sense of deprivation. Because high income and high occupational status are rare among Negroes, the middle-status Negro (by white standards) ranks above most other Negroes and therefore enjoys high prestige in the Negro community.[1] As long as he evaluates his economic status in relation to other Negroes, he may be fairly well satisfied, but when he begins to judge his status in relation to whites, he ranks himself lower and is less satisfied. To use the hackneyed metaphor, he is no longer a big frog in a little pond but a little frog in a big pond.

THE TURNING POINT: WORLD WAR II

Neither the occupational nor the economic gap between Negroes and whites was markedly closed between emancipation and the entry of the United States into World War II. In 1890, when the Census Bureau first gathered data on Negro occupations, almost

[1] Norval D. Glenn, "Negro Prestige Criteria: A Case Study in the Bases of Prestige," *American Journal of Sociology*, 68 (May, 1963), pp. 645–657.

90 percent of Negro workers were in agriculture and domestic and personal service; about 60 percent of the native white workers were so employed. Early in the twentieth century, large numbers of Negroes moved from agriculture and domestic service into industrial occupations. However, there was an even greater movement of white workers, so that by 1940 only 20 percent of white workers remained in agriculture and domestic and personal service, compared with about 55 percent of Negro workers. In addition, many more white than Negro workers moved into skilled and white-collar occupations, resulting in a somewhat wider occupational gap between Negroes and whites in 1940 than in 1890. Accurate data on Negro and white incomes are not available for years prior to 1939, but there is little reason to believe that in 1939 Negro income compared more favorably with white income than it did late in the nineteenth century.

With the entry of the United States into World War II, Negro workers for the first time took a giant step toward equality with whites. The drafting of hundreds of thousands of civilian workers into the Armed Services created an acute labor shortage, and the dearth of qualified white males led to the recruitment of white women and Negroes of both sexes into types of work that previously had been largely closed to them. President Roosevelt's Executive Order 8802 in June 1941 forbade discrimination on the basis of race, creed, or national origin by employers who held government war contracts. The Fair Employment Practices Committee was set up to implement the order, and in several cases the committee was able to prevent discrimination and to open new jobs to Negroes. With the return of veterans to the civilian labor force at the end of the war, with the end of the Fair Employment Practices Committee in 1946, and with the decline of industries that mainly served the war effort, Negroes suffered losses in occupational status. However, not all wartime gains were lost, and conditions remained more favorable for Negro advancement than they had been before the war. Negro servicemen and workers in war industries gained valuable training and experience that enabled them to compete more effectively, and their employment in large numbers in unionized industries during the war left them in a stronger position in the labor movement. (Negroes first joined labor unions in large numbers after the founding of the CIO in 1935.)

However, the continuation of Negro gains after the war was not so much due to the residual effects of the war as to the nearly continuous prosperity and sustained growth of the whole economy. During and since the war, hundreds of thousands of new jobs have been created at intermediate and upper levels, and many Negroes

have been able to move up without displacing whites.[2] Between
1940 and 1960, the total number of employed white-collar workers
increased by nearly 12 million, or 81 percent, while the total
employed labor force increased by only 37 percent. Hundreds of
thousands of white workers have moved into new higher-level jobs,
leaving vacancies at intermediate levels that could be filled by
Negroes. For instance, of white males 25 through 34 years old in
1950 who were employed as clerical and kindred workers, 61,000—
or 9 percent—had moved out of these occupations or died by 1960
and had not been replaced by other white males of the same cohort
(a "cohort" is made up of all persons born during a given period
of time). Some of these whites were replaced by younger whites,
but many were replaced by Negroes. Because Negro gains could
occur without loss to whites, white resistance to Negro advancement
was less than it otherwise would have been. Expansion of jobs at
the upper levels is not a new trend; it goes back to the start of
industrialization, but until recently the upward movement of workers
generated by this change did not greatly benefit Negroes. As long
as large numbers of European immigrants were entering the
country, they, rather than Negroes, replaced most of the native-born
whites who moved up. World War I slowed European immigration
and the Immigration Act of 1924 reduced it to a mere trickle, so
that by the 1940s there was no longer a large pool of immigrants
at the lowest occupational levels to replace the upward-moving
native workers. The opportunity for the first great occupational
advancement of Negro Americans was at hand.

THE OCCUPATION GAP

Some aspects of the occupational advancement of employed
Negroes in relation to employed whites from 1940 to 1960 are
shown in Table 1. The "expected" proportion of Negroes in each
occupational group is the proportion of Negroes in the total employed labor force. For instance, 8.4 percent of all employed males
in 1960 were Negro, and one might "expect" 8.4 percent of employed
males in each occupational group to be Negro. If the actual proportion of Negroes in an occupational group was more than this
parity the ratio is greater than 1.00; if the actual proportion was
less than expected, the ratio is less than 1.00.

The greatest gains for both Negro males and females from

2 Norval D. Glenn, "Some Changes in the Relative Status of American Nonwhites, 1940 to 1960," *Phylon*, 24 (Summer, 1963), pp. 111–113.

1940 to 1960 were in intermediate-level occupations, such as clerical workers, craftsmen, foremen, and operatives. There was negligible increase in the representation of Negro males in the highest-level occupations during the two decades. The ratio of the actual to expected proportion of employed Negro males who were managers, officials, and proprietors increased only slightly, from .13 in 1940 to .17 in 1960. The ratio for professional and technical workers declined, from .33 in 1940 to .30 in 1960.

TABLE 1: Ratio of Actual to Expected Proportion of Employed Workers Who Were Negro, in Each Occupational Group, United States, 1940, 1950, and 1960[a]

Occupational group	Male			Female		
	1940	1950	1960	1940	1950	1960
Professional, technical, and kindred workers	.33	.29	.30	.33	.45	.55
Farmers and farm managers	1.44	1.28	.77	2.20	2.24	1.06
Managers, proprietors, and officials, except farm	.13	.19	.17	.19	.30	.28
Clerical and kindred workers	.19	.47	.70	.04	.14	.25
Sales workers	.13	.17	.19	.07	.16	.19
Craftsmen, foremen, and kindred workers	.30	.42	.50	.16	.41	.54
Operatives and kindred workers	.69	1.05	1.23	.34	.76	.82
Private household workers	7.00	5.71	5.32	3.38	4.87	4.60
Service workers, except private household	1.92	2.27	2.32	.92	1.55	1.58
Farm laborers and foremen	2.44	2.14	2.55	4.49	2.61	2.47
Laborers, except farm and mine	2.44	2.92	2.96	.96	1.88	1.85

SOURCE: Computed from data from the 1940, 1950, and 1960 census of U.S. population.
[a] The "expected" proportion of Negroes in each occupational group is the proportion of Negroes in the total employed labor force.

This decline is accounted for by a large decrease in Negro clergymen, from 17,102 in 1940 to 13,955 in 1960. The number of male clergymen per 10,000 population declined from 13.3 in 1940 to 7.4 in 1960 for Negroes but increased from 9.8 to 11.4 for whites. This decline in Negro clergymen reflects the passing from the scene of the older traditional minister, perhaps a declining interest in religion among Negro Americans, and increased opportunities for young Negroes in more lucrative lines of work. Since most Negro clergymen in 1940 were poorly educated, poorly paid, and professional workers only in the extended sense, a decline in their numbers may be regarded as a gain for Negroes.

If clergymen are excluded from the professional and technical category, there was a slight increase in the ratio from .24 for 1940 to .27 for 1960. In contrast to males, the ratio for Negro females increased appreciably in each of the highest-level occupational categories, from .33 in 1940 to .55 in 1960 as professional and technical workers, and from .19 to .28 as managers, officials, and proprietors.

In spite of Negro gains in the 1940s and 1950s, both males and females in 1960 were far from proportionally represented in all of the white-collar occupational groups and as craftsmen and foremen. Furthermore, the recent rate of Negro increase in these occupations is not great enough to lead to occupational equality in the near future. For instance, assuming that the representation of Negro males as professional, technical, and kindred workers (excluding clergymen) were to continue to increase at the 1940–1960 rate, it would not be for *530 years* after 1960 (until the year 2490) that proportional representation would be attained. By the same calculations, proportional representation of Negro males would not be attained as managers, officials, and proprietors within 415 years and as sales workers not for 270 years. Since these projections extend several generations beyond the lifetime of Negroes now living, it is small wonder that Negroes imbued with the ideal of equality are less than satisfied with the recent pace of occupational gains. To be sure, neither Negroes nor whites are aware of the arithmetic of trends nor their harsh implications, but some Negroes may sense the rate of change. (The reader must be cautioned that these figures are projections, not predictions. Alterations in the rates of change probably will occur and we point to some of the conditions that may cause such changes. Nevertheless, the projections do dramatize the gap that remains.)

Small as the ratios were in the higher-level occupational groups in 1960, they do not fully reveal the extent of inequality. Within each occupational group, Negroes were relatively concentrated in the lower-paying and lower-prestige occupations. For instance, the occupational group of professional, technical, and kindred workers includes such diverse occupations as physicians, engineers, school teachers, social workers, and medical and dental technicians. In 1960, only 11.4 percent of the employed Negro male professional, technical, and kindred workers were architects, dentists, engineers, lawyers, judges, physicians, and surgeons. In contrast, 31.4 percent of the employed white male professionals had these higher-paying occupations. In addition, the rate of increase of Negroes in the higher-level professional and technical occupations has generally been less (see Table 2). For instance, from 1940 to 1960 there was no increase in the representation of Negro males as physicians and surgeons or as college presidents, professors, and instructors, and the increase in Negro representation as dentists was very small. The big gains were in relatively low-paying semi-professional occupations, such as welfare and recreation workers and medical and dental technicians.

Not only are Negroes concentrated in the lower-paying occupations; they generally earn less than whites in the same occupations. The 1959 median earnings of white and nonwhite males in selected occupations are shown in Table 3. The gap between whites and nonwhites was generally less in governmental occupations such as postal workers, firemen, and policemen. For the seven occupations of this type in the table, the average ratio of nonwhite to white median earnings was .92, whereas for the other occupations the average was only .72. Present-day discrimination in government employment, where it exists more often takes the form of exclusion than of lower pay. Even at the state and local levels, wages and salaries are fairly well standardized, and Negroes and whites with similar jobs and similar seniority are usually paid about the same. Highly trained Negro workers, such as engineers and electronics technicians, who are employed mainly by private industry also are paid almost as much as their white counterparts. In contrast, an appreciable earnings gap existed in 1959 between Negroes and whites in most manual occupations and in those occupations in which Negroes serve other Negroes as enterpreneurs or as employees of Negro institutions. Some, but not all, of the Negro-white disparity in earnings within occupations is due to greater unemployment of Negroes in most occupations.

The Negro-white occupational gap obviously is still very wide, and it is closing so slowly that it will not disappear within the next century unless the rate of Negro gains sharply accelerates. Some acceleration, especially at the highest levels, is likely and may already have occurred since 1960. The increased race consciousness of Negroes is making the opening of higher-level government jobs to Negroes a political necessity and is making the hiring of Negroes by private firms requisite to the attraction and holding of a large Negro clientele. There will be some discrimination in favor of Negroes, but unless it becomes more widespread than seems probable, near equality in occupational status must await near equality in occupational qualifications. As we point out above, near equality in qualifications is at least several decades away.

TABLE 2: Ratio of Actual to Expected Proportion of Negro Males in Selected Occupations, United States, 1940, 1050, and 1960

	1940	1950	1960
Accountants and auditors	n.a.[a]	.04	.07
Architects	.05	.07	.10
Artists and art teachers	.08	.14	.20
Authors, editors, and reporters	.09	.09	.11
Bookkeepers	n.a.	.06	.12
Chemists	.06	.12	.24
Clergymen	1.48	1.31	.85
College presidents, professors, and instructors (not elsewhere classified)	.30	.30	.30
Dentists	.24	.24	.30
Designers and draftsmen	.01	.05	.13
Engineers			
—aeronautical	n.a.	.02	.07
—civil	.01	.05	.10
—electrical	.01	.03	.08
—mechanical	.01	.03	.05
Insurance agents and brokers	n.a.	.23	.18
Lawyers and judges	.07	.09	.12
Mail carriers	.54	.87	1.24
Medical and dental technicians	n.a.	.44	.95
Musicians and music teachers	.82	.86	.83
Natural scientists (not elsewhere classified)	n.a.	.16	.18
Pharmacists	.12	.16	.20
Physicians and surgeons	.25	.24	.24
Real estate agents and brokers	.13	.20	.20
Salaried managers, officials, and proprietors (not elsewhere classified)			
—in manufacturing	n.a.	.03	.05
—in retail and wholesale trade	n.a.	.13	.11
—in finance, insurance, and real estate	n.a.	.10	.12
Salesmen and sales clerks			
—in manufacturing	n.a.	.05	.06
—in wholesale trade	n.a.	.05	.06
—in retail trade	n.a.	.20	.25
Self-employed managers, officials, and proprietors (not elsewhere classified)			
—in construction	n.a.	.20	.21
—in manufacturing	n.a.	.06	.10
—in wholesale trade	n.a.	.17	.24
—in eating and drinking places	n.a.	.46	.45
—in other retail trade	n.a.	.19	.18
Social scientists	n.a.	.15	.19
Social, welfare, and recreation workers	n.a.	.73	1.17
Teachers (not elsewhere classified)	.63	.76	.77

SOURCE: Computed from data from the 1940, 1950, and 1960 censuses of U.S. population.
[a] Not available.

TABLE 3: Ratio of Nonwhite to White Median Earnings of Males in Selected Occupations, United States, 1959

Occupation	Ratio of nonwhite to white	Occupation	Ratio of nonwhite to white
Electrical and electronics technicians	.98	Secondary school teachers	.76
Firemen, fire protection	.96	Foremen (not elsewhere classified)	.74
Mail carriers	.96	Compositors and type-setters	.73
Postal clerks	.95	Automobile mechanics and repairmen	.71
Policemen and detectives	.95	Dentists	.70
Aeronautical engineers	.94	Linemen and servicemen, telegraph, telephone, and power	.69
Electrical engineers	.91		
Inspectors, public administration	.90	Laborers, except farm and mine	.69
Bookkeepers	.90	Musicians and music teachers	.67
Designers and draftsmen	.88		
Airplane mechanics and repairmen	.88	Painters, construction and maintenance	.64
Mechanical engineers	.88	Clergymen	.64
Bus drivers	.87	Barbers	.64
Electricians	.86	Insurance agents, brokers, and underwriters	.63
Civil engineers	.86		
Accountants and auditors	.84	Salesmen and sales clerks (not elsewhere classified)	.63
Officials and administrators, public administration	.83	Brickmasons, stonemasons, and tile setters	.61
Office machine operators	.83	Truck and tractor drivers	.59
Elementary school teachers	.82	Cement and concrete finishers	.59
Medical and dental technicians	.80	Plumbers and pipe fitters	.58
Radio and television mechanics and repairmen	.79	Plasterers	.56
Chemists	.78	Carpenters	.55
College professors and instructors	.77	Farm laborers, wage workers	.52
Mine operatives and laborers (not elsewhere classified)	.77	Physicians and surgeons	.39
Shipping and receiving clerks	.77	Farmers and farm managers	.33

SOURCE: Computed from data from *U.S. Census of Population: 1960,* Final Report PC(2)-7B, Table 1 (U.S. Bureau of the Census, Washington, D.C.).

THE INCOME GAP

Until recently, the moderate closing of the occupational gap between employed Negroes and whites was accompanied by a similar narrowing of the income gap. The income gap closed appreciably during World War II but very slowly and erratically during the postwar period. White and nonwhite median family incomes in constant (1965) dollars are shown for each year from 1947 to 1965 in Figure 1. Incomes for both races went up steeply during the period, but the ratio of the nonwhite to the white median hardly changed; it was exactly the same in 1965 as it was in 1955. The absolute gap between the white and nonwhite medians increased. The data in Table 4 on the median income of individuals show greater improvement in the relative standing of nonwhites. However, these data are only for persons *with* income, and since a greater percentage of Negro than of white adult males had no income, the comparison of family incomes is more meaningful. Nevertheless, it is important that the ratio of Negro to white median income of males with income did not increase from 1949 to 1959.

TABLE 4: Median Income of Persons with Income, by Race and Sex, United States, 1949 and 1959

	Negro	White	Ratio of Negro to white
Both sexes			
1949	961	2,058	.47
1959	1,519	3,026	.50
Male			
1949	1,356	2,582	.53
1959	2,254	4,338	.52
Female			
1949	703	1,139	.62
1959	905	1,509	.60

SOURCE: *U.S. Census of Population: 1960,* Final Report PC(1)-1D, p. 578 (U.S. Bureau of the Census, Washington, D.C.).

The slower rate of income gains as compared to occupational gains of Negroes is largely accounted for by (1) an increase in the difference between white and nonwhite unemployment rates and (2) an increase in the income gap between lower-level and other occupations. The ratio of nonwhite to white percentage of workers unemployed increased from 1.18 in 1940 to 1.73 in 1950, to 1.85 in 1960. The absolute differences between the percentages for the same three years were 2.6, 3.3, and 4.0. Mechanization of industrial processes that eliminated many jobs in occupations in which Negroes are concentrated largely accounts for this widening of the unemployment gap.

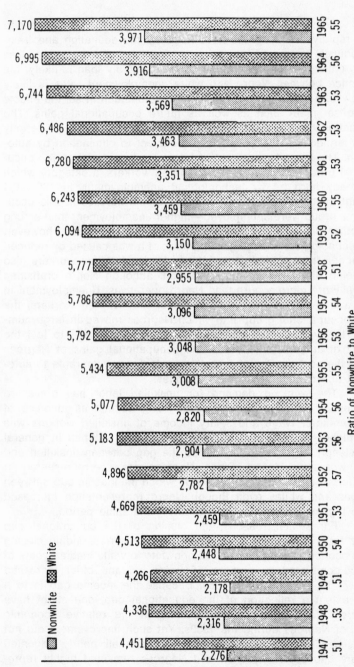

FIGURE 1. Median Family Income in Constant (1965) Dollars, by Color, United States, 1947-1965

SOURCE: Computed from data reported annually by the U.S. Bureau of the Census in Current Population Reports, Series P-60.

Ratio of Nonwhite to White

■ Nonwhite
▨ White

Year	Nonwhite	White	Ratio
1965	7,170	3,971	.55
1964	6,995	3,916	.56
1963	6,744	3,569	.53
1962	6,486	3,463	.53
1961	6,280	3,351	.53
1960	6,243	3,459	.55
1959	6,094	3,150	.52
1958	5,777	2,955	.51
1957	5,786	3,096	.54
1956	5,792	3,048	.53
1955	5,434	3,008	.55
1954	5,077	2,820	.56
1953	5,183	2,904	.56
1952	4,896	2,782	.57
1951	4,669	2,459	.53
1950	4,513	2,448	.54
1949	4,266	2,178	.51
1948	4,336	2,316	.53
1947	4,451	2,276	.51

Demand for unskilled and semiskilled labor has declined more rapidly than Negroes have acquired the education and training requisite to upgrading into expanding lines of work, and unless Negro education and skills improve more rapidly than is likely, the difference between Negro and white unemployment rates is likely to grow with further mechanization and automation. If so, the effects may offset many past as well as future occupational gains. The occupational advances of Negro workers after 1940 were largely into intermediate-level jobs that are subject to elimination by automation. The largest movement of Negro workers was into the occupational group of operatives and kindred workers, a category which is already hard hit by technological unemployment. In 1960, 6.4 percent of the males and 9.9 percent of the females in this occupational group were unemployed—higher unemployment than among any other class of workers except laborers. (Only part, however, was technological unemployment; much of it was caused by reduced production in some industries.) Many kinds of skilled workers also are being displaced by mechanization, although Negro craftsmen generally are more secure than Negro operatives. Unemployment in 1960 was relatively low among clerical and kindred workers, the other occupational group into which Negroes moved in large numbers. However, clerical jobs appear to be next in line to feel the impact of automation. Most of the occupational gains of Negroes during the past quarter of a century, in fact, are vulnerable to automation and other technological changes.

The reduced demand for unskilled labor has prevented incomes of unskilled workers from rising as fast as incomes of other workers. Wage and salary income of unskilled workers was little higher in 1959 than in 1949. Wages and salaries in general rose steeply during the decade, so the gap between unskilled and other workers widened. Since Negroes are overrepresented in unskilled work, this change tended to widen the income gap between Negroes and whites even though Negro representation increased at the higher occupational levels during the same period.

For similar reasons, the closing of the educational gap during the 1950s was not accompanied by a corresponding closing of the economic gap. The ratio of nonwhite to white median years of school completed by persons 25 years old and older increased from .71 in 1950 to .75 in 1960. Because the income gap is to a large extent a reflection of the educational gap, one might have expected similar marked improvement in the relative economic status of Negroes during the 1950s. Yet such improvement did not occur, because the economic gap between all poorly educated workers and others widened and Negroes remained highly represented among the poorly educated. In 1949, the median income of males who had completed one to four years of elementary school was 43 percent of the median income of those who had completed high school and was 31 percent of the median income of those who had completed four or more years of college. By 1959, these percentages had declined to 34 and 24.

Negro Americans are on a treadmill. They must keep gaining on whites in education and occupation simply to stay the same distance behind in income. Undoubtedly, this condition adversely affects Negro morale. Many Negroes find it increasingly difficult to get and keep jobs, and many who manage to remain employed most of the time do not share in the general increase in real income in the United States. While their own economic condition becomes worse or improves only slowly, their appetite for a more affluent style of life is whetted by direct observation of increased consumption by other Americans (both whites and the growing number of middle-class Negroes) and by increased exposure to the mass media of communication. Their feelings of deprivation increase even if their absolute economic condition improves.

The increased sense of deprivation of poorly educated Negroes is not unique but is shared by many poorly educated and unskilled whites. However, the consequences of Negro discontent are different. Negroes tend to define their troubles in racial terms, especially since the recent increased publicity given to the struggle for equal rights. The plight of the large percentage of Negroes who are poorly educated and unskilled has appreciable effects upon other Negroes. Self-employed Negro businessmen and professionals are dependent upon other Negroes and can hope to improve their economic condition only as the economic condition of the entire Negro population improves. Middle-class Negroes employed in the integrated economy have less reason to be concerned about the plight of poor Negroes, but whether they care or not, their fates are linked in important ways. Middle-class Negroes often must live in neighborhoods with lower-class Negroes, send their children to schools in which most of the pupils come from lower-class families, and in general have more frequent and closer contacts with lower-class people than do middle-class whites. An increasing number of middle-class Negroes owe their jobs to the political influence and buying power either of the entire Negro population or of the local Negro community. In addition, these people know that whites are likely to judge them on the basis of stereotypes that reflect the characteristics of the lower class. Therefore, a condition that adversely affects any segment of the Negro population has some adverse effects on all. Negroes are apparently becoming more sensitive to this fact, and the plight of unskilled workers causes some unrest among all classes.

As we suggest above, improvement in the relative occupational status of Negro Americans since the beginning of World War II seems, to a large extent, to be an outgrowth of a high level of nationwide prosperity, a high rate of economic growth, and changes in the occupation structure generating many upper- and intermediate-level jobs. The evidence for this reasoning is convincing if not conclusive. For example, Negroes generally made their greatest occupational gains in lines of work in which the number of jobs increased most rapidly.[3] Their relative economic status improved during years of rapid economic growth and generally declined or was static during years of little or no economic growth. These facts might lead one to conclude that future Negro gains are largely contingent upon continued economic growth and changes in the economic structure. Such changes probably are necessary for Negro gains, but they are hardly sufficient, and there is reason to believe that they will be less beneficial to Negroes than they have been. Rapid economic growth in the past has helped Negroes mainly by reducing unemployment. The economic status of Negroes has generally risen during years of full employment in the total labor force and fallen during years of high unemployment. Now, however, a rapid rate of economic growth does not reduce unemployment as much as it once did; high rates of economic growth and high rates of unemployment recently have occurred together. For instance, the rate of economic growth in the United States from 1958 to 1959 was about 8.5 percent, well above the average for the previous decade, but unemployment in 1959 was 5.5 percent, also well above the average for the previous decade. (The rate of economic growth is defined roughly as the annual percentage increase in the value, in constant dollars, of all goods and services purchased for final use.)

In the future, unemployment may actually increase during years of rapid economic growth, and if so, rapid expansion of the economy may no longer tend to improve the relative status of Negroes. Furthermore, the opening of new jobs at the higher and intermediate occupational levels may no longer be greatly beneficial to the Negro population as a whole if there is an accompanying large decrease in jobs at the lower levels. The number of Negroes displaced from lower-level jobs may be larger than the number who are qualified to take advantage of openings at intermediate and higher levels. In short, economic and occupational trends of the

[3] *Ibid.,* p. 112.

future may benefit Negroes appreciably only if their occupational qualifications improve very rapidly. And the improvement of Negro occupational qualifications depends largely, although not completely, upon improvement in the quantity and quality of Negro education. The obstacles to rapid improvement in Negro education are formidable; and perhaps the obstacles to rapid improvement of the occupational qualifications of adult Negroes who have completed their formal education are even greater. Therefore, the relative economic status of Negroes may drop below its present level within the next few years. Only unforeseen developments could bring about a rapid increase in the near future.

4
The Social Dynamics of the Ghetto

Kenneth B. Clark

White America is basically a middle-class society; the middle class sets the mores and the manners to which the upper class must, when it wishes influence, seek to conform, at least in appearances, and which the lower class struggles to attain or defensively rejects. But dark America, of the rural and of the urban Negro, has been automatically assigned to be a lower-class society; the lower class sets the mores and manners to which, if the Negro upper class wishes influence, it must appeal; and from which the Negro middle class struggles to escape. As long as this chasm between white and dark America is allowed to exist, racial tensions and conflict, hatred and fear will spread. The poor are always alienated from normal society, and when the poor are Negro, as they increasingly are in American cities, a double trauma exists—rejection on the basis of class and race is a danger to the stability of society as a whole. Even though Negroes are a minority in America— approximately one-tenth of the population—a minority that is sick with despair can poison the wellsprings from which the majority, too, must drink. The social dynamics of the dark ghettos can be seen as the restless thrust of a lower-class group to rise into the middle class.

The problem of the American Negro, once predominantly Southern, has gradually over the past few decades become predominantly a Northern problem. Millions of Negroes have come North seeking escape from the miasma of the South, where poverty and oppression kept the Negro in an inferior caste. Three out of every four Negroes live in cities; approximately one of two lives in Northern cities. A million and a half left the South in the years 1950–1960, the largest number heading for California, New York, Illinois, and Michigan. Of the Negroes who live in the North, 95 percent now live in cities (in 1890 it was 65 percent).

There are Negro residential areas in such Southern cities as Atlanta, Birmingham, and New Orleans, but the Negro ghetto in America is essentially a Northern urban invention. There are racially mixed residential areas in a number of Southern cities, few in Northern cities. Although the South often criticizes the North for its urban segregation and explains its own comparatively mixed residential patterns as illustrative of a more intimate and more tolerant relationship to the Negro, the fact is that in the South mixed neighborhoods are permitted only so long as Negroes are not seen as a threat. In Charleston, South Carolina, for example, racial residential patterns reflect slavery days, and whites and Negroes tend to live in the same area as they did before Emancipation. Negro servants can come into any area and live in white homes without a lifted eyebrow. Racial problems have not been problems of racial contact—despite the implications of those who refuse to join Negroes at a college dormitory table or to use the common washroom in a factory. It is not the sitting next to a Negro at a table or washing at the next basin that is repulsive to a white, *but the fact that this implies equal status.* Historically, the most intimate relationships have been approved between Negro and white so long as status of white superiority versus Negro inferiority has been clear. Trouble comes only when Negroes decide not to be servants or mistresses and seek a status equal to that of whites. When Negroes start to assume symbols of upward mobility, then a pattern of residential segregation develops in the South, too. In Little Rock and Pine Bluff, Arkansas, and Atlanta, Georgia, to illustrate, as the status of Negroes improved, housing segregation increased. The South is today becoming more "Northern" in its discriminatory pattern. As its economic level rises, it will steadily become more and more like the North. Then urban ghettos will be created, and the Negro will be forced to deal with a different kind of rejection. Part of the social dynamics of the ghetto is the tension between those Negroes who wish to resist and eventually to destroy the ghetto and those whites who seek to maintain and strengthen it.

Eleven metropolitan areas have Negro communities of between 200,000 and one million: New York, Chicago, Los Angeles, Detroit, Philadelphia, Washington, D.C., St. Louis, Baltimore, Cleveland, Houston and New Orleans. (See Tables 1, 2, 2A, 3.) In Wash-

TABLE 1: Residential Concentration of Negroes

Tracts with 90 percent + Negro population	City	In city	In tracts 90 percent + Negro	Percentage in tracts 90 percent + Negro
122	Chicago, Ill.	812,637	533,214	65.6
31	Baltimore, Md.	325,589	184,992	56.8
27	Cleveland, Ohio	250,818	134,142	53.5
29	Washington, D.C.	411,737	200,380	48.7
10	St. Louis, Mo.	214,377	94,041	43.9
8	Houston, Texas	215,037	87,222	40.6
27	Philadelphia, Penn.	529,240	207,627	39.2
17	New Orleans, La.	233,514	85,968	36.8
71	New York, N.Y.	1,087,931	362,370	33.3
45	Detroit, Mich.	482,223	140,546	29.1
19	Los Angeles, Calif.	334,916	68,715	20.5

SOURCE: U.S. Census of Population: 1960. The data presented in Tables 1 through 3 were prepared by James A. Jones, research director of Haryou, for this book.

TABLE 2: Cities with 200,000 or More Negroes

City	Total Population	Negroes			Percent Negro
		Total	Males	Females	
New York, N.Y.	7,781,984	1,087,931	498,167	589,764	% 14.0
Chicago, Ill.	3,550,404	812,637	387,718	424,919	22.9
Philadelphia, Penn.	2,002,512	529,240	250,256	278,984	26.4
Detroit, Mich.	1,670,144	482,223	232,829	249,394	28.9
Washington, D.C.	763,956	411,737	196,257	215,480	53.9
Los Angeles, Calif.	2,479,015	334,916	160,118	174,798	13.5
Baltimore, Md.	939,024	325,589	157,130	168,459	34.7
Cleveland, Ohio	876,050	250,818	120,873	129,945	28.6
New Orleans, La.	627,525	233,514	110,096	123,418	37.2
Houston, Texas	938,219	215,037	103,471	111,566	22.9
St. Louis, Mo.	750,026	214,377	100,159	114,218	28.6
A Sampling of Other Cities					
Pittsburgh, Penn.	604,332	100,692	48,670	52,022	% 16.7
Kansas City, Mo.	475,539	83,146	39,723	43,423	17.5
Boston, Mass.	697,197	63,165	30,081	33,084	9.1
Rochester, N.Y.	318,611	23,586	11,491	12,095	7.4
Minneapolis, Minn.	482,872	11,785	5,792	5,993	2.4

TABLE 2A: Cities with 200,000 or More Negroes in Terms of Percentages of Negroes

City	Percent Negro
Washington, D.C.	% 53.9
New Orleans, La.	37.2
Baltimore, Md.	34.7
Detroit, Mich.	28.9
Cleveland, Ohio	28.6
St. Louis, Mo.	28.6
Philadelphia, Penn.	26.4
Chicago, Ill.	22.9
Houston, Texas	22.9
New York, N.Y.	14.0
Los Angeles, Calif.	13.5
Sample Cities in Terms of Percentage of Negroes	
Kansas City, Mo.	% 17.5
Pittsburgh, Penn.	16.7
Boston, Mass.	9.1
Rochester, N.Y.	7.4
Minneapolis, Minn.	2.4

SOURCE: U.S. Census of Population: 1960.

ington, D.C., Negroes are in the majority; in Philadelphia, one in four persons is Negro. In the half century between 1910 and 1960 when the nation's Negro population doubled, New York City's Negro population multiplied ten times over.[1] Now the largest concentration of Negroes in an urban ghetto area is in Chicago; the largest number of Negroes lives in New York; and the largest percentage of Negroes (of total population) is in Washington, D.C.

In every one of these cities, Negroes are compelled to live in concentrated ghettos where there must be a continuous struggle to prevent decadence from winning over the remaining islands of middle-class society. A possible exception to this picture of creeping blight seems to be the Bay Area of San Francisco, Berkeley, and Oakland, where the Negro residential areas do not stand out from the other middle-class areas; the usual signs of congestion, deterioration, dirt, ugliness are not yet present there. In all of these ghettos whites had lived before and, as Negroes came, gradually moved away. The origin of Harlem—symbol of Negro ghettos everywhere—is, in many ways, typical of the blight that has already affected almost all.

[1] E. Franklin Frazier noted in *Condition of Negroes in American Cities,* when the first federal census was taken, Negroes constituted 13.1 percent of the New York City population and 5.7 percent of Philadelphia's.

TABLE 3: Negro Residential Concentration by Areas of Cities

City and Area	Population	Negroes	Percent
New York, N.Y.			
Brooklyn ghetto	91,391	87,654	% 95.9
Queens ghetto	20,324	19,091	93.9
Manhattan ghetto	241,125	236,051	97.9
Los Angeles, Calif.			
Area I	48,806	46,865	96.0
Area II	15,489	14,990	96.8
Baltimore, Md.			
Area I	149,197	143,849	96.4
Washington, D.C.			
Area I	120,060	115,552	96.2
Area II	66,043	64,196	97.2
Cleveland, Ohio			
Area I	70,060	68,700	98.1
Area II	49,815	46,863	94.1
St. Louis, Missouri			
Area I	97,144	93,807	96.6
New Orleans, Louisiana			
Area I	45,111	44,044	97.6
Chicago, Illinois			
Area I	347,806	340,599	97.9
Area II	105,307	102,096	97.0
Area III	21,133	20,401	96.5
Area IV	22,168	21,347	96.3

SOURCE: U.S. Census of Population: 1960.

In the early years of the century an upper-class community of luxury, Harlem by World War I became a moderately populated area of middle-class Jews, Italians, Irish, Germans, and Finns and then, during the twenties and thirties, was transformed into one of the largest and most densely populated Negro communities in the country.

The Negro came to Harlem, as all migrants do, seeking better living conditions and expanded economic opportunities. Harlem became the center of Negro culture and talent. It is here that most Negro artists and intellectuals lived, drawing their ideas and inspiration from the life of the community. But the Negro in Harlem found himself increasingly isolated culturally, socially, and economically by a wall of racial prejudice and discrimination. He was blocked from the training necessary to prepare himself for the highly skilled jobs in private industry or government, and he was pushed into the most menial occupations. His housing and schools deteriorated, and he was forced to pay more for less. He discovered that his new neighbors resented his presence, his aspirations, and his talents. They left in droves, and Harlem became a prison of its new residents. During the thirties Harlem seethed with discontent and racial strife, gaining an exaggerated reputation as a center of vice and crime. White persons ventured into the community only in search of exotic primitive glamour. Today, Harlem, no longer the mecca for white bohemia, is a center both of trouble and potential talent, the fountainhead of Negro protest movements. Despite the apathy and despair of many of its residents, it is a vibrant, exciting and, all too frequently, a turbulent community.[2]

In most important ways—social and economic structure, community culture, quality of education, and the like—all urban ghettos in America are similar. As one Negro told a Haryou interviewer: "I don't limit the black man to Harlem alone. Harlem is only one of the accidents in time that have beset the children along the way. Problem of the black man is universal, the world over."

ECONOMIC AND SOCIAL DECAY

The symptoms of lower-class society afflict the dark ghettos of America—low aspiration, poor education, family instability, illegitimacy, unemployment, crime, drug addiction and alcoholism, frequent illness and early death. But because Negroes begin with the primary affliction of inferior racial status, the burdens of despair and hatred are more pervasive. Even initiative usually goes unrewarded as relatively few Negroes succeed in moving beyond menial jobs, and those who do find racial discrimination everywhere they go.

The most concrete fact of the ghetto is its physical ugliness—the dirt, the filth, the neglect. In many stores walls are unpainted, windows are unwashed, service is poor, supplies are meager. The parks are seedy with lack of care. The streets are crowded with the people and refuse. In all of Harlem there is no museum, no art gallery, no art school, no sustained "little theater" group; despite the stereotype of the Negro as artist, there are only five libraries—but hundreds of bars, hundreds of churches, and scores of fortune tellers. Everywhere there are signs of fantasy, decay, abandonment, and defeat. The only constant characteristic is a sense of inadequacy. People seem to have given up in the little things that are so often the symbol of the larger things.

[2] The name "Harlem," as used in this book refers to that section of Manhattan sometimes referred to as Central Harlem, and excluding Spanish Harlem. Its boundaries are: 110th Street on the south; Third Avenue on the east; Harlem River, northeast; the parks bordering St. Nicholas, Morningside, and Manhattan avenues on the west.

The dark ghetto is not a viable community. It cannot support its people; most have to leave it for their daily jobs. Its businesses are geared toward the satisfaction of personal needs and are marginal to the economy of the city as a whole. The ghetto feeds upon itself; it does not produce goods or contribute to the prosperity of the city. It has few large businesses. Most of the businesses are small, with what that implies in terms of degree of stability. Even the more substantial-appearing businesses (e.g., real estate and insurance companies) are, by and large, marginal. Of 1,617 Harlem businesses listed in the yellow pages of Manhattan's telephone directory, 27 percent are barber shops, beauty shops, or cleaning establishments—all devoted to tidying up, a constantly renewable service. Thirty-five percent are involved in the consumption of food and drink (bakeries, caterers, grocery stores, liquor stores, luncheonettes, restaurants, bars, and taverns). In general, a ghetto does not produce goods of lasting worth. Its products are used up and replaced like the unproductive lives of so many of its people. There are 93 funeral homes in Harlem.

Even though the white community has tried to keep the Negro confined in ghetto pockets, the white businessman has not stayed out of the ghetto. A ghetto, too, offers opportunities for profit, and in a competitive society profit is to be made where it can.

In Harlem there is only one large department store and that is owned by whites. Negroes own a savings and loan association; and one Negro-owned bank has recently been organized. The other banks are branches of white-owned downtown banks. Property—apartment houses, stores, businesses, bars, concessions, and theaters—are for the most part owned by persons who live outside the community and take their profits home. Even the numbers racket, a vital and indestructible part of Harlem's economy, is controlled by whites. Here is unproductive profit-making at its most virulent, using the Negro's flight from despair into the persistent dream of quick and easy money as the means to take from him what little money he has.

When tumult arose in ghetto streets in the summer of 1964, most of the stores broken into and looted belonged to white men. Many of these owners responded to the destruction with bewilderment and anger, for they felt that they had been serving a community that needed them. They did not realize that the residents were not grateful for this service but bitter, as natives often feel toward the functionaries of a colonial power who, in the very act of service, keep the hated structure of oppression intact. Typical of this feeling are the following views expressed to Haryou investigators in 1962 and 1963. None who heard their contempt, their anti-Semitic overtones, would have been surprised at the looting of 1964—rarely does a social revolt occur without decades of advance warning.

> That Jew, he's got a wagon out here, and he will send his son through college, you understand? Nothing but a wagon, selling to these people in this junky neighborhood right here, and he's got a house in the Bronx, and he's paying for it, and the child is going to college, and he's selling you stringbeans at fifteen cents a pound.
> —Man, age 27

> Another thing I am sick and tired of, I am sick and tired of all these Jew business places in Harlem. Why don't more colored business places open? This is our part of town. They don't live here but they got all the businesses and everything.
> —Woman, age 38

Negroes have left business in the ghettos to whites not from a dislike of business but for a complex of other reasons. In those Southern cities like Birmingham, Atlanta, and Memphis, where the pattern of segregation is so complete that the dark ghettos must be almost self-sufficient, there are a number of Negro-owned stores, restaurants, and banks. But, in the North, the Negro is allowed to involve himself partially in the total city, and whites are willing to open businesses within the ghetto, sensing a profit among the tenements. The white power structure has collaborated in the economic serfdom of Negroes by its reluctance to give loans and insurance to Negro business. Eugene P. Foley, administrator of the Small Business Administration, told a meeting called in August 1964 to encourage economic investment among minorities that, before its field office opened in Philadelphia in that year, "I am ashamed to admit that my agency had made seven loans to Negroes in ten years." The situation has somewhat improved since then: in the six months after the field office opened fifty-five loans were granted and sixteen new businesses opened; new field offices were organized, also, in Harlem and in Washington, D.C.

There are insufficient economic resources within the ghetto to support its future development. Therefore any economic growth —as in fact is true of suburbs—must be supported and developed from without. But unlike the suburbs, where residents have high income and good credit, the ghetto has inadequate resources to command the attraction of economic power outside and cannot lure capital into its limits. Most ghetto residents are permitted only menial jobs and marginal income. The suburbs drain the economy of the city—through subsidized transportation, housing development, and the like. The economy of the ghetto is itself drained and is not replenished.

HOUSING DECAY

Another important aspect of the social dynamics of the Northern urban ghettos is the fact that all are crowded and poor; Harlem houses 232,792 people within its three and one half square miles, a valley between Morningside and Washington Heights and the Harlem River. There are more than 100 people per acre. Ninety percent of the 87,369 residential buildings are more than thirty-three years old, and nearly half were built before 1900. Private developers have not thought Harlem a good investment: Few of the newer buildings were sponsored by private money, and almost all of those buildings erected since 1929 are post-World War II public housing developments, where a fifth of the population lives.

The condition of all but the newest buildings is poor. Eleven percent are classified as dilapidated by the 1960 census; that is, they do "not provide safe and adequate shelter," and thirty-three percent are deteriorating (i.e., "need more repair than would be provided in the course of regular maintenance"). There are more people in fewer rooms than elsewhere in the city. Yet the rents and profits from Harlem are often high, as many landlords deliberately crowd more people into buildings in slum areas, knowing that the poor have few alternatives. The rent per room is often higher in Harlem than for better-equipped buildings downtown. Slum landlords, ready enough when the rent is due, are hard to find when repairs are demanded. Even the city cannot seem to find some of them, and when they go to trial for neglect, they are usually given modest and lenient sentences—compared to the sentences of Harlem teen-agers who defy the law. Cruel in the extreme is the landlord who, like the store owner who charges Negroes more for shoddy merchandise, exploits the powerlessness of the poor. For the poor are not only poor but unprotected and do not know how to seek redress. One is reminded of the Biblical admonition: "For whosoever hath, to him shall be given, and he shall have more abundance: but whosoever hath not, from him shall be taken away even that he hath."

The effects of unsafe, deteriorating, and overcrowded housing upon physical health are well documented and understood.[3] The multiple use of toilet and water facilities, inadequate heating and ventilation, and crowded sleeping quarters increase the rate of acute respiratory infections and infectious childhood diseases. Poor facilities for the storage of food and inadequate washing facilities cause enteritis and skin and digestive disease. Crowded, poorly equipped kitchens, poor electrical connections, and badly lighted and unstable stairs increase the rate of home accidents and fires. Nor is the street any safer. Harlem's fourteen parks, playgrounds, and recreational areas are inadequate and ugly, and many of the children play in the streets where heavy truck traffic flows through the community all day. Far more children and young adults are killed by cars in Harlem than in the rest of the city (6.9 per 100,000 population compared to 4.2 per 100,000 for New York City as a whole).

The physical health of the residents of the ghetto is as impaired as one would expect based on knowledge of its housing conditions. The best single index of a community's general health is reputed to be its infant mortality rate. For Harlem this rate in 1961 was 45.2 per 1,000 live births compared to 25.7 for New York City. For Cleveland's Hough area the infant deaths are also about double that of the rest of the city. Poor housing conditions, malnutrition, and inadequate health care are undoubtedly responsible; where flies and maggots breed, where the plumbing is stopped up and not repaired, where rats bite helpless infants, the conditions of life are brutal and inhuman. All are symptoms of the underlying fact of poverty. Perhaps even more extraordinary than the high rate of disease and death is the fact that so many human beings do survive.

The effect of housing upon the social and psychological well being of its occupants is much discussed but less well documented. The most careful of the few relevant studies (those by Wilner, Walkley, Pinkerton and Tayback) on the psychological effects of poor housing have produced findings less dramatic than one would expect. The link between housing and mental health is not clearly

---

[3] Among others, see D. M. Wilner, R. P. Price, and M. Tayback, "How Does the Quality of Housing Affect Health and Family Adjustment?" *American Journal of Public Health,* June 1956, pp. 736–744; "Report of the Subcommittee on Housing of the Committee on Public Health Relations," *Bulletin of the New York Academy of Medicine,* June 1954; M. Allen Pond, "The Influence of Housing on Health," *Marriage and Family Living,* May 1957, pp. 154–159; Alvin L. Schorr, *Slums and Social Insecurity,* Social Security Administration, Division of Research and Statistics, no date; D. M. Wilner, R. P. Walkley, T. Pinkerton, and M. Tayback, *The Housing Environment and Family Life: A Longitudinal Study of the Effects of Housing on Morbidity and Mental Health,* Baltimore, Johns Hopkins Press, 1962.

established, but residents of public housing do have higher morale and greater pride in their neighborhoods than those who live in slums, and they are more likely to say that they have improved their lot in life and are "rising in the world." Nevertheless, their pride is generally not followed by genuine aspiration. They often express hope, but it usually is, alas, a pseudohope unaccompanied by an actual struggle to win better jobs, to get their children into college, to buy homes. Real hope is based on expectations of success; theirs seems rather a forlorn dream. Wilner and Walkley point out that "for all the housing improvement, many other circumstances that would be expected to affect the way of life [of these families] remained substantially the same. These were still families at the lowest end of the economic scale; practical family situations remained materially unimproved; in one-third of the families there was no husband present; and one-third were on public welfare."[4] Housing alone does not lead to sound psychological adjustment, for to build new housing or to spruce up the old is not to abolish the multiple pathology of the slums. Still, at the very least, good housing improves health, lifts morale, and thereby helps to generate a restless eagerness for change, if not in the adult generation then in their children; a fact, incidentally, that might give pause to some of those in society who support aid to public housing believing it will decrease the demands of Negroes. It will, in fact, stimulate them to further demands, spurred by hope for a further identification with middle-class society. Housing is no abstract social and political problem, but an extension of a man's personality. If the Negro has to identify with a rat-infested tenement, his sense of personal inadequacy and inferiority, already aggravated by job discrimination and other forms of humiliation, is reinforced by the physical reality around him. If his home is clean and decent and even in some way beautiful, his sense of self is stronger. A house is a concrete symbol of what the person is worth.

In Harlem, a Haryou interviewer had a conversation with a little girl about her home that revealed both the apathy and the hope of the ghetto:

Interviewer: *Tell me something about you— where you were born, you know, where you grew up, how everything went for you?*
Gwen D: *When I was born I lived on 118th Street. There was a*

man killed in the hallway, and a man died right in front of the door where I lived at. My mother moved after that man got killed.

I liked it in 97th Street because it was integration in that block. All kinds of people lived there.

Interviewer: Spanish people? White people?

Gwen D: *Spanish people, Italian people, all kinds of people. I liked it because it wasn't one group of whites and one group of Negroes or Spanish or something like that; everybody who lived in that block were friends.*

Interviewer: How come you moved?

Gwen D: *Well, my mother she didn't like the building too well.*

Interviewer: What didn't she like about it?

Gwen D: *Well, it was falling down!*

Interviewer: In your whole life, has anything happened to you that you really got excited about?

Gwen D: *I can't remember.*

Interviewer: Tell me about some real good times you've had in your life.

Gwen D: *In Harlem?*

Interviewer: In your life, that you've really enjoyed.

Gwen D: *One year we was in summer school, and we went to this other school way downtown, out of Harlem, to give a show, and everybody was so happy. And we were on television, and I saw myself, and I was the only one there with a clean skirt and blouse.*

Interviewer: And you really got excited about that. Anything else ever happen to you that you had a really good time?

Gwen D: *No.*

Interviewer: What kind of changes would you want to make? Changes so that you can have a better chance, your sisters can have a better chance and your brother?

Gwen D: *Well, I just want a chance to do what I can.*

THE DYNAMICS OF UNDER-EMPLOYMENT

The roots of the pathology of ghetto communities lie in the menial, low-income jobs held by most ghetto residents. If the occupational level of the community could be raised, one would expect a corresponding decrease in social pathology, in dependency, disease and crime.

With the growth of the civil rights movement, Negroes have won many footholds earlier forbidden to them, and it would seem logical to conclude, as many do, that Negroes are better off than ever before in this gradually desegregating and generally affluent society. But the fact is that in many ways the Negro's situation is deteriorating. The Negro has been left out of the swelling prosperity and social progress of the nation as a whole. He is in danger of becoming a permanent economic proletariat.

About one out of every seven or eight adults in Harlem is unemployed. In the city as a whole the rate of unemployment is half that. Harlem is a young community, compared to the rest of New York, and in 1960 twice as many young Negro men in the labor force, as compared to their white counterparts, were without jobs. For the girls, the gap was even greater—nearly two and one-half times the unemployment rate for white girls in the labor force. Across the country the picture is very much the same. Unemployment of Negroes is rising much faster than unemployment of whites. Among young men eighteen to twenty-four, the national rate is five times as high for Negroes as for whites.

An optimist could point to the fact that the average family income of Negroes has increased significantly within the two decades 1940–1960, but a more realistic observer would have to qualify this with the fact that the *discrepancy* between the average family income of whites and that of Negroes has increased even more significantly. The real income, the relative status income, of Negroes has gone down during a period when the race was supposed to have been making what candidates for elective office call, "the most dramatic progress of any oppressed group at any period of human history."

The menial and unrewarding jobs available to most Negroes can only mean a marginal subsistence for most ghetto families. The median income in Harlem is $3,480 compared to $5,103 for residents of New York City—a similar gap exists in the country as a whole. Half the families in Harlem have incomes under $4,000 while 75 percent of all New York City residents earn more than $4,000. Only one in twenty-five Negro families has an income above $10,000, while more than four in twenty-five of the white families do.

Nor do Negroes with an education receive the financial benefits available to whites. Herman P. Miller in his book, *Rich Man, Poor Man,*[5] states that Negroes who have completed four years of college *"can expect to earn only as much in a lifetime as whites who have not gone beyond the eighth grade."* This is true both in the North and in the South. The white high school graduate will earn just about as much as a Negro who has gone through

[5] New York, Thomas Y. Crowell Co., 1964.

college and beyond for graduate training. One young man in Harlem asked: "What is integration into poverty?" The question is not easy to answer.

Both the men and the women in the ghetto are relegated to the lowest status jobs. Sixty-four percent of the men in Harlem compared to only 38 percent of New York City's male population, and 74 percent of the women, compared to 37 percent for New York City, hold unskilled and service jobs. Only 7 percent of Harlem males are professionals, technicians, managers, proprietors, or officials. Twenty-four percent of the males in the city hold such prestige posts.

An eighteen-year-old Negro boy protested: "They keep telling us about job opportunities, this job opportunity, and that, but who wants a job working all week and bringing home a sweat man's pay?" Most of the men in the dark ghetto do work for a "sweat man's pay," and even *that* is now threatened by the rise of automation.

Many of the jobs now held by Negroes in the unskilled occupations are deadend jobs, due to disappear during the next decade. Decreases, or no expansions, are expected in industries in which more than 43 percent of the labor force in Harlem is now employed (i.e., transportation, manufacturing, communication and utilities, and wholesale and retail trades). Employment in those industries and occupations requiring considerable education and training is expected to increase. As the pressure of unemployed white workers in the few expanding areas of unskilled jobs grows, the ability of ghetto residents to hold on to such jobs becomes doubtful. And by 1970 there will be 40 percent more Negro teenagers (16–21) in Harlem than there were in 1960. The restless brooding young men without jobs who cluster in the bars in the winter and on stoops and corners in the summer are the stuff out of which riots are made. The solution to riots is not better police protection (or even the claims of police brutality) or pleas from civil rights leaders for law and order. The solution lies in finding jobs for the unemployed and in raising the social and economic status of the entire community. Otherwise the "long hot summers" will come every year.

By far the greatest growth in employment in New York City is expected in professional, technical, and similar occupations —some 75,000 to 80,000 jobs by the end of the present decade.[6]

---

[6] *Manpower Outlook 1960–1970*, New York City Department of Labor, 1962, pp. 1 and 12, provides the projections that pertain to job expectations.

Of the 3 percent of Harlem residents in this group, the major portion are in the lower-paying professions: clergymen, teachers, musicians, and social welfare and recreation workers. A substantial increase of 40 percent in the number of managers, officials, and proprietors is expected in business and government, but the Negro has made few advances here. This will be offset by declines expected in retail business, where the trend toward bigness will result in fewer small store proprietors, another prophecy with grim implications for Negroes since the only business where Negro ownership exists in number is small stores. The number of clerical positions is due to grow in New York by 35,000 to 40,000 jobs. Approximately 14 percent of the residents of Harlem have such jobs, but most of them are in the lower-paying positions. Electronic data-processing systems will soon replace many clerks in routine and repetitive jobs, such as sorting, filing, and the operation of small machines—the kind of jobs Negroes have—while workers in jobs requiring contact with the public, such as claim clerks, complaints clerks, and bill collectors—usually white—will be least affected by office automation. The number of sales workers will decline as self-service increases, and here too, Negroes who have been successfully employed will lose out.

Jobs for skilled workers are due to grow in New York State by 28,000 yearly. Building trades craftsmen will be particularly in demand. But the restrictions to apprenticeship training programs in the building trades industry have kept Negroes from these jobs. Semiskilled and unskilled jobs (excluding service workers) will decrease by 70,000 to 80,000 jobs between 1960 and 1970. Thirty-eight percent of the Negro male workers living in Harlem have such jobs now. If present employment patterns persist, Negro and white workers who might ordinarily qualify for semiskilled jobs will undoubtedly be pushed into the unskilled labor force or become unemployed in the face of increasing competition with those who are better trained. Negro unemployment will rise as the unskilled labor supply exceeds the demand. The only jobs that will increase, and in which Negroes now dominate, are jobs as servants, waitresses, cooks—the traditional service jobs which have added to the Negro's sense of inferiority. But as the requirements for skilled jobs grow stiffer and as semiskilled jobs decline, Negroes will face strong competition from whites to hold even these marginal jobs.

It is illegal in New York to deny a job to anyone on the basis of skin color, but it is common practice anyway. First, Negro applicants are often said to lack the qualifications necessary for a particular job. Who can prove this to be disguised racial discrimination? Like any charge with some truth, the extent of the truth is hard to determine. Second, often working against the Negro applicant, though sometimes in his favor, are ethnic quotas applied to certain types of jobs, employed with the conscious intent of maintaining an "ethnic balance" in the work force. When the quota is filled, the Negro applicant, no matter how well qualified, is told that there are no openings. Third, and much more subtle, although no less discriminatory, is the practice employed by some unions of requiring that a member of the union vouch for an applicant. When the union has no Negro members, the possibility of finding someone to vouch for a Negro applicant is extremely remote.

Through historical processes certain ethnic or religious minority groups come to predominate in certain kinds of jobs: in New York, the waterfront for the Italians, the police force for the Irish, the school system for Jews, and the personal services for Negroes.[7]

A study by the Bureau of Social Science Research, Inc., showed a fourth technique of exclusion; that employers tend to label some jobs, usually the lowest, as "Negro jobs"—Negroes are hired by many firms, but at "Negro jobs," with menial status, minimum wages, and little if any security.

Furthermore, many Negroes are discouraged before they begin. Guidance counselors often in the past advised Negro students not to prepare for jobs where employment opportunities for Negroes were limited. Doubtless they believed they did so in the best interests of the youth—better not to encourage him to pursue a career which is likely to end in bitter frustration and unemployment. There is some evidence that this form of root discrimination is now being reduced under persistent pressure from groups like the Urban League and the National Scholarship Service and Fund for Negro Students. The plethora of ineffective antidiscrimination and equal opportunities legislation—contrasted with the clear evidence of actual exclusion—leads one to suspect that this type of discrimination works in such a way as to be relatively immune to laws. It would appear that effective techniques for reducing discrimination in employment must, therefore, be as specific, subtle, and as pervasive as the evil they seek to overcome.

It has been charged over and over again that Negro youth lack motivation to succeed. To the extent that this is true, it is largely a consequence of ghetto psychology. Teen-age boys often help to support their families, and they have neither the time nor money nor encouragement to train for a white-collar job or skilled craft.

---

[7] A similar conception has been formulated by Eli Ginsberg in *A Policy for Skilled Manpower,* New York, Columbia University Press for the National Manpower Council, 1954, especially p. 249.

Negroes often dread to try for jobs where Negroes have never worked before. Fear of the unknown is not peculiar to one racial group, and Negroes have had traumatic experiences in seeking employment. The Negro youth is caught in a vicious cycle: Poor preparation means poor jobs and low socio-economic status. Low status and poor jobs result in poor preparation for the next generation to come.

A comprehensive employment program for the youth of dark ghettos everywhere must be geared toward revamping the various systems which feed upon one another. It must upgrade the educational system which spawns functional illiterates and which helps perpetuate personnel practices which exclude Negro youth. Even if a personnel officer is free of racial prejudice, the majority of Negro applicants can be rejected for jobs which require basic educational skills. Inferior schools, which discriminate against the masses of Negroes, have made Fair Employment Practices regulations virtually irrelevant. A crash program of rehabilitation with specific skill training is imperative. So, too, is a systematic procedure to inform ghetto youth about the occupations for which they might qualify. A realistic and comprehensive occupational training and employment program would include a counseling service not only to develop motivation and self-respect but also to help young people with concrete problems related to getting and keeping a job—many do not know how to apply for a job, how to speak to an employer, how to fill in an application blank. Many must learn the importance of promptness, appropriate dress and speech, and to modify habits that had been appropriate in the menial jobs to which Negroes had been relegated in the past. They must learn to appear and to behave like other middle-class applicants with whom they will be required to compete.

The Haryou proposal[8] to the City of New York included such a many-pronged attack. Over a three-year period, 7,000 Harlem youths, ages 16 through 21, were to receive job training. In on-the-job training the youth was to be paid the standard wage of the job for which he was being trained, with the employer and the project sharing the cost. As he improved, the employer would assume more of the salary costs. Also part of the Haryou plan was to establish a special counseling and guidance program for high school dropouts, for those who could be encouraged to re-enter high school. Those who chose not to return to school were to be referred to training pro-

[8] See author's introduction and *Youth in the Ghetto, A Study of the Consequences of Powerlessness and a Blueprint for Change,* Harlem Youth Opportunities Unlimited, Inc., New York, 1964.

grams appropriate to their specific needs and interests. High school graduates with marketable work skills were to be referred for employment through the program placement services. Graduates in need of further training would get it.

The young people associated with Haryou during its planning stage (the Haryou Associates) pointed out that Negro youth in Harlem did not have the opportunity to learn how to manage even a small business or store since, unlike other lower-middle-class groups in the city, their parents did not own stores. They believed that this was a major handicap and suggested the organization of a Harlem Youth Enterprises, Unlimited, which would sponsor a cluster of local business enterprises owned by youth so as to provide them with on-the-job training opportunities.

For those who have been so severely damaged that they are not at present able to profit from organized job training and not able to benefit from the small-business management program, Haryou proposed to recruit in the poolrooms and other hangouts for a Community Service Corps, designed to perform various needed community services at whatever level of competence these young people had. The corps would try to raise their level of competence so that they would eventually be able to move into a more demanding job training program. Since each corps trainee would get enough money to meet his normal living needs, it might turn out that in a time of severe job scarcity, young people would "make a career" of job training. The alternative—larger welfare rolls, more jails, bigger police force to constrain hordes of desperate, jobless young people —is clearly more expensive. But the emphasis in all these programs would not be on "make-work" jobs designed to provide pocket money or to keep youths out of trouble during the stormy adolescent years. Rather, they would concentrate on providing young people with salable skills and insure a boost to the socio-economic status of ghetto residents of all America's urban ghettos, crucial if the pathology rooted in social and economic inferiority is to be remedied. One man expressed to a Haryou interviewer the view of many in the dark ghettos of America:

> Most of all, I am trying to impress on them that
> the people are not chaining themselves to posts,
> that demonstrations are not being held, that people
> are not exposing themselves to dogs and tear gas so
> they can go on being delivery boys forever.

And another said with wistfulness:

If you go down and say well, man, I want a job,
and showed that you really want to work and were
given a job, then that's hope.

The main hope, however, may be that stated by Gunnar Myrdal in
his book, *The Challenge to Affluence:*[9]

... at this juncture of history there is a striking
convergence between the American ideals of liberty
and equality of opportunity on the one hand, and of
economic progress on the other. Indeed, the chief
policy means of spurring economic progress will
have to be huge reforms that are in the interests of
social justice.

WHITE UNIONS, BLACK PROLETARIAT

America does not like to admit—seldom does admit—that it
is divided by social and economic classes. This fantasy has persisted in large measure because of the presence of Negroes, without whom low-income and low-status whites would see they themselves have been relegated to the lower rungs of the ladder; and
that for many the ladder is not a ladder at all: The presence of the
Negro obscures the facts.

The white worker has felt much less a proletariat psychologically than his counterpart in Europe because of the existence of
a black proletariat in subjugated status beneath him. From a psychological point of view it was correct that he should. Whites will have
to risk their own status if Negroes are to be admitted into the world of
work as peer, and the white worker has understood this instinctively.
The white worker is vulnerable because he has only the reality of his
wish to give some security to his assumed status. When the Negro
starts moving he threatens almost total collapse of white status and
of the white worker's world. This is a matter of bread and butter and
self-respect to the white worker. Unlike so many who have opposed
the Negro—in the churches and elsewhere—the worker is really vulnerable. He feels his own job is at stake, that his family's future is
endangered, that in an automated society there will be fewer jobs for
the white man as well as the black. He has no time for a stereotyped liberal response in behalf of civil rights.

[9] New York, Pantheon Books, 1963.

Racism has been one of the persistently debilitating facts in the American labor movement. After Eugene Debs, the American labor movement was never really a solid force, a movement in which the total rights and concerns of all workingmen were protected. The American Federation of Labor's position was one of no direct involvement in politics and one of apology when it did hesitatingly enter the political arena. It refused to become a significant part or core of any labor party. The Congress of Industrial Organizations was more politically active but also uninterested in a labor party. After the initial stages the labor movement organized itself in terms of respectable nonproletarian models. As it grew strong it took on the appearance and manner of management, with large salaries, palatial offices, and privileges and prerogatives for leadership competing with the luxury symbols of management. The American labor movement is basically a vehicle by which the workingman seeks to realize his aspirations to be a boss. It is a ringing refutation of the Marxian premise of categorical cleavages between economic classes. It is inextricably bound up in the American dream of success, of upward mobility. Unions are seen as escalators to management, not just as the protector of the workingclass. The presence of Negroes on the American scene has given some objective support to this belief, for whites have moved up—in large measure—by excluding Negroes from the competition, from the unions, and hence from the better-paying jobs.

In the highest levels of labor unions, the status of Negroes is weak and almost invisible. In New York City no Negro holds a position of primary power in organized labor. Negroes have been effectively segregated in American labor, much as in American churches, with their "own" unions, such as the railroad Brotherhood of Sleeping Car Porters, for workers in jobs almost exclusively reserved for Negroes. Where Negroes are singled out as labor representatives, they hold these posts at the pleasure of white leadership. Even in unions where most workers are Negro or Puerto Rican, the actual top leadership is predominantly white and often seems responsive more to the wishes of management than to the people they allegedly serve.

A significant example of the powerlessness of the Negro worker in a major trade union with a "liberal" reputation is found in the status of Negroes in the International Ladies' Garment Workers Union in New York City. The ILGWU is unique in many respects. The ILGWU is probably the most decisive force in the ladies' garment industry in New York City because it has rationalized and stabilized industry practices and established union control over a scattered multiplicity of small, highly competitive shops. Both em-

ployers and the workers regard the union as the major power in
the industry.

The ILGWU and its leaders are important politically in New
York City and State through their pivotal position in the Liberal
party and the role of the Liberal party in city and state democratic
politics. The ILGWU is generally considered to be a major liberal
social and political force. This liberal image, however justified in
other respects, does not extend to the protection of the economic
status of Negro and Puerto Rican workers in the garment industry.
Although there are thousands of Negroes employed in garment manufacturing in New York City, they are concentrated, with few exceptions, in the low wage, unskilled classifications and with very little
job mobility. For example, Negroes are concentrated in such categories as "push boys" and shipping clerks in what amounts to a
segregated ILGWU "auxiliary unit" known as 60-A and which operates under the control of the predominantly white Pressers Local 60.

Herbert Hill, National Labor Secretary of the National Association for the Advancement of Colored People, in testifying before
a subcommittee of the House Committee on Education and Labor on
August 17, 1962, referred to 60-A as the "Jim Crow auxiliary of
local 60" and stated that:

> The racial practices of the ILGWU are seen most
> clearly in relationships to the Cutters and Pressers
> locals. Local 60, the Pressers local, controls jobs
> within its jurisdiction that on an hourly rated basis
> are the highest paying jobs in the entire garment in-
> dustry in New York City. The average wage being
> almost $5.00 an hour. Local 60 has an all-white mem-
> bership. On the other hand, there is 60-A which is
> simply an appendage to Local 60 and which has a
> membership which is almost entirely Negro and
> Puerto Rican. The members of 60-A are shipping
> clerks, push boys and delivery men. These workers
> earn in the vicinity of $50.00 per week. Yet, 60-A
> with twice the membership of Local 60 has never
> been chartered by the International as a separate
> local and the manager of 60, who is a presser,
> functions also as the manager of 60-A. One must
> ask, why should a local of shipping clerks and push
> boys, whose members are paid extremely low wages,
> be attached as an auxiliary unit to the pressers local
> whose members make the highest wages in the
> garment industry?

Hill has charged that:

—there is not a single Negro who is an officer of the international union;

—there is not a single Negro on the twenty-three member General Executive Board;[10]

—there is not a single Negro or Puerto Rican vice president of the union;

—there are no Negro or Puerto Rican local managers;

—only 11 percent of the unionized garment workers in New York earn enough to maintain a "modest but adequate" standard of living;

—the wages of workers in the New York City ladies' garment industry have declined relative to the total manufacturing average.

None of these charges was refuted by the top leadership or spokesmen of the ILGWU.

Daniel Bell, sociologist of Columbia University, said in an article in the *New Leader* (January 21, 1963):

> . . . The fact is—and this is the "bite" in Hill's charges—that the Negroes are underrepresented in the leadership of many of the unions where they form a significant proportion of the membership. In the case of these unions, what the Negroes want is "recognition" at the level of top leadership and a growing share of the spoils of office. . . . For one thing, the realistic political process in the United States, at least in the northern urban centers, has been one of ethnic groups advancing themselves precisely in this fashion; by organizing on bloc lines, electing their own kind, and using the patronage system to enhance the wealth and status of their group. . . .

Bell concludes:

> . . . In economic and educational opportunity, the Negro is in a position of inequality, and the government is bound to help him move ahead. But doesn't the trade union movement have a *special* obligation to help redress the balance . . . ?

---

[10] Until recently, there was not a Puerto Rican on the Board. In March 1964, however, as a result of exposure and pressure, a Puerto Rican was appointed to the ILGWU General Executive Board.

The predicament of Negroes and Puerto Ricans in the ILGWU reflects the powerlessness of their general educational, economic, political, and social status. Earlier immigrants have used labor unions, public schools, and the control of political organizations as ladders of economic and social mobility. As they became successful through the use of these institutions and instruments of power, they tended to assume leadership positions and dominate them. As the numbers of Negroes and Puerto Ricans increased in the city as a whole to a "significant proportion" of the voting strength and union membership, older ethnic groups who had already consolidated their educational, economic, and political power are reluctant to share this with Negroes and Puerto Ricans. As the sheer weight of numbers of these new minorities increases, older minorities are required to set up institutional, bureaucratic, or even moral and ideological blocks to the fulfillment of the demands of Negroes and Puerto Ricans for a share in the spoils and patronage power. Within the conflict between the past and the present lie the seeds for serious social problems and tensions of the future.[11]

There are a few indications that labor unions are beginning to reexamine the role of Negroes. A. Philip Randolph, one of the AFL-CIO vice presidents, has played a crucial part in bringing the problem to the attention of labor leadership. So, too, the pressures of Hill, labor secretary of the NAACP, have been effective. The early resistance of George Meany seems to be giving way to recognition of the fact that inclusion of Negroes in the labor movement will, in fact, not be a threat but will strengthen it. If this is a new positive development in American labor it matches the recognition by leaders of business and industry that exclusion of Negroes from full participation in the economy saps the strength of the economy, artificially restricts the skilled labor supply, and thereby grants to labor unions control over that supply. The cooperation of management in the President's Committee on Equal Employment in opening job opportunities for Negroes is based on the knowledge that as one provides better jobs for Negroes one increases the number of consumers, one expands the domestic markets and the national productivity and the general level of prosperity. Labor, too, will be strengthened because as long as Negroes are kept out of labor unions they remain a vast reservoir of cheap labor which, in effect, is more of a threat to the

[11] For a documentation of the status of nonwhite workers in the ladies garment industry in New York City and in the ILGWU see Herbert Hill, Testimony Before the House Committee on Education and Labor, 88th Congress, 1st Sess. 1569–72 (Jan. 31, 1963 Congressional Record, House, pp. 1496–1499); see also Hill, *The ILGWU, Fact and Fiction,* New Politics, Winter, 1963, pp. 7–27.

workingman than Negro competition could be within the union. Bringing Negroes in will make the unions morally and pragmatically more powerful.

If labor unions do not fully let down the barriers of apprenticeship and membership to Negroes on an open and free competitive basis, management and ownership will have to bring pressure to bear. If management transforms its own policies, compensating for past injustice by more active hiring of Negroes at higher status levels, the labor unions themselves will heed the demands of social change. But if Negroes gain at the expense of whites, racial hostility will increase and force a regression. It is incumbent upon economic power to supply jobs for all who need and wish them. The consumer potential of the urban Negro is, in this effort, an untapped resource. The American economic society is vigorous and can respond imaginatively to threats against its own security and the stability of society itself.

The resistance of labor to automation can be tolerated up to a point, but when the economic imperatives are clear, neither management nor labor can hold the clock back in automation and in civil rights. The total economy is threatened by the decay of the heart of American cities, long the creative centers of industry, transportation, communication, and education, and by the dangers of Negro unemployment, and Negro concentration in low-status menial service jobs. No longer can the potential consuming power of one-tenth of the American people be ignored, and the power of consumption be artificially limited by the low wages of Negroes and the heavy load of Negro welfare dependency, a product of broken families caused in turn in large part by male unemployment.

THE CYCLE OF FAMILY INSTABILITY

One of the inevitable results of the unemployment and menial job status of urban Negroes is family instability. Family breakdown occurs among the white poor, too, but inferior racial status that makes escape seem impossible and damages the core of personality adds impetus to the problem. Once again, the Negro poor are forced to be different. As the Haryou report indicated, approximately one out of every five men in Harlem is separated from his wife, and about two out of every seven women are separated from their husbands. In the city as a whole, only one in thirty men is separated from his wife, and approximately one in sixteen women from her husband. Only about half of the children under eighteen in the Harlem community are living with both parents, compared with 83 percent in New York City as a whole. The child without a secure family life is often forced either into aggression and delinquency or into apathy and despair. As one mother said to a Haryou interviewer:

> When you see an obedient child, he will come home when you tell him to be home in an hour or two. But when he comes home, the mother has the door locked and the father is gone someplace half drunk. The child can't come home like he wants to. Maybe the child wants to say something to his parents, but his parents are not home. He has no one to talk to but perhaps an older brother. When the parents are not home, the children are lost. Perhaps he's hurt. He wants to come home and talk to either his father or mother, but they are out. He can't even get in the house to use the lavatory, so they do what they have to do in the halls.

Children and young people who grow up in a community in which a large proportion of families have no father in the home, a community in which 40 percent of the men and 47 percent of the women aged 14 or over are unmarried,[12] find it difficult, if not almost impossible, to know what an "adequate" family is like. The cycle of family instability continues uninterrupted.

Broken families and poverty also usually mean reliance upon public assistance. In 1961, 226.5 per 1,000 Harlem youth under eighteen years of age—nearly one in four—were supported, in part, by aid-to-dependent-children (ADC) funds, three times as many as in the city as a whole (72 per 1,000). In that same year in Cleveland's Hough area, three times as many families received General Assistance and about four times as many received ADC help as for the city as a whole. Similar trends could doubtless be discovered in the other urban ghettos.

Therefore, the Negro's despair at his racial rejection is reinforced by the knowledge that he is often a heavy financial burden to himself and to the community. Fear of the poor, in turn, reinforces the white's prejudice against the Negro. Many white people have come to fear the "influx" of Negroes, from the South into Northern

---

[12] This statistic for Harlem is roughly the same proportion of unattached adults as obtains for the city as a whole, but in New York, especially Manhattan, a large number of single young people congregate at the start of their careers and a large number of elderly persons find living convenient—conditions not true of Harlem.

cities and from the large urban ghettos into smaller cities and
suburbs, as a threat of social and economic dimension—the threat of
higher taxes to care for the dependent, lowered property values, and
the like. Few look at the causes of the vicious cycle, which lie in the
white community—the low-paying menial jobs unskilled Negroes are
compelled to take; the chronic rising Negro unemployment rate, the
poor education of Negro children; the compulsive bargain selling of
property, encouraged by "block-busters," i.e., unscrupulous real
estate agents (Negro as well as white); and many other factors.

The white society which has to deal with massive social
problems of poverty and despair tends to rely on the temporary ex-
pedients of counseling and emergency help rather than on direct
social change. The poor, and especially the Negro poor, often seem
ungrateful and resist what help is offered.

> The poor, thought of as being ignorant, illiterate,
> and unimaginative, have developed a variety of ways
> of coping with the welfare worker; evasion is fre-
> quent as recipients become "welfare wise."
> And so we have a typical situation of a great deal
> of police and control efforts on one side and a con-
> siderable amount of matching efforts at evasion on
> the other. The stalemate that is reached is one
> where frequently there is repugnance on the part of
> the authorities and a lack of respect on the part of
> the recipients.[13]

One family service agency director observed that the energy
of "multiproblem" families of the lower socio-economic class seems
directed almost entirely to giving social workers the "run-around."
She felt the explanation lay in the fact that such persons are not
"geared to talking," and do not know how to "make good use" of
social agencies.

A young man who has, for months, sought work in vain
would be expected to be pleased by the offer of a decent job or
training in a desired skill. But the alienation of the Negro poor is
such that the "hustler" or "bop" or unwed ADC mother, the members of the "deviant subculture," often respond with an attitude of
"include me out," which reflects the cynical desire to "cash in" on a
less demanding mode of adjustment. In the ghetto to "cash in"
means to earn a livelihood for imaginary services, or for an outright

[13] S. M. Miller, *Poverty, Race and Politics,* Syracuse University
Youth Development Center, 1963.

disservice, and it means that one must establish a mutually exploita- tive relation with others—one must have a "hustle." "Cashing in" and the "hustle" reflect the belief that one cannot make a living through socially acceptable vocations in a complex and rejecting racist society. "Cashing in" tends to be seen as the way the world is.

Agencies that encourage their clients to accept dependency or to accept transparent "make-work" contribute to the perpetuation of the pathology of the ghetto communities. It is reasonable to as- sume that people who have not already been severely damaged want wholesome work. When the client cannot find such work, the profes- sional cannot have wholesome work of his own either. This neces- sarily leads to a mutually protective estrangement of client and worker, to the "flight from the client" illustrated by the exodus of most of the family service agencies out of Harlem. It may also in- crease the contempt of the "client" for all who claim to be willing to help him.

For social service and social agencies to be relevant to the pressing problems of the ghetto, those who are in control of this part of our society must have the courage to re-examine ruthlessly their present assumptions, methods, and programs and prune those postures and pretenses which reflect only traditional and bureau- cratic lags or fund-raising gimmicks. To be relevant, social service agencies must above all accept and respect the humanity of those in need of help—and express this acceptance and respect through courtesy and the warmth, cleanliness, and beauty of the physical surroundings in which the help is offered. Social service cannot be relevant to the pathology of the ghetto, except to reinforce it, if it encourages even subtly the dependency of the people of the ghetto —because to encourage dependency is to rob the individual of the sense of his own dignity and to strengthen his feelings of inferiority. Relevant and human social services must dare to run the risks of being a part of a real and comprehensive program of social action and social change.

REALISTIC INTERVENTION

The Haryou program was based upon the above rationale and the finding that piecemeal, isolated, and peripheral social agency programs neither helped individuals nor stemmed the tide of ghetto pathology.

To build a new culture designed to enable the ghetto to service itself would cost far less in the long run than the present list of human casualties. The ghetto needs to replace hostility and alienation with a creative, constructive culture.

Who are the most effective workers in such programs? As catalysts in this enterprise, Haryou found during its planning explorations that it could make use of artists and ex-delinquents as well as trained social workers. The advisability of recruiting large numbers of professionally trained social workers and teachers has been seriously questioned. Often it appears that professional training itself enhances the "flight from the client." Furthermore, large numbers of trained personnel are not available. The best recruits for these jobs may be residents of the community themselves who stand to benefit not only financially but also by gaining status, self-esteem and the new satisfaction of "meaningful" work. With such workers there is less of a possibility, also, that the communication barrier will be a factor, since they are literally part of the world of their clients. They will probably be more willing to endure the long hours which some of the programs require, since they have not developed a working tradition which shies away from sustained relationship with clients, from week-end and night work. They have not yet developed professional ennui.

Many of the ghetto's working mothers who now work outside the community, taking care of other people's children, could be paid instead to work within their own community as aides in preschool academies. Other potential recruits would be young mothers who have recently left school, many of whom are just beginning the aid-to-dependent-children treadmill to apathy. This plan seems more economical than the family-by-family casework approach particularly in view of the tragic fact that many ghetto parents may be "too far gone" to be reclaimed as a wholesome influence in the lives of their children. For those persons in the community who are not yet too far gone, but who lack the personal and social skills for sound influence over their children, training may serve as a substitute for "treatment." It may be that many lower-class persons who now refuse the role of client will accept the same therapeutic help if it is offered in a course of training as part of a position as paid or volunteer trainee.

It may also prove more feasible to train sensitive lower-class persons in the necessary skills to overcome the demoralizing impact of cultural shock in middle-class workers. Most social workers and teachers are themselves middle class, some far enough removed in time and circumstance to cause an inevitable sense of strangeness between themselves and the client; others too close themselves in time and circumstance to accept without anxiety the reminders of a rejected past. The problems are not merely ones of psychological alienation between the two groups but more concrete ones of speaking different languages and responding to different standards of behavior.

In training schools and community centers in which deviant peer group codes dominate, the would-be influentials, the professionals, are often stymied by a communication barrier. The point cannot be overstressed that in Harlem, and probably elsewhere, there are people in the helping services, probation and parole officers, group workers, caseworkers, and others in presumably influential roles who have abandoned any meaningful attempt to help the people who are in need. When they show any insight into this fact, these professionals almost always explain it by pointing to some lack or deficiency in the clients whom they cannot reach or cannot help. These clients are commonly called "unreachables" or those "hard to reach." Whatever the label, it means that the professionals have abandoned hope.

Yet many of these new recruits may later decide to complete their education and qualify for professional training, and it would be one of the risks of a program of encouraging such endeavor that the workers would quickly become middle class themselves.

The problem of class and race alienation is more difficult to solve than to understand. Bureaucratic organization is such that promotion and status are related to moving up the ladder to administration, and administration in social work, in education, as in many other professions, means supervising the work of other staff personnel. It is ironic that the further "up" one goes, the further one moves from the persons for whose service the profession exists— the client in the social casework agency, the child in the classroom. Yet this movement up the ladder to status, title, and higher pay is hard to resist. Perhaps it would be important for all administrators of programs dealing with human beings to keep in touch by some degree of direct involvement—the supervisor keeping a few clients, the school principal teaching an occasional class. Yet this, too, may be impractical, for the stance of authority upon which administrative success depends is itself related to a certain distance between the "top" and "bottom" levels in the hierarchy. In any event, one must be conscious of the danger of the flight from the client and insure that personal advancement does not rest on escape from the essential service.

To insure that the ghetto gets its share of social and community services, a large group of citizens of the ghetto, both youth and adult, who are disciplined and politically sensitive, would need to be organized. Otherwise, these vast and wide-ranging programs of reform would only amount to a benevolence from outside the community, vulnerable to control and abuse, and tending to encourage further dependency.

Given a community climate of indifference and apathy, even simple services like those of the Department of Sanitation will not be efficiently performed, as Harlem's many dirty streets make obvious. That the Department of Sanitation neglects to clean Harlem's streets as frequently as it cleans the streets in other communities may be seen as a simple sin of omission. On the other hand, genuine exploitation may be at work in such neglect as when building inspectors fail to inspect, or accept bribes from landlords to overlook violations. The ghetto community fails to get necessary public services and yet, through taxation, it is also involved in subsidizing its own deterioration.

The Haryou Associates Leadership Training Workshop in the summer of 1963 combined a paid job in social service with an unpaid training period in community action projects that helped to teach Harlem youth how to insist upon and get public services their taxes had already paid for. Unfortunately, these workers often lose the very qualities for which they were recruited from the community once they are placed on the payroll and brought into contact with professional colleagues whose style they sought to imitate.

Local neighborhood boards of adults and youth who live or work in the neighborhood could help change the patterns of community immobility and impotence by defining problems and by accepting responsibility for evaluating public and private services to the community. Such neighborhood boards would have powers of patronage from the outset—recruiting staff, providing service—but if they are to become a potent voice in the local neighborhood, patronage is not enough. They must have imagination and daring, and they must assume the risk of demanding real social change.

It may well turn out that a major role in insuring that the local boards do not begin to "play it safe" could be assumed by an organization run by the youth themselves. Since young people have less to lose by a radical stance and have fewer vested interests in "the system" than most adults, hopefully they could lend the clear and fresh vision, enthusiasm, and courage of youth to the adult members of the local boards and the adult staff alongside whom they would work.

Without such grass-roots activity in the neighborhoods, no comprehensive program, no matter how imaginative, will be safe from bureaucratic dry rot and exploitation. Neighbor would be responsible for neighbor. Individuals would come to have confidence in their ability to assess conflict, incompetence, and stagnation, and their right to do so. If the youth and adults of a neighborhood cannot be brought into the actual operation of reform programs, the programs themselves, no matter how elaborately and thoroughly planned, will merely contribute to the proliferation of irrelevance.

"The resentment of the weak," writes Eric Hoffer in *The Ordeal of Change*,[14] "does not spring from any injustice done to them, but from the sense of their inadequacy and impotence. Our healing gift to the weak is the capacity for self-help. We must learn to impart to them the technical, social and political skills which would enable them to get bread, human dignity, freedom and strength by their own efforts."

There is harnessable power to effect profound social change in the generally repressed rage of the alienated. There is much energy and imagination in the deviant subcultural forms in which this rage presently finds expression. Initially operating as close to the marginal world as is possible, a successful program of social rehabilitation must help the poor and the delinquent rehabilitate others like themselves and, in the process, effect their own salvation. This is one of the hopes for the ghetto. But if it is to work, the people of the ghetto must be respected and must learn to respect themselves through evidence of actual success in attempts at improving their condition. They cannot have this opportunity without serious risks and the many forms of turbulence inevitably associated with genuine social change.

BLACK SOCIAL MOBILITY

In response to white society's criticism of Negro family instability and the patterns of poverty, many middle-class Negroes have tended to accept the judgment of many whites that they are responsible for their own troubles, that economic dependency is related directly to immorality. As one Negro woman put it:

> Whenever a woman has a child of course she will do anything to provide for it, even to accepting welfare, but family breakdown and the moral state that we find ourselves in as a people has accounted for this development of the welfare programs.
> Now we could develop ourselves morally, perhaps, and this can only come about through an economic development. If we had some of the better things in life, that is, if we had the necessary leisure to

14 New York, Harper & Row, 1963.

develop ourselves intellectually, or if we had enough
money to provide for ourselves and enjoy life, and
to be happy, then the family would become stronger,
and the moral development of the people would
increase, and these welfare programs would be
done away with.

The middle-class prisoners of the ghetto are ashamed of
these elements in the community which bring disgrace to that community. They view themselves as an example of respectability and
are viewed by others in the same way. After the summer revolts of
1964, it was they who called for counterrallies of religious commitment to show the world "the other Harlem." They often preach that
if the lower class would work hard and clean up their homes and
not litter their streets and show more interest in their children, the
Negro predicament would be solved.

One such rather influential woman leader, in a talk to a
Negro church in Harlem, urged Negro women to organize for community reform. On every block in Harlem, she said, a committee
should be rallied to buy brooms; squads of women and children
would be recruited to sweep the streets. She argued that people who
live on dirty streets could not hope to gain the respect of others.
Negro children, she said, should be taught to respect cleanliness
and this would in turn give them pride in their parents and in
themselves.

She did not understand that it is not the job of the people to
sweep the streets; it is the job of the Department of Sanitation. It
had not occurred to her to advise these women to organize to gain
these services to which they were entitled. In a middle-class neighborhood, the people see to it that government does provide services.
To lecture the miserable inhabitants of the ghetto to sweep their
own streets is to urge them to accept the fact that the government
is not expected to serve them. But to force the government to provide sanitation and care is an effort beyond their capacity for, in
such ghettos, people are so defeated that their sense of powerlessness becomes a reality. They are immobilized against action even in
their own behalf.

Most disturbing of the implications of her advice was that
Negroes are responsible for their own condition, that dirt reflects
defects in the inhabitants. She was buying the position of many
middle-class whites that social victims are responsible for their
plight. She was in error, but even more important was the fact that
she was, in effect, presenting an apology for oppression.

Ghetto residents, particularly members of the middle class,

are often obsessed with what they feel to be a lack of initiative and moral fiber on the part of other Negroes. In a ghetto each member identifies, to some degree, with the other, and feels shame at the other's plight as though a member of the family had gone wrong. Often he resents the troublesome lower-class Negro, and then responds to this dislike by a pervasive sense of guilt—particularly when he finds there is no escape, after all. Although in the days of extensive European immigration, the second generation often felt guilt at its wish to escape the language and habits of their parents' "old country," a white person who moves into the middle class or upper class today can afford to forget his origins; he no longer needs to identify with those he has left behind. But in a society where wealth, aristocratic bearing, and talent are insufficient to overcome the stigma of the color of one's skin, there is no such escape for any generation. While this sense of relatedness may have its points, it also imposes a heavy psychological burden upon people whose own lives are hard enough to bear without the additional shame they feel the white community asks them to feel for their neighbors. Shame and despair, unlike anger, seldom lead to effective social or personal reform.

There are few middle-class sections in the central urban ghetto of Harlem. One of them is the Riverton Development and its residents are proud of the fact that it is an oasis in the slums in an area that was once one of the worst slum neighborhoods in the city. The middle-class Negro points with pride to the fact that the grounds are well kept, that the halls are scrupulously clean, that the elevators are in working order. Neighbor vies with neighbor in Riverton for the most luxuriously furnished apartment. As a consequence, James Baldwin's article in *Esquire* about Riverton outraged most of Harlem's middle-class residents.[15] Actually Riverton is not a slum, but James Baldwin was right that in an important sense it *is.* It is a spiritual slum, a paradoxical symbol of the phenomenon it seeks to deny, a symbol of Jim Crow. Riverton exists because at one time the Metropolitan Life Insurance Company's policy excluded Negroes from Stuyvesant Town on Manhattan's East Side, containing them in the ghetto. Today there are only a token number of Negroes in Stuyvesant Town, and there are no white families in Riverton. Thus residents of Riverton are as much prisoners of the ghetto as their neighbors in rat-infested tenements across the street or in the low-income public housing on the other side. Their very attempt to exist in isolated defiance inevitably involves them in the total system of the ghetto. They constantly fight the slum but can

[15] "Fifth Avenue Uptown," *Esquire,* 1960, Vol. 54, p. 70.

never be victorious. The ghetto is all-encompassing, a psychological as well as a physical reality. It consumes all its residents.

Yet the struggle of the middle-class Negro against the ghetto cannot be cynically dismissed. It is from this group of upwardly mobile Negroes that outstanding Negroes come. These are the young people who are stimulated by the desire and determination for personal success in spite of or because of the handicaps of rejected racial status. If they succeed, many whites nod approvingly: "I said so all along; American racial oppression is not unbearable; it can be overcome." The masses of lower-class Negroes regard this movement up the ladder with mixed feelings, both proud and resentful of the success of "one of their own."

Such middle-class Negro youth spend a considerable amount of their human energy seeking to mold their lives in rigid conformity to the prevailing middle-class values and standards. They are clean, they dress well, they speak well, they strive very hard to make good grades in school and to get a good education. They dedicate their lives to the task of becoming walking refutations of negative racial stereotypes. They are the opposite of the flamboyantly rebellious ghetto youth, more likely to withdraw passively and seek to repress any sign of hostility. Many express a subtle form of self and group hatred by denying awareness of any racial problems, or even by interpreting racial discrimination as an understandable response to the uncouth "lower-class" street Negro.

One poignant example was reflected in the response of a Negro undergraduate at Columbia College. An interview in the college magazine described and quoted him, as follows:

A sophomore who was raised in Harlem, Henry graduated third in his class of 400 ("beaten by two girls, as you might suspect") from Benjamin Franklin High School, which is 90 per cent Negro and Puerto Rican. His parents migrated from South Carolina; his father is a power press operator. Although his high school had no football team, he is out for the lightweight football squad. He lives in a single room in John Jay. Henry shuns demonstrative protests, preferring to participate in such projects as SEER, a Columbia College-initiated national program to help prepare Negro students for college during the summers. He likes social studies, but is toying with the idea of becoming a physician.

"Most people in Harlem, and, I suspect, other Negroes, feel very discouraged and are full of resentment against whites—too much so, I think. Negroes have to stop feeling so sorry for themselves and start trying to help themselves. Harlem could actually be a nice place to live. My parents have taught me not to expect to have things handed to me, but to work hard and get what I wanted. My teachers have encouraged me in the same way. But maybe if I had different parents and teachers I would feel trapped and bitter too. I really like Columbia, but I sometimes wish it had a lake."[16]

As adults they embark on the competitive cycle of conspicuous consumption and seek to share the good life of American middle-class suburbia. Some struggle to break through into nonsegregated communities in order to escape the ghetto, prepared to run the risks of overt hostility or even of violence. Others accept the easier escape to one of the middle-class suburban Negro ghettos. On the surface, the ghetto population in New York—unlike that in other cities—seems to be declining. (Harlem's population has decreased by 27,000 between 1950 and 1960, roughly a 10 percent loss despite the high birth rate.) But the fact is that Harlem's Negroes are merely shifting to other ghetto pockets in the city—Brooklyn's Bedford-Stuyvesant, the Lower Bronx, or Queens, or to suburban ghettos, such as those in Englewood, New Rochelle, Mount Vernon, and elsewhere. Many of those who move away from the central city are young couples—another drain on the ghetto's sources of energy and leadership.

Middle-class Negroes do not generally react with the overt, active hostility prevalent in many members of the "working class," but they, too, are often hostile, in ways similar to the larger pattern of white middle-class competitiveness, yet complicated by the persistent problems of racial anxiety, hypersensitivity, and defensiveness.

Negroes who do succeed in reaching the point of real competition with whites and who are rewarded with high-status jobs do not find that they have thereby resolved the problem of being Negro in a white society. Negroes brought into high-status jobs must be significantly above the norm, but feel they must adopt a style of compensatory gentility, allowing the whites to feel less threatened and even causing many to assume a protective role toward them. Negroes who do take this precautionary step must be certain that it

[16] Negroes and the College. *Columbia College Today*. New York: Columbia College, Columbia University, Vol. 12, No. 1, Fall 1964, p. 32.

is appropriate to the nature of the job itself, for a "show Negro" cannot afford to play, in an executive management job, a comic or subservient role. He needs an air of authority or he will lose status. If he adopts a stance or role of subtle deference, he will also be successful in protecting himself by assuaging the fears of whites. He must be constantly careful not to make his white colleagues uncomfortable, either by apparent arrogance or inappropriate obsequiousness.

Other Negroes in status jobs choose to protect themselves by keeping a careful distance between themselves and others, by neither asking for nor granting favors, by remaining aloof so that no one can be effectively patronizing. This pattern of overcompensation often leads to great productivity and intense concentration on the job. Less time and energy are available for socializing with others. Both closeness and acceptance are feared. Cliques are avoided as risky involvement. Friendship—with its danger of rejection—is not sought. When solicitousness is offered, it is regarded with disdain. The reputation sought is one of remoteness, single-minded dedication to the job, unremitting self-respect. If the Negro seems also to be cold and to lack concern for persons, he will accept this as evidence that his stance of invulnerability is effective. Colleagues are expected to be sophisticated enough not to intrude beyond the limits the Negro has set. If one sets the boundaries oneself, excluding others, one cannot oneself be excluded.

These protective devices to which high-status Negroes often resort are evidence of the depth of damage which racism has done. Such defenses must be seen for what they are—a response to fear of rejection and the anticipation of pain.

The middle-class Negro is demanding the right to share in the status symbols of personal success—quality education for his children; white-collar, managerial, or executive jobs; a fine home in one of the better neighborhoods. Having accepted the same value system which the middle-class whites live by, middle-class Negroes are forced to compete with them even at the risk of conflict. The demand for nonsegregated public schools comes largely from upwardly mobile middle-class Negroes; the demands for better white-collar, managerial, and executive jobs and for better nonsegregated housing come from the more successful and stable middle-class Negroes. If whites respond without mere grudging tokenism—"We already have a Negro in our firm (in our block) (in our school) (in our church)"—the masses of workingclass and lower middle-class Negroes will benefit. Other Negroes, too, will come to believe that the average Negro can win rewards through persistence, hard work, thrift, and character.

The competitive demands of the growing Negro middle class, if successful, would open more doors for all Negroes. A Negro in a managerial or executive position tends, also, to reduce the novelty of a Negro foreman or Negro salesman. A Negro professor might increase the employment chances for Negro secretaries on a college payroll. The tendency of white Americans to lump all Negroes together could lead ironically to major social advances, as Negroes in high-status jobs prepare the way for gradual acceptance of all Negroes. Still, whites who otherwise generalize about Negro racial traits ("All Negroes look alike to me") are often inconsistent when confronted with a Negro in a high-status post, viewing him as an exception to the rule.

To leave the heart of the ghetto is the goal of the average young educated Negro. The retreat of young professional Negro men and women—doctors, nurses, lawyers, engineers, teachers— from the central ghetto to the opening suburbs imposes a burden of decay of leadership upon the central city; yet the psychological stability of these families often seems to depend upon just such flight. The reminders of the ghetto, however, are never far away, for as Negroes—educated, clean, dignified, self-respecting families, the elite of Negro society—come to a formerly white community where whites had earlier retreated, white families often flee before them as though they were the carriers of a dread disease. The only contagion they carry is freedom, but what could be more dangerous than freedom to those who themselves live insecure, unhappy lives bound to frequently abhorred routines of family duty, unfulfilling job, and status-seeking? The insecure try to enhance their own personal status by denying others the very security and status which they seek for themselves.

This flight of the middle-class white to suburban, presently all-white communities, is a temporary stopgap only, unrealistic in view of the constant pressure of middle-class minority group members to escape the ghetto's deterioration and distress. Suburban communities can only be temporary havens for whites who desire racial homogeneity. The pressure for open occupancy in the suburbs will increase in the next decade with rising momentum. The pressure for integrated suburban schools will follow, as the struggle to abolish de facto school segregation in Orange, Englewood, and Teaneck, New Jersey, and in New Rochelle, White Plains, Manhasset, and Malverne, in New York, already demonstrate. It would indeed be a pathetic repetition of social, economic, and political folly if whites respond by techniques of exclusion that "worked" in the past, by developing suburban ghettos. But such a routine, unimaginative, and fearful response is all too likely—people tend to follow familiar patterns of behavior unless interrupted. An immediate systematic plan is needed to introduce minority group members into the suburbs without, at the same time, building new suburban ghetto substitutes. Such a plan could "interrupt" accustomed patterns of response to anxiety and break the cycle.

But though many middle-class residents of the ghetto do have a constant wish for physical and psychological escape, the ghetto has a devouring quality and to leave provokes a curious struggle. In an important sense no one can ever leave. Those who do not try feel that those who *do* try should have some feeling of guilt and a sense of betrayal. They demand allegiance to the pathology of the ghetto. The ghetto develops the sinister power to perpetuate its own pathology, to demand conformity to its norms; it ridicules, drives out, or isolates those who seek to resist those norms or even to transform them. This is an almost irresistible social Gresham's Law that none is allowed to escape with impunity.

That Negroes continue to seek to imitate the patterns of middle-class whites is a compliment, not the threat it may seem, but a compliment in large part undeserved, and the scars inflicted upon Negroes who are constantly confronted by the flight of those they encounter are deep and permanent. The wounded appear to eschew bitterness and hatred, but not far below the often genial, courteous surface lies a contempt that cannot easily be disguised.

In an article which was first published in 1943 and has subsequently become a classic, Hortense Powdermaker presented a subtle analysis of the means by which the American cultural process caused the Afro-American to play a role of accommodation. Utilizing the techniques of history, anthropology, sociology, and psychoanalysis, Powdermaker examined the mechanisms which enabled "the Negro to play this meek, deferential role." Professor Powdermaker concluded that the decline in Negro religious faith, the improvement of black education, and the migration of Negroes to urban areas would make the repression of black aggression more difficult to maintain. This conclusion has proven to be prophetic.

The selections which follow confirm Powdermaker's prediction that "unless some other form of adaptation takes place and unless discriminations are lessened, we may expect a trend toward greater overt aggression." The second selection, a study by psychiatrists Jacob Fishman and Fredric Solomon, was published in 1963, exactly twenty years after the initial appearance of Powdermaker's article. During this interim, massive changes occurred in American race relations. Of particular importance, the discrediting of racist theories had undermined the cultural basis for the black role of accommodation. In the 1940s and 1950s, the principle of racial equality was preached in the mass media and most of the nation's schools. This ideal was given further legitimacy by such governmental actions as President Truman's order to desegregate the nation's armed forces, the Supreme Court's 1954 decision that school segregation was unconstitutional, and President Eisenhower's enforcement of that decision in Little Rock, Arkansas. Finally, Negro leaders were gaining national prominence in areas other than sports and the arts. Adam Clayton Powell became a major Congressional figure, while the 1955 Montgomery bus boycotts produced a truly charismatic black leader, Martin Luther King.

As Fishman and Solomon demonstrate, these social changes had a profound effect on the black self-image. Black children who grew up during this transition period were affected the most. In their study of the student sit-in demonstrations which took place in Washington in the early 1960's, Fishman and Solomon show that "the Negro student in the sit-in movement proves he is neither childlike nor contented." They argue that the ability of young black college students to "express publicly the frustration and resentment that has been so long hidden" represented the "emergence of a new social character." While the student protests indicated new found pride, the nonviolent nature of these demonstrations represented continuity with the Negro past.

In the third selection, these changes are analyzed from the perspective of political science. Using survey data collected in 1960, Dwaine Marvick describes the rising level of expectations among northern and young Negroes. Marvick attributes these findings to postwar social changes; he argues that only in the period following World War II did "Negro youths . . . think seriously about claiming their birthrights." The process of political socialization described by Marvick could have led to the expression of black demands through conventional political channels if the dominant white society had been more responsive to black needs. Instead, the development of black pride took place in the context of little socioeconomic progress and white unwillingness to make a major commitment to eliminate black poverty and powerlessness. The alienation which resulted led to widespread rioting in the mid-1960's.

Although on the level of personality blacks had become more like whites in the postwar period,[1] relations between the two races worsened on the group level once blacks rebelled openly against the inequalities between the two groups. The final expression of black manhood, based on the premise that blacks were as good as whites, came in the form of open rebellion against the status quo. By the middle 1960s, black aggression was no longer repressed, as in the slavery and Jim Crow periods, nor was it expressed in a passive-aggressive manner, as it was during the days of the civil rights movement. Black rage was expressed directly against white oppression.

In the final selection, the psychiatrist Frederick Hacker criti-

[1] Bertram P. Karon, *The Negro Personality: A Rigorous Investigation of the Effects of Culture,* New York, Springer, 1958.

cizes the report of the McCone Commission (the "official" study of the August, 1965, Watts riot) for its failure to examine the real motivations of the black participants in that rebellion. Hacker sees the Watts rebellion as "the metamorphosis of the Negroes of southeastern Los Angeles from victims—historical objects—to masters." And Hacker concludes that while "the emotionally liberating effects of the riots have not lasted, . . . they have been replaced by a strange sense of pride and accomplishment which is actually the finding of a national and racial identity."

5
The Channeling of Negro Aggression by the Cultural Process

Hortense Powdermaker

We shall attempt in this article to look at one small segment of our cultural process—namely, a changing pattern of aggressive behavior—caused by the interracial situation. We limit ourselves to considering, at this time, only the Negro side of this complex of interpersonal relations; and we shall do no more than offer a few rather broad hypotheses on the relation between the forms aggression has taken during different historical periods and changes in the cultural processes at these times. For our hypotheses we are indebted to history, anthropology, sociology, and psychoanalysis; to the first three for understanding how social patterns come into being at a given point in time and how they are related to each other; and to the fourth, psychoanalysis, for a clue to the mechanisms by which individuals adopt particular social patterns. We shall concentrate on an analysis of two forms of adaptation where the aggression seems to have been concealed and, therefore, less understood. The two forms are that of the faithful slave and that of the meek, humble, unaggressive Negro who followed him after the Civil War. Since there is much more data on the latter role, this is the one we shall discuss in detail.

Education includes learning to play certain roles, roles which are advantageous to the individual in adapting himself to his particular culture. As the culture changes, so does the role. Adaptation to society begins at birth and ends at death. Culture is not a neatly tied package given to the child in school. It is an ever chang-

Reprinted by permission of University of Chicago Press and the author from Hortense Powdermaker, "The Channeling of Negro Aggression by the Cultural Process," *American Journal of Sociology*, 48 (May, 1943), pp. 750–758.

ing process, gropingly and gradually discovered.[1] The family, church, movies, newspapers, radio programs, books, trade-unions, chambers of commerce, and all other organized and unorganized interpersonal relations are part of education. All these are part of the cultural process, which determines how behavior and attitudes are channeled.

The cultural milieu of the Negro in the United States has run the gamut from slavery to that of a free but underprivileged group, who are slowly but continuously raising their status. From the time slaves were first brought to this country until today there have been barriers and restrictions which have prevented the Negro from satisfying social needs and attaining those values prized most highly by our society. How the resentment against these deprivations is channeled depends largely on cultural factors. Each historical period has produced certain types of adaptation.

Much has been written as to whether slaves emotionally accepted their status or whether they rebelled against it, with the consequent aggressive impulses turned against their masters. There is no categorical answer. Aggression can be channeled in many ways, and some of these are not discernible except to the trained psychiatrist. But others are quite obvious. The fact that thousands of slaves ran away clearly indicates dissatisfaction with their status.[2] Crimes committed by the slaves are another evidence of lack of acceptance of status and of aggressive feelings toward the whites.

Many people have assumed that there was little or no crime by Negroes during the slave regime. The impression will be quickly dispelled if one consults the elaborate studies contained in *Judicial Cases concerning American Slavery and the Negro.* . . . In these lists can be found cases of murder, rape, attempted rape, arson, theft, burglary, and practically every conceivable crime.[3]

[1] For further elaboration of this point see Edward Sapir, "The Emergence of the Concept of Personality in a Study of Cultures," *Journal of Social Psychology,* V, 408–415.

[2] From 1830 to 1860 about fifty thousand escaped, chiefly through Ohio and Philadelphia. In an earlier period many escaped to near-by Indian tribes, others to Canada and the free states (see E. B. Reuter, *The American Race Problem* [New York, 1938], pp. 117–118).

[3] Quoted in W. D. Weatherford and C. S. Johnson, *Race Relations* (New York, 1934), p. 265.

The fact that these crimes were committed in the face of the most severe deterrents—cutting-off of ears, whipping, castration, death by mutilation—bears witness to the strength of the underlying aggression. Equally cruel was the punishment of those slaves who broke the laws against carrying firearms, assembling, and conspiring to rebel. The Gabriel conspiracy in Richmond, the Vesey conspiracy in Charleston, the Nat Turner rebellion, and others resulted in the massacre of whites and in the burning, shooting, and hanging of the Negroes. These attempts were undertaken despite the fact that the superior power of the whites made it virtually impossible for a slave revolt to be successful.

But the overt aggression was very probably only a small part of the total hostility. The punishments imposed by the culture for failure were too severe and the chances for success too slight to encourage the majority of slaves to rebel to any considerable extent. There were large numbers of loyal and faithful slaves, loyal to the system and to the masters. It is this loyalty that we try to understand.

Psychologically, slavery is a dependency situation. The slave was completely dependent upon the white master for food, clothing, shelter, protection—in other words, for security. If he could gain the good will or affection of the master, his security was increased. In return for this security the Negro gave obedience, loyalty, and some-times love or affection. With certain limitations the situation of slave and master corresponds to that of child and parent. The young child is completely dependent on his parents for food, shelter, love, and everything affecting his well-being and security. The child learns to be obedient because he is taught that disobedience brings punishment and the withdrawal of something he needs for security. Basic infantile and childhood disciplines relating to sex are imposed on this level. In our culture, parents forbid and punish deviations by a child, who in turn renounces his gratification to gain the parent's approval. "The parent is needed and feared, and must therefore be obeyed; but the hatred to the frustrating parent, though suppressed, must be present somewhere."[4]

We mentioned above that there are certain limitations to our analogy. Obviously, the bondage is greater for the slave than for the child. Equally obviously, while there was love in some master-slave relationships, it was certainly not so prevalent as between parents and children. Again, the child always has a weak and under-

---

[4] A. Kardiner and R. Linton, *The Individual and Society* (New York, 1939), p. 24.

developed ego while the adult slave may have a strong, developed one. But most important is the difference in the reasons for the dependency attitude. The limited strength and resources of the child and his resulting helplessness and anxiety are due to biological causes. But the slave's dependency is imposed on him by culture and has nothing to do with biological factors. The structure of the two dependency situations is, therefore, very different. Nevertheless, functionally they have something in common. To attain the only security available to them, both the slave and the child repress, consciously or unconsciously, their hatred for the object which restricts their desires and freedom. At this late date it is impossible to determine to what degree aggression occurred in slaves' fantasies or in minor overt acts.[5] It probably varied from one slave to another, as it does for children. Neither all children nor all slaves repress their aggression all the time. Running away is a pattern for both groups. Disobedience is followed by punishment for both. Another alternative for both is open rebellion. Finally, children and slaves may accept their dependency and repress their aggression when compensations are adequate. They may even identify with the frustrating object. The picture of the faithful slave who helped the white mistress run the plantation while the master was away fighting, fighting the men who would liberate the slave, is only superficially paradoxical.

Data from psychoanalysis indicate that those children who do not permit their aggressive impulses to break through even in fantasy, not to mention overt behavior, have great difficulty as adults in entering into any personal relationship which does not duplicate the dependency pattern of parent and child. A legal edict of freedom did not immediately change the security system for the slave, conditioned over years to depend on the white man for all security. Time was needed for the compensations of freedom to become part of the ex-slave's security system. The process of growing up, or becoming less dependent, is a long and difficult one.

With emancipation the slave, from being a piece of property with no rights at all, attained the status of a human being—but an underprivileged one. Psychological dependency did not vanish with the proclamation of freedom. In the period following the Civil War the slave's illiteracy, his complete lack of capital and property, the habituation to the past, and the continuous forces wielded by the whites in power created new conditions for the continuance of the

[5] I know of no accurate way of getting data on this point. The memories of old ex-slaves would be colored by what has happened to them since slavery was abolished. Aggressive impulses which may have been completely repressed during slavery could be released and brought into consciousness after slavery ceased.

old dependency. The recently freed Negro was dependent on the whites for jobs, for favors, for grants of money to set up schools, and for much of his security. In the South, following the Reconstruction Period, it was by obtaining favors from whites rather than by insisting on his rights that the Negro was able to make any progress or attain any security. The set of mores which insured the colored man's status being lower than that of the whites was and is still firmly intrenched. The denial of the courtesy titles (Mr., Mrs., Miss); the Jim Crowism in schools, buses, and trains, in places of residence; the denial of legal rights; the threat of lynching—these are among the more obvious ways of "keeping the Negro in his place." He is deprived of what are considered legal, social, and human rights, without any of the compensations for his deprivation which he had under slavery.

The same questions we asked about the slave occur again. Did the Negro really accept his position? Or was aggression aroused, and, if so, how did the culture channel it? This is an easier situation to study than the slavery of the past; for varied ways of reacting or adapting to this situation became stereotyped and still persist today. They are therefore susceptible of direct study.

First, there is direct aggression against its true object. Since the whites had, and still have, superior power and since Negroes are highly realistic, they rarely use this method on any large scale except in times of crisis, and then as a climax to a long series of more indirect aggressive behavior patterns. The knocking-down of a white overseer, the direct attack on other whites, has occurred, but only occasionally. One of the reasons advanced by many southern white planters for their preference for colored share-croppers to white ones is that the former do not fight back like the latter.

A second method consists in substituting a colored object for the white object of aggression. This was, and still is, done very frequently. The high degree of intra-Negro quarreling, crime, and homicide, revealed by statistics and observation, can be directly correlated with the Negro's frustration in being unable to vent his hostility on the whites. The mechanism of the substitution of one object of aggression for another is well known to the scientist and to the layman.[6] The substitution of Negro for white is encouraged by the culture pattern of white official and unofficial leniency toward intra-Negro crime. Courts, more particularly southern ones, are mild

---

[6] This is reflected in the jokes and stories about the man who has a bad day at the office and then "takes it out" on his wife or children when he comes home in the evening.

in their view of intra-Negro offenses, and the prevailing white attitude is one of indulgence toward those intra-Negro crimes which do not infringe on white privileges.[7]

A third possibility is for the Negro to retreat to an "ivory tower" and attempt to remain unaffected by the interracial situation. But this type of adjustment is very difficult and consequently a rare one.

Another form of adaptation consists in the Negro's identification with his white employer, particularly if the latter has great prestige. Some of the slaves also identified themselves with the great families whom they served. This pattern may likewise be observed in white servants. Still another adaptation is the diversion of aggression into wit, which has been and still is a much-used mechanism. We have not sufficient data on these two mechanisms to discuss them in detail.

But we do want to analyze in some detail a very frequent type of adjustment which occurred after the Civil War and which has persisted. We mean the behavior of the meek, humble, and unaggressive Negro, who is always deferential to whites no matter what the provocation may be. The psychological mechanism for this form of adaptation is less obvious than some of the other types, and a more detailed analysis is therefore needed. We have called this Negro "unaggressive," and that is the way his overt behavior could be correctly described. All our data, however, indicate that he does have aggressive impulses against whites, springing from the interracial situation. He would be abnormal if he did not have them. Over and over again field studies reveal that this type of Negro is conscious of these resentments. But he conceals his true attitude from the whites who have power. How has he been able to conceal his aggression so successfully? His success here is patent. What is the psychological mechanism which enables the Negro to play this meek, deferential role?

A clue appears in certain similarities of this kind of behavior to that of the masochist, particularly through the detailed analysis of masochism by Dr. Theodor Reik in his recent book on that subject.[8] The seeming paradox of the masochist enjoying his suffering has been well known to psychoanalysts. He derives pleasure, because, first, it satisfies unconscious guilt feeling. Second (and here is where Dr. Reik has gone beyond the other psychoanalysts in his interpretation), the masochist derives another kind of pleasure, because his suffering is a prelude to his reward and eventual tri-

[7] For further elaboration see H. Powdermaker, *After Freedom* (Viking Press, 1939), pp. 172–174.

[8] *Masochism in Modern Man* (New York: Farrar & Rinehart, 1941).

umph over his adversary. In other words, he gets power through his suffering. We must not be misunderstood at this point. The meek Negro is neither neurotic nor masochistic any more than the slave was biologically a child. But the unaggressive behavior has some elements in common with (and some different from) the behavior of the masochist; and a comparison of the two gives a clue to an understanding of the strength behind the meek, humble role played by so many Negroes.

First, there are essential differences between the Negroes we are describing and the masochists analyzed by Dr. Reik and others. The Negro's sufferings and sacrifices are not unconsciously self-inflicted (as are those of the masochist) but are inflicted on him by the culture. The Negro plays his social masochistic role consciously, while the psychologically compulsive masochist does it unconsciously. These two important differences should be kept in mind while the similarities are discussed.

Our hypothesis is that the meek, unaggressive Negro, who persists today as a type and whom we have opportunity to study, feels guilty about his conscious and unconscious feelings of hostility and aggression toward the white people. These Negroes are believing Christians who have taken very literally the Christian doctrine that it is sinful to hate. Yet on every hand they are faced with situations which must inevitably produce hatred in any normal human being. These situations run the scale from seeing an innocent person lynched to having to accept the inferior accommodations on a Jim Crow train. The feeling of sin and guilt is frequently and openly expressed. In a Sunday-school class in a southern rural colored church a teacher tells the tale of a share-cropper who had worked all season for a white planter, only to be cheated out of half of his earnings. The teacher's lesson is that it is wrong to hate this planter, because Christ told us to love our enemies. The members of the class say how hard it is not to hate but that since it is a sin they will change their hate to love. They regard this as possible, although difficult.[9]

One woman in the same community, who plays the deferential role to perfection and who, whites say, never steps out of "her place," tells me she feels guilty because she hates the whites, who do not seem to distinguish between her, a very moral, respectable, and law-abiding person, and the immoral, disreputable colored prostitutes of the community. She says that God and Jesus have told her not to hate but to love—and so she must drive the hatred and bitterness away. Almost every human being in our culture carries a

[9] Cf. Powdermaker, *op. cit.*, pp. 247–248.

load of guilt (heavy or light as the case may be) over his conscious and unconscious aggressive impulses. It is easy then to imagine how heavy is the load of guilt for the believing Christian Negro who lives in an interracial situation which is a constant stimulus to aggressive thoughts and fantasies. By acting in exactly the opposite manner— that is, meekly and unaggressively—he can appease his guilt feelings consciously and unconsciously. It is this appeasement which accounts, in part, for his pleasure in the unaggressive role he plays with the whites.

But only in part. The unaggressive Negro enjoys his role also because through it he feels superior to the whites. Like the masochist, he thinks of his present sufferings as a contrasting background for his future glory. His is the final victory, and so he can afford to feel superior to his white opponent who is enjoying a temporary victory over him. My own field work and the work of others give many examples. Dr. Charles S. Johnson, in his recent book on rural colored youth in the South, discusses the dissimulation of many of the young people studied. He says:

> Outward submissiveness and respect may thus be, as often as not, a mask behind which these youth conceal their attitude. George Cator is an example of this behavior. He has learned to flatter as a means of preserving his own estimate of himself. . . . "When I'm around them, I act like they are more than I am. I don't think they are, but they do. I hear people say that's the best way to act."[10]

Any expression of antagonism would be dangerous, but this is not the whole story. It is not just that this boy and others avoid danger by meek negative behavior. There is a positive element in that he and others are insuring eventual victory. This was expressed by a colored servant who is a model of deferential behavior when with the whites. However, to me she says, partly scornfully and partly jokingly, that she considers it ridiculous that having cleaned the front porch and entrance she has to use the back entrance. She hates having to walk in the back door, which in this case is not only the symbol of status for a servant but the symbol that a whole race has a servant status. She adds that she expects to go to Heaven and there she will find rest—and no back doors.[11]

[10] Charles S. Johnson, *Growing Up in the Black Belt* (American Council on Education, 1941), pp. 296–297.
[11] From the author's field notes in rural Mississippi.

The Christian doctrines, "The last shall be first, and the first shall be last" and "The meek shall inherit the earth," and all the promises of future reward for suffering give strong homiletic sanction to the feeling that the Negroes' present status and suffering is a prelude to their future triumph. Colored ministers give very concise expression to this attitude. A sermon heard in a colored church in rural Mississippi related

> the story of a rich woman who lived in a big house and had no time for God. When she went to Heaven she was given an old shanty in which to live and she exclaimed: "Why that's the shanty my cook used to live in!" The cook, who on earth had given all her time to God, was now living in a big house in Heaven, very much like the one in which her former mistress used to live.[12]

The Christian missionaries of the pre-Civil War period emphasized the reward for the meek and their contrasting glories in the future partly because it was an important part of Christian doctrine and partly because it was only by negating the present and emphasizing the future that the evangelists could get permission from the planters to preach to the slaves. The general theme of many of these sermons was that the greater the suffering here, the greater would be the reward in the world to come. One minister, referring to the case of a slave who was unjustly punished by his masters, says, "He [God] will reward you for it in heaven, and the punishment you suffer unjustly here shall turn to your exceeding great glory thereafter."[13] Sermons, past and current, quite frequently picture Heaven as a place where whites and Negroes are not just equal but where their respective status is the opposite of what it is here.

This fantasy of turning the tables on the oppressor is not always confined to the other world; sometimes the setting is our own world. An example of this is the fantasy of a young colored girl in a northern town who had publicly taken quite meekly a decision that the colored people could not use the "Y" swimming pool at the same time white people were using it. Privately she shows her anger and says that she wishes the colored people would build a great big, magnificent "Y," a hundred times better than the white one, and make that one look like nothing. Her fantasy of triumph

[12] Powdermaker, *op. cit.,* p. 243.
[13] Revor Bowen, *Divine White Right* (1934), p. 111.

over the whites obviously gives her real pleasure and allows her to carry the present situation less onerously. Another example of the same type of fantasying occurs in the joking between two colored teachers who obey a disliked white official with deferential meekness. The joking consists of one of them boasting in some detail about how he has fired the white official; and the other one, in the same tone, describing how he "cussed out" the white official over the telephone.

Another aspect of the unaggressive Negro's pleasure is his feeling of superiority because he thinks he is so much finer a Christian than his white opponent. He, the Negro, is following Christ's precepts, while the white man does the opposite. The white man oppresses the poor and is unjust; in other words, he sins. He, the Negro, is virtuous and will be rewarded. One Negro, referring to a white man's un-Christian behavior, says, "It reflects back on him."

This feeling of superiority is a third characteristic of the unaggressive Negro's pleasure and is not limited to the feeling of Christian virtue. He feels superior to the whites because he is fooling them. His triumph is not completely limited to the distant future, but he enjoys at least a small part of it now. One of my informants in Mississippi, who plays this role to perfection, told me how he has the laugh on the whites because they never know his real thoughts. He quite consciously feels that he and the other Negroes like him have the upper hand through their dissimulation. He says very clearly that it makes him feel superior. One woman who presents an appearance of perfect meekness laughs with a kind of gleeful irony when she tells me how she really feels, and her meekness drops away from her as if she were discarding a cloak. Another chuckles when she relates how much she has been able to extract from white people, who would never give her a thing if they knew how she really felt about them. A Negro official who holds a fairly important position in his community knows that he is constantly being watched to see that he does not overstep his place, that his position and contact with whites has not made him "uppity." As he goes around humbly saying, "Yes, ma'am" and "Yes, sir," waiting his turn long after it is due, appearing not to heed insulting remarks, he is buoyed up with a feeling of superiority because he is really fooling all these whites. He is quite aware of his mask and knows it is such and not his real self. This mask characteristic comes out particularly when one of these individuals is seen with the whites and then later with his own group. One woman who has been particularly successful in the deferential, humble role with the whites gives a clear impression of meekness and humility. Her eyes downcast, her voice low, she patiently waits to be spoken to before she speaks, and then her tone is completely deferential. An hour later she is in the midst of her own group. No longer are her eyes downcast. They sparkle! Her laugh flashes out readily. Instead of patiently waiting, she is energetically leading. Her personality emerges, vibrant and strong, a complete contrast to the picture she gives the whites. These people enjoy wearing their mask because they do it so successfully and because its success makes them feel superior to the whites whom they deceive.

The deferential, unaggressive role just described and well known to students of Negro life has a very real function besides the obvious one of avoiding trouble. As Dr. Reik says in his book on masochism, "The supremacy of the will is not only expressed in open fights." It is, as he says, likewise expressed "in the determination to yield only exteriorly and yet to cling to life, nourishing such phantasies anticipating final victory."[14] Our unaggressive Negro, like the masochist, imagines a future where his fine qualities are acknowledged by the people who had formerly disdained him. This, in good Christian manner, will be brought about through suffering. This philosophy and its resulting behavior obviously make the Negroes (or any minority group) who have them very adaptable to any circumstance in which they find themselves, no matter how painful. They continue to cling to life, in the assurance of ultimate victory. They cannot be hurt in the way that people without this faith are hurt. The adaptability of the Negro has often been noted. This hypothesis may give some further clue to understanding it.

A special combination of cultural factors—namely, oppression of a minority group and a religion which promises that through suffering power will be gained over the oppressors—has channeled one type of adaptive behavior similar to that of the masochist. This behavior pattern has given the Negro a way of appeasing his guilt over his aggressive impulses and a method of adapting to a very difficult cultural situation. Because of the understanding given us by psychoanalysis of the pleasure derived through suffering, of the near and distant aims of the masochist, we are given a clue to the psychological mechanism underlying the so-called "unaggressive" Negro's behavior. This Negro is not a masochist, in that his sufferings are not self-inflicted and he plays his role consciously. He knows he is acting, while the masochist behavior springs from inner compulsion. Again, there is a real difference in structure, as there was in the dependency situations of the child and the slave; and again there is a real similarity in function. The masochist and the meek, unaggressive Negro derive a similar kind of pleasure from

[14] *Op. cit.,* p. 322.

their suffering. For the Negro as well as for the masochist there is pleasure in appeasing the guilt feeling; for each there is the pleasure derived from the belief that through his suffering he becomes superior to his oppressors; and, finally, for each the suffering is a prelude to final victory.

Neither the slave nor the obsequious, unaggressive Negro, whom we have described, learned to play his role in any school. They learned by observation and imitation; they were taught by their parents; they observed what role brought rewards. Since the Civil War the Negro has likewise seen the meek, humble type presented over and over again with approval in sermons, in literature, in movies, and, more recently, through radio sketches. By participating in the cultural processes, the Negro has learned his role. This was his education, far more powerful than anything restricted to schools; for the kind of education we are discussing is continuous during the entire life of the individual. It is subtle as well as direct. One part of the cultural process strengthens another part, and reinforcement for the role we described comes from every side.

But the cultural process continues to change with resulting changes in behavior. Just as the completely loyal and faithful slave disappeared, so the meek, unaggressive, and humble Negro, the "good nigger" type, is declining in numbers. In the rural South, and elsewhere too, the tendency of Negro young people (in their teens and twenties) is to refuse to assume the unaggressive role. The passing of the "good nigger" from the scene does not entail a civil war as did the passing of the faithful slave. But it does indicate a psychological revolution. For the slave the Civil War altered the scope of the dependency situation. Today, without a Civil War, equally significant cultural changes are taking place. The Negro is participating now in a very different kind of cultural process from that which he underwent fifty years ago.

Some of the differences occurring today are here briefly indicated. There is a decline in religious faith. The vivid "getting-religion" experience prevalent in the past has become increasingly rare for young people. Today they use the church as a social center. Gone is the intensity of religious belief that their parents knew. The young people are not atheists, but they do not have the fervor and sincerity of belief in a future world. They are much more hurt by slights and minor insults than are their parents, because they do not put their faith in the promise of a heavenly victory.

Along with changes in the form of religious participation have come many other changes. The illiteracy of the past has disappeared. A lengthening of schooling and a steady improvement in educational standards tend to give the Negro the same knowledge and the same tools enjoyed by the white man and to minimize cultural differences between the two. A more independent and rebellious Negro type is making its appearance in literature, as, for instance, the character of Bigger in the best seller, *Native Son.*

The steady trek of the rural Negroes to cities, North and South, has changed the milieu of masses of Negroes from the rural peasant life to the industrial urban one.[15] Here they come under the influence of the trade-union movement, which slowly but gradually is shifting its attitude from one of jealous exclusion to one of inclusion, sometimes cordial and sometimes resigned. The shift is not anywhere near completion yet, but the trend is there: In the city the Negro is influenced by the same advertisements, the same radio sketches, the same political bosses, the same parties (left or right), and all the other urban forces which influence the white man.

The Negro's goals for success are thus becoming increasingly the same as those of the white person; and these goals are primarily in the economic field, although those in other fields, such as art and athletics, are not to be minimized either. The securing of these goals is in this world rather than in a future one. They are attained through the competition and aggressive struggle so characteristic of our culture rather than through meekness and subservience. The compensations available to the loyal slave and the humble, unaggressive, free Negro no longer exist or, at least, are steadily diminishing. The white man can no longer offer security in return for devotion, because he himself no longer has security. The whites of all classes have known a mounting social insecurity over the past decade, and they obviously cannot give away something which they do not possess. Thus the material rewards for obsequiousness and unaggressiveness are fading away. Gone, too, is the religious emphasis on rewards in Heaven. When the cultural process takes away rewards for a certain type of behavior, dissatisfaction with that behavior appears and there is a gradual change to another form which is more likely to bring new compensations. Obviously, one can expect, and one finds, a growing restlessness and uncertainty which occur in any transition period, when old goals have been lost. The new goals are the standard American ones. But the means for attaining these goals are not yet as available to the Negro as they are to the white. Economic and social discriminations still exist. Unless some other form of adaptation takes place and unless discriminations are lessened, we may expect a trend toward greater overt aggression.

[15] Between 1920 and 1930 over a million Negroes migrated from the country to the cities. The figures for the past decade are not yet available.

However, there are no sudden revolutions in behavior patterns, and this holds for the patterns of aggression. They change slowly; the old ones persist while new ones are being formed, and opposing patterns exist side by side. But change occurs. The cultural process in which the Negro has participated from the time when he was first brought to this country until today has involved a constant denial of privileges. The denial has taken various forms, from the overt one involved in slavery to the more subtle ones of today. The compensations for the denial have varied from different degrees of material security to promises of future blessings in Heaven, and from the feeling of being more virtuous than the white to the feeling of fooling him. Today these compensations are fading away. Equally important, ideological fetters of the past have been broken by the Negro's increasing participation in the current urban industrial processes.

The Negro's education, formal and informal, has consisted of his participation in this ever changing cultural process, one small part of which we have briefly examined. Slavery, religion, economic and other social factors, have channeled his activities, offering him alternatives within a certain cultural range. We have examined only two of the alternatives in any detail—namely, the roles of the faithful slave and of the humble, meek Negro who was a fairly common stereotype following the Civil War; we have concentrated on the latter because he still exists and we therefore have more data on him. Both appear unaggressive. A functional comparison with the psychoanalytical analysis of the dependency situation of the child and of the problem of masochism has indicated how the aggression may have been present, although concealed, in these two roles.

6
Youth and Social Action: Perspectives on the Student Sit-in Movement

Jacob R. Fishman, M.D.
Fredric Solomon, M.D.

This is the initial report of a study of the psychodynamics of adolescent and student participation in public, risk-taking activities for racial desegregation. The major participants in this movement have been Negro and white college students in the Southern United States. Their most dramatic and perhaps most effective weapon has been a form of public passive resistance known as the sit-in demonstration. Indeed, the whole movement has come to be known as the student sit-in movement, and the term has quickly become part of our contemporary culture.

The original targets of these demonstrations were variety stores, which customarily welcome Negro patrons in most departments but exclude them from service at lunch counters. The first student sit-in took place on February 1, 1960, when four freshmen at an all-Negro college in Greensboro, North Carolina, deliberately decided to request service at such a segregated lunch counter.[18] When service was denied them because of their color, they refused to leave; instead they remained seated, reading schoolbooks and Bibles. Since that time demonstrations have spread through many parts of the country where such policies are in effect and have been aimed at all kinds of segregated public facilities.

There are several possible results from a sit-in. At one extreme, the segregation policy may be promptly ended and the stu-

An earlier version of this paper was presented at the Third World Congress of Psychiatry, Montreal, Canada, June 1961. Reprinted by permission from Jacob R. Fishman and Fredric Solomon, "Youth and Social Action: 1. Perspectives on the Student Sit-in Movement," *American Journal of Orthopsychiatry*, 33, no. 5 (October, 1963), pp. 872–882. Copyright, 1963 the American Orthopsychiatric Association, Inc.

dents served. At the other, the demonstrators may be heckled and assaulted, or arrested, jailed and charged with trespassing or disorderly conduct. Whatever the outcome, the pattern of social crisis is always the same. The students aggressively cross the color line, and then passively allow the consequences to rest on the co-operation of other like-minded people and on the decisions of civic authorities and businessmen in the dominant white majority. In the space of three years the South has witnessed thousands of demonstrations, which have also included boycotts, picketing, mass marches, hunger strikes of jailed students and the "freedom rides" on interstate buses. As of April, 1961 (before the freedom rides), demonstrators had numbered in the tens of thousands and had been active in some 75 Southern towns and cities. Three thousand five hundred demonstrators had been arrested; of these, an estimated 95 per cent were young people of both sexes in their teens or early twenties, both Negro and white.*

These demonstrations have resulted in the desegregation of more than 5,000 eating facilities, as well as hundreds of libraries, places of recreation and churches. The local, national and international news media have provided wide coverage, and the impact has been felt on campuses all over the country. For the Southern United States, this has represented a rate of social change far more rapid than any it has known since the Negro people were emancipated from slavery nearly 100 years ago.[6,17,21] In view of the social significance of this student movement, an understanding of the psychodynamic background and motivation of these young people should illuminate some of the relationships among personality, society and social change.

During the past two years we have studied the development of this movement, particularly in the Washington, D.C., area. The present paper represents our tentative psychosocial formulations of some motivational and personality factors in these students. Further data collection and analysis is under way.[5,18–20] This report focuses mainly on young Negroes, whereas future papers will deal more extensively with the white student demonstrators, as well as with opponents and supporters in surrounding communities. Reports have already been presented on the very first of the organized sit-in demonstrations[18] and on the dynamics of nonviolent action.[20]

Picketing demonstrations in the Washington area have on occasion attracted as many as 200 participants, including, at one point in the summer of 1960, five United States Congressmen. However, the decision-making core of regular demonstrators consisted

* Statistics provided by the Congress of Racial Equality, New York, N.Y.

of about 40 students, calling themselves "NAG," "Nonviolent Action Group." They felt this name exemplified the group's determination to "nag the conscience of the community." (It also symbolizes the recurrent theme of a passive-aggressive, persevering style of action.) White and Negro students, both male and female, were about evenly represented in the group. The average age was 18 years and six months, most members having completed one year in college, with little or no comparable prior experience with interracial organizations. In its first year of activity, the group succeeded in desegregating about 25 facilities, including restaurants, lunch counters, a movie theatre and the area's only amusement park. In addition, they were an important factor in stimulating the development of a council on human relations in suburban Montgomery County. During the course of these activities, about 100 arrests of demonstrators were made by local authorities. Several members of the original group later went on to become involved in freedom rides and other risk-taking actions for desegregation in the Deep South.[20]

Seventeen students (7 Negroes and 10 whites) in the Washington group were interviewed both indiviudally and in groups. Three others (2 young Negro men who were major leaders, and one young white woman) were interviewed individually in some depth over a period of six months. Of primary interest in the interviews were those factors leading up to a student's decision to involve himself in a public, risk-taking activity for desegregation: a second focus was on family background and parental reactions to the student's participation. The demonstrators readily volunteered to discuss these and related matters, and two of the young Negro leaders have continued to maintain close contact with us.[20] In addition to interviews, direct observations were made of demonstrations and other group activities, and public reaction was followed through the extensive coverage of the local news media.

EMERGENCE OF A NEW SOCIAL CHARACTER

One of the 19-year-old Negro students recalled his reaction, which was typical, when he read the newspaper report of the very first organized sit-in in Greensboro, North Carolina. He and his friends at Howard University "all rejoiced, and we all felt the opportunity was here; and the fact that college students were doing it is one of the powerful reasons for participating ourselves . . . but more than anything . . . we all realized we had been *wanting to do something* and now was the time." Many of these students remembered that they first began "wanting to do something" in 1954 when they

first heard about the Supreme Sourt decision for school desegregation; the student quoted above was 13 years old at that time, as
were most of the young demonstrators in this study.

Thus it was at the threshold of their adolescence that the
United States Supreme Court ruled unanimously that the segregated
schools these youngsters had been attending were illegal. The
Court had decided that systems of separate schools for Negroes
and whites were inherently unequal because they generated in
Negro students "a feeling of inferiority as to their status in the community that may affect their hearts and minds in a way unlikely
ever to be undone." A unique and significant precedent was set in
the use of statements of psychologists and social scientists to support this ruling.

This Supreme Court decision immediately received widespread publicity, discussion, denunciation and praise. It was apparent from talking to all of our Negro subjects that its message had
been deeply imprinted on their minds and outlook. This public and
legal recognition of the desirability of desegregation and its possible achievement in the near future was an experience in the
adolescent development of these young people quite different from
that of their parents and older siblings. They felt that the older
generation had come to accept segregation and social inferiority
as the natural order of things. They were aware of the Southern
tradition that, when dealing with white people, one should present
the appearance of a contented subordinate. However, feeling that
desegregation was now their right, these students experienced
increasing frustration with its painfully slow implementation and
with the seeming hypocrisy of adults who paid lip service to principles but took no risks for implementation. Such feelings were
intensified by the contrast of their own situation with that of many
African peoples who were aggressively achieving independence
and total public recognition as adults in the family of nations.

Many observers have pointed out that the psychosocial
history of the Southern Negro has been largely characterized by
his need to suppress and displace elsewhere his feelings of hostility
toward the dominant whites.[1, 15, 16] Similarly he has had to suppress
and displace any motivation to compete in economic and social
spheres. He has been forced to assume a manifest role of passivity
and submission, a role which has its social roots in economic and
legal dependency on the white majority as well as in fear of puni-
tive retaliation for overstepping color boundaries. These characteristics are expressed and further reinforced through the incorporation
by the Negro of certain aspects of Christianity—especially the
childlike trust in God, acceptance of one's lot in life, turning the

other cheek and a belief in a happy afterlife coming to those good Christians who suffer and endure.[15]

Outbreaks of this bottled-up aggression in the South through crimes directed against whites have been dealt with traditionally in an extraordinarily harsh manner, for example, lynchings. Crimes within the Negro community, however, have received greater toleration from the white authorities, who viewed them as the behavior of irresponsible children who could be taught no better. The inhibited anger against the whites commonly has been turned on the self and displaced into the greatly disguised, stereotyped patterns of laziness, apathy, passivity and unreliability. The hostile roots of such behavior have been so well masked and denied by the defensive operations of both racial groups that, until very recently, the prevalent Southern white's view of the Negro was that of a rather irresponsible but essentially contented child. The Negro's needs were thought to be amply taken care of by a paternal system of social relationships modeled on the traditions of slavery. It comes as a real shock to many Southerners to see a discontented Negro forcefully displaying his discontent in a public, vocal manner. This confrontation is very threatening to some white Southerners, as shown in some of their violent reactions to sit-ins.

The Negro student in the sit-in movement proves he is neither childlike nor contented. The protests are neither indirect nor patient, as tends to be the behavior of the older generation. At the same time they express publicly the frustration and resentment that has been so long hidden. Through the force of the moral and democratic principles they invoke to justify their action, they channel aggression into a positive identification with the traditional ego-ideal of the white majority, as well as with that of the world community. Using the terms of Erich Fromm, we may describe this as the emergence of a new social character for the Southern Negro.[8] One prominent white Southern politician has remarked, "These kids seem to be completely new Negroes, the likes of which we've never seen before." This new social character has emerged from the psychological reaction of adolescent members of a social group to changed external realities. It is built upon certain long-standing personality and cultural traits shared by the group's members, as well as the changing events, ideas and circumstances around them.

IDENTITY FORMATION AND "PROSOCIAL ACTING OUT"

Along with these factors of changing social history and new social character, an additional perspective is necessary to understand the student sit-in movement. One must take into account certain features of the developmental and group psychology of late adolescence—with special emphasis on interrelationships between action and identity formation. As Erik Erikson has intimated, the unique needs and strengths of late adolescence frequently focus on the social and intellectual crises of the era, translating issues into the ideology and action of the youth movement. Thus ideology and social action may have a fundamental role in the development of identity in adolescents.

We have already remarked the childlike nature of the Negro stereotype in the eyes of the white Southerners (vividly symbolized in the custom of hailing any adult Negro male as "Boy," instead of "Mister" or "Sir"). Until recently the Negro could either accept that role, or move to the North. In the South he has been largely denied the opportunity to express normal aggressive and masculine strivings through dignified and respected occupations in the general society and in competition with the white male. Under these conditions the Negro male is degraded and depreciated and cannot serve as an adequate ego ideal or model for identification for his children.[12]

The young Negro demonstrators are acutely aware of the lack of adult identity that has characterized their fathers in the South. Both the conscious and unconscious strivings for potent male identification became very apparent in talking to them. In 1955, Rev. Martin Luther King led the entire Negro community of Montgomery, Alabama, in a boycott of the city's transit buses; after one year's struggle, the buses were desegregated.[13] This occurred when many of the students were only 15, two years after the Supreme Court had told them that their anger against segregation was justified and sanctioned. Young people all over the South were vastly impressed with the Montgomery boycott. They felt it was a lesson in the practical and emotional "advantages of direct action" in expressing legitimate Negro discontent.* King became the image of an assertive Negro male assuming freedom of action with dignity, and achieving respectful recognition through successful struggle with the white community (that is, male community). In a sense he became the figure the Negro adolescent wished his father might have been, and as such he was incorporated as part of the ego-ideal. Three years later, soon after leaving home for college, Negroes

* It is interesting to note reports that indicate a sharp decline in the incidence of crime among the Negro population of Montgomery, Alabama, during the year of the boycott.[11]

were acting on the dictates of this identification model through the sit-in. Thus, for the late adolescent in the vanguard of the sit-in movement, the search for recognition as an adult that so characterizes his age group has been intimately interwoven with the struggle of Southern Negroes as a social group for recognition as mature human beings. For the 19-year-old student, then, the creation of a new social character for his people has become identical with the development of his own personality as a young adult.

As part of their struggles to achieve emancipation and identity, many of the Negro students seem to display significant ego-syntonic processes that suggest an acting out through the sit-ins of early childhood frustrations and parental conflicts and wishes. Although the concept of acting out has been used primarily in connection with certain forms of antisocial behavior[10] and problems of psychotherapy,[9] data in the current study suggest a more general role for acting out in character and identity formation.[5, 18] This is illustrated in the following description of B., a seemingly typical, poor, ambitious 19-year-old male Negro college freshman from the Deep South who became a leader of the Washington group of demonstrators. The data and formulations are based on a six-month series of research interviews and subsequent followups.

B. was brought up in a matriarchal family in which his step-father was absent most of the time, or jobless and degraded when home. His real father had left when he was still an infant. He is the oldest of eight brothers and sisters. His mother worked as a domestic for a white Southern family. He grew up feeling contemptuous and resentful of his father, but guilty about this resentment and perhaps responsible for the father's failures and absences. B. has ambivalent feelings toward his mother whom he fantasies really loved him most, but was forced to give prime attention to his younger siblings as well as the white family that employed her. He wore the white family's cast-off clothing. His mother was quite harsh with him if ever he expressed resentment about their status or about white people. She told him that they must know their place, and it would do no good to antagonize the whites. She feared losing the meager job which was their only source of income. He associates the lives of his parents with submission to the white community, and displaces onto this social submission much of the resentment, frustration and deprivation he experienced within his family. At the same time he recognizes his parents' passive-aggressive ambivalence to the whites and the different levels of meaning in his mother's prohibitions against open hostility. This perception helps him develop an idealized image of his parents in which they are really eager for and capable of self-assertion (which would mean more love, attention and recognition for him); but their self-assertion is blocked by circumstance or fear.

B.'s decision to participate in a sit-in demonstration was at first quite impulsive, with a great deal of subsequent rationalization. His personal involvement and dedication have been intense, and actions result in much discharge of affect, as anger and depression are transformed into elation. This discharge of affect is related not only to the stimuli of immediate circumstances but also to symbolic mastery of childhood frustrations. Thus, on the one hand, he acts out his long-standing resentment of his parents derived from his repeated experiences of deprivation and displacement as a youngster, which he now sees as a consequence of his parents' social role. On the other hand, when he takes risks and tests the retaliatory dangers of which he has been warned by his family, he may threaten his mother, but he also wins her secret approval. He thereby enhances his self-esteem as an autonomous, masculine adult. He has acted out his family's suppressed resentment of the social system in a dignified and passive-aggressive manner and has responded to his mother's fantasied need for a socially potent male. (It is of interest that, in follow-up interviews two years later, he reports that his whole family has "come around" to open support of his activities.) It can be inferred that for some adolescents acting out has an important role in identity formation and progressive development of ego functions.

In an historical context, B. feels "caught between Uncle Tom and Jim Crow." Uncle Tom represents the internalized ambivalence of his parents in telling him he must be passive. Jim Crow represents the traditional pattern of segregation and sanctions applied by the whites, which also thwarts his aggressive strivings. He is able successfully to act out unconscious parental hostility to the whites that they themselves have been unable to express overtly. Consciously he has an idealized image of what his parents "really" feel or ought to feel about what is right. He also perceives that he is acting according to the dictates of the conscience of the total community and that he is doing what others fear, hesitate or are "too hypocritical" to do.* This perception of the super-ego or conscience of the community and of his parents allows him to rationalize his rebellion against his own family thereby decreasing guilt and anxiety. He feels he is doing what his parents (and the nation)

* An interesting parallel may exist between the messianiclike feelings and identification of this young Negro leader and those formulated about Moses by S. Freud.[7]

really want him to do but they are afraid to say so openly. We have found similar dynamics in all but two of the young white demonstrators as well. One after another they reported that their parents were both definitely against racial segregation and definitely against doing anything about it. Some were consciously aware of the mixture of anxiety and pride their parents felt about their activities. As it were, they are acting out the conscience of the community.

The acting out of suppressed parental wishes and problems of deprivation, frustration and moral ambiguity has been frequently reported in the psychodynamics underlying adolescent delinquency and antisocial behavior.[10] However, the acting out we have observed here is consciously based on moral imperatives, that is, on the perceived super-ego or conscience of the community, which becomes incorporated into the individual and group functional self-image. Since this perception began in childhood and, as we have shown, was dramatically reinforced during early adolescence, it becomes part of the ego-ideal; action based on its dictates becomes an important source of self-esteem. Therefore, we suggest the term "prosocial" acting out to describe this behavior.[5] This distinction is important. Delinquent acting out is described as antisocial precisely because of its opposition to the morality of the community. Acting out occurs through the delinquent's rebellion against severe super-ego dictates or in the framework of defective super-ego development (for example, "lacunae").[10] In prosocial acting out, however, the ego-ideal and resultant functional self-image are much more in accord with the dictates of the community morality and conscience. Those involved in the latter require some level of social or moral approval, and their goals are rationalized in the direction of social welfare. This allows a gratifying and self-enhancing resolution of emotional conflict and social identity formation. They feel they are "doing society's work for it." The answers to the typical adolescent questions of autonomy, time perspective, work and ideals[2] are vastly different in these two forms of behavior. However, the dynamics seem to have many similarities. It may be that a more detailed understanding of the differing determinants of these two adolescent pathways would have significant implications for the social health of a community, as well as for a new approach to the prevention and treatment of delinquency.

One aspect of the group dynamics of acting out is worthy of note here. Through the conversion of their own anger into a seemingly passive and pious stance these students threaten the bigoted and volatile defenses of the white extremists. In so doing, the demonstrators accomplish a remarkable psychosocial feat, much to their advantage. The white extremists are provoked by the young

Negroes to act out for them the very anger and resentment that they (the Negroes) have themselves felt. However, the anger and violence have now been externalized and projected onto the "aggressor," so that the students feel guiltless and even exhilarated in their justifiable indignation. It also helps win the sympathy of the observing public and reduces the fears of whites that Negroes intend to retaliate violently for past suppression.[13] This is probably a prominent feature of the dynamics of nonviolent action as a political weapon.

It is extremely important for these young students to be able to express publicly and directly their discontent and indignation against restriction, dependency and inequity. It allows them to identify their aggressive strivings for independence and recognition, which are intrinsic to the adolescent phase of development, with their desperate need for social emancipation and equality. These demonstrations are certainly aggressive. However, the dignified, well-disciplined, nonviolent style of the student action is calculated to be an effective propaganda weapon that will encourage the more moderate white southerners to accept some measure of desegregation, as well as win the sympathy and support of news media and public in other parts of the country. The students are also keenly aware of the attention they receive in news media in other parts of the world; they are surprisingly sophisticated in their political and social awareness. Although they are preoccupied with the task at hand, they readily identify with students and movements for recognition and emancipation in other parts of a total world community.

IDEOLOGY AND IDENTITY

The use of nonviolent resistance means that the students will picket, sit-in, ride buses and use facilities that are segregated, but they will not resist when heckled, attacked or arrested. It is consciously conceived of by many as a pragmatic political weapon applicable to the problem of segregation, and is consistent with Christian religious training. Although Biblical and Christian teachings and the traditions of Gandhi and civil disobedience are incorporated into their ideology as formulated by Martin Luther King,[13] these students are generally not pacifists. This is exemplified in the remarks of B., who was very much committed and dedicated to the principles of nonviolence in the sit-in. Soon after quoting from the Scriptures and Gandhi in support of nonviolence, he went on to talk with pride of his own personal ambitions to be a jet pilot in the U.S. Air Force.

At the same time, the philosophy of nonviolence is consistent with the long tradition of minimizing offense to the white community. It is a natural outgrowth of the traditional passive and submissive role in the face of white domination and potential retaliation. The internal prohibition against hostility to the whites is deep-seated; this hostility is more readily expressed by first being transformed into love for those who hate you. This process reduces guilt and anxiety and makes easier the students' departure from parental stereotypes; yet at the same time it allows them to identify with the parental religious ego-ideal. The ideology helps the adolescent maintain super-ego control over angry impulses while simultaneously internalizing an ego-ideal of love and respect for all human beings including the enemy, which in turn enhances the sense of identity and self-esteem. This illustrates the connection of ideology and identify formation for many adolescents.[3]

In one sense, then, the sit-in can be described as a passive-aggressive act. For a few it provides the arena for masochism and martyrdom. For all it is a demand to be seen, heard and recognized. As is usual with adolescent movements, it is never anonymous. Names are freely given and no one hides his face when pictures are taken. However, one should not underestimate the intensity of the aggression and hostility being channeled here, especially in the Negro students. We did not need to probe very deeply to find resentment and hostility built on layers of social and personal frustration in the demonstrators we interviewed. The aggression is manifest in the very circumstance that they are coercing people to accept or react to the accomplished fact of sitting-in at a segregated establishment, as well as in the evident satisfaction at stirring social turmoil by what seems to be such a small, quiet initial action; moreover, this is done frequently in areas where the violent and explosive potential of white segregationists is well known.

In our interviews with them, all these students, both Negro and white, saw its high moral purpose as a major feature of their activity. Desegregation and the philosophy of nonviolent resistance are seen primarily as moral rather than political principles.[20] As Erikson has pointed out in describing the process of ideology formation in adolescents,[3] these students take literally the moral commitment of the community and, denouncing what are perceived to be the hypocrisies of the current social and political situation, demand a substantial change. Here the goals of conscience of the students represent not only the traditional Christian morality of the nation but also the well-known and basic American social and political principles of equal rights and freedom of choice. Thus the Negro sit-in youth thinks of himself as more Christian than the white community in the South. He also thinks of himself as more in accord with the highest principles of American democracy than the white hecklers on the sidelines. He derives considerable ego support from thus identifying with the ideals of the white majority and a great feeling of compensatory gratification from the experience of superior moral dedication. This helps him offset traditional feelings of racial inferiority that have been so long a part of the Southern milieu.

Although the ideology is highly moral, this is by no means an intellectual movement. There is a heavy orientation to action and work, even to the point of impatience with prolonged intellectual discussion. During the organization of the first sit-in in the Washington area, the original students, in recruiting others in their dormitory to join them, used as their rallying cry, "There's work to be done." Again and again there was an emphasis on getting down to the work at hand, the picketing or sitting-in, with a minimum of fuss or preliminary discussion. A great deal of gratification was derived from their sense of dedicated work, and it undoubtedly has an important function in the formation of individual and group identity.[2] However, it also illustrates the impulsive urge to immediate action so characteristic of adolescent time perspective and so different from that of the older generation. This sense of immediacy is exemplified in the students' frustration with "plenty of ideals but no action." Such an action orientation leads to considerable risk taking. Since deciding to take a risk is done by an individual student quite on his own (albeit with group support), such a decision helps to develop a feeling of autonomy, as well as proving bravery and the willingness to endure suffering on behalf of one's principles.[4] The mutual experience of action, risk taking and injury does a great deal to solidify the feelings of unity and identity of the group and to assure individual loyalties. Thus the sit-in groups derive great strength from their experiences in jail or in the midst of hostile crowds.

The assertion of freedom of choice in one's own behavior is interestingly parallel to the emphasis on freedom of choice in the principle of desegregation. For example, an 18-year-old white girl with a mixed group being arrested at a suburban bowling alley asked simply, "If these are my friends and I want to bowl with them, why should we be arrested?" For this girl, the need for freedom of choice and action so typical of the adolescent has become identical with the strivings of Negroes in the community at large.

It seems that an element of renunciation of former dependency gratifications is almost always present in the process of growing up. As they approach maturity, social groups as well as individuals must lose some of the security of their former social and economic relationships. A young person feels most free or independent only after having done something active and aggressive to win that independence. In this context, perhaps an "independent" identity can never be freely given—it must be at least partially *taken* by adolescents and, possibly, by young nations as well.

In summary, we would emphasize that one can find in the student sit-in movement patterns of adolescent identity strivings similar to those in many other adolescent groups. These young people, however, are caught on a wave of psychosocial transition and upheaval. For the Negroes, inferiority, submission and deprivation are their childhood experience; passive-aggressive resolutions their heritage; Christianity their moral background; the Supreme Court decision and the coming of age of new African nations part of the tempo of change. Through these influences are filtered the typical internal pressures and new ego capacities of early and late adolescence. Public action for social goals is their way of at least temporarily resolving issues of identity formation, conscience and aggression. They see themselves as prodders of the national conscience, and derive satisfaction and self-esteem from this role. As a result, they have been forced into synthesizing a new social character with its new problems and anxieties, with its risks and violence, but also with a vitality and optimism for a future that they feel they have had a hand in shaping.

Recent student activities in this and other countries suggest that the motivation and psychodynamics of student involvement in political and social action represents an important area of study.[14, 19, 22] Such studies may help in understanding the effects of social change and crises on personality and identity formation, as well as the converse effects of adolescent striving for recognition and identity on social and political change.

References

[1] Dollard, J. 1939. Caste and Class in a Southern Town. Harper & Bros., New York, N.Y.

[2] Erikson, E. 1956. The problem of ego identity. J. Amer. Psychoanal. Assn. 4(1): 56–121.

[3] Erikson, E. 1958. Young Man Luther. W. W. Norton & Co., Inc. New York, N.Y.

[4] Erikson, E. 1962. Youth; fidelity and diversity. Daedalus 91(1):5.

[5] Fishman, J. R. and F. Solomon. Pro-social Acting out. In preparation.

[6] Fleming, H. 1960. The new South and the sit-ins. J. Intergroup Relations 2(1): 56–60.

[7] Freud S. 1934. Moses and Monotheism. Hogarth Press. London, Eng.

[8] Fromm, E. 1941. Appendix: Social character and social process. *In* Escape from Freedom. Farrar & Rinehart. New York, N.Y.

[9] Greenacre, P. 1950. General problems of acting-out. Psychoanal. Quart. 19: 455–467.

[10] Johnson, A. M. and S. A. Szurek. 1952. The genesis of antisocial acting-out in children and adults. Psychoanal. Quart. 21(3): 323–343.

[11] Kahn, T. 1960. Unfinished Revolution (Pamphlet). Igal Rodenko, Printer. New York, N.Y. :28.

[12] Kardiner, A. and L. Ovesey. 1951. The Mark of Oppression: A Psychosocial Study of the American Negro. W. W. Norton & Co., Inc. New York, N.Y.

[13] King, M. L. 1958. Stride Toward Freedom: The Montgomery Story. Harper & Bros. New York, N.Y.

[14] Laquer, W. Z. 1962. History of the German Youth Movement. Basic Books, Inc. New York, N.Y.

[15] Myrdal, G. 1944. An American Dilemma. Harper & Bros. New York, N.Y.

[16] Powdermaker, H. 1943. The channeling of Negro aggression by the cultural process. Amer. J. Sociol. 48: 750–758.

[17] Rexroth, K. 1960. The students take over. The Nation. 191(1): 4–9.

[18] Solomon, F. and J. R. Fishman. Identity formation and crisis in student demonstrators against racial segregation. Presented at the Annual Meeting of the American Psychiatric Association, Toronto, Canada. May 7, 1962.

[19] Solomon, F. and J. R. Fishman. Youth and social action: students participating in a large "peace" demonstration. Presented at the Annual Meeting of the American Orthopsychiatric Association, Washington, D. C. March, 1963.

[20] Solomon, F. and J. R. Fishman. Non-violence in the South: a psychosocial study. Presented at the Annual Meeting of the American Psychiatric Association, St. Louis, Mo. May 6, 1963.

[21] Wilson, J. Q. 1961. The strategy of Negro protest. J. Conflict Resolution. 5(3): 291–303.

[22] Youth: change and challenge (a symposium). 1962. Daedalus 91(1).

7

The Political
Socialization
of the
American Negro

Dwaine Marvick

In the middle of the twentieth century, the political socialization of the American Negro is rapidly and drastically changing.
In part, the trends involve and reflect a massive migration from the
rural South into Northern metropolitan slums. In part the trends
are embodied in the perspectives of successive generations—those
under forty today, whose awareness of American political life is
therefore exclusively post-World War II, and their elders, who grew
up in a prewar or wartime climate of opinion.

These key dimensions—migration and generation—will be
repeatedly considered as we sift the findings available from recent
research into how people are inducted into their political culture,
which is what we mean by the phrase "political socialization." And
because change is the outstanding feature in considering both
dimensions, the findings raise questions about "resocialization"
quite different from those involved in teaching civics to children
or in other ways giving young people a "feel for politics." Protest,
alienation, reconciliation, reintegration: these are all relevant terms
when we examine how Negroes adjust to the rules and arrangements of American politics.

Political socialization refers to one's induction into a political culture, and perhaps one's capacity to change it. As a learning
process, it needs to be seen as often painful, embarrassing, and
even stultifying. It is a school of hard knocks for those on the
receiving end as American Negroes are. It is not a pleasant aca-

Reprinted by permission from Dwaine Marvick, "The Political
Socialization of the American Negro," *Annals* of the American Academy
of Political and Social Science, 361 (September, 1965), pp. 112–127.

demic routine of lessons learned and grades achieved in a civics class. It is the process by which adults come to learn what is expected of them as citizens and, perhaps, leaders.

Political socialization, then, is concerned with how a person "comes to terms" with the roles and norms of the concentric political worlds—local, regional, and national—into which he passes as he grows up. Necessarily it focuses on formative experiences—in the family, school, and primary group contexts of childhood—that shape ideals and give insight into political aspects of life. It requires consideration of a set of motivational factors—rooted in each individual's private problems of psychic management, including also the patterned goals and goads to which he responds with some regularity. Negro Americans in many ways are excluded from the dominant political culture of their community and nation, and are denied its rewards. Norms and roles for political performance are learned in a special Negro subculture, which is at present undergoing basic changes, creating for the next Negro generation new prototypes for political action, and creating also new tensions and new frustrations for the individual.

But the psychological transformation—the "internalized revolution"—in the way Negroes are being inducted into American political life still confronts the would-be "new Negro" with some practicalities that can make all the difference. The study of political socialization requires attention also to situational insights and beliefs—sets of ideological, group-oriented, or self-interested calculations made by a person which largely determine the level of his involvement and participation in any specific occasion or process. Attitudes of skepticism may be widely prevalent among Negro citizens, but they are surprisingly differentiated from person to person, and from situation to situation. And linked to these situational appraisals also is the question of what resources can be marshaled. A full analysis of the changes occurring in Negro political socialization would take into account a long list of capabilities—skills, knowledge, contacts, style, energy, strength, reputation, access, control of organizations—each of which is distributed unequally within the Negro population, and each of which implies control by an active intelligence to be effectively invoked.

Finally, political socialization is not simply the study of how people come to terms with the conventional practices and arrangements which are manifestly referred to as "political" or "governmental" in the institutional sense. It involves examination also of a set of functional equivalents, ways of doing indirectly what cannot be done directly. Because of the history of Negro exclusion—both nationally and in his residence localities—from active and accepted participation in the conventional processes of governance, it is especially relevant to look at his political education as it is functionally acquired, even though the ostensible processes are those of community-service groups, fraternal associations, or church affairs.

This, then, is a brief inventory of the range of problems embraced by the study of political socialization. Applied to an inquiry about the American Negro, it is, perhaps, a useful approach. But certain risks should be pointed out. First, learning what is expected and how to perform in either basic or specialized roles is an undertaking that seems to imply a rather homogeneous political culture, housed in monolithic institutions and with standardized induction norms. Second, it is likely to suggest that the things to be learned are, on the surface, straightforward, manifest political events and governmental patterns. Third, these, in turn, imply that learning depends upon the initiative of each student; some will get *A*'s and others *F*'s. Fourth, it conveys a rather static picture. Allowing for variations in milieu, the old textbook should continue to apply; if one is not politically inducted into the same culture, at least it is into a progressively unfolding political culture. These are all comfortable illusions.

In any extensive society there is a plurality of political milieus into which a person coming to adulthood passes. They are not equally challenging, nor easy, nor stable. In the South, a Negro "knew where he stood" and what to expect—or he used to. In the North, impersonal treatment is functional on the surface. It means access to public accommodations, a chance to vote, due process of law, and so forth. It also means isolation, exclusion, hypocrisy, and ambiguity about where the Negro stands socially.

Change does not necessarily mean revolutionary change. The actions of those in a political culture *are* largely what reaffirm or modify its norms and practices, and incidentally serve to integrate or disjoin it from other political cultures. The accretion of small changes in political practice, moreover, includes not only innovations made on purpose and by forceful leaders, but the modifications as well that result from improvisation, from fumbling, from shortsighted maneuvers, from unwillingness to continue in familiar roles, and so forth.

To learn the political game only once is not enough, whether one treats it as a spectator sport, a hobby, or a vocation. Change is too basic; resocialization is too necessary. Especially is this so in the rapidly changing arenas of America's racial politics. Recent collective efforts at direct action have multiplied Negro opportunities for political experience; the organizational scaffolding of leader-

ship and cadre roles has vastily increased the list of political tasks
to be done at the same time that it has made those roles more
desirable and more differentiated. New organizing skills, analytical
abilities, and communication talents are being found and encouraged in the distinctive circumstances of "protest politics." Yet, in
looking at the changing patterns of Negro role-playing and Negro
skill-acquisition, it is still difficult to gauge the changes in Negro
attitudes and motivations. It is necessary to remember the backlog
of frustration, self-doubt, and anger which the neophyte must somehow control if he is to learn anything effectively. That he often fails,
and in the process learns other lessons about himself and the political system, are other aspects of the problem.

This inquiry, then, becomes a case study in the use of a
new conceptual paraphernalia—that of "political socialization"—
applied to the complexity and recalcitrance of actual politicizing
situations, as reported by Negro informants. Analyzing some of the
available data in these terms is at least a way of highlighting the
flimsiness of our theoretical apparatus in this area. And because
it is impossible to consider the acquisition of political capacities,
skills, and beliefs by a sizable segment of the population without
asking what difference it is likely to make to the political system
in which they will be used and are being used, this inquiry also
links interpretation of Negro potentialities to the developmental
prospects for the American polity. Let us turn then to a consideration of the resources and difficulties of Negro Americans in coming
to terms with the political worlds that surround them.

THE NONCOMPATIBILITY OF NEGRO AND
WHITE CIRCUMSTANCES

In special ways as well as common ones, American Negroes
occupy inferior statuses. Almost from birth they are discriminated
against and made to feel inadequate, useless, and undesirable by
the dominant white community. As a group also they tend to be
poor, marginally educated, and maladapted economically.

In these latter respects, many whites living in the same
localities are in similarly depressed circumstances. Some of the
apathy and skepticism about American political life which we expect
to find among Negroes is probably due to these socioeconomic dis-
abilities. At the same time, the political viewpoints and roles of
typical Negro citizens must substantially be seen as a response to
the animosities and prejudices they experience because of their
ethnic distinctiveness.

Within the Negro community as elsewhere, there is a spectrum of affluence and poverty, prominence, and ordinariness. It is increasingly hard to find a "typical" Negro. How old should he be? Does he live in a Northern city? Does he work at a menial job? Does he earn less than $5,000 a year? For every such Negro, an equal number can be found in contrasting circumstances.

Only a composite picture begins to convey at once the "central tendencies" and the "scatter" in Negro characteristics. Sample surveys, by interviewing representative cross-sections of the citizenry, secure just this kind of composite picture for the nation as a whole. Complications arise, however, when a segregated and disadvantaged subgroup like the Negroes in such a sample are compared with the larger majority-status sample of whites.

In the spring of 1960, the National Opinion Research Center (NORC) undertook a national survey of the United States, as part of a five-nation study of contemporary patterns of political socialization. Reported elsewhere, that project has disclosed many fascinating parallels and contrasts between American, British, German, Italian, and Mexican publics.[1] Many subsidiary problems were scarcely touched upon in their transnational study, although their data are directly relevant. One such problem area concerns the American Negro's past and potential induction into politics.

To investigate carefully those aspects of Negro political socialization that seem distinctive for the ethnic group, and at the same time identify attitudes and beliefs about political matters that equally characterize a set of whites in comparable socioeconomic circumstances, a matching procedure was followed. One hundred interviews had been taken with Negro respondents, as part of the NORC survey. These were now classified by region (South or North), by urban or rural residence, by age (over and under forty), by income levels (over and under $5,000 a year for family units), and by sex. Invoking all five points of distinction as either-or dichotomies produced thirty-two exclusive categories, each with two to five Negro respondents. The 870 white respondents in the national sample were then divided into the same thirty-two subsets. Random selection methods were used to choose as many white counterparts in each subset as there were Negro cases. Thus a composite group of one hundred whites was defined, deliberately matched with the Negro group on five dimensions.

In each component, hereafter called the Negro and the Counterpart groups, approximately half were male under forty,

[1] Gabriel Almond and Sidney Verba, *The Civic Culture* (Princeton, N.J.: Princeton University Press, 1963).

big-city dwellers, Northerners, and earning over $5,000 a year. The
other half were not. So far as the national white cross-section was
concerned, proportions quite different from fifty-fifty were found on
most of these same counts (Table 1).

TABLE 1: Composition of Negro and White Counterpart Samples and
National White Cross-Section (1960 Survey)[a]

(Cases)	Matched subsamples		National white cross-section (870) %
	Negro (100) %	White (100) %	
1. Sex: Male	49	49	47
2. Age: Under forty	47	47	40
3. Residence: Big-city dwellers	53	53	42
4. Region: Southern	55	55	30
5. Income: Less than $5,000 a year	57	56	24
6. Rearing place: Rural or small town	50	55	54
7. Married	67	67	73
8. Dependents: Three+ children	38	38	35
9. Intend to stay in current locale	76	78	83
10. Birth region: South	89	50	27
11. Lived in current locale "always"	36	46	47
12. Occupation:			
Unskilled workers	37	30	20
Operatives and service workers	39	28	20
Craft and white collar workers	19	28	41
Business and professional	6	13	19
13. Education:			
Only some grammar	37	25	16
Full grammar (8 grades)	19	19	16
Only some high school	22	15	18
Full high school	16	24	29
Some college	6	17	21
14. Group membership:			
Belong to no organizations	41	57	43
Belong to one organization	36	23	24
Belong to several organizations	23	20	33
15. Interviewer SES Rating: Low	48	37	15

[a] Data from NORC survey of American electorate in the spring of 1960 for
Almond-Verba five-nation project.

A few other points of comparability deserve mention. In
both Negro and Counterpart samples, approximately half grew up
in rural, small-town, or farm environments. In both samples, two-

thirds were married, and just under two-fifths had large families—three or more children. In both groups, also, at least three-fourths intended to stay in their current locality of residence.

On all of these points, moreover, the national white cross-section registered quite similar levels. Once having come to terms with a community, a young adult marries, raises a family, and intends to stay there. In all these respects, both the Negro and Counterpart groups are typically American.

Looked at from another vantage point, what sociologists call status-crystallization operates in ways that are dysfunctional to the Negro's most elementary solution—to move. This is illustrated by the impossibility—using the kinds of matching procedures noted —of securing a good match between Negroes and their Counterparts on either occupational or educational counts; there were simply not enough whites in menial job categories or with limited educational backgrounds, once age, sex, region, income, and residence area dimensions were stipulated.

Cumulative social constraints box in an American Negro. Unskilled or semiskilled (76 per cent) and poorly educated (56 per cent), his problem is further exacerbated by the region and locality in which he lives and *wants to remain living.* Of the Counterpart group, only 58 per cent hold similarly low-status jobs, and only 44 per cent had comparable educational handicaps. For the larger white cross-section, these percentages dropped to 40 per cent and 32 per cent respectively. The Counterparts are considerably closer to the Negroes on these counts than are most white Americans. Their disadvantages, nevertheless, are not so cumulative; they are not so "locked in."

The "first solution"—migration—is, of course, widely used by Negroes. In our sample, only half now live in the South, but nine-tenths were born there. Nearly half the Counterparts but only 36 per cent of the Negroes reported that they had always lived in their current locality.

The underlying point, however, relates to the generational aspect of the socialization phenomenon. For many Negroes, although not for all, "coming to terms" with a political world is almost irreversible. Basic life premises are involved. Some kinds of adult activity are so difficult, once foresworn, as to be impossible to undertake later in life. Some sets of events are so remote that they do not really touch one's daily life, however relevant, as news developments about public policy or group demonstrations, they may seem to the observer. Politics is the "art of the possible." And in school, on the job, in dealings with police or government officials, learning the art of the possible is not an abstract problem.

Instead, it is a practical question of getting along with a specific teacher, a particular foreman, a well-known sheriff, a certain postal clerk or building inspector.

Consider the evidence in Table 2. Asked in 1960 whether government officials were likely to give them "equal treatment" in matters like housing regulations or taxes, 49 per cent of the Negro sample and 90 percent of the white Counterpart group said yes. On a parallel question, asking about encounters with the police over traffic violations or similar minor offenses, a slightly reduced margin was found with 60 per cent of the Negroes and 85 per cent of the Counterparts expecting "equal treatment."

Probing to learn what kind of treatment was expected, that is, how considerate and reasonable, the same patterns were found. Among both Negro and Counterpart groups, substantially fewer persons expected either bureaucrats or policemen to "give serious consideration" to their explanations. Counterparts are close to the scores registered on these counts by the larger white cross-section; the Negroes are about half again as likely to be pessimistic. This is a level of caution and distrust among Negro Americans toward representatives of the law with whom they have dealings which may well be substantially realistic.

It is when North-South contrasts and younger-older comparisons are made that the dynamics of Negro resocialization are suggested. While 60 per cent of the Northern Negroes expected equal treatment from officials in government agencies, only 40 per cent of the Southern Negroes were so optimistic. And, however equal the treatment might be, only 44 per cent of the Northern group and 18 per cent of the Southern expected agency officials to take their viewpoint seriously. Not only has the trek north to the metropolitan slums been accompanied by a measurable growth in confidence of equal official treatment, but also it represents a heightened feeling that the character of official treatment is not deaf or insensitive to their points of view.

Northern Counterpart whites to be sure, are more confident (93 per cent) than Northern Negroes (60 per cent) of equal treatment. When the quality of that treatment is brought into question, however, they register only 49 per cent confidence of being listened to. The 44 per cent level on this point among Northern Negroes thus approaches parity.

If we look next at the parallel question of police treatment, the direction of change is just opposite. While only 47 per cent of the Northern Negroes expected equal handling by the police, 76 per cent of the Southern Negroes did. Moreover, this latter figure approaches parity with the level of confidence scored by the white Counterpart—and even the white cross-section.

Only 29 per cent of the Northern Negroes expected the police to listen to their story. Here again the level of confidence registered by Southern Negroes (44 per cent) matches that found among the Southern Counterpart. In sum, in the South of 1960 a random sample, economically and socially, of Negroes and their white counterparts reported roughly equal treatment by the police in their home communities. Equally, too, they reported that treatment to be reasonable and considerate.

A glance at the generational breakdown on these points is useful. It is younger Negroes, not those over forty, whose confidence in the police had risen to a near parity with that registered by their white Counterparts. It is younger Negroes, too, whose expectations of considerate attention from officials—although not equal treatment—had risen to a parity level.

TABLE 2: Expected Treatment by Officialdom: Comparisons of Negro and White Counterparts, with Regional and Generational Breakdowns

	National white cross-section %	Matched sub-samples		Regional breakdown[a]				Generational breakdown[b]			
		Negro %	White %	Negro		White		Negro		White	
				N %	S %	N %	S %	Y %	O %	Y %	O %
1. Government officials would give equal treatment	87	49	90	60	40	93	87	57	42	89	91
2. Police would give equal treatment	88	60	85	47	76	84	87	77	47	87	83
3. Official would listen and take views seriously	50	30	45	44	18	49	42	36	25	43	47
4. Police would listen and take views seriously	58	36	48	29	44	51	44	45	28	55	42

[a] N = North, S = South.
[b] Y = Younger (under forty), O = Older.

THE NEGRO MIGRATION INTO AMERICAN URBAN LIFE

By 1960 half of America's Negro population lived outside the states of the old Confederacy, and nearly a third lived in the twelve largest metropolitan centers. More than half of the residents of Washington, more than a third of those in Detroit, Baltimore, and

Cleveland, and easily a quarter in Chicago and Philadelphia were Negroes. In a ten-year period, a million and a half Negroes had left the South. No immigrant wave in American history was ever so large or came so quickly into the urban centers of the nation. In 1930, half of the Negro population lived in rural Southern areas and another quarter in the towns and cities of the South. By 1940, the ratio was one Northern to every two Southern Negroes. And while the proportion living in Northern localities went, decade by decade, from a quarter to a third to half, the size of the Negro population in absolute numbers had nearly doubled.

This massive influx of Negro citizens flooded the metropolitan slums with newcomers who, by reason of their opportunity-deprived upbringing, often lacked the incentives and goads to get ahead found among previous immigrant groups. Earlier ethnic minorities had come from culturally intact backgrounds in Europe which provided them with distinctive but, usually, well-defined standards of conduct for political life. The slave-period traditions for Negroes who had been field hands in the Delta, members of a domestic class in a plantation system, or personal servants for white masters in the urban South were quite disparate, but in all cases were heavily weighted in terms of imitating white patterns.

While this long spiral of migration continued, other trends were also at work. Technological advances in industry and commerce were displacing unskilled and semiskilled labor—Negro labor—at an accelerating pace. Metropolitan programs for meeting transportation, education, recreation, and housing demands were inevitably displacing families—both long-established and newly come—from blighted neighborhoods.

Table 3 provides some glimpse of the magnitudes involved in the attitudinal reorientation of Negroes toward local government. In 1960, asked how important was its impact on their daily lives, nearly the same proportion—one-third—of Negroes and whites felt that the answer was "great impact." Among Northerners, whites (41 per cent) were somewhat more inclined to this view than Negroes (29 per cent).

Asked to evaluate the contribution of local government, only 50 per cent of the Negroes, compared with 72 per cent of their Counterparts, felt it had generally been helpful in their lives. In the North, however, the 60 per cent scored by Negroes was rather close to the Counterpart figure of 69 per cent. On the other hand, only 42 per cent of the Southern Negroes made this evaluation, while 75 per cent of their white Counterparts did so. When generations are compared, the margin by which whites make more favorable evaluations is similar for younger and older sets.

TABLE 3: Expectations about Local Government: Comparisons of Negro and White Counterparts, with Regional and Generational Breakdowns

	National white cross-section %	Matched sub-samples		Regional breakdown[a]				Generational breakdown[b]			
				Negro		White		Negro		White	
		Negro %	White %	N %	S %	N %	S %	Y %	O %	Y %	O %
1. Local government has "great impact" on daily lives	35	31	37	29	33	40	35	36	26	38	36
2. Local-government actions are usually helpful	71	50	72	60	42	69	75	55	45	77	68
3. It is almost impossible to change a bad local regulation by own efforts	24	38	31	20	53	36	27	28	47	26	36
4. Very unlikely to try to change bad local regulation	26	43	38	31	53	50	27	34	51	26	49
5. Never have tried to influence local policy decision	70	86	73	76	95	76	71	89	83	68	77

[a] N = North, S = South.
[b] Y = Younger (under forty), O = Older.

Those interviewed were asked to consider what could be done to prevent the village or city council from adopting a regulation which "you considered very unjust or harmful." For the national white cross-section, only 24 per cent felt it was impossible for them to change a bad local ordinance. Somewhat more (31 per cent) of the Counterpart whites and fully 38 per cent of the Negroes felt this way. Asked whether they had, in fact, ever tried, 70 per cent of the national cross-section of whites and 73 per cent of the Counterpart whites admitted never having done so, but 86 per cent of the Negroes had never tried.

When attention is given to the regional and age breakdowns, again the attitudinal transformation can begin to be seen. Not alienation, but heightened involvement and substantial realism in the choice of methods and targets seem to be disclosed. While fully 53 per cent of the Southern Negroes felt that changing a bad local law was virtually impossible, only 20 per cent of the Northern Negroes did so—a figure rather similar to that of Counterpart whites. The contrast in optimism was correspondingly great also between younger and older Negroes, with "virtually impossible" being the reaction of 28 per cent and 47 per cent, respectively, a substantially greater age difference than registered by white Counterparts.

As to whether they, personally, would actively try to change a bad local law if the occasion arose, sharp contrasts are found between North and South. More than half of the Southern Negroes felt it was unlikely they would ever try; only 27 per cent of Southern Counterparts were so passive. Conversely, only 31 per cent of the Northern Negroes felt they would never try to influence such a matter, but 50 per cent of the Northern Counterparts admitted their probable inaction. For both Negroes and Counterpart whites, the younger age groups showed markedly greater propensities toward local political agitation. And when the question was posed, had any actual attempt to influence a local ordinance issue ever been made, 95 per cent of the Southern Negroes said "never." On the same question, only 76 per cent of the Northern Negroes had never tried, the same proportion as for Northern Counterparts.

THE LOCALLY CIRCUMSCRIBED POLITICAL WORLD OF AMERICAN NEGROES

In the study of American race relations today, intellectuals tend to assume that Negroes all along have felt oppressed and constrained at the mold of second-class citizenship, in 1895 as much as 1935 or 1965. Yet, little is known about their political socialization patterns, and a few cautionary points are pertinent. Ordinary Negroes lived mostly in the South. About 1890, open efforts began to disfranchise Negro voters and to impose Jim Crow circumscriptions with the force of law on Negro use of public facilities. By 1910 the political rules had been reformulated; the Supreme Court's "separate but equal" doctrine helped to quiet public concern about what was happening, while political realities ensured a steady deterioration in the public services and accommodations available in their home communities to Negroes. Incidental to this triumph of nasty-mindedness, much race hatred was preached and countenanced, apparently in part to reassure the poor whites that they were not the next target.

Frederick Douglass, the most militant national Negro leader, fought in vain after 1880 against the trend to disengage all national machinery capable of aiding the Negro. After his death in 1894, others founded the NAACP and the Urban League, conceived as instruments for rallying the racial elite, of training the "Talented Tenth" as race spokesmen and cadres for future struggles, of pursuing political goals not in political arenas but in academic, philanthropic, religious, and journalistic modes. Themselves the products of a selective social mobility process within the Negro world, most of the Negro publicists, lawyers, academics, and others on the national scene struggled to get and to keep open elite communication lines. Their efforts reflected a middle-class presumption that the Negro masses, when mobilized, would accept their lead. There is dignity and restraint, rather than anger and impatience, in the formulation of tasks confronting the NAACP by the militant leader, W. E. B. DuBois: "By every civilized and peaceful method, we must strive for the rights which the world accords to men."[2]

Nationally, the "accommodationist" style of Negro leadership was set by Booker T. Washington. The head of Tuskegee was a man of humble origins, a self-made man who had met the world on its own terms. He was realistic. Negroes lacked the skills and knowledge to succeed economically; education was the crucial resource needed, and education was provided by local governing bodies; Southern whites would only provide that crucial resource if the "products" were reliably docile.

Just when the use of governmental machinery to enforce disadvantages on the Negro was at its peak, Washington counselled submission. Work hard, in the service of the community, and you will become accepted in proper time. His advice and example were for Negroes to give up their interest in political power as a way of securing their rights. Industrial education and an appropriate station in the emerging industrial work of twentieth-century America, were the objectives he used.

De facto segregation in the North was not implemented by state laws and local ordinances as in the South; nor were prejudices so openly proclaimed by militant whites. But the Northern reception system has been a pale facsimile of its Southern prototype in many ways, and especially at the local community level.

Until the postwar years it can be argued that, North and South alike, Negro adults became politically socialized almost exclusively to the circumscriptions and indirect channels of the localities in which they lived. It was irrelevant to speak of national

[2] Quoted in Charles E. Silberman, *Crisis in Black and White* (New York: Random House, 1964). p. 129.

or even state-bestowed citizen status for Negro Americans. In the outlook of educated Negro elite figures, no doubt, an awareness of the life in the national and state superstructure of American politics existed. At the same time, it is quite understandable that most events occurring in the central institutional complex of American democracy would not touch the ordinary Negro American emotionally, nor arouse desires to participate. And for the Negro poor, during this whole century of segregation and lower-caste treatment, politics was white man's business; even in the local arenas of political life Negroes often could secure no electoral footing. The gambit of Negro influence was thus severely limited; it took only a primer to learn the rules of how to behave. Compliance with imposed norms was rudimentary but necessary, even when fellow-Negroes called it "Toming."

Myrdal's massive codification in 1942 of the circumstances of Negro life informs us about the extent to which Negroes of that and previous generations were a minority harder than Italians, Poles, or Jews to assimilate.[3] His study stressed themes that continue to preoccupy discussion today. Myrdal believed that Negroes were "exaggerated Americans," who believed in the American Creed more passionately than whites, and who should exploit their common bonds of belief with white Americans more effectively. It would not be possible for white Americans to sustain their corporate belief system unless those who asked their due were granted it, once heard. Negroes had not strenuously asked their due; avoiding scenes and temporizing had been the style.

The Negro community was dependent on the white community; whites were committed to their egalitarian, optimistic, democratic creed, as were the Negroes; by playing upon the beliefs of whites, Negroes could gain their objectives.

Did Negroes consciously or persistently aspire to full citizenship? Had they been politically socialized to want citizen status, but somehow left untutored in how to manipulate and persuade whites to grant them what was due?

Or had they undergone a harsher socialization process, one which left them not prepared to believe that the American political system, for all its protestations, would support them in their aspirations?

The argument here is *not* that Negroes were passive, apathetic, and for generations unable to protest effectively because they had become disenchanted with the American Creed—alienated

[3] Gunnar Myrdal, *An American Dilemma* (New York: Harper & Brothers, 1944).

from American society. Probably more commonly, Negro adults had never allowed themselves to become enchanted with "democracy" in the first place, so far as their own community and private lives went. Traditionally, Negro civic leaders occupying symbolic positions of respect were "tapped" by leaders in the white community as contact points. The influence of such "anointed" figures often depended more on their near-monopoly over liaison channels to the all-important white community's decision-makers than on any spontaneous following within the Negro community which they might have generated. Undertakers, insurance men, bankers, teachers, a few professional men—above all, ministers of Negro churches: these were the men who traditionally were treated as spokesmen for their local Negro communities. Accommodationist, conservative, dignified, personally successful men: they have been for more than half a century the prime models for Negro children asking to be shown *local* "men of influence."[4]

With the mobilization of electoral strength, the decline of Negro ministers and leaders of fraternal organizations as sources for community leadership—whether in the liaison or symbolic sense— has steadily been taking place in Southern localities. "Street lights, sidewalks, and paved streets are more common in communities where Negroes vote in substantial numbers. Such things as Negro civic centers, bandshells, playgrounds, libraries, hospital annexes, and even swimming pools are found in increasing numbers."[5]

The dynamics of political *rapprochement* in Louisiana communities, according to Fenton and Vines, have occasionally involved an alliance of "shady white and underdog Negro" elements. Local politics centers around the sheriff's office. If a sheriff permits gambling, he is charged with corruption by middle-class residents of the community; to offset their electoral threat, the sheriff in such instances has catered to the marginal Negro vote for support. "The reward . . . is respect from the politicians and attendance at Negro political meetings, cessation of police brutality, and promises made and often kept regarding such matters as street improvements and better school facilities."[6]

---

[4] See Silberman, *op. cit.,* chap. vii. Also M. Elaine Burgess, *Negro Leadership in a Southern City* (Chapel Hill: University of North Carolina Press, 1962); E. F. Frazier, *The Negro in the United States* (New York: The Macmillan Company, 1949), and G. Franklin Edwards, *The Negro Professional Class* (Glencoe, Ill.: Free Press, 1959).

[5] H. D. Price, "The Negro and Florida Politics, 1944–1954," *Journal of Politics* (May 1955).

[6] J. H. Fenton and K. N. Vines, "Negro Registration in Louisiana," *American Political Science Review* (September 1957).

Thus, in Southern communities where voter registration has progressed to a point sufficient to create a substantial potential bloc, a new, self-taught, and white-tutored breed of professional Negro politicians has begun to emerge. Specifically equipped with the organizing and campaigning skills appropriate to electoral politics, these new political journeymen bargain with some effectiveness among the rival white politicians anxious for their vote.

In Northern metropolitan centers, too, professional Negro politicians have emerged, men who work inside the party machine dominating their city, men who accept the terms of political life laid down by white counterparts who are scarcely less ethnic-minded—Irish, Italian, Polish, Jewish, and Puerto Rican "spokesmen" also judged by their readiness and reasonableness in making bargains, and by their ability to deliver votes as promised. Considerable variations remain, of course, in style, in methods used, and in results obtained.[7] In Chicago, Dawson's political strength within the Democratic machine, like that of other ethnic politicians, has depended on the historical "fit" between ward boundaries and Negro ghetto limits. Working in a solidly Negro area, he deals in tangible and divisible benefits, few of which pose clear moral questions. In New York City, on the other hand, Powell's role is also system-specific, but here a much weaker and less unified alliance of politicians runs the dominant party apparatus. There is therefore scope for Powell's agitational style. He deals in moral questions, in intangible ideals and indivisible causes which must not be compromised. His dramatic skills link these to his personal leadership. Dr. Kenneth B. Clark, himself an occasional rival of Powell in Harlem, has this to say:

> In his flamboyant personal behavior, Powell has been to the Negroes a symbol of all that life has denied them. . . . The Negro masses do not see Powell as amoral but as defiantly honest in his protest against the myths and hypocrisies of racism. . . . He is important precisely because he is himself a caricature, a burlesque of the personal exploitation of power.[8]

The growth of militancy among Negroes—with the decline of "accommodation"—in the modal leadership style is a double-edged

---

[7] See James Q. Wilson, *Negro Politics* (Glencoe, Ill.: Free Press, 1960) for a comparative inquiry which develops these points systematically.
[8] K. B. Clark, *Dark Ghetto* (New York: Harper & Row, 1965), p. 210.

blade. On the one hand, it reflects a shift away from the habit of evaluating their social position primarily within the nonpolitical, "intramural" range of Negro rivals, and a shift toward evaluating it instead by explicit comparison to a counterpart group—their opposite numbers in the white middle class.[9] On the other hand, it is a behavior pattern which, once initiated, generates its own reputation. It is far more conspicuous than the older pattern of accommodationist leadership, and it is reinforced powerfully by the way in which other Negroes, both peers and elders, respond by endorsing and accepting it. The "accommodating" style is established by a sequence of occasions when aggressive confrontations were avoided; the "militant" style is more rhetorical, and tends to be *predicted* on the basis of even a very small set of occasions when aggressive leadership options are used. Negro leaders drift into the former; they assert the latter kind of role.[10]

THE SKILLS AND HABITS OF CITIZENSHIP

Learning about political life, then, is not a simple, static, or finished process. Instead, it is highly complex; it is dynamic and changing; and, at best, it is imperfectly realized. Many Negro adults never become very effective at organizing and improving their daily lives. How much less likely that the methods used to socialize them to onerous predetermined political rules and arrangements should regularly be effective! Indeed, if Negroes had internalized the American dream and seriously wanted it for themselves, it is hard to believe they would not long since have been radically disenchanted and militantly alienated. Instead, it is only in recent years that a new generation of Negro youths begins to think seriously about claiming their birthrights.

In 1910, for a young Negro to study the program of the then-fledgling NAACP was not to review an impressive sequence of judicial victories, as the task is for his 1965 counterpart. The 1910 program was a recital of watered-down hopes and carefully worded aims. Even so, Booker T. Washington and William E. B. DuBois debated the proper goals and strategy for Negroes in polemical

[9] Ruth Searles and J. A. Williams, Jr., "Negro College Students' Participation in Sit-Ins," *Social Forces*, 40 (1962), pp. 215–220.

[10] See the insightful participant-observer case study by Allan P. Sindler, "Youth and the American Negro Protest Movement," prepared for the 1964 International Political Science Association Meetings in Geneva, Switzerland.

terms that made the former's call for self-improvement seem at odds with the latter's demand for Negro civil rights at once.

Today, also, there are rivalries and polemics among Negro leaders on the national scene, conflicts brought home to Negro citizens by television and radio rather than in exclusively Negro news media. But perhaps there is now a stronger sense of the need for a division of labor: the need for militant direct action protests, to arouse the Negro poor from apathy and self-hate, and the simultaneous need for persistent integrative efforts—through the courts, in union-management bargaining and in government personnel practices, in community service organizations, and through partisan political activities. Not only the symbolic struggles that eventuate in decisions to desegregate a school, permit voter registration, make public accommodations equally accessible, or create job opportunities, but also the practical tasks of implementing and consolidating each such victory are coming to be seen by the young Negro of 1965 as part of the political world with which he must come to terms.[11]

But what does it mean to "come to terms"? One view expects each generation to produce a distinctive style, seizing new opportunities which older generations have yielded or neglected. Another view, not necessarily incompatible with the first, expects realism. Systematic adjustment to changing circumstances seems mostly to come from the older people, while youth refuse to come to terms and instead appear idealistic and unreasonable.

Not many studies of political socialization have yet been made, of Negroes or any other grouping. We have examined some systematic evidence about the attitudes and self-conceptions held by adult Negroes and their white Counterparts concerning American politics. But we know little of how those notions were first acquired, when today's adults were growing up and were gradually coming to understand their place in a white democracy. Neither for Negroes nor for other categories do we know much about the differentiation and attenuation of childhood attitudes and beliefs. Yet adults have to behave in response to situational insights, and adults have to acquire the experience and skills as well as the nerve and desire to mount fresh assaults on complacency and indifference.

Memorable experiences, for example, whether they arise in the midst of electoral campaigns, in moments of public crisis, or in the workaday context of civic co-operation, are hard to plan ahead

[11] See the sympathetic sketches by Howard Zinn, SNCC: The New Abolitionists (Boston: Beacon Press, 1964) and the careful case study of biracial co-operation and protest activities in a Southern community by Lewis Killian and Charles Gregg, Racial Crisis in America (Englewood Cliffs, N. J.: Prentice-Hall, 1964).

of time. They tend to be memorable because of accidental and unexpected developments. The Montgomery bus boycott of 1955 began spontaneously when a weary Negro seamstress refused to yield her seat to a white. For more than a year, 17,000 Negroes refused to ride, cutting the bus line's patronage to a fourth of normal. From such unplanned rejection of roles and defiance of norms, in the ten subsequent years, boycotting has become a formidable political weapon for American Negroes. With notice spread by word of mouth or from the pulpits of Negro churches, the boycott has provided a community-level focus and has helped to create leadership-communication networks that are transforming Northern metropolitan slum areas as well as Southern colored quarters. In 1963, a third of a national cross-section of Negroes and more than two-thirds of a panel of Negro leaders reported that they had boycotted certain stores in their local communities.[12]

The syndrome of dejection, self-contempt, a sense of worthlessness, and hopelessness is what Kardiner and Ovesey called the Negro's "mark of oppression." It has been repeatedly noted in studies since their work dealing with Negro psychological adjustment problems.[13] The problems of Negro personality formation are often traced to the "identity crises" through which Negro children perforce must pass: the color-bias they develop even in pre-school play, often linked with a tense reluctance to acknowledge that they are Negro; the postpuberty estrangement of Negro youths from their white playmates, enforced by white parental racist fears of miscegenation; in young adulthood, too, after the relatively sheltered years of school and familiar neighborhood, "the full awareness of his social devaluation in the larger society" can cause severe emotional distress.[14]

Little is known about how the emotional wellsprings of love and hate, hunger and vitality are linked persistently to a set of socially "given" goals and goads. The levels of need achievement among Negroes vary substantially, perhaps as much as among whites, although the standards of behavior, life-plans, and career objectives are manifestly different in the ghetto subculture into which most Negroes are born and in the American society which isolates them from awareness of those norms and denies them the rewards of compliance with those norms.

It is in interracial dyadic relationships that Negroes have

---

[12] William Brink and Louis Harris, *The Negro Revolution in America* (New York: Simon & Schuster, 1964), p. 203.
[13] A. Kardiner and L. Ovesey, *The Mask of Oppression* (1951); see also the comprehensive survey by Thomas F. Pettigrew, *A Profile of the Negro American* (Princeton, N.J.: D. Van Nostrand, 1964).
[14] *Op. cit.*, p. 8.

usually learned manipulative strategies, situational tactics, and bargaining ploys. It has been in response to the emotional strain of interracial contacts that Negroes have generated double standards of fair play, humor, and even relaxation.

Almost every Negro adult—not only his organizational leaders—has been schooled in ways to get along in superior-subordinate relationships. Moreover, the picture he has acquired very commonly puts him in the latter role. The extent to which the mental outlook of oppressed people tends toward fantasies, childlike incompetence, and passive dependence is hard to measure; available evidence suggests that a pervasive pattern of such behavior has historically laid its imprint on Negro America.

But when people acquire skills and sensitivities in how to sense the mood of superiors, how to parlay advantages, how to conceal their emotions, how to accomplish a thousand political artifices, they often find such assets portable to new circumstances and applicable in quite unexpected situations. American Negroes learned these skills under persistent conditions of duress. Perhaps many never have mastered techniques that could be used on anyone but a white superior; many have probably repressed all sensitivities to similar opportunities in intraracial organizational relations. Even so, given this kind of schooling, American Negroes must often make very acute political followers, able to appreciate very well the difference between a leader's pretensions and his actual performances.

The Negro revolution in America has been manifest in headlines and news bulletins for more than ten years. It is tempting to speculate about the ways in which scenes of militant direct action, showing parental courage and group discipline in the face of mindless hatred, affect young Negro children today—in the choice of their ego ideals, in the games they play, the stories they read, the fantasies they have, the careers they want, the nightmares they endure, and in their heightened awareness of political rules and possibilities, now that such awareness carries an instrumental rather than an academic tag.

There is perhaps no single event that marks the watershed in American race relations better than the 1954 Supreme Court decision calling for "all deliberate speed" in desegregating the nation's schools. Yet it was ten years later, in the Birmingham riots of 1964, before the Negro poor entered the protest movement:

> The riots . . . were waged not by the disciplined
> cadres of relatively well-educated "middle-class"
> Negroes but by the apathetic poor who had previ-
> ously remained completely on the outside, and

whose potential for violence frightened Rev. Martin
Luther King's lieutenants as much as the whites.[15]

Moreover, the nonviolent direct action methods of the new
protest groups—CORE, SCLC, SNCC—represent also only part of a
ten-year prelude to the far more fundamental revolution that is
coming in the politics of neighborhoods and communities, of school
districts and residential blocks, a revolution that began in scattered
localities during the 1950's and received large financial and direc-
tional support from the 1964 Civil Rights Act and the resultant anti-
poverty program of the Office of Economic Opportunity. In states of
the South as well as of the North, and at county and municipal levels, biracial area human resources councils are being formed, to
co-ordinate and sponsor programs for community action, establish
and run youth job corps and urban centers, and encourage private
nonprofit groups and universities to contribute to neighborhood improvement and adult education projects.

The importance of these experiences, both to acquire new
skills and play new roles in civic affairs, can scarcely be overesti-
mated. The full, genuine, and mundane "political resocialization" of
American Negro citizens awaits the proliferation of such institutional
scaffolding for public-spirited action.

---

[15] Silberman, *op. cit.,* p. 143.

8
What the McCone Commission Didn't See

Frederick J. Hacker, M.D.
with
Aljean Harmetz

The Watts rebellion in Los Angeles has now been tidily swept into the 101 pages of the McCone Report. The report cost $250,000 and is obviously well-meaning and respectable. It suggests better education, more employment, and nicer relations between Negroes and the police department to avoid "the dull, devastating spiral of failure that awaits the average disadvantaged child."

It will also, in essence, be treated as a "white man's" report. It labels the rebellion "a formless, quite senseless, all but hopeless violent protest—engaged in by a few but bringing great distress to all." The McCone Commission, firmly on the side of God, country, and our present law and order, reached this judgment: "Yet, however powerful their grievances, the rioters had no legal or moral justification for the wounds they inflicted." What the McCone Commission fails to understand is that, from the standpoint of the lower-class Negroes living in Watts, the "disorderly and immoral" riots were neither senseless nor hopeless. The rebellion brought them enormous and immediate psychological benefits, or at least so they thought.

In all 101 pages of the report there is little consideration of the psychological reasons why the Negroes revolted and no appreciation of the psychological changes that occurred within the Negroes during the riots. As the only dissenting member of the commission, the Rev. Mr. James E. Jones, said in an interview, the report did not consider attitudes.

For the Negroes, what happened in southeastern Los Angeles last August *was* justified legally and morally. Where the police

Reprinted by permission of *The Nation* from Frederick J. Hacker with Aljean Harmetz, "What the McCone Commission Didn't See," *Frontier*, March, 1966, pp. 10–15.

saw black criminals tearing apart law and order with a cascade of Molotov cocktails, the Negroes of Watts watched freedom fighters liberating themselves with blood and fire. The McCone Report says that only 2 percent of the Negroes patricipated in the rioting. It implies that the rest of the Negro community was cowering in darkened houses waiting for the forces of law and order to rescue them. Actually, the majority of the 400,000 Negroes in the area supported the riots. As one high school girl said afterwards, "Every time I looked out of my window and saw another fire, I felt new joy."

NOT "BAD" OR "CRIMINAL"

The most distinctive generally shared feeling of the Negroes about the riots is that they were not criminal. To some, they were the explosion of a powder keg; to others, a rationally planned demonstration against sustained injustice; to others, a full-scale rebellion; to others, an assertion of racial independence, a kind of racial identity struggle; and for others, a protest against intolerable poverty. For none of the Negroes, however, were the riots "bad" or "criminal" in the sense these words are used by the McCone Commission.

For the Negroes, there was no reason to feel guilt, shame, or regret. Although most of the rioters interviewed believe that it is wrong to "burn," "loot," "break down the law," they felt the looting and burning were merely excesses of a just cause and thus justified. In that respect, the Watts riots were psychologically analagous to the Hungarian Revolution and the Boston Tea Party, where the participants also did not try to excuse the single acts considered "bad" but felt fully justified by their over-all cause.

Some psychoanalysts tend to belittle violence as *sickness.* They—like the members of the McCone Commission—ignore the uncomfortable historical evidence that violence can unite, particularly if the violence occurs once and is not repeated. As in the mythology of bull fighting, violence—the ultimate violence that could or does lead to death—is the great unifier, the strange symbol of reality confronted with an ultimate truth. When one is nakedly facing one's destiny, presumably all falsehood and pretense falls away and one is—as described by rioters—"close to God."

"ALTERNATIVE TO DESPAIR"

Conventional psychoanalytic theory says that resorting to violence, particularly collective violence, is a regression and a projection of inner feelings of panic and despair. This is undoubtedly true. What is overlooked is that violence is also an effective defense. In other words, violence is an alternative to despair. Through violence, you can rid yourself of a torturing feeling of helplessness and nothingness. Violence makes you feel good—at least for a while. And it could be argued that the "mental health" of the Negro community was much better after the riots than before, because the riots served as a safety valve against the feeling of apathy that was the strongest characteristic of life in Watts.

Life in Watts before the riots was not only deprived. It was dull. Anyone familiar with the psychology of modern crime knows that the search for novelty and the desire to escape monotony is by no means willful, arbitrary, or fanciful. The hunger and search for new experiences—popularly known as "kicks"—indicates just as legitimate a need as the search for food or sexual satisfaction.

The psychological climate of Watts last summer was one of apathy tangled with an acute sense of injustice. The Negroes felt that all the storekeepers were Jews and Italians, who, having suffered exploitation, were out to exploit Negroes. They felt all the policemen assigned to Watts were recent immigrants recruited from the South and therefore sadistic and brutal. Both reactions were serious misconceptions. But most of the carefully collected injustices did result from real deprivation and major suffering, although the suffering was often expressed in trivial terms.

It cost seventy-five cents to cash a check in Watts, while in nearby white communities it cost nothing. Food cost more in Watts. For example, canned peaches cost three cents more than they do in white neighborhood supermarkets. In Watts, there was no promise or possibility of real change. In Watts, there was no "action." In Vietnam people were dying; in Hollywood people were living the sweet life; in Watts nothing ever happened.

To the white Angelenos driving the freeways in their Monzas and Barracudas and Mustangs, Watts was invisible. By an accident of geography, it was underneath the freeway. It was underneath the freeway in the very center of their city, and the white Angelenos roared over it daily without noticing its existence. (Over and over again after the riots, the participants used the same words: "We put ourselves on the map." It was almost as though the riots had been planned as a tourist attraction and the inhabitants were now happy and proud that photographers and curiosity seekers were descending from the freeways to see where it all took place.)

In Watts, the police often reached for their guns if a Negro approached them even if he only wanted to ask directions. Few cared what happened to Negroes as human beings. To a great extent, only their women could get jobs—usually as servants. The police were continually harassing them—humiliating them by making them spreadeagle over a car hood to be searched, by mimicking their speech, by refusing to call them "Mister" and substituting the insults of "Hey, boy," or "Come here, monkey."

HOW NEGRO MEN SAW THEMSELVES

The Negroes of Watts were constantly degraded in the presence of their wives and children. Children need to see their fathers as strong and omnipotent. Negro children saw their fathers as helpless and frightened objects of the arbitrariness of white men in uniform. In school, the children were taught urban, middle-class white values with their emphasis on aggressiveness, responsibility, and the assertion of masculinity. But adult Negro men were barred from responsibility and treated as though they were irresponsible children; and they were punished for aggressiveness. As a result, the children were contemptuous of their fathers. "Our dads didn't count," they said. "When we wanted anything, we asked our mothers." And the Negro men felt an even deeper sense of being victimized.

But the sense of injustice started to breed a feeling of hope. It is a curious and now often-discussed fact that riots occur precisely at a time when—objectively and subjectively—the situation is not only improving, but improving more rapidly than was believed possible.

Riots never break out when the situation is considered hopeless. Action then appears senseless, and the reduction of people to historical objects is so complete and internalized—and thus regarded as inevitable—that no resistance is possible. When black people or yellow people or white people think of themselves as born servants, helpless victims, there can be no rioting. People who say, "Give the Negroes a finger and they want the whole hand," and who blame the rioting on desegregation and liberal court decisions are, in part, right. So is Police Chief William H. Parker of Los Angeles when he blames *permissiveness* and the *over-regard for civil rights.* If the American Negroes were still slaves, there would have been little chance of rioting in the summer of 1965.

The trigger for the riots might have been anything. In fact, it was the arrest by the police of a drunken driver in the middle of a heat wave. For days the thermometer had stayed just under 100 degrees. The weather was as chronically muggy and oppressive as was the life of the average Watts Negro. In a heat wave, everyone feels like a helpless object battered by forces he cannot control. The riot started almost as a temper tantrum against the heat and the despair. In a short while, this feeling proved contagious. It spread to Chief Parker who had a tantrum against the liberals and to Mayor Samuel W. Yorty who had a tantrum against the state government. And, like a child's temper tantrum which has succeeded in attracting attention, the riot flowered under the attention of newspaper headlines and national television.

For the rioters, the riots were fun. The conventional explanation by middle-class parents to their children about sex skips over the important point that sex also can be fun. In much the same way, observers have not understood or have withheld the fact that the riots were fun. There was a carnival in the midst of carnage. Rioters laughed, danced, clapped their hands. Many got drunk. Violence was permissible. Children stayed out all night. Several children between the ages of ten and fourteen (who first asked the permission of their mothers to talk to a white man) later admitted defensively that it was "great fun." . . . "It was a little scarey but mostly it was great because everybody had a good time, sort of a ball." . . . "Nobody cared if we ever went to bed."

Contrary to the usual pattern of riots, there was hardly any sexual delinquency or increase in sexual activities. Usually rioting, and the uncontrolled, unrestrained, and thus pleasurable descent into repressed and suppressed emotion and the release of all tension in the absence of ordinary inner and outer controls, brings with it sexual promiscuity. But when the lower-class Negro says he "wants to feel like a man," he is talking about status—not sex. The rioters constantly volunteered the information that "we never had to worry about sex." . . . "Sex is nothing to get excited about." . . . "Whitey makes too much of it." Sex has always been the lower-class Negro's one free pleasure. Homosexual and heterosexual experience starts young. And from the time a boy is ten or eleven, girls are always available. So the release of tension in rioting led not to sexual delinquency, but to looting.

MIXED FEELINGS ABOUT THE LOOTING

The looting also was fun. There was great glee about the breakdown of a law-enforcement system identified with suppression and injustice. The objects looted from stores were often taken as a symbol of the Mardi Gras atmosphere of liberation from injustice. Some rioters said over and over again that they didn't need the things they stole and could not use them. In many cases, the stolen refrigerators, stoves, television sets and stereo sets were divorced completely from their utilitarian use. They had been coveted for a long time, but after they were stolen, they were often taken apart and abandoned. It was the ultimate in waste, in contempt for the white man's objects—a determined NO to acculturation, to the white man's world. Rather than useful instruments that had to be guarded and protected and cared for, the looted objects actually became toys.

During the riots there was, to paraphrase Coleridge, "a willing suspension of conscience." In rioting, one loses personal individuality by gaining collective individuality. One "becomes like the others" and this "makes you happy." . . . "I don't think any more." . . . "I had the good feeling that this was right and it was wonderful."

This liberation from conscience and from conscientiousness made possible for the rioters an involvement and an extreme commitment usually denied them. The most important resource the lower-class Negro lacks is the resource to get involved in something or committed to something, including the ordinary values of society that are unhesitatingly accepted by the middle-class white—and the middle-class Negro—American.

Bayard Rustin says that the black body has to be used precisely because democratic channels are denied to the Negro, and he has nothing but his body to fight with. During the Watts rioting, the apathy—which is a form of chronic mild depression—was swept away. Real feeling was restored to the Negroes by the full involvement of their bodies and by actual danger. There was ecstatic body involvement. ("It felt good all over." . . . "We were whole again." . . . "We were whole people, not just servants." . . . "We were new.")

Again and again one phrase was repeated: "At last we were where the action was." At last something was happening, and what was happening was extraordinarily important. It was the metamorphosis of the Negroes of southeastern Los Angeles from victims—historical objects—to masters. They were now men. As one explained the change: "It made our males men," and another said, "I saw children respect their fathers for the first time."

A SHARED FEELING OF IDENTITY

The people of Watts felt that for those four days they represented all Negroes; the historic plight of the Negroes; all the rebellions against all injustice. They were doing the job that other

Negroes were prevented from doing. They were setting an example, starting a pattern. Being able to watch themselves on television screens in store windows, even as they smashed the stores, reinforced their feelings of self-importance. In their simultaneous participation and watching their participation, they felt that the whole nation—black and white—watched them too. They felt the emotional involvement of the nation in the riot as a symbol. Like lighting the Christmas tree on the White House lawn, it was a shared experience.

There was an extraordinary religious—almost mystical—fervor. Economic and social injustices took on religious meaning. "All God's children got shoes," said one rioter, explaining his looting of a shoe store. The injustices had betrayed the promises of the Bible that all people should be equal and that the lowest is as good as the highest. Watts stood for every deprived Negro community. Frequently there was overt identification with Christ as a sacrificial being who by his suffering takes upon himself and atones for the sins of everybody. But the role of Christ was rejected in the next breath in favor of "being where the action is."

A STRANGE SENSE OF PRIDE

The emotionally liberating effects of the riots have not lasted, but they have been replaced by a strange sense of pride and accomplishment which is actually the finding of a national and racial identity. National identity, racial identity, and, often, religious identity are accepted ingredients of personality structure and seem to have been always present to those who have them. They forget that what now appears as given and predestined had to be taken and grabbed in the past. National identity is not a gift but an active and often violent deed. Were Americans not colonial Englishmen prior to their becoming Americans by violent action? Did not the Jews experience themselves as the arch-symbol of unwanted yet persistent guests in foreign countries until they grabbed their own country and forged their national identity in the assertive belligerence that had previously been considered "un-Jewish"?

There is an exhilarating feeling in the rioters that they have finally found and forged a new sense of identity. The riots welded them together, and now they feel capable of carving a new fate, not just passively enduring their present existence. Perhaps every national and racial identity derives from the fact—or at least the legend—of an aggressive rising. Is not every revolution a sudden and abrupt break with the past and the potential beginning of a new tradition? Destructiveness can lose its negative connotation when it has become successful in welding people together. The destruction of society becomes, by a change of function, the building of a new and different society. The rioters believe—and have to believe even if it isn't true—that a new era has started. The new era was foreshadowed by Montgomery and Birmingham, but they believe it really started with the violent uprising of Watts.

There is pride that now everybody knows *what* Watts is and *where* Watts is. Before, not even the people who live in Los Angeles knew. Now the whole nation knows. Before, nobody cared what happened to them. Now, by God, people have to care. Each of the rioters interviewed said something like, "You don't want to talk to my kind of Negro," meaning a proud, aggressive Negro who talks back. And each of the rioters interviewed assumed that the interviewer had had experience only with submissive Negroes.

The rioters now look upon themselves as self-respecting, fighting Negroes who would not be pushed around any longer, or, as they put it: "We're men now." . . . "We won't take any more from Whitey." . . . "It's finally happened. They can't get away with everything."

Assertive and masculine, the "new Negro" fights and does not necessarily wait to fight back. He fights first. And due to the easy manufacture of Molotov cocktails, there is now a constant threat of the repetition of violence. (Possibly, Molotov cocktails are more significant for our period, and, socially, a more important fact than the atom bomb.) To this "new Negro," the only good Negro is a destructive Negro. This feeling does not apply to the middle-class Los Angeles Negro who most often lives in an integrated neighborhood like Baldwin Hills, works with white lawyers or accountants, and pickets with white liberals for the Congress of Racial Equality (CORE). To him, this "new Negro" is enormously embarrassing. The middle-class Negro believes in passive resistance, in gradualism, in the melting-pot approach—the things which the Watts Negro calls "phoney hope solutions." Middle-class Negroes have tried to explain away the riots by saying "there are good and bad in every society." The rebellious, assertive Negro is—in their eyes as in the eyes of almost the whole community—the "bad Negro." They speak of him in the same stereotypes the whites use: "uncontrolled," "undisciplined," "childish," "close to the jungle."

"WE WILL NEVER BE THE SAME AGAIN"

The rioters overemphasize the significance and importance of the riots: "The whole world knows and will never forget." . . . "Now we have something to remember." . . . "This is where our calendar starts." They have taken their fate into their own hands, and they feel that what happened is irreversible. "Our children and grandchildren will remember Watts." . . . "The world isn't the same." . . . "We aren't the same." . . . "We'll never be the same again." . . . "The world will never be the same."

To exactly the extent that the riots contributed to the enhancement of the self-image of the Negroes, it gave whites a furious feeling of impotence. Inwardly, they experienced the feeling of an inevitable surrender to Negro demands and the fear of "mongrelization," of "the black danger" which is so similar to "the yellow danger" of Spengler's *Decline of the West.*

Before the riots there were many subtle sociological and psychological distinctions within the white community, within the black community, and even within the police department. But the riots polarized everyone into two groups: black and white.

One of the functions of aggressive action is precisely this simplification. As the German kaiser once said, "I don't know any parties any more. I only know Germans." In Los Angeles, there was only white against black. This simplification and polarization relieves anxiety and solves moral problems by giving each party the same firm conviction in the justness of its fight. The line between good and bad is obvious to each side; nothing is blurred. Whoever is not on *our* side is either too stupid, too wicked or too depraved to be regarded as a human being. Why else is he not on *our* side, the side of the angels that has so obviously pre-empted all goodness, justice, and truth? All specific individual acts are justified and sanctioned if committed by the right side. *Our* side is idealized. The opponents, however, are satanized, made into devils. By their opposition to *us,* they have forfeited their place as human beings. They are less than human. Therefore, all laws respecting their human dignity can be suspended.

During the riots, the whites felt that Negro grievances did not have to be discussed or remedied. They feared the unleashing of uncontrollable forces that could sweep us all under. People who had previously been critical of Police Chief Parker rallied to his defense. Law and Order must be re-established and enforced. It did not matter what kind of Law and Order. As Chief Parker said, "They're on the bottom, we're on top," and he announced that he did not bargain with hoodlums. After the riots, some rioters were picked arbitrarily as culprits. They were treated as ordinary criminals. On the other hand, all police officers were cleared of charges. Their acts leading to deaths were declared justifiable homicide. *War crimes are committed only by the opponent.*

The rebels, during the riots, felt justified no matter what

aggressive and destructive acts they committed because law enforcement itself was something evil and oppressive to them. Every act against the law or an officer of the law was, a priori, justified. (For a different example, remember the spy movies during World War II in which personally innocent wearers of the hated Nazi uniform were killed to the applause of the audience.)

In a polarized situation, there is a common enemy, and the enemy is easily recognizable. In Watts, the Negroes were black, the police wore uniforms. Polarization melts away all inner conflicts. The participants feel free and guilt-free, while the external conflict is exaggerated, serving the purpose of eliminating inner turmoil.

When the riots were over, the polarization also receded. The old fronts within the Negro community and within the white community reappeared. There was name calling. Guilt distribution started according to a foreseeable and extremely repetitious pattern. There were immediate charges on every side of "playing politics," or "making hay out of the situation."

THE "DELUSION OF PARTICULARISM"

In one sense, the rioters and the police stood together against the rest of the community. They shared a strange delusion of particularism. They believed their problems to be unparalleled, inconceivable to any outsider. Only someone with special understanding, long acquaintance and local participation could understand. For this reason the Negroes resented Dr. Martin Luther King's visit to Los Angeles, although they otherwise respected him as an effective Negro leader. The social agencies in Watts insisted on handling all reconstruction since they believed that only they knew the real situation and had the confidence of the Negroes. This attitude was strangely matched by the insistence of Chief Parker that the police did not need outside advice because they knew more than any outsider.

After the riots, Negroes of the area showed resentment because the white community sent middle-class Negroes to Watts as agents. There are two Negro assemblymen in Los Angeles and three Negroes on the fifteen-member Los Angeles City Council, but these five "Negro leaders" were ineffective in stopping the riots because the rioters considered any middle-class Negro submissive to white people and white values. They consider middle-class Negroes as "Uncle Toms" toadying to the white people and afraid to lose their positions with "Whitey."

The rioters had no particular desire for communication with

the white community, yet they expected that the white community would and must help them and was actually compelled to help them to prevent further riots. They said that Black Muslims and Communists had not been involved in the riots, but, they added, who could say what might happen if the situation didn't improve. This hint of radicalization was a blackmail threat to the white community.

The ugliness of Watts had become intolerable, and they meant to burn the buildings partly as a kind of attempt at urban renewal. As they saw it, "The whites will now have to build better buildings because we don't have any." . . . "If we hadn't destroyed them, we would never get new ones." They believed the white community, and particularly the federal government, had to clothe them, feed them, and rebuild for them.

This magical expectation of full outside help to redress all the injustices that led to the outbreak was in strange contrast to the nearly unanimous insistence that all real improvement has to come from local leaders, local agencies, and people living in the community. Their insistence on "local leaders" reflects a resentment against middle-class Negroes who have moved from Watts, leaving the community with hardly any Negro lawyers, doctors or other professionals. ("How can we have pride when the successful Negroes don't stay?")

SHATTERING A "NEGATIVE IMAGE"

Before the riots, the underprivileged and psychologically castrated Negro male of Watts had accepted and incorporated the contemptuous value judgment that considered him not quite human. He had actually seen himself as a negative copy of white values. He had prided himself on his lack of control, on his unwillingness to obey the rules of a game that he had not chosen. He had experienced himself as more real, more untamed, more natural than white people.

That negative image broke apart in the riots. Consciously and unconsciously, most of the rioters knew that the riots could not succeed and that they would have to pay for their defiance. The riots actually were an accident, the explosive coincidence of trivial events. Yet in the courage of a rebellion that attracted worldwide attention, the Negroes acquired a taste of autonomy. They were not any longer either positive or negative copies of the white man's values. They asserted a will of their own, no matter how little they knew what this will actually meant. Their rebellion left deep marks, even if it did not fully succeed. Perhaps the most amazing thing to the author was how often unsophisticated and uneducated rioters spoke about identity and about their pride in the national and international prominence they felt was gained by their rebellion.

What the McCone Commission didn't see is that the desire of Negroes for a proud image of themselves is as vital to them as the fulfillment of their economic needs. If the recommendations of the McCone Report are implemented by people who continue to think of the riots as only criminal and the rioters as ordinary criminals, the result will be disastrous.

A few days after the McCone Report, a committee of the Los Angeles Grand Jury, declaring that the riot was merely a crime spree, said, "There can be no extenuating circumstances to rationalize this ruthless outbreak of lawlessness and those who are convicted of leadership or participation in this riot should be punished to the fullest extent of the law."

Whatever the Grand Jury and the McCone Commission and middle-class Americans may think, the riot was *not* "equally abhorred and resented by all good, law-abiding citizens, regardless of race or status." For the overwhelming majority of the Negroes in Watts it was better to be feared than to be treated with contempt. What must be understood by the rest of America is that, for the lower-class Negro, riots are not criminal but are a legitimate weapon in a morally justified civil war. Already, the Watts riots have given the Negro a sense of personal and national identity. For the ghetto-Negro in the second half of the 20th Century, anything—even a new American revolution—is better than being invisible.

In the years following World War II, the Federal government intervened seriously, if intermittently, on behalf of Negro rights for the first time since Reconstruction. Perhaps the first major black victory of this "second Reconstruction" era was President Harry Truman's decision to order the integration of the armed forces. This decision was not made in a political vacuum; it reflected growing pressure on Truman from members of his own party to attack the problems of racial discrimination. Spurred by a swelling northern Negro vote and white sympathy for the Negro's plight in the South, many northern politicians—most of them Democrats—had become champions of the causes of civil and political rights for southern blacks and welfare measures to aid blacks in the North. Rhetorical support for this movement came from leading liberal Democrats, like Adlai Stevenson, Hubert Humphrey, Paul Douglas, and G. Mennon Williams, who had risen to national prominence in the late 1940s. However, in spite of this support, comprehensive federal legislation on behalf of black people did not emerge from Congress until the 1960s. Prior to passage of the 1964 Civil Rights Act, the most important victory of the civil rights movement came from the judicial branch of the federal government when the Supreme Court, in 1954, unanimously declared public school segregation to be unconstitutional. Nevertheless, despite this decision, school desegregation proceeded at a snail's pace during the ensuing decade.

Although *Brown vs. Board of Education* and the actions taken by the executive branch on behalf of Negroes in the late 1940s and 1950s had only a limited effect on racist practices, these federal moves did have a significant indirect result. Southern black people were encouraged to demonstrate against racial discrimination. Starting with the Montgomery bus boycotts of 1955 and culminating in the massive 1963 March on Washington, black Americans demanded rights which had been enjoyed by their white counterparts for centuries. Journalists termed this period of black protest the "Negro Revolution" and praised its nonviolent nature. When Congress passed the 1964 Civil Rights Act, it was generally concluded that the Negro Revolution had reached its successful conclusion.

But no real revolution had occurred with respect to black wealth and power in the United States. And black realization of this fact contributed to the development of movements which sought, as Malcolm X would have put it, "a real revolution." In this and the following section, the development of the "Negro Revolution" is traced, first in the arena of politics, and second in the area of protest. The recurrent theme of the diverse selections which follow is that despite the symbolic gains made by black people in the postwar period, neither black political activity, nor nonviolent protest, succeeded in ending black poverty and powerlessness.

The first selection is from E. Franklin Frazier's critical study of the Negro middle class, *Black Bourgeoisie*. Frazier wrote that study in the early 1950s on the eve of the Negro Revolution. His selection reviews the history of black politics since Reconstruction, and describes the nature of black political leadership in the decade following World War II. Frazier concluded that this leadership was subservient to white interests and unresponsive to the needs of the black masses. While Frazier may have been overly critical of black politicians, his portrayal of Negro political leadership as powerless and middle-class oriented was basically correct.

The second selection, by Edward Banfield and James Q. Wilson, describes Negro urban politics in the early 1960s. Their detailed analysis tends to confirm the conclusions made by Frazier; Banfield and Wilson argue that the numerous constraints on Negro politicians force them "to be politicians first and Negroes second." Black politicians are constrained by such factors as the lack of cohesion among the black masses, class polarity within the black community, the weaknesses of Negro civic organizations, and the stake which many black leaders have in the status quo. But perhaps of greatest importance, black politicians must operate in political systems which are controlled by the white majority; "the nature of Negro politics . . . depends largely upon the nature of white politics."

At first glance, the 1967 elections of Negro mayors in Cleveland, Ohio, and Gary, Indiana, appeared to represent a reversal of the pattern described by Frazier and Banfield and Wilson. Yet in a detailed case study of the Cleveland election in which Carl Stokes was elected mayor, Jeffrey Hadden, Louis Masotti, and Victor Thiessen conclude that "Stokes and Hatcher [the present black mayor of Gary] won because black-voter power coalesced with a relatively small minority of liberal whites. It was not a victory of acceptance or even tolerance of Negroes, but a numerical failure of the powers of discrimination, a failure that resulted in large part because of the massive exodus of whites from the central city." Subsequent urban elections—particularly those of 1969—have confirmed this assessment. In Los Angeles, after a campaign in which race was *the* issue, a black candidate for mayor with strong bipartisan political support lost election to the incumbent whose administration had been beset by scandal. In Minneapolis, a former policeman was elected mayor on a strong "law and order" platform, while in the New York City primaries, white liberal candidates for mayor were defeated in both the Republican and Democratic primaries. Mayor John Lindsay had to face the general election as an independent; his victory resulted from the fact that he faced *two* candidates who were unsympathetic to black aspirations.

Although black politicians appear to be able to accomplish little on behalf of their constituents, it has been argued by some observers that blacks can achieve their goals by entering into political coalitions with sympathetic whites. In the final selection, a chapter from *Black Power: The Politics of Liberation in America*, Stokely Carmichael and Charles Hamilton criticize the position that black alliances with "liberal" political elements will bring about substantial Negro gains. While Carmichael and Hamilton feel that blacks *should* enter political coalitions under certain conditions, they argue forcefully that black people should be wary of such alliances because a mutuality of interests does not exist between black and white Americans. The failure of conventional politics to have more than a marginal effect on the problems facing black Americans suggests that their analysis cannot easily be dismissed.

9
Serving
Two
Masters

E. Franklin Frazier

Since the wealth of the black bourgeoisie is too inconse-
quential for this class to wield any political power, the role of Negro
politicians has been restricted to attempting to satisfy the demands
of Negro voters while acting as the servants of the political machines supported by the propertied classes in the white community
When the Negro enjoyed the right of suffrage in the South during
the Reconstruction period, the Negro political leaders were a part of
the Republican Party machine supported by northern industrial capitalism. The state constitutions which the Negro leaders helped to
draw up embodied middle-class interests and ideals. With the exception of a few political leaders who were concerned with making land
available for the freedmen, the Negroes' political leaders, many of
whom belonged to the class of Negroes who were free before the
Civil War, were interested primarily in securing civil and political
rights for the freedmen.

After the disfranchisement of the Negro in the South, the
Republican Party continued to maintain a mere skeleton of an organization in most of the southern States.[1] In these organizations, which
played no real role in local political struggles, Negro politicians
continued to have influence. Although the Republican Party organizations did not have much influence locally except in the matter of
federal appointments, they were important in the Republican National
Conventions where candidates were nominated for the presidency
and vice-presidency of the United States. A candidate who could be
sure of the support of the southern delegates to the Republican

Reprinted with permission of The Macmillan Company from
E. Franklin Frazier, *Black Bourgeoisie,* pp. 91–97. Copyright © The Free
Press, a Division of The Macmillan Company, 1962.

National Convention would have a good chance of securing the nomination. The only rewards that Negroes received for their support of the Republican Party were a few federal appointments that went to middle-class Negroes. The most important rewards included the appointment of Negroes as minister to Liberia, as recorder of deeds in the District of Columbia, and as registrar of the United States Treasury. A few Negroes were also appointed as consular agents, postmasters in small towns, and as a collector of a port until President Taft inaugurated the policy of not appointing Negroes to posts in the South because of the opposition of the southern whites. These appointments did not affect the economic or social welfare of the Negro in American life, though Negro leaders made the appointments appear to be of great importance to the Negro. Southern Negro politicians continued to be the most important political leaders among Negroes until the mass migrations to northern cities where the masses gained once more the right to vote.

When the Negro masses acquired the right to vote in northern cities, they continued for a while to give their support to the Republican Party, chiefly on sentimental grounds, though there were some good reasons for their sentimental attachment to the Republican Party. The Republican Party was the party of Lincoln; it was the party which had given them their freedom. The Democratic Party was the party of the southern white men who had been responsible for lynching, disfranchisement, and segregation.[2] Negroes had respect for the words of the great Negro abolitionist leader, Frederick Douglass, who once said, "The Republican Party is the ship. All else is the open sea." But gradually the Negro masses began to demand more than the appointment of middle-class Negroes to honorific posts. A part of their re-education was due to the activities of the Communist Party.[3] The Communists began to attack the religiosity and other-worldly outlook of the Negro masses. They organized Negroes in demonstrations against racial discrimination; they nominated Negroes for political office; they gave special attention to Negro workers in their attempt to capture organized labor. However, the Communists succeeded only in enlisting the support of relatively small numbers of Negroes. The small gains which the Communists were able to make resulted in an anti-Communist campaign on the part of the municipal authorities and middle-class Negro leaders, especially the Negro preachers. Negroes who were active in Communist activities were subjected to special brutality on the part of the police. Because of their traditional religious background, the Negro masses were easily persuaded by Negro preachers that the irreligious Communists were using Negroes as tools.

The Communists had less influence in directing the political development of the Negroes than did the inauguration of the New Deal program during the Depression years. The situation in Chicago provides an excellent study of the change in the Negro's political outlook. At the time of the presidential election in 1932, less than a fourth of the Negro vote as compared with three-fifths of the white vote in Chicago went to Roosevelt.[4] But in 1933, when more than 80,000 Negroes or 34.4% of the entire Negro population were on relief, Negroes began to shift their support to the Democratic Party which utilized its strategic position to capture Negro votes. In the 1935 election of the Democratic mayor, four-fifths of the Negro vote went to the Democratic candidate; and in 1936 half of the Negroes voted for Roosevelt. From then on the Negro voters supported the Democratic candidates. Oscar DePriest, a leading Negro Republican, had been elected to the United States Congress in 1928; but in 1934 Arthur Mitchell was elected to Congress on the Democratic ticket and thus became the first Negro Democratic congressman in the history of the United States.

The political leaders who have emerged as a consequence of the new role of Negroes in the political life of America are men and women with a purely middle-class outlook. In the rough and tumble politics of American cities, it has often been Negroes associated with the underworld who have been able to organize the Negro voters and wring concessions from white society.[5] These Negro leaders often operate behind the façade of a legitimate business, very frequently the undertaking business. The undertaking business brings them into intimate contact with the Negro masses. Among the Negro masses they gain a reputation for generosity and humanity by giving money to the poor and to churches and by enabling criminals to escape punishment. Behind the façade of their legitimate business, they carry on illegitimate businesses such as gambling, vice, and the lottery known as the "numbers." Therefore, their interest in the political machines is mainly to secure protection for their business enterprises. They often make financial contributions to both the Democratic and Republican Party machines in order to insure protection for their businesses. Their political affiliation or leadership has no relation to the needs of the Negro masses.

Except in the case of a crisis such as that created by the Depression when the Negro masses changed their political affiliation, the Negro politician may even mobilize the masses to vote against their economic interests.[6] In his role as leader, the Negro politician attempts to accommodate the demands of the Negro masses to his personal interests which are tied up with the political machines. He may secure the appointment of a few middle-class

Negroes to positions in the municipal government. But when it comes to the fundamental interests of the Negro masses as regards employment, housing, and health, his position is determined by the political machine which represents the propertied classes of the white community. The position which the Negro political leader generally occupies in relation to the Negro masses and the dominant white community is shown in the following typical case.

The economic and political life of this small northern city, which borders a southern State, is dominated by a large manufacturing corporation.[7] This corporation provides employment for many Negroes as unskilled laborers and a large proportion of the whites as professional and white-collar workers. The white political leader is an official of the large corporation. At the same time, he is the owner of several local business enterprises including a cinema and a restaurant, neither of which admits Negroes. The white political leader finances the business enterprises of the Negro political leader who owns a cinema attended solely by Negroes. When the Negroes started a campaign for their admission to the "white" cinema and the "white" restaurant, the Negro political leader discouraged them and urged them to be loyal to Negro business enterprises. On the national scene, the white political leader played the role of a friend of Negroes. He is influential in securing a contribution from the large corporation to a fund-raising campaign for Negro education, of which he is a director. Moreover, he consented to become a trustee of a Negro college in the South which receives money from the fund-raising campaign. In the eyes of the black bourgeoisie of this city, some of whom send their children to the Negro college, he is a friend of the Negro. The few Negro intellectuals who have dared to express disapproval of the existing system of control over race relations have been labeled Communists.

Footnotes

[1] V. O. Key, *Southern Politics* (New York: Knopf, 1949), pp. 286–291.

[2] See St. Clair Drake and Horace R. Clayton, *Black Metropolis* (New York: Harcourt, Brace & World, 1945), pp. 348 ff.; and Harold F. Gosnell, *Negro Politicians* (Chicago: University of Chicago Press, 1935), pp. 24 ff.

[3] See Gosnell, *op. cit.,* Chapter XV.

[4] See Elmer W. Henderson, "Political Changes Among Negroes in Chicago During the Depression," *Social Forces,* XIX (May, 1941), 538–546. See also Drake and Cayton, *op. cit.,* pp. 353 ff.

[5] See Gosnell, *op. cit.,* pp. 125 ff., concerning Negro political leaders who have been associated with the underworld.

[6] One Negro political leader, who has many "business" operations in a northern city, said that he used to pay the Negro voters to vote against Roosevelt and the New Deal, but they were so *untrustworthy* that when alone in the voting booths they voted for Roosevelt. Therefore, he adopted the policy of paying them to refrain from voting.

[7] It has been necessary to conceal the identity of this city as well as that of the Negro college in order to protect all persons concerned in this situation.

10

Negroes
in
City
Politics

Edward C. Banfield
James Q. Wilson

In five major cities outside the South, Negroes comprise more than one fourth of the population; in two others, more than one fifth; and in five others, around one sixth. The number of Negroes in the larger central cities has been increasing rapidly. Between 1950 and 1960, the twelve largest had a net loss of more than two million whites and a net gain of nearly two million Negroes. In view of all this, one would expect to find Negroes figuring prominently in the political life of the city. They often do, but rarely because of the elective positions they hold. As Table 1 shows, remarkably few of them are elected to office.

Not only are few Negroes elected to office, but those who *are* elected generally find it necessary to be politicians first and Negroes second. If they are to stay in office, they must often soft-pedal the racial issues that are of the most concern to Negroes as Negroes. Of course, white politicians are not indifferent to the interests—or at any rate, the votes—of Negro constituents, but to the extent that the Negro wants to be represented in the sense of "symbolized" rather than "spoken on behalf of," the white politicians are obviously unable to do it. Since the Negroes do not always represent Negroes as Negroes, and since whites can and do represent Negroes to some extent, the underrepresentation of the Negro is in some respects greater and in some respects less than the figures in Table 1 suggest.

The anomaly of the Negro's numerical strength and political

weakness can be explained largely in terms of two interrelated factors: the class structure of Negro society and the character of urban political systems. Because of these factors, much of the Negro's civic action takes place, not in the city's electoral or legislative systems, but in the courts or (more recently) in the streets. And often even this "direct action" (e.g., protest marches and mass meetings), though it occurs in the cities, has the federal rather than the city government as its ultimate target.

TABLE 1: Negro representation on city councils in selected non-Southern large cities

City	Total city council seats	Seats held by Negroes in 1961	Percent of seats held by Negroes	Negroes as percent of population, 1960
Detroit	9	1	11.1	28.9
Cleveland	33	8	24.2	28.6
St. Louis	29	6	20.7	28.6
Philadelphia	17	1	5.9	26.4
Chicago	50	6[a]	12.0	22.9
Cincinnati	9	0	0	21.6
New York City	25	2	8.0	14.0
Los Angeles	15	0[b]	0	13.5
Boston	9	0	0	9.1

[a] Results of preliminary elections in 1963 indicated that Chicago would add one more Negro to its council.
[b] Results of preliminary elections in 1963 indicated that Los Angeles would probably elect two Negroes to its council.

NEGRO CLASS STRUCTURE

The most crucial fact about Negro class structure in the larger cities is that (as compared to white) the lower class is large and economically backward. So far as we are aware, no analytical comparative studies have been published in recent years. However, the Census figures in Table 2, which compare whites and nonwhites with respect to income and education, are indicative.

Lower-class people generally are withdrawn from politics, but lower-class Negroes may be especially so. To some extent, their failure to participate can be explained by the uncertainties of their situation. Uncertainty about jobs and housing and in a good many cases fear of the police keep many Negroes on the move. It is instructive that many of the Negroes participating in the 1963 demonstrations in Birmingham, Alabama, and Greenwood, Mississippi, were unemployed and therefore immune to economic reprisals by white employers. The high rate of turnover in lower-income Negro areas makes their full political mobilization particularly difficult.

TABLE 2: Distribution of income and education among whites and non-whites in Chicago, 1960

	Whites	Nonwhites
Income of families		
Percent under $3,000 per year	9.9	28.4
Percent $10,000 per year or more	26.3	8.7
Education of persons 25 and over		
Percent with less than 1 year of high school	41.6	48.0
Percent with 4 years of college or more	6.6	3.6

SOURCE: 1960 Census of Population, PC (1)-15C (Illinois).

More important than transiency, however, is the social disorganization which is characteristic of lower-class Negroes and which is reflected in their high rates of crime, delinquency, desertion, divorce, and illegitimacy. This is in great part the result of the weakness of the family unit. The plantation system during the period of slavery made it difficult to form stable Negro families; the continuing lack of economic opportunities since then has made it difficult for Negro men to acquire the economic self-sufficiency to become the head and breadwinner of a family. Female-centered households are common among Negroes, and the "wandering male" who is only a part-time worker and a part-time husband has contributed to the high percentage of Negro families supported by either working mothers or welfare checks or both.[1]

The cultural and economic factors which make the lower-class Negro's family life so uniquely precarious also make his sense of attachment to the community uniquely weak. The attributes which community life presupposes—education, self-respect, personal skills, a belief in the efficacy of one's own efforts, and a sense of attachment to social entities larger than oneself—are often in short supply because there is no strong family unit to inculcate them. Consequently, the social institutions of the city, and especially its govern-

[1] For vivid accounts of the lower-class Negro world and the family system see E. Franklin Frazier, *The Negro Family in the United States* (Chicago: University of Chicago Press, 1939); and St. Clair Drake and Horace R. Cayton, *Black Metropolis* (New York: Harcourt, Brace, 1945), chaps. xx and xxi.

ment, are often looked upon by Negroes as (at best) remote forces to be ignored or (at worst) hostile forces to be reckoned with.

The inability to feel himself part of a larger community may extend to the neighborhood and "the race" as well; these may be no more able to command his loyalty than is the city. In such circumstances, it is not surprising that, however much a lower-class Negro may talk of abstract racial issues, they have a good deal less meaning to him than specific material considerations—a job, a place to live, a bed in the county hospital, and help when he is in trouble with the police.

Like all people who respond to specific material inducements, the lower-class Negro is a natural potential supporter of the political machine. As we have explained, there are now few white neighborhoods where a ward leader's offers of jobs, favors, and patronage have much appeal. Among the large and relatively disadvantaged Negro lower class, however, the situation is still very much as it was among immigrant whites two generations ago. But there is one very important difference. Because most white voters have ceased to want the machine's favors and have even come to feel contempt for it, the machine is a thing of the past in most cities and the ward politician has few if any favors to offer. Not having the material wherewithal to organize lower-class Negro voters, many party organizations rely instead on generalized loyalties to party labels, on the attraction of well-known national candidates, or (in rare cases) on developing "race issues"—like allegations of "police brutality"—which are considered relevant by these voters.

Often, however, a party which has been stripped of patronage resources by the reform movement and therefore cannot offer specific material incentives will endeavor to woo the lower-class Negro vote with *general* material incentives particularly welfare payments of various kinds. For example, Negroes are the prime beneficiaries of the program of aid to dependent children. To curtail (or even to re-examine) such programs carries the greatest risks for a party in power because Negro voters, rightly or wrongly, will interpret such actions as "anti-Negro."

There have been some efforts to organize the Negro lower classes. The most conspicuous of these is the Black Muslim movement which uses frankly nationalistic, racist, and antiwhite sentiments to instill a sense of self-respect in Negroes.[2] By persuading the Negro that he is superior to whites, the "Muslim" leaders give

---

[2] See the account in E. U. Essien-Udom, *Black Nationalism* (Chicago: University of Chicago Press, 1962).

him a sense of his own dignity sufficient to make him behaviorally, if not economically, middle-class. And often this transformation in style of life is accompanied by an improvement in the Negro's material circumstances because he becomes more strongly motivated to acquire an education, useful skills, and a stable family. The Muslim movement disavows political or civic action, however, on the grounds that it is demeaning and disadvantageous to participate in a political and civic system which is the creation of whites and which ultimately can only serve their ends. But even if the Muslims should seek to wield influence in the cities, the nature of the movement is such that its enrolled membership can never be large. The ideology on which its appeal is based is sufficiently esoteric, restrictive, and even absurd that it cannot enlist large numbers of members.

Thus the first and most important feature of Negro social structure is the predominance of a lower class lacking a strong sense of community. And a second feature is the relative inability, or unwillingness of the middle class to identify with the lower class and to provide leadership for it. In any community, of course, it is the middle and upper classes who provide most of the civic and political leadership. But in this respect the Negro faces not only those constraints which affect any group seeking to wield influence, but an additional set which arises out of the particular nature of the Negro community.

A middle-class Negro wears a badge of color that is associated with lower-class status, and therefore cannot take for granted that the difference between him and the lower-class Negro will be appreciated. Close contact with the lower class tends to obscure the status difference which he has been at enormous pains to establish. To eat spareribs on the street would entail psychic burdens for the educated and well-to-do Negro of a kind which, it is safe to say, eating blintzes does not entail for Governor Nelson Rockefeller. At any rate, the Negro middle class conspicuously avoids contact with the lower class.[3] The Negro politician, when not

[3] The Negro middle class, according to Essien-Udom (*ibid.,* esp. p. 304), looks upon the Negro masses with contempt and shame, and the masses have no confidence in the middle class. "Most Northern lower-class Negroes do not share in any significant way the opportunities which integration 'victories' are supposed to bring them. Northern Negroes have the right to vote where they please; yet this has not brought them nearer to the 'promised land.' They are conscious of the inequality of fortunes between them and the Negro middle class and whites in general. A great many Negroes know (and are discouraged by this awareness) that they will live and die in the Black Belt. They are beginning to resent the Negro middle-class leadership. They even feel elation when a middle-class Negro is humiliated, harassed, or actually prevented by whites in his effort to enter

a member of the lower class, tends to be drawn from among those members of the middle class who are least averse to such contact. He seldom is a member of the elite of wealth and education. Often he is a new recruit to the middle class; as a politician, his class standing is likely to be marginal.

The relatively small Negro middle class is separated from the lower by differences of interest and ethos. Whereas the lower-class Negro is concerned with "welfare" goals, the middle-class Negro is concerned with "status" goals.[4] He wants the opportunity to move into an unsegregated suburb, to send his children to an unsegregated school, to join an exclusive club, to patronize the better hotels and restaurants, to have equal opportunities in his profession (to practice in an unsegregated hospital if he is a physician, for example). Needless to say, these things that are so important to the middle-class Negro rarely enter into the life of the lower-class one at all.

In some matters there is a clear conflict of interest between the two groups. The middle-class Negro, for example, may oppose establishment of a public housing project which will bring lower-class Negroes into his neighborhood, or he may support (perhaps not in a very conspicuous way) an urban renewal project which will clear out lower-class Negroes and so "upgrade" his neighborhood.[5] Police activity which the lower-class Negro finds harassing may be vigorously supported by the middle-class Negro who wants to live in peace and quiet. Such conflicts of interest are multiplied and exacerbated by residential segregation, which forces the middle class to live in the high-density slum in close proximity to the lower class.

The Negro middle class, like the white, places a relatively high value on community-regarding goals. To many of its members the primary "community" is the racial one, not the city. The preoccupation of these Negroes with status is not simply with their individual status; it is also—and often primarily—with the status of the race. To vindicate the principle of equal rights is generally at least as important to the middle-class Negro as to win concrete benefits, especially benefits of the "welfare" kind. In Chicago, for example,

---

the white society. They are indignant and humiliated when the 'exceptional' Negro marries a white person." Essien-Udom believes that a class struggle may impend between "a semisatisfied Negro middle class and the Negro masses."

[4] On this distinction, see James Q. Wilson, *Negro Politics: The Search for Leadership* (Glencoe, Ill.: Free Press, 1960), chap. viii.

[5] See Martin Meyerson and Banfield, *Politics, Planning, and the Public Interest* (Glencoe, Ill.: Free Press, 1955), p. 234.

"race men" opposed the building of a new county hospital in the hope that overcrowding of the old one would lead to the breakdown of segregation in private hospitals. To them the most important thing was to destroy the principle of discrimination, not to provide better facilities for hospital care. Probably most of the middle class —but very little of the lower class—agreed with this view.[6]

A third important feature of Negro social structure is the fairly large and growing number of young people who have more education than the job market enables them to use. Between 1940 and 1960 the Negro's education improved greatly. His relative income improved also, but by no means as much, and most of the improvement occurred as long ago as World War II. Table 2 indicates that although Negro-white disparities in income are great, in education they are much less.

The consequence is that there are now a great many Negroes who are, so to say, half in and half out of the middle class. Some have college degrees but can find nothing better to do than work as postmen, clerks, and the like. Others find jobs in their chosen fields—they are lawyers, professors, and journalists, for example—only to discover that their employers will not promote them. Most of these young people live in the larger cities. Having plenty of time and nothing much to lose, they become the activists in Negro civic associations. As such they are dedicated, militant, and highly articulate.

A fourth important feature of Negro social structure is the relative fewness of entrepreneurs and the consequent importance of professionals. There are very few Negro-owned businesses of any size; most of the large businesses Negroes patronize—even illegitimate ones like "policy" (a form of gambling for small amounts)— are run by whites. Few Negroes, therefore, are wealthy enough to support large-scale political undertakings. Most of the proprietors are owners of very small retail stores and service establishments. The prosperous members of the middle class are mostly professionals. Negro professionals, like white ones, often tend to be antipolitical in outlook and to come under pressure from the institutions they work for—especially schools and government agencies—to stay clear both of partisan politics and of controversy of any kind.

A fifth feature of Negro social structure is that many important individuals and institutions have a vested interest in the maintenance of discrimination and segregation. Negro churches, political organizations, voluntary associations, schools, and businesses

    [6] See Banfield, *Political Influence* (New York: Free Press of Glencoe, 1961), chap. ii, esp. p. 43.

—and therefore, of course, the individuals whose jobs and status depend upon them—benefit from discrimination both because it is their reason for being and because it frees them from the necessity of competing on equal terms with whites. Residential segregation benefits them additionally by affording economies of scale: the more that members or customers are concentrated in one place, the better the opportunities to organize or serve them. "Had it not been for segregation," a Negro alderman in Chicago was quoted as saying, "Negroes would not have been able to advance politically here. It's the same with Negro business—segregation has been a Godsend to Negro business. It's nothing new. The Poles seek out the Poles, the Germans seek out the Germans. Why shouldn't Negroes seek out Negroes?"[7]

That Negro institutions and leaders have this vested interest does not mean, of course, that they can be depended upon to support discrimination and segregation. To do that would get them in trouble with the large sector of Negro opinion that is influenced by "race" men. As a rule, moreover, antidiscrimination and antisegregation measures take effect so slowly and incompletely as not to endanger them greatly anyway. The Negro politician or minister can support a bill for "open occupancy" secure in the knowledge that its passage (which in itself may be unlikely) will not precipitate a mass exodus from the slum to the white suburbs. The individuals and institutions with a vested interest in discrimination and segregation are seldom to be found among the most aggressive fighters for reform, but they are not likely to be open opponents of it either unless it touches them very closely.

Negro civic organizations are small in size and short on resources. This is a sixth feature of Negro social structure, and one that is to a large extent explained by the other five.

In most cities that have substantial numbers of Negroes there are only one or two permanent Negro civic associations. The National Association for the Advancement of Colored People (NAACP), a militant Negro-rights organization, has (as of 1959) 1,366 branches and about 350,000 members. The Urban League, which until a few years ago was mainly occupied in finding jobs for selected Negroes but which now concerns itself with a wide range of problems, exists in most large cities. Although staffed and led by Negroes, it is largely financed by whites.

Recently four other organizations, all utilizing a protest

[7] *Chicago Sun-Times,* Jan 6, 1963, p. 36. The alderman, Kenneth E. Campbell, was described as the heir apparent to the political power of Congressman William E. Dawson.

strategy to advance their ends, have become an important part of Negro civic affairs. One is the Congress of Racial Equality (CORE); another is the Student Nonviolent Co-ordinating Committee (SNCC). Both utilize the "sit-in" and other forms of direct protest action. A third is the Southern Christian Leadership Conference (SCLC), the organizational extension of the personality of its founder, the Rev. Martin Luther King, Jr., the leader of the Montgomery, Alabama, bus boycott and later of the Birmingham protest marches. These three groups have been primarily (although not exclusively) active in Southern cities where the targets for protest are many and obvious and where little in the way of Negro political organization exists to impede them. The fourth group is scarcely an organization at all but rather a deliberately amorphous boycott movement led, in various Northern cities, by Negro ministers—a group which for many years has played a relatively small role in militant Negro civic action of this kind. The ministers have induced Negroes, often with surprising effectiveness, to boycott certain business firms which failed to respond to Negro demands for jobs or promotions. The movement, which began in Philadelphia, is called the "selective patronage campaign." It is a frank effort to compel businesses to re-divide the existing supply of jobs.

Lower-class Negroes play little part in most of these organizations. Nor can the middle class be said to support them very well. NAACP's membership is small (see Table 3). Moreover, of the few Negroes who contribute money to NAACP, still fewer contribute time and effort. A large NAACP branch is doing well if it turns out 10 percent of its membership for a meeting and 2 percent for active committee work. The average member contributes only his two-dollar minimum membership fee. Because of the indifference of most members, it is usually easy for a handful of militants to dominate the activities of a branch, at least until there is a general membership meeting. Then conservatives, who often control blocs of votes through affiliation with churches, businesses, labor unions, and ward political organizations, are likely to join forces to sweep the militants out.

The older, permanent Negro civic association, like the permanent white one, tends to be immobilized in matters of importance by conflict over the concrete meaning of its goals. The newer, often *ad hoc* organizations, the memberships of which are more cohesive because they are concerned with only one issue, are usually readier to take a stand and to act; however, they suffer the disadvantage of having few allies and little money.

Negro civic associations, both permanent and *ad hoc* ones, are generally most effective (in the North) when acting as "veto groups," trying to block a measure harmful to Negro interests. They have succeeded in preventing transfers of children from one school to another, in stopping land clearance projects, and in checking mistreatment of individuals by the police. They have been least effective in initiating new policies and programs, particularly ones the importance of which is mainly symbolic or ideological and which would benefit not specifiable individuals but the "race" in general.[8]

TABLE 3: NAACP membership relative to Negro population in selected cities

City	NAACP membership, 1959	NAACP members as percent of 1960 Negro population
Boston	4,859	7.7
Cleveland	12,318	4.9
Detroit	16,746	3.5
St. Louis	7,234	3.4
Baltimore	8,830	2.7
San Francisco	1,583	2.1
Chicago	12,051	1.5
Los Angeles	4,328	1.3
Philadelphia	6,797	1.3

Source of membership figures: Files of national headquarters, NAACP (New York City).

Given all these circumstances, what is remarkable is that any effective Negro civic action occurs at all. Yet it does, and more so each year. The source of much of this activity can be found in the college-educated but underemployed young men and women who constitute in many cities the backbone of the Negro volunteer activists in the NAACP, the "selective patronage campaign," and similar movements. And the successes of this group have raised the level of expectations governing the behavior of other, more conservative Negroes, with the result that the tempo and militancy of Negro civic action as a whole increases steadily. But because of the nature of these activists, the goals sought and methods employed are often of a special kind—status rather than welfare goals, protest rather than bargaining tactics, and with middle-class rather than lower-class backing. Institutions most susceptible to such campaigns are typically those such as city agencies which have legal power over

[8] See on this James Q. Wilson, "The Strategy of Protest: Problems of Negro Civic Action," *Journal of Conflict Resolution,* September 1961, pp. 291–303.

some community activity and which in turn are vulnerable to lawsuits, political pressures, and adverse public sentiment. Thus, boards of education and police departments find themselves increasingly under attack in Northern cities by militant Negroes concerned about *"de facto"* school segregation and police treatment of minorities.

Finally, it must be said that the Negro middle class has always been the beneficiary of civic action undertaken in its behalf by white liberals (often Jews) whose political ethos is markedly Anglo-Saxon Protestant. In Chicago, agitation for a state fair employment practices act was for many years led almost entirely by Jewish organizations (even though few Jews expected to benefit from such a law); the campaign for integrated public housing projects was waged largely by an *ad hoc* group of white liberals; opposition to an urban renewal project (on the grounds that it was anti-Negro) was primarily the result of efforts of a Catholic monsignor and a few Jewish allies. In New York, where Jewish and liberal organizations are even more abundant, race relations have been even more an activity of whites. The organization which led the successful fight for various "open occupancy" laws to eliminate discrimination in private housing was created largely by Jews and (although it had several prominent Negro officers) relied on white financing and white staffs.

Many Negroes regard this assistance as a mixed blessing. No one likes to take advice or be placed in a subordinate position in a cause which he feels is peculiarly his own. But perhaps more importantly, Negroes are beginning to feel that their white allies will not go "all the way" with them in efforts (such as selective patronage campaigns and other direct action rather than legalistic programs) to attain something more than purely symbolic victories.

THE EFFECT OF THE POLITICAL SYSTEM

These features of the social structure set certain boundaries (so to speak) on the nature of the Negro's participation in the politics of the city. Within these boundaries, however, a considerable variety of styles of Negro politics is possible. Which style will exist in a particular city depends mainly upon the nature of that city's political system. In other words, the nature of Negro politics (within the bounds set by social structure) depends largely upon the nature of white politics.

We will amplify and illustrate this general proposition by characterizing briefly the style of Negro politics in cities whose political systems are of the following kinds: (1) ward-based,[9] machine; (2) ward-based, weak organization or factions and followings; (3) proportional representation; and (4) nonpartisan, at-large.

Ward-based, Machine

In a city with a partisan, ward-based machine, Negroes will be organized as a sub-machine and will have as many representatives in the council as there are wards dominated by the sub-machine. The councilmen will not (at least publicly) take a "race" point of view, however, or indeed any point of view not tolerated by the leaders of the citywide machine. Chicago is a case in point. Negroes there have long had machine-style politics.[10] For many years the most powerful Negro boss has been Congressman William L. Dawson, who controls five all-Negro wards and therefore a large contingent of ward committeemen, aldermen, and state representatives. Control of these wards gives Dawson a safe seat in Congress (he is chairman of the House Government Operations Committee) and a place in the high councils of the Democratic National Committee.

Dawson maintains his machine in the usual way, by exchanging jobs, favors, and protection for votes. Almost every weekend he flies to Chicago to sit in a shabby ward office in the midst of the slums and to listen to all who come to him. Where the direct, material interests of his constituents are at stake, he and his organization are ready to help; they will get a sick man into the county hospital, find out why an old lady's welfare check has not arrived, defend a beleaguered homeowner against the urban renewal authority, and go to the police commissioner, and if necessary the mayor, to see to it that a case of alleged police brutality is properly investigated. Matters involving Negro rights in the abstract do not interest them, however. These concern the militants, but they are not the base upon which the machine builds.

In the realm of general principles, Dawson is virtually apolit-

[9] We use the word "ward" in a broad sense here to refer to any arrangement that enables a Negro candidate to face a geographically drawn constituency that is entirely, or mainly, Negro. The ward system is in contradiction to the at-large one, in which the candidate faces the (predominantly white) electorate of the whole city.

[10] For the history of Negro participation in Chicago politics, see Harold Gosnell, *The Negro Politician* (Chicago: University of Chicago Press, 1935). For an account of contemporary Negro politics there and of Congressman Dawson in particular, see Wilson, *Negro Politics:* and Wilson, "Two Negro Politicians: An Interpretation," *Midwest Journal of Political Science,* November 1960, pp. 346–369.

ical. He very rarely speaks in the House (although he is highly regarded by the House leadership). On occasion he has publicly opposed the "race" position on important questions and at least once he and his lieutenants packed a membership meeting of the Chicago NAACP chapter in order to unseat a militant officer. In the city council it is the Jewish alderman from the University of Chicago ward who takes the initiative in race relations. The Negro aldermen vote for the measures he introduces, but they do not fight for them.

The Dawson machine is only part of the larger one controlled by Mayor Daley. In order to maintain his sub-machine, Dawson has to depend on Daley for patronage. He and those whom he controls must therefore support the candidates slated by Daley and the legislation proposed by him. No Negro aldermen connected with the organization would seriously propose any measure that had not been cleared with Daley, and no Democratic Negro precinct captain would fail to urge a voter to vote against a Negro and for a white if the white was the organization candidate. "Ticket splitting," a Negro ward leader explained in a newspaper interview, "weakens my force." He was quoted as follows: "When I report to the central committee that 15 to 20 percent of the people in my ward split their tickets, I'm not as strong as the man with 95 percent straight ballots. The Negro gains more by voting for a party and not for a Negro candidate. Candidates on a partisan ticket should get all of the votes of that party—not just the Negro ones, or the Irish ones, or those of some other group."[11]

Ward-based, Weak Organization

In a partisan city with ward constituencies but a weak party organization (e.g., a decayed machine) or a coterie of factions and followings, as many Negroes will be elected to office as there are wards in which Negroes are in a majority, and the Negro politicians will be those who can develop personal followings or take advantage of intraparty factionalism. Manhattan is one example. Its political system does not provide Harlem politicians with sufficient patronage and other resources to build strong organizations, nor does it give city-wide politicians sufficient resources to control the Negro leaders.[12] Because of the lack of party-controlled material resources, Negro politicians in Harlem compete with personal followings (sometimes based on racial demagoguery) and with club-based factions.

[11] *Chicago Sun-Times,* Jan. 6, 1963, p. 38.
[12] Elsewhere in New York City—Brooklyn, for example—there is a party machine, and Negro politics is much as it is in Chicago. See Wilson, "Two Negro Politicians: An Interpretation."

Congressman Adam Clayton Powell, Jr., the principal Harlem politician, is an example of the kind of politician such a system produces. For many years the pastor of a large and fashionable church, he is entirely without ward or precinct organization. A constituent would not go to him for a job or a favor (although they might go to one of his aides in his *church*). His appeal is almost entirely personal and ideological. He is handsome, eloquent, flamboyant and—at least as he appears to his public—passionately and uncompromisingly dedicated to the cause of racial justice. This being the basis of his power, Powell is beyond the reach of party discipline. Whereas Mayor Daley and Dawson can talk to each other as two executives of the same organization and whereas Daley as head of the organization can give orders to Dawson, Mayor Wagner can do little or nothing to influence Powell.

Also in Harlem is J. Raymond Jones, a Negro politician whose stock in trade is not ideology or racism but rather his exceptional ability to survive and even prosper in the bitter factional warfare of the community. He has usually been able, by carefully timed alliances, to obtain enough patronage, favors, and nominations for elective office to maintain a firm hold on one part of Harlem but not to dominate for long all parts of Harlem. He was almost the only Tammany leader who foresaw that Mayor Wagner was going to defeat Tammany in the 1961 primary and who joined with the mayor in time to take advantage of that victory.

The factional politics of Cleveland is somewhat similar. There, most of the eight Negro councilmen maintain followings in all-Negro neighborhoods by being good fellows, by providing the associational attractions of political clubs, and by distributing limited amounts of patronage and favors. A few, however, are race-conscious, issue-oriented leaders whose appeal cuts across neighborhood lines. If the neighborhood-based councilmen had more patronage and other resources at their disposal they would doubtless convert their followings into full-fledged machines and take the seats of the issue-oriented councilmen. By the same token, if their political resources were less, they would probably be supplanted themselves by the issue-oriented politicians. As matters stand, both lower-class and middle-class elements of the Negro community are represented in the council; for that very reason, of course, the Negro councilmen do not constitute a unified bloc.

Proportional Representation

Proportional representation deserves brief mention here (despite the fact that it is used in only one city) because it leads by a different route to a result like that just described. Under PR, a Negro candidate appeals to what is for all practical purposes an all-Negro constituency (election is at-large, but the Negro expects to attract mainly Negro votes). In a PR city, too, the candidate has no patronage or other political resources with which to build an organization; therefore he too must depend upon showmanship and racial ideology. In Cincinnati, PR produced a Negro councilman as militant as Congressman Powell (although neither as flamboyant nor as unpredictable). This, indeed, was the principal reason why it was abandoned there in 1957.[13]

Nonpartisan, At-large

In a city with a nonpartisan, at-large system the nature of Negro politics is radically affected by the fact that the candidate must face the whole (predominantly white) electorate and must do so without benefit of a party label. Detroit is a city with a system of this kind. In order to have any chance of success, a Negro candidate for the Detroit city council must have the support of a newspaper or of some important city-wide civic associations. This means that he must be acceptable to middle-class whites. A Negro who is light-skinned, Harvard-educated, and "reasonable" on racial questions stands the best chance. Although almost 30 percent of the people of Detroit are Negroes, there is only one Negro councilman among nine.

A Negro elected under the circumstances that prevail in Detroit is in an extremely difficult position. Without a strong Negro vote he cannot hope to be re-elected, and to get a strong Negro vote he must (since he has no jobs, favors, or other material inducements to offer) be aggressive on at least some racial issues. But he must also have the support of the press and the civic associations in order to be re-elected, and he will not have this unless he is "reasonable" from the standpoint of conservative, middle-class whites. Recently, Detroit's one Negro councilman narrowly escaped being crushed between these two forces. Charges were made of police brutality. The Negro councilman introduced a measure empowering the Human Relations Commission to investigate the police department. This became an election issue. Somewhat surprisingly,

---

[13] On Negro politics under PR in Cincinnati, see Ralph A. Straetz, *PR Politics in Cincinnati* (New York: New York University Press, 1958), esp. chap. viii. The circumstances under which PR was abandoned are described in Kenneth Gray, *A Report on City Politics in Cincinnati* (Cambridge, Mass.: Joint Center for Urban Studies, 1959, mimeo).

a newspaper supported him and he was re-elected. Whether he can survive many such issues is hard to say.

NEGRO POLITICS IN THE SOUTH

What we have said applies to Northern cities; the situation in the South is different. In the smaller Southern cities, Negroes have generally been denied the right to vote or to hold office, and consequently their influence in civic affairs has been negligible. This has not been the case everywhere, however. In Atlanta, where almost a third of the population is Negro, Negroes have voted for many years and they have often held the balance of power between white candidates.[14]

After the school desegregation decision of 1954, the race issue came to dominate the politics of many Southern cities and the power of the Negro increased. Negroes registered to vote in large numbers, partly because federal laws and court orders gave them protection at the polls and partly because the urbanization and industrialization of the South raised their income and educational level and made them more politically conscious and assertive. Today about 25 percent of the eligible Negroes in the South are registered to vote. These are heavily concentrated in the larger cities.

In these cities, Negro political associations are forming and growing at a rapid rate. In Florida, for example, where between 1944 and 1956 Negro registration rose from 5.5 per cent to 37.5 percent of eligibles, many political leagues, or voters' associations, have sprung up. In some instances these began under church auspices and then soon broke away. They have developed effective tactics for identifying to the Negro voter the candidates who are preferable without at the same time running the risk of hurting the candidates' standing with their anti-Negro white constituents, and they have organized the Negro voters to make their endorsements effective at the polls.[15] Unlike the ethnic associations that have long existed in the North, these leagues do not seek "recognition" by electing their own representatives to office. That is out of the question in most places, and therefore the Southern Negro political league concentrates on trading votes for commitments from white politicians. In the nature of the case, they cannot rely on financial contributions

---

[14] See Floyd Hunter, *Community Power Structure* (Chapel Hill: University of North Carolina Press, 1953), pp. 49–50.

[15] H. D. Price, *The Negro and Southern Politics: A Chapter of Florida History* (New York: New York University Press, 1957), pp. 67–81.

from Negroes who expect to be elected to office or who are already in office (there are too few of them); to a considerable extent, therefore, they get them from whites who want their endorsement.

In the North the goals of lower-class and middle-class Negroes are often in conflict and the political process tends to exacerbate the conflict. In the South, by contrast, Negroes of all social classes want very much the same things—especially desegregation of schools and public accommodations, access to buses and eating places, and voting rights—and their common struggle tends to unify them. In the South, too, the issues confronting the Negro are of a kind that lend themselves well to the use of the tactics of mass protest and litigation. There is evidence that Negro civic leaders in the South are more nearly in agreement on goals and have more support from their followers than in the North.[16]

HUMAN RELATIONS AGENCIES

More and more large cities have created, as either independent agencies or as committees under the office of the mayor, public human relations organizations whose task it is to supervise the enforcement of civil rights ordinances and to act as fact-finding and mediation agencies. The Chicago Commission on Human Relations, established in 1943, was the first of these and it is still one of the largest. It has a staff of about thirty professional and clerical employees, and a budget of about a quarter of a million dollars a year. As of 1961, forty or so other cities in the United States had created, by ordinance, such commissions. Fifteen of these are in Illinois. Comparable commissions can be found in New York, Detroit, Philadelphia, and elsewhere. In addition, there are committees—not endowed with statutory authority—which advise mayors on race matters. Because cities in many cases do not have the constitutional authority to enact laws in this field, legislation barring discrimination in public accommodations, housing, employment, medical facilities, and such areas has often been enacted by the state; and state agencies such as New York's State Commission Against Discrimination have been created to supervise enforcement.

[16] See M. Elaine Burgess, *Negro Leadership in a Southern City* (Chapel Hill: University of North Carolina Press, 1962). Compare the case histories of issues reported there with those discussed in Wilson, *Negro Politics,* which deals with a Northern city. More data will be available upon the publication by Donald R. Matthews and James W. Prothro of their large-scale study of Negro political participation and community action in the South.

Indeed, so many public and private agencies have sprung up in this field that the staff members of such groups have formed a professional society, the National Association of Intergroup Relations Officials (NAIRO), and are publishing a journal.

A public human relations commission occupies a crucial but ambiguous role in the politics of race relations. On the one hand, it is a staff agency created to advise the mayor; on the other hand, it is looked to for "action" by various individuals and groups who have grievances in this field. Furthermore, it has its own conception—ingrained in the staff—of its mission to remedy certain conditions even if no one organizes a formal complaint and the mayor does not ask for advice; in such cases, the human relations agency does not act as the transmission belt which carries reports of outrages suffered from the point of grievance to the mayor, city council, or city attorney, nor does it provide the mayor with advice on what remedial policies are needed and then sit back and wait while the mayor drafts an appropriate ordinance or executive order. On the contrary, the commission is usually engaged simultaneously in stimulating protest and then proposing solutions to the mayor to eliminate the protest thus stimulated. This, of course, entails an elaborate pattern of negotiation and an organizational ability to face in several directions at once.

The very structure of Negro civic life means that a public race relations agency, if it does anything at all, must act in part as a combination of NAACP and Urban League. When Negro organizations are prevented by internal constraints from pressing for a certain goal, the commission must organize pressure of its own. When the Negro organizations *are* spontaneously exerting influence, the commission often discovers that action in the particular area is not feasible and it thus must find some way of stopping or diverting the protest activity. At the same time, the commission must maintain good relations with affected private white organizations—businesses, labor unions, hospitals, schools, and so forth—so that it can negotiate some kind of acceptable solution to a given race problem which the mayor can then ratify. In the circumstances it is hardly surprising that city human relations commissions are seldom completely successful.

Race becomes an issue in other kinds of city agencies as well, not just in those primarily charged with human relations work. In most large cities, it is an unwritten but unbreakable rule that a Negro must be appointed to certain kinds of boards and commissions—the public housing authority, the school board, the urban renewal or land clearance agency, perhaps the police commission, and so forth. The extent to which such Negro "representation" has an effect on the substance of public policy in these areas is problematical; in any case, it is sure to vary greatly from city to city. Everything depends on the terms on which the appointment is made.

In a city such as Chicago, where the Democratic party is powerful and where politics controls rewards sought by many, the mayor can appoint a Negro almost on his own terms. There are plenty of lawyers who depend on the party for business, advancement, and judicial appointments, even though they may hold no public or party office. Their service on a public commission is shaped by their expectations of future rewards and penalties and—what is equally important—by habits and attitudes acquired over years of intimate acquaintance with political leaders and deep involvement in the party's style of life.

In cities where there is no controlling party, where politics is nonpartisan or factional, and where each person must build his own career on an individual basis, Negroes may be able to dictate the terms on which they will accept appointment. Every city administration needs to legitimize its decisions; every city administration resorts, in some measure, to group representation as a way of achieving this legitimacy; but cities vary greatly in the extent to which they really depend on this sort of "front." Where the city administration lacks other sources of authority—where it has no machine and no faithful followers—it may attach a very high value indeed to the legitimacy that group representation can confer. In such a case it must seek out those representatives, including Negroes and other minorities, who have the greatest prestige as a result of their participation in *nonpolitical* activities—voluntary associations, businesses, churches, education, and so forth. The price the city must pay to obtain such men, of course, is a willingness to alter substantive policies to take into account the objections and recommendations of the members of the commission.[17]

[17] Philip Selznick makes a similar argument when he distinguishes between "formal" and "informal" co-optation in the TVA. "Formal" co-optation reflects the need to establish the legitimacy of the institution without actually sharing power (this corresponds to Negro appointments in Chicago). "Informal" co-optation refers to the need to adjust the institution to specific centers of power in the community by actually sharing power. Selznick, *TVA and the Grass Roots* (Berkeley: University of California Press, 1953), pp. 259 ff.

11
The Making of the Negro Mayors 1967

Jeffrey K. Hadden
Louis H. Masotti
Victor Thiessen

Throughout most of 1967, black power and Vietnam kept this nation in an almost continual state of crisis. The summer months were the longest and hottest in modern U.S. history—many political analysts even felt that the nation was entering its most serious domestic conflict since the Civil War. Over a hundred cities were rocked with violence.

As the summer gave way to autumn, the interest of the nation shifted a little from the summer's riots to the elections on the first Tuesday of November. An unprecedented number of Negroes were running for office, but public attention focused on three elections. In Cleveland, Carl B. Stokes, a lawyer who in 1962 had become the first Democratic Negro legislator in Ohio, was now seeking to become the first Negro mayor of a large American city. In Gary, Ind., another young Negro lawyer, Richard D. Hatcher, was battling the Republican Party's candidate—as well as his own Democratic Party—to become the first Negro mayor of a "medium-sized" city. And in Boston, Louise Day Hicks, a symbol of white backlash, was conducting a "You know where I stand" campaign to capture the mayoralty.

Normally, the nation couldn't care less about who would become the next mayors of Cleveland, Gary, and Boston. But the tenseness of the summer months gave these elections enormous significance. If Stokes and Hatcher lost and Hicks won, could

Reprinted by permission from Jeffrey K. Hadden, Louis H. Masotti, and Victor Thiessen, "The Making of the Negro Mayors 1967," *Trans*-action 5, no. 3 (January/February, 1968) pp. 21–30. Copyright © by *Trans*-action Magazine, New Brunswick, N.J.

Negroes be persuaded to use the power of the ballot box rather than the power of fire bombs?

Fortunately, November 7 proved to be a triumphant day for racial peace. Stokes and Hatcher won squeaker victories, both by margins of only about 1500 votes; in Boston, Kevin H. White defeated Mrs. Hicks by a 12,000 plurality. Labor leader George Meany was exultant—"American voters have rejected racism as a political issue." Negroes in the three cities were also jubilant. In Gary, the most tense of the cities, Richard Hatcher urged the mostly Negro crowd at his headquarters to "cool it." "I urge that the outcome of this election be unmarred by any incident of any kind. . . . If we spoil this victory with any kind of occurrence here tonight, or any-where in the city, it will be a hollow victory." The evening *was* cool: Joyous Negroes danced and sang in the streets.

But beyond the exultation of victory remain many hard questions. Now that Cleveland and Gary have Negro mayors, just how much difference will it make in solving the many grave prob-lems that these cities face? Will these victories cool militancy in urban ghettos next summer, or will the momentum of frustration prove too great to put on the brakes? A careful analysis of *how* these candidates won office may help provide the answers.

The focus of this report is on Cleveland because:

• As residents of Cleveland, we are more familiar with the campaign and the election.

• Cleveland is unique because, in 1965, it had a special census. By matching voting wards with census tracts, we can draw a clearer picture of voting behavior than we could in the other cities, where rapid neighborhood transitions have made 1960 census data quite unreliable in assessing voting patterns. Having examined Cleveland in some detail, we will draw some comparisons with the Gary and Boston elections, then speculate about their significance and impli-cations.

CLEVELAND—CITY IN DECLINE

Cleveland has something less than 2,000,000 residents. Among metropolitan areas in America, it ranks eleventh in size. Like many other American cities, the central city of Cleveland is experiencing an absolute decline in population—residents are flee-ing from the decaying core to the surrounding suburbs. The city certainly ranks high both in terms of absolute and proportional decline in the central-city population.

Between 1950 and 1960, the population of the central city declined from 914,808 to 876,050, a loss of almost 39,000. By 1965 the population had sunk to 810,858, an additional loss of 65,000. But these figures are only a partial reflection of the changing composition of the population, since new Negro residents coming into the central city helped offset the white exodus. *Between 1950 and 1960, nearly 142,000 white residents left the central city, and an additional 94,000 left between 1960 and 1965—nearly a quarter of a million in just 15 years.*

During the same period the number of Negro residents of Cleveland rose from 147,847 to 279,352—an increase from 16.1 percent to 34.4 percent of the city's population. There is no evidence that this dramatic population redistribution has changed since the special 1965 census. Some suburbanization of Negroes is beginning on the east and southeast side of the city, but the pace is not nearly so dramatic as for whites. In 1960, approximately 97 percent of the Negroes in the metropolitan area lived in the central city. This percentage has probably declined somewhat since then—16,000 Negro residents have moved to East Cleveland. But the basic pattern of segregation in the metropolitan area remains. The development in East Cleveland is little more than an eastward extension of the ghetto, and the older, decaying residential units the Negroes have moved to are hardly "suburban" in character.

While the population composition of Cleveland is changing rapidly, whites are still a significant majority—about 62 percent. Again like many other central cities, a significant percentage of the white population comprises nationality groups that live in segregated sections, with a strong sense of ethnic identity and a deep fear of Negro encroachment. (In 1964, the bussing of Negro students into Murray Hill, an Italian neighborhood, resulted in rioting.)

In 1960, the census classified 43 percent of the central city's white residents as "foreign stock." In that year, five groups—Germans, Poles, Czechs, Hungarians, and Italians—had populations of 25,000 or greater; at least 20 other nationality groups were large enough to have to be contended with in the political arena. But today these ethnic groups—although unwilling to admit it—have become less than the controlling majority they constituted before 1960.

The Cuyahoga River divides Cleveland, physically as well as socially. When Negroes first began to move into the city, during World War I, they occupied the decaying section to the south and east of the central business district. As their numbers grew, they continued pushing in this direction and now occupy the larger part of the eastside (except for some ethnic strongholds). There are no stable, integrated neighborhoods in the central city—only areas in transition from white to black. To the west, the Cuyahoga River constitutes a barrier to Negro penetration.

Ever since 1941, when Frank Lausche was elected, Cleveland has had a succession of basically honest but unimaginative Democratic mayors. These mayors have kept their hold on City Hall by means of a relatively weak coalition of nationality groups. At no point in this 26-year Lausche dynasty did a mayor gather enough power to seriously confront the long-range needs and problems of the city.

By early 1967, the city had seemingly hit rock bottom. A long procession of reporters began arriving to write about its many problems. The racial unrest of the past several years had, during the summer of 1966, culminated in the worst rioting in Cleveland's history. This unrest was continuing to grow as several militant groups were organizing. Urban renewal was a dismal failure; in January, the Department of Housing and Urban Development even cut off the city's urban-renewal funds, the first such action by the Federal Government. The exodus of whites, along with business, shoved the city to the brink of financial disaster. In February, the Moody Bond Survey reduced the city's credit rating. In May, the Federal Government cut off several million dollars of construction funds—because the construction industry had failed to assure equal job opportunities for minority groups. In short, the city was, and remains, in deep trouble. And while most ethnic groups probably continued to believe that Cleveland was the "Best Location in the Nation," the Negro community—and a growing number of whites— were beginning to feel that Cleveland was the "Mistake on the Lake," and that it was time for a change.

Carl Stokes's campaign for mayor was his second try. In 1965, while serving in the state House of Representatives, he came within 2100 votes of defeating Mayor Ralph S. Locher. Stokes had taken advantage of a city-charter provision that lets a candidate file as an independent, and bypass the partisan primaries. Ralph McAllister, then president of the Cleveland School Board, did the same. For his hard line on *de facto* school segregation, however, McAllister had earned the enmity of the Negro community. The Republican candidate was Ralph Perk, the first Republican elected to a county-wide position (auditor) in many years. A second generation Czech-Bohemian, Perk hoped to win by combining his ethnic appeals with his program for the city (Perk's Plan). He had no opposition for his party's nomination. The fourth candidate was

Mayor Locher, who had defeated Mark McElroy, county recorder and perennial candidate for something, in the Democratic primary.

It was in the 1965 Democratic primary that the first signs of a "black bloc" vote emerged. The Negroes, who had previously supported incumbent Democratic mayoral candidates, if not enthusiastically at least consistently, made a concerted effort to dump Locher in favor of McElroy. There were two reasons.

• Locher had supported his police chief after the latter had made some tactless remarks about Negroes. Incensed Negro leaders demanded an audience with the mayor, and when he refused, his office was the scene of demonstrations, sit-ins, and arrests. At that point, as one of the local reporters put it, "Ralph Locher became a dirty name in the ghetto."

• Stokes, as an independent, and his supporters hoped that the Democratic primary would eliminate the *stronger* candidate, Locher. For then a black bloc would have a good chance of deciding the general election because of an even split in the white vote.

Despite the Negro community's efforts, Locher won the primary and went on to narrowly defeat Stokes. Locher received 37 percent of the vote, Stokes 36 percent, Perk 17 percent, and McAllister 9 percent. Some observers reported that a last-minute whispering campaign in Republican precincts—to the effect that "A vote for Perk is a vote for Stokes"—may have given Locher enough Republican votes to win. The evidence: The popular Perk received only a 17 percent vote in a city where a Republican could be expected to receive something closer to 25 percent. Had Perk gotten anything close to 25 percent, Stokes would have probably been elected two years earlier.

Although he made a strong showing in defeat, Carl Stokes's political future looked bleak. No one expected the Democratic leaders to give Stokes another opportunity to win by means of a split vote. Nor were there other desirable elected offices Stokes could seek. Cleveland has no Negro Congressman—largely because the heavy Negro concentration in the city has been "conveniently" gerrymandered. The only district where Stokes might have had a chance has been represented by Charles Vanik, a popular and liberal white, and as long as Vanik remained in Congress Stokes was locked out. Stokes's state Senate district was predominantly white; and a county or state office seemed politically unrealistic because of his race. So, in 1966, Stokes sought re-election to the State House unopposed.

Between 1965 and 1967, Cleveland went from bad to worse, physically, socially, and financially. With no other immediate possibilities, Stokes began to think about running for mayor again. The big question was whether to risk taking on Locher in the primary—or to file as an independent again.

THE PRIMARY RACE

In effect, Stokes's decision was made for him. Seth Taft, slated to be the Republican candidate, told Stokes he would withdraw from the election entirely if Stokes filed as an independent in order to gain the advantage of a three-man general election. Taft had concluded that his best strategy was to face a Negro, *alone,* or a faltering incumbent, *alone,* in the general election. But not both. In a three-man race with Locher and Stokes, Taft correctly assumed that he would be the man in the middle with no chance for victory. (Taft would have preferred to run as an independent—to gain Democratic votes—but the county Republican leader threatened to file *another* Republican candidate unless Taft ran as a Republican.)

Meanwhile, Locher committed blunder after blunder—and Democratic party leaders began to question whether he could actually win another election. In the weeks before filing for the primary, Democratic leaders even pressured Locher to accept a Federal judgeship and clear the way for the president of the city council to run. But the Democratic leaders in Cleveland are not noted for their strength or effectiveness, as is evidenced by the fact that none of the Democratic mayors since 1941 were endorsed by the party when they were first elected. When Locher refused to withdraw, the party reluctantly rallied behind him.

Another Democratic candidate was Frank P. Celeste, former mayor of the Republican westside suburb of Lakewood. Celeste established residency in the city, announced his candidacy early, and—despite pressure from the Democratic Party—remained in the primary race.

There was always the possibility that Celeste would withdraw from the primary, which would leave Stokes facing Locher alone. But the threat of Taft's withdrawal from the general election left Stokes with little choice but to face Locher head-on in the primary. A primary race against Locher and a strong Democrat was more appealing than a general election against Locher and a weak Republican.

Now, in 1965 Stokes had received only about 6000 white votes in the city in a 239,000 voter turnout. To win in the primary, he had to enlarge and consolidate the Negro vote—and increase his white support on the westside and in the eastside ethnic wards.

The first part of his strategy was a massive voter-registration drive in the Negro wards—to reinstate the potential Stokes voters dropped from the rolls for failing to vote since the 1964 Presidential election. The Stokes organization—aided by Martin Luther King Jr. and the Southern Christian Leadership Conference, as well as by a grant (in part earmarked for voter registration) from the Ford Foundation to the Cleveland chapter of CORE—did succeed in registering many Negroes. But there was a similar drive mounted by the Democratic Party on behalf of Locher. (Registration figures are not available by race.)

The second part of the Stokes startegy took him across the polluted Cuyahoga River into the white wards that had given him a mere 3 percent of the vote in 1965. He spoke wherever he would be received—to small groups in private homes, in churches, and in public and private halls. While he was not always received enthusiastically, he did not confront many hostile crowds. He faced the race issue squarely and encouraged his audience to judge him on his ability.

Stokes's campaign received a big boost when the *Plain Dealer,* the largest daily in Ohio, endorsed him. Next, the *Cleveland Press* called for a change in City Hall, but declined to endorse either Stokes or Celeste. But since the polls indicated that Celeste was doing very badly, this amounted to an endorsement of Stokes.

More people voted in this primary than in any other in Cleveland's history. When the ballots were counted, Stokes had 52.5 percent of the votes—he had defeated Locher by a plurality of 18,000 votes. Celeste was the man in the middle, getting only 4 percent of the votes, the lowest of any mayoral candidate in recent Cleveland history.

What produced Stokes's clear victory? Table 1 reveals the answer. The decisive factor was the size of the Negro turnout. While Negroes constituted only about 40 percent of the voters, 73.4 percent of them turned out, compared with only 58.4 percent of the whites. Predominantly Negro wards cast 96.2 percent of their votes for Stokes. (Actually this figure underrepresents the Negro vote for Stokes, since some of the non-Stokes votes in these wards were cast by whites. Similarly, the 15.4 percent vote for Stokes in the predominantly white wards slightly overestimates the white vote because of the Negro minority.)

Newspaper and magazine reports of the primary election proclaimed that Stokes could not have won without the white vote.

TABLE 1

	City totals			Negro wards		
	1965 General	1967 Primary	1967 General	1965 General	1967 Primary	1967 General
Registered Voters	337,803	326,003	326,003	103,123	99,885	99,885
Turnout	239,479	210,926	257,157	74,396	73,360	79,591
% Turnout	70.9	64.7	78.9	72.1	73.4	79.7
Stokes Votes	85,716	110,769	129,829	63,550	70,575	75,586
% Stokes Votes	35.8	52.5	50.5	85.4	96.2	95.0

Our own estimate—based on matching wards with census tracts, and allowing for only slight shifts in racial composition in some wards since the 1965 special census—is that Stokes received 16,000 white votes. His margin of victory was 18,000. How would the voting have gone if the third man, Celeste, had not been in the race? Many white voters, feeling that Stokes could not win in a two-man race, might not have bothered to vote at all, so perhaps Stokes would have won by an even larger margin. Thus Stokes's inroad into the white vote was not the decisive factor in his primary victory, although it was important.

Stokes emerged from the primary as the odds-on favorite to win—five weeks later—in the general election. And in the first few days of the campaign, it seemed that Stokes had everything going for him.

• Stokes was bright, handsome, and articulate. His opponent, Seth Taft, while bright, had never won an election, and his family name, associated with the Taft-Hartley Act, could hardly be an advantage among union members. In addition, he was shy and seemingly uncomfortable in a crowd.

• Both the *Plain Dealer* and the *Cleveland Press* endorsed Stokes in the general election.

• The wounds of the primary were quickly (if perhaps superficially) healed, and the Democratic candidate was endorsed by both the Democratic Party and Mayor Locher.

• Labor—both the A.F.L.-C.I.O. and the Teamsters—also endorsed Stokes.

• He had a partisan advantage. Of the 326,003 registered voters, only 34,000 (10 percent) were Republican. The closest any Republican mayoral candidate had come to winning was in 1951, when—in a small turnout—William J. McDermott received 45 percent of the vote.

TABLE 1: (Continued)

	White wards			Mixed wards		
	1965 General	1967 Primary	1967 General	1965 General	1967 Primary	1967 General
Registered Voters	159,419	152,737	152,737	75,261	73,421	73,421
Turnout	111,129	88,525	119,883	53,962	49,105	57,113
% Turnout	69.7	58.0	78.5	71.7	66.9	77.8
Stokes Votes	3,300	13,495	23,158	18,866	26,699	30,872
% Stokes Votes	3.0	15.2	19.3	35.0	54.4	54.1

• Stokes had 90,000 or more Negro votes virtually assured, with little possibility that Taft would make more than slight inroads.

• Perhaps most important, voting-behavior studies over the years have demonstrated that voters who are confronted by a dilemma react by staying home from the polls. Large numbers of life-long Democrats, faced with voting for a Negro or a Republican by the name of Taft, were likely to stay home.

Had this been a normal election, Democrat Carl Stokes would have won handily. But this was not destined to be a normal election. During the final days of the campaign, Stokes knew he was in a fight for his political life. Those who predicted that the cross-pressures would keep many voters away from the polls forgot that the variable "Negro" had never been involved in an election of this importance.

On Election Day, an estimated 90 percent of those who voted for Locher or Celeste in the Democratic primary shifted to Taft—many pulling a Republican lever for the first time in their life. Was this clearly an unequivocally bigoted backlash? To be sure, bigotry *did* play a major role in the election. But to dismiss the campaign and the election as pure overt bigotry is to miss the significance of what happened in Cleveland and the emerging subtle nature of prejudice in American society.

THE NON-ISSUE OF RACE

A closer look at the personal characteristics and campaign strategy of Seth Taft, the Republican candidate, reveals the complexity and subtlety of the race issue.

In the final days of the Democratic primary campaign, Taft repeatedly told reporters that he would rather run against Locher and his record than against Carl Stokes. On the evening of the primary, Taft appeared at Stokes's headquarters to congratulate him. As far as he was concerned, Taft said, the campaign issue was, Who could present the most constructive program for change in Cleveland? Further, he said he didn't want people voting for him simply because he was white. A few days later, Taft even presented a strongly-worded statement to his campaign workers:

> "The Cuyahoga Democratic party has issued a number of vicious statements concerning the candidacy of Carl Stokes, and others have conducted whisper campaigns. We cannot tolerate injection of race into this campaign. . . . Many people will vote for Carl Stokes because he is a Negro. Many people will vote for me because I am white. I regret this fact. I will work hard to convince people they should not vote on a racial basis."

Seth Taft's programs to solve racial tensions may have been paternalistic, not really perceptive of emerging moods of the ghetto. But one thing is clear—he was not a bigot. Every indication is that he remained uncomfortable about being in a race in which his chances to win depended, in large part, upon a backlash vote.

Whether Taft's attempt to silence the race issue was a deliberate strategy or a reflection of deep personal feelings, it probably enhanced his chances of winning. He knew that he had the hard-core bigot vote. His task was to convince those in the middle that they could vote for him and *not* be bigots.

Stokes, on the other hand, had another kind of problem. While he had to draw more white votes, he also had to retain and, if possible, increase the 73 percent Negro turnout that had delivered him 96 percent of the Negro votes in the primary. Stokes's campaign leaders feared a fall-off in the voter turnout from Negro wards—with good reason. The entire primary campaign had pushed the October 3 date so hard that some Negroes could not understand why Carl Stokes was not mayor on October 4. Full-page newspaper ads paid for by CORE had stated, *"If you don't vote on Oct. 3rd, forget it. The man who wins will be the next mayor of Cleveland!"* So Stokes felt he had to remobilize the Negro vote.

The moment came during the question-and-answer period of the second of four debates with Taft in the all-white westside. Stokes said:

> "The personal analysis of Seth Taft—and the analysis of many competent political analysts—is that

> Seth Taft may win the November 7 election, but
> for only one reason. That reason is that his skin
> happens to be white."

The predominantly white crowd booed loudly and angrily for several minutes, and throughout the rest of the evening repeatedly interrupted him. Later, Stokes's campaign manager revealed that his candidate's remark was a calculated risk to arouse Negro interest. Stokes probably succeeded, but he also gave Taft supporters an excuse to bring the race issue into the open. And they could claim that it was *Stokes,* not Taft, who was trying to exploit the race issue.

To be sure, *both* candidates exploited the race issue. But, for the most part, it was done rather subtly. Stokes's campaign posters stated, "Let's Do Cleveland Proud"—another way of saying, "Let's show the world that Cleveland is capable of rising above racial bigotry." A full-page ad for Stokes stated in bold print, "Vote for Seth Taft. It Would Be Easy, Wouldn't It?" After the debate, Taft was free to accuse Stokes of using the race issue—itself a subtle way of exploiting the issue. Then there was the letter, signed by the leaders of 22 nationality clubs, that was mailed to 40,000 members in the city. It didn't mention race, but comments such as "protecting our way of life," "safeguard our liberty," and "false charges of police brutality" were blatant in their implications. Taft sidestepped comment on the letter.

No matter how much the candidates may have wanted to keep race out of the picture, race turned out to be the most important issue. Both Taft and Stokes could benefit from the issue if they played it right, and both did use it. And although the Stokes remark at the second debate gave white voters an excuse to vote for Taft without feeling that they were bigots, many whites probably would have found another excuse.

TAFT AS A STRATEGIST

The fact is that Taft, for all his lackluster qualities, emerged as a strong candidate. He was able to turn many of his liabilities into assets.

• Taft was able to insulate himself against his Republican identity. He successfully dissociated himself from his uncle's position on labor by pointing to his own active role, as a student, against "right to work" laws. At the same time, he hit hard at Stokes's record as an off again-on again Democrat. This strategy neutralized, at least in part, Taft's first political disadvantage—running as a Republican in a Democratic city.

• A second liability was that he came from a wealthy family. Taft was an Ivy League intellectual, cast in the role of a "do-gooder." He lived in an exclusive suburb, Pepper Pike, and had bought a modest home in Cleveland only a few weeks before declaring his candidacy. How, it was frequently asked, could such a man understand the problems of the inner-city and of the poor? Almost invariably the answer was: "Did John F. Kennedy, Franklin D. Roosevelt, and Nelson Rockfeller have to be poor in order to understand and respond to the problems of the poor?" Taft's campaign posters were a side profile that bore a striking resemblance to President Kennedy. Whether he was consciously exploiting the Kennedy image is an open question. But there can be little doubt that when Taft mentioned his Republican heritage, he tried to project an image of the new breed of Republican—John Lindsay and Charles Percy. This image didn't come across very well at first, but as he became a seasoned campaigner it became clearer.

• Another liability was that Taft had never held an elected office. His opponent tried to exploit this—unsuccessfully. Taft could point to 20 years of active civic service, including the fact that he was one of the authors of the Ohio fair-housing law. Then too, the charge gave Taft an opportunity to point out that Stokes had the worst absentee record of anyone in the state legislature. Stokes never successfully answered this charge until the last of their four debates, when he produced a pre-campaign letter from Taft commending him on his legislative service. But this came moments *after* the TV cameras had gone off the air.

• Still another liability emerged during the campaign. Taft's strategy of discussing programs, not personalities, was seemingly getting him nowhere. He presented specific proposals; Stokes, a skilled debater, succeeded in picking them apart. Stokes himself discussed programs only at a general level and contended that he was best-qualified to "cut the red tape" in Washington. His frequent trips to Washington to confer with top Government officials, before and during the campaign, indicated that he had the inside track.

Taft, realizing at this point that his campaign was not gaining much momentum, suddenly switched gears and began attacking Stokes's record (not Stokes personally). Stokes had claimed he would crack-down on slumlords. Taft discovered that Stokes owned a piece of rental property with several code violations—and that it had not been repaired despite an order from the city. He hit hard at Stokes's absenteeism and his record as a "good" Democrat. He put a "bird-dog" on Stokes and, if Stokes told one group one thing and another group something else, the public heard about it.

TABLE 2: Percent Stokes Vote by Ward

White wards	% Negro	1965 General	1967 Primary	1967 General
1	.6	3.2	17.2	20.5
2	.3	1.9	12.8	17.4
3	.9	2.5	13.6	22.1
4	.3	3.0	18.2	20.9
5	.6	1.7	11.8	17.8
6	.8	2.3	15.1	16.7
7	.6	3.4	16.5	23.7
8	3.0	6.1	24.7	29.3
9	.2	1.9	12.4	16.4
14	1.4	1.1	12.7	13.0
15	1.4	1.2	9.2	14.1
22	5.7	8.1	22.5	26.3
26	1.1	2.8	16.3	19.9
32	2.4	2.9	10.0	15.3
33	.3	2.5	17.7	21.4
Average		3.0	15.2	19.3
Negro wards				
10	91.3	88.7	97.3	96.7
11	91.8	86.3	95.9	96.0
12	82.7	76.9	90.4	90.5
13	75.2	75.8	90.7	88.4
17	99.0	86.6	98.1	97.9
18	89.3	84.0	96.0	95.7
20	91.0	83.0	95.0	92.8
24	92.6	90.6	98.1	98.1
25	90.9	91.3	98.4	98.2
27	85.7	85.2	95.6	94.0
Average		85.4	96.2	95.0
Mixed wards				
16	56.6	50.7	69.9	70.1
19	25.3	29.2	48.0	39.9
21	61.1	55.2	66.3	68.9
23	20.3	9.8	18.2	23.2
28	28.5	26.5	54.8	57.3
29	24.4	26.8	43.2	42.3
30	51.7	51.5	75.3	71.4
31	21.8	16.9	31.8	39.0
Average		35.0	54.4	54.1

The upshot was that in the final days of the campaign Taft captured the momentum. Stokes was easily the more flashy debater and projected a superior image; but Taft emerged as the better strategist.

SHOULD TAFT HAVE WITHDRAWN?

One may ask whether all of this discussion is really relevant, since the final vote was sharply divided along racial lines. In one sense it *is* irrelevant, since it is possible that a weaker candidate than Taft might have run just as well. It is also possible that a white racist might actually have won. Still, this discussion has buttressed two important points.

• Taft was not all black, and Stokes was not all white. Taft proved a strong candidate, and—had he been running against Locher instead of Stokes—he might have amassed strong support from Negroes and defeated Locher.

• By being a strong candidate, Taft made it much easier for many white Democrats, who might otherwise have been cross-pressured into staying home, to come out and vote for him.

Some people felt that Taft should have withdrawn and let Stokes run uncontested. But many of the same people also decried white liberals who, at recent conferences to form coalitions between black-power advocates and the New Left, let black militants castrate them. It is not traditional in American politics that candidates enter a race to lose. Taft was in to win, and he fought a hard and relatively clean campaign—as high a compliment as can be paid to any candidate.

Yet all of this doesn't change the basic nature of the voting. This is clear from the evidence in Table 2. Stokes won by holding his black bloc, and increasing his white vote from 15 percent in the primary to almost 20 percent in the general. An enormous amount of the white vote was, whether covert or overt, anti-Negro. It is hard to believe that Catholics, ethnic groups, and laborers who never voted for anyone but a Democrat should suddenly decide to evaluate candidates on their qualifications and programs, and—in overwhelming numbers—decide that the Republican candidate was better qualified. The implication is that they were prejudiced. But to assume that such people perceive themselves as bigots is to oversimplify the nature of prejudice. And to call such people bigots is to make their responses even more rigid—as Carl Stokes discovered after his remark in the second debate with Taft.

This, then, is perhaps an important lesson of the Cleveland election: Bigotry cannot be defeated directly, by telling bigots that they are bigoted. For the most part Stokes learned this lesson well, accumulating as many as 30,000 white votes, nearly five times the number he received in 1965. But another slip like the one in the second debate might have cost him the election.

A few words on the voting for Stokes ward by ward, as shown in the table. Wards 9, 14, and 15—which gave Stokes a comparatively low vote—have the highest concentration of ethnic groups in the city. Not only is there the historical element of prejudice in these areas, but there is the ever-present fear among the residents that Negroes will invade their neighborhoods. (This fear is less a factor in ward 9, which is across the river.)

Wards 26 and 32 also gave Stokes a low percentage of votes, and these wards are also the ones most likely to have Negro migration. They are just to the north of East Cleveland, which is currently undergoing heavy transition, and to the east of ward 27, which in the past few years has changed from white to black. In these two wards, then, high ethnic composition and a fear of Negro migration would seem to account for Stokes's 19.9 and 15.3 percentages.

The highest percentage *for* Stokes in predominantly white areas was in wards 8 and 22. Ward 8 has a growing concentration of Puerto Ricans, and—according to newspaper polls—they voted heavily for Stokes. Ward 22 has a very large automobile-assembly plant that employs many Negroes. Now, in 1965 the ward was 5.7 percent Negro—a large increase from 1960. Since 1965, this percentage has probably grown another 2 or 3 percent. Therefore, if one subtracts the Negro vote that Stokes received in this ward, the size of the white vote is about the same as in other wards.

"IMMINENT DANGER" IN GARY

The race for mayor in Gary, Ind., was not overtly racist. Still, the racial issue was much less stable than it was in Cleveland. When Democratic chairman John G. Krupa refused to support Richard D. Hatcher, the Democratic candidate, it was clear that the reason was race. When the Gary newspaper failed to give similar coverage to both candidates and sometimes failed to print news releases from Hatcher headquarters (ostensibly because press deadlines had not been met), it was clear that race was a factor.

Even though race was rarely mentioned openly, the city polarized. While Stokes had the support of the white-owned newspapers and many white campaign workers, many of Hatcher's white supporters preferred to remain in the background—in part, at least, because they feared reprisals from white racists. Hatcher didn't use the black-power slogan, but to the community the election was a contest between black and white. And when the Justice Department supported Hatcher's claim that the election board had illegally removed some 5000 Negro voters from the registration lists and added nonexistent whites, the tension in the city became so great that the Governor, feeling that there was "imminent danger" of violence on election night, called up 4000 National Guardsmen.

Negroes constitute an estimated 55 percent of Gary's 180,000 residents, but white voter registration outnumbers Negroes by 2000 or 3000. Like Stokes, Hatcher—in order to win—had to pull some white votes, or have a significantly higher Negro turnout.

The voter turnout and voting patterns in Cleveland and Gary were very similar. In both cities, almost 80 percent of the registered voters turned out at the polls. In the Glen Park and Miller areas, predominantly white neighborhoods, Joseph B. Radigan—Hatcher's opponent—received more than 90 percent of the votes. In the predominantly Negro areas, Hatcher received an estimated 93 percent of the votes. In all, Hatcher received about 4000 white votes, while losing probably 1000 Negro votes, at most, to Radigan. This relatively small white vote was enough to give him victory. If Stokes's miscalculation in bringing race into the Cleveland campaign gave prejudiced whites an excuse to vote for Taft, the glaring way the Democratic Party in Gary tried to defeat Hatcher probably tipped the scales and gave Hatcher some white votes he wouldn't have received otherwise.

THE SCHOOL ISSUE IN BOSTON

The Boston election, unlike the Cleveland and Gary elections, didn't pose a Negro against a white, but a lackluster candidate—Kevin White—against a 48-year-old grandmother who had gained national attention over the past several years for her stand against school integration. On the surface, Mrs. Hicks seems to be an obvious racial bigot. But she herself has repeatedly denied charges that she is a racist, and many who have followed her closely claim that this description is too simple.

Mrs. Hicks, perhaps more than any other public figure to emerge in recent years, reflects the complex and subtle nature of prejudice in America. Her public denial of bigotry is, in all probability, an honest expression of her self-image. But she is basically unaware of, and unwilling to become informed about, the way her views maintain the barriers of segregation and discrimination in American society. In 1963, when the N.A.A.C.P. asked the Boston School Committee to acknowledge the *de facto* segregation in the schools, she refused to review the evidence. Meeting with the N.A.A.C.P., she abruptly ended the discussion by proclaiming: "There is no *de facto* segregation in Boston's schools. Kindly proceed to educational matters." Later, when the State Board of Education presented a 132-page report on racial imbalance in Massachusetts schools, she lashed out at the report's recommendations without bothering to read it.

Mrs. Hicks, like millions of Americans, holds views on race that are born out of and perpetuated by ignorance. John Spiegel, director of Brandeis University's Lemberg Center for the Study of Violence, has summed up the preliminary report of its study of six cities:

> ". .. the attitude of whites seems to be based on ignorance of or indifference to the factual basis of Negro resentment and bitterness. . . . If white populations generally had a fuller appreciation of the just grievances and overwhelming problems of the Negroes in the ghetto, they would give stronger support to their city governments to promote change and to correct the circumstances which give rise to strong feelings of resentment now characteristic of ghetto populations."

Prejudice is born not only out of ignorance, but also out of fear. There is much about the Negro ghettos of poverty that causes whites, lacking objective knowledge, to be afraid, and their fear in turn reinforces their prejudice and their inability to hear out and understand the plight of the Negro in America.

In Boston, the voter turnout was heavy (71 percent) but below the turnouts in Cleveland and Gary. White accumulated 53 percent of the vote and a 12,000 plurality. Compared with Stokes and Hatcher, he had an easy victory. But considering Mrs. Hicks's lack of qualifications and the racial overtones of her campaign, Boston also experienced a massive backlash vote. Had it not been for the final days of the campaign—when she pledged, unrealistically, to raise police and firemen's salaries to $10,000 without raising taxes, and came back from Washington with "positive assurance" that nonexistent Federal monies would cover the raises—she might even have won. But throughout the campaign Mrs. Hicks repeatedly revealed her ignorance of fiscal and political matters. Mrs. Hicks had another handicap: She is a woman. The incredible fact that she ran a close race demonstrated again the hard core of prejudice and ignorance in American society.

Now let us consider the broader implications these elections will have on the racial crisis in America. To be sure, the immediate implications are quite different from what they would have been

if Stokes and Hatcher had lost and Mrs. Hicks had won. If the
elections had gone the other way, Summer '68 might well have
begun November 8. As Thomas Pettigrew of Harvard put it a few
days before the election, "If Stokes and Hatcher lose and Mrs.
Hicks wins, then I just wonder how a white man in this country
could ever look a Negro in the eye and say, 'Why don't you make
it the way we did, through the political system, rather than burning
us down?' "

THE MEANING OF THE ELECTIONS

But do these victories really alter the basic nature of the
racial crisis? There is, true, some reason for hope. But to assume
that anything has been fundamentally altered would be disastrous.
First of all, it is by no means clear that these elections will pacify
militant Negroes—including those in Cleveland, Gary, and Boston.
In Boston, some militants were even encouraging people to vote
for Mrs. Hicks—because they felt that her victory would help unify
the Negro community against a well-defined foe. In Cleveland,
most militants remained less than enthusiastic about the possibility
of a Stokes victory. Of the militant groups, only CORE worked hard
for him. In Gary alone did the candidate have the solid support of
militants—probably because Hatcher refused to explicitly rebuke
Stokely Carmichael and H. Rap Brown, and because his opponents
repeatedly claimed that Hatcher was a black-power advocate.

If the Stokes and Hatcher victories are to represent a turning point in the racial crisis, they must deliver results. Unfortunately,
Hatcher faces an unsympathetic Democratic Party and city council.
Stokes has gone a long way toward healing the wounds of the
bitter primary, but it remains to be seen whether he will receive
eager support for his programs. Some councilmen from ethnic wards
will almost certainly buck his programs for fear of alienating their
constituencies.

Stokes and Hatcher themselves face a difficult and delicate
situation.
• Their margins of victory were so narrow that they, like Kennedy
in 1960, must proceed with great caution.
• Enthusiasm and promises of change are not the same as the
power to implement change. And the two mayors must share power
with whites.
• They must demonstrate to Negroes that their presence in City Hall
has made a difference. But if their programs seem too preferential
toward Negroes, they run the risk of massive white resistance.

This delicate situation was clearly seen in the early days of the Stokes administration. Of his first ten appointments, only two were Negroes. Although relations with the police have been one of the most sensitive issues in the Negro ghetto, Stokes's choice for a new police chief was Michael Blackwell, a 67-year-old "hard-liner." This appointment was intended to ease anxieties in the ethnic neighborhoods, but it was not popular in the Negro ghetto. Blackwell, in his first public address after being sworn in, lashed out at the Supreme Court, state laws, and "publicity-seeking clergy and beatniks" for "crippling law enforcement." Cleveland's Negroes are already beginning to wonder whether a Negro in City Hall is going to make any difference.

Some observers believe that Stokes is basically quite conservative, and point to his sponsorship of anti-riot legislation. To be sure, Stokes's position on many issues remains uncertain, but what does seem fairly clear from his early days in office is that his efforts to gain support in white communities is going to lead to disaffection among Negroes. How much and how quickly is a difficult question.

Race relations is only one of many problems that these two new mayors must face. Stokes has inherited all of the problems that brought national attention to Cleveland last spring—poverty, urban renewal, finance, transportation, air and water pollution, and so on. Hatcher faces similar problems in Gary, and must also cope with one of the nation's worst strongholds of organized crime. If they fail, the responsibility will fall heavier on them than had a white man failed. Some whites will generalize the failures to all Negro politicians, and some Negroes will generalize the failures to the "bankruptcy" of the American political system.

Almost certainly, Washington will be a key factor in determining if these two men succeed. The national Democratic Party has a strong interest in making Stokes and Hatcher look good, for it desperately needs to recapture the disaffected Negro voters before the 1968 national election. But how much can the party deliver? The war in Vietnam is draining enormous national resources and Congress is threatening to slash poverty programs. Even if Federal monies were no problem, there is the question whether *any* of Washington's existing programs are directed at the roots of ghetto unrest. Many informed administrators, scientists, and political analysts feel they are not. And the chances for creative Federal programs seem, at this moment, fairly dim.

Another clear implication of these elections is that white resistance to change remains large and widespread. More than 90 percent of the Democrats in Cleveland who voted for a Democrat in the primary switched, in the general election, to the Republican candidate. Now, not many American cities are currently composed of as many as 35 percent Negroes; the possibility of coalitions to elect other Negro candidates appears, except in a handful of cities, remote. Additional Negro mayoral candidates are almost certain to arise, and many will go down to bitter defeat.

Stokes and Hatcher won because of black-voter power coalesced with a relatively small minority of liberal whites. It was not a victory of acceptance or even tolerance of Negroes, but a numerical failure of the powers of discrimination, a failure that resulted in large part because of the massive exodus of whites from the central city. The election of Stokes and Hatcher may break down white resistance to voting for a Negro, but this is, at best, problematical. Also problematical is how bigoted whites will react to the election of a Negro mayor. Their organized efforts to resist change may intensify. As we have already indicated, the pace of white exodus from the central city of Cleveland is already alarming. And an acceleration of this pace could push the city into financial bankruptcy.

AMERICA HAS BOUGHT A LITTLE TIME

In short, while the implications of the November 7 elections are ambiguous, it does seem that the victories of Stokes and Hatcher, and the defeat of Mrs. Hicks, have kept the door open on the growing racial crisis. America has, at best, bought a little time.

On the other hand, we do not find much cause for optimism in those elections—unlike George Meany, and unlike the *New York Times,* which, five days after the election, published a glowing editorial about "the willingness of most voters today to choose men solely on personal quality and impersonal issues." To us, it would seem that the elections have only accelerated the pace of ever-rising expectations among Negroes. And if results don't follow, and rather rapidly, then we believe that the Negro community's frustration with the American political system will almost certainly heighten.

The hard task of demonstrating that Negroes can actually achieve justice and equality in America still lies ahead.

12
The
Myths
of
Coalition

Stokely Carmichael
Charles V. Hamilton

There is a strongly held view in this society that the best—indeed, perhaps the only—way for black people to win their political and economic rights is by forming coalitions with liberal, labor, church and other kinds of sympathetic organizations or forces, including the "liberal left" wing of the Democratic Party. With such allies, they could influence national legislation and national social patterns; racism could thus be ended. This school sees the "Black Power Movement" as basically separatist and unwilling to enter alliances. Bayard Rustin, a major spokesman for the coalition doctrine, has written:

> Southern Negroes, despite exhortations from SNCC to organize themselves into a Black Panther Party, are going to stay in the Democratic party—to them it is the party of progress, the New Deal, the New Frontier, and the Great Society—and they are right to stay.[1]

Aside from the fact that the name of the Lowndes County Freedom Party . . . is *not* the "Black Panther Party," SNCC has often stated that it does not oppose the formation of political coalitions *per se;* obviously they are necessary in a pluralistic society. But coalitions

Reprinted by permission of Random House, Inc., from Stokely Carmichael and Charles V. Hamilton, *Black Power*, Copyright © 1967 by Stokely Carmichael and Charles V. Hamilton.

[1] Bayard Rustin, "Black Power and Coalition Politics," *Commentary* (September, 1966).

with whom? On what terms? And for what objectives? All too frequently, coalitions involving black people have been only at the
leadership level; dictated by terms set by others; and for objectives
not calculated to bring major improvement in the lives of the black
masses.

. . . We propose to reexamine some of the assumptions of
the coalition school, and to comment on some instances of supposed
alliance between black people and other groups. In the process
of this treatment, it should become clear that the advocates of
Black Power do *not* eschew coalitions; rather, we want to establish
the grounds on which we feel political coalitions can be viable.

The coalitionists proceed on what we can identify as three
myths or major fallacies. *First,* that in the context of present-day
America, the interests of black people are identical with the interests
of certain liberal, labor and other reform groups. Those groups accept the legitimacy of the basic values and institutions of the society,
and fundamentally are not interested in a major reorientation of the
society. Many adherents to the current coalition doctrine recognize
this but nevertheless would have black people coalesce with such
groups. The assumption—which is a myth—is this: what is good
for America is automatically good for black people. *The second
myth* is the fallacious assumption that a viable coalition can be
effected between the politically and economically secure and the
politically and economically insecure. *The third myth* assumes that
political coalitions are or can be sustained on a moral, friendly,
sentimental basis; by appeals to conscience. We will examine each
of these three notions separately.

The major mistake made by exponents of the coalition
theory is that they advocate alliances with groups which have never
had as their central goal the necessarily total revamping of the
society. At bottom, those groups accept the American system and
want only—if at all—to make peripheral, marginal reforms in it.
Such reforms are inadequate to rid the society of racism.

Here we come back to an important point . . . the overriding sense of superiority that pervades white America. "Liberals,"
no less than others, are subjected and subject to it; the white
liberal must view the racial scene through a drastically different
lens from the black man's. Killian and Grigg were correct when
they said in *Racial Crisis in America:*

> . . . most white Americans, even those white leaders
> who attempt to communicate and cooperate with
> their Negro counterparts, do not see racial in-

> equality in the same way that the Negro does. The
> white person, no matter how liberal he may be,
> exists in the cocoon of a white-dominated society.
> Living in a white residential area, sending his chil-
> dren to white schools, moving in exclusively white
> social circles, he must exert a special effort to
> expose himself to the actual conditions under which
> large numbers of Negroes live. Even when such
> exposure occurs, his perception is likely to be
> superficial and distorted. The substandard house
> may be overshadowed in his eyes by the television
> aerial or the automobile outside the house. Even
> more important, he does not perceive the subjec-
> tive inequalities inherent in the system of segrega-
> tion because he does not experience them daily as
> a Negro does. Simply stated, the white American
> lives almost all of his life in a white world. The
> Negro American lives a large part of his life in a
> white world also, but in a world in which he is
> stigmatized [p. 73].

Our point is that no matter how "liberal" a white person might be,
he cannot ultimately escape the overpowering influence—on himself and on black people—of his whiteness in a racist society.

Liberal whites often say that they are tired of being told
"you can't understand what it is to be black." They claim to recognize and acknowledge this. Yet the same liberals will often turn
around and tell black people that they should ally themselves with
those who can't understand, who share a sense of superiority
based on whiteness. The fact is that most of these "allies" neither
look upon the blacks as co-equal partners nor do they perceive
the goals as any but the adoption of certain Western norms and
values. Professor Milton M. Gordon, in his book, *Assimilation in
American Life,* has called those values "Anglo-conformity" (p. 88).
Such a view assumes the "desirability of maintaining English institutions (as modified by the American Revolution), the English language, and English-oriented cultural patterns as dominant and
standard in American life." Perhaps one holding these views is not
a racist in the strict sense of our original definition, but the end
result of his attitude is to sustain racism. As Gordon says:

> The non-racist Anglo-conformists presumably are
> either convinced of the *cultural* superiority of Anglo-

Saxon institutions as developed in the United States, or believe simply that regardless of superiority or inferiority, since English culture has constituted the dominant framework for the development of American institutions, newcomers should expect to adjust accordingly [pp. 103–104].

We do not believe it possible to form meaningful coalitions unless both or all parties are not only willing but believe it absolutely necessary to challenge Anglo-conformity and other prevailing norms and institutions. Most liberal groups with which we are familiar are not so willing at this time. If that is the case, then the coalition is doomed to frustration and failure.

The Anglo-conformity position assumes that what is good for America—whites—is good for black people. We reject this. The Democratic Party makes the same claim. But the political and social rights of black people have been and always will be negotiable and expendable the moment they conflict with the interests of their "allies." A clear example of this can be found in the city of Chicago, where Mayor Daley's Democratic "coalition" machine depends on black support and unfortunately black people vote consistently for that machine. Note the results, as described by Banfield and Wilson in *City Politics:*

> The civic projects that Mayor Daley inaugurated in Chicago—street cleaning, street lighting, road building, a new airport, and a convention hall, for example—were shrewdly chosen. They were highly visible; they benefited the county as well as the city; for the most part they were noncontroversial; they did not require much increase in taxes; and they created many moderately paying jobs that politicians could dispense as patronage. The *mayor's program conspicuously neglected the goals of militant Negroes,* demands for the enforcement of the building code, and (until there was a dramatic exposé) complaints about police inefficiency and corruption. *These things were all controversial, and, perhaps most important, would have no immediate, visible result; either they would benefit those central-city voters whose loyalty could be counted upon anyway* or else (as in the case of police reform) they threatened to hurt the machine in a vital spot [p. 124; authors' italics].

As long as the black people of Chicago—and the same can be said of cities throughout the country—remain politically dependent on the Democratic machine, their interests will be secondary to that machine.

Organized labor is another example of a potential ally who has never deemed it essential to question the society's basic values and institutions. The earliest advocates of unionism believed in the doctrine of *laissez faire.* The labor organizers of the American Federation of Labor (AFL) did not want the government to become involved in labor's problems, and probably for good reason. The government then—in the 1870's and 1880's—was anti-labor, pro-management. It soon became clear that political power would be necessary to accomplish some of the goals of organized labor, especially the goals of the railroad unions. The AFL pursued that power and eventually won it, but generally remained tied to the values and principles of the society as it was. They simply wanted in; the route lay through collective bargaining and the right to strike. The unions set their sights on immediate bread-and-butter issues, to the exclusion of broader goals.

With the founding and development of mass industrial unionism under the Congress of Industrial Organizations (CIO), we begin to see a slight change in overall union orientation. The CIO was interested in a wider variety of issues—foreign trade, interest rates, even civil rights issues to an extent—but it too never seriously questioned the racist basis of the society. In *Politics, Parties and Pressure Groups,* Professor V. O. Key, Jr. has concluded: ". . . on the fundamental question of the character of the economic system, the dominant labor ideology did not challenge the established order." Professor Selig Perlman wrote: ". . . it is a labor movement upholding capitalism, not only in practice, but in principle as well."[2] Organized labor, so often pushed as a potential ally by the coalition theorists, illustrates the pitfalls of the first myth; as we shall see later . . . its history also debunks the second myth.

Yet another source of potential alliance frequently cited by the exponents of coalitions is the liberal-reform movement, especially at the local political level. But the various reform-politics groups—particularly in New York, Chicago and California—frequently are not tuned in to the primary goals of black people. They establish their own goals and then demand that black people identify with them. When black leaders begin to articulate goals in the

[2] Selig Perlman, "The Basic Philosophy of the American Labor Movement," *Annals of the American Academy of Political & Social Science,* Vol. 274 (1951), pp. 57–63.

interest of black people *first,* the reformers tend, more often than not, to term this "racist" and to drop off. Reformers push such "good government" programs as would result in posts being filled by professional, middle-class people. Wilson stated in *The Amateur Democrat,* "Blue-ribbon candidates would be selected, not only for the important, highly visible posts at the top of the ticket, but also for the less visible posts at the bottom" (p. 128). Black people who have participated in local reform politics—especially in Chicago—have come from the upper-middle class. Reformers generally reject the political practice of ticket balancing, which means that they tend to be "color blind" and wish to select candidates only on the basis of qualifications, of merit. In itself this would not be bad, but their conception of a "qualified" person is usually one who fits the white middle-class mold. Seldom, if ever, does one hear of the reformers advocating representation by grass-roots leaders from the ghettos: these are hardly "blue-ribbon" types. Again, when reformers push for elections at large as opposed to election by district, they do not increase black political power. "Blue-ribbon" candidates, government by technical experts, elections at large—all these common innovations of reformers do little for black people.

Francis Carney concludes from his study of California's liberal-reform Democratic clubs[3] that although those groups were usually strong on civil rights, they were nonetheless essentially middle-class oriented. This could only perpetuate a paternalistic, colonial relationship—doing *for* the blacks. Thus, even when the reformers are bent on making significant changes in the system, the question must be asked if that change is consistent with the views and interests of black people—as perceived by those people.

Frequently, we have seen that a staunch, militant stand taken by black leaders has frightened away the reformers. The latter could not understand the former's militancy. "Amateur Democrats (reformers) are passionately committed to a militant stand on civil rights, but they shy away from militant Negro organizations because they find them 'too race-conscious'" (p. 285), says Wilson in *The Amateur Democrat,* citing as one example the Independent Voters of Illinois, who felt they could not go along with the desire of some black members to take a very strong, pro-civil rights and anti-Daley position. The liberal-reform politicians have not been able fully to accept the necessity of black people speaking forcefully and for themselves. This is one of the greatest points of tension between these two sets of groups today; this difference must be

---

[3] Francis Carney, *The Rise of the Democratic Clubs in California,* Eagleton Institute Cases in Practical Politics. New York: McGraw-Hill, 1959.

resolved before viable coalitions can be formed between the two.

To sum up our rejection of the first myth: . . . the political and economic institutions of this society must be completely revised if the political and economic status of black people is to be improved. We do not see how those same institutions can be utilized —through the mechanism of coalescing with some of them—to bring about that revision. We do not see how black people can form effective coalitions with groups which are not willing to question and condemn the racist institutions which exploit black people; which do not perceive the need for, and will not work for, basic change. Black people cannot afford to assume that what is good for white America is automatically good for black people.

The second myth we want to deal with is the assumption that a politically and economically secure group can collaborate with a politically and economically insecure group. Our contention is that such an alliance is based on very shaky grounds. By definition, the goals of the respective parties are different.

Black people are often told that they should seek to form coalitions after the fashion of those formed with so-called Radical Agrarians—later Populists—in the latter part of the nineteenth century. In 1886, the Colored Farmers' Alliance and Cooperative Union was formed, interestingly enough, by a white Baptist minister in Texas. The platform of this group was similar to that of the already existing Northern and Southern Farmers' Alliances, which were white. But upon closer examination, one could see substantial differences in interests and goals. The black group favored a Congressional bill (the Lodge Federal Elections Bill) which aimed to guarantee the voting rights of Southern black people; the white group opposed it. In 1889, a group of black farmers in North Carolina accused the Southern Alliance of setting low wages and influencing the state legislature to pass discriminatory laws. Two years later, the Colored Alliance called for a strike of black cotton pickers. Professors August Meier and Elliot Rudwick ask a number of questions about these two groups, in *From Plantation to Ghetto:*

> Under what circumstances did Negroes join and to what extent, if any, was participation encouraged (or even demanded) by white employers who were members of the Southern Alliance? . . . Is it possible that the Colored Alliance was something like a company union, disintegrating only when it became evident that the Negro tenant farmers refused to follow the dictates of their white employers? . . . And how was it that the Alliance men and Populists

were later so easily led into extreme anti-Negro actions? In spite of various gestures to obtain Negro support, attitudes such as those exhibited in North Carolina and on the Lodge Bill would argue that whatever interracial solidarity existed was not firmly rooted [pp. 158–59].

The fact is that the white group was relatively more secure than the black group. As C. Vann Woodward writes in *Tom Watson, Agrarian Rebel,* "It is undoubtedly true that the Populist ideology was dominantly that of the landowning farmer, who was, in many cases, the exploiter of landless tenant labor" (p. 18). It is difficult to perceive the basis on which the two could coalesce and create a meaningful alliance for the landless, insecure group. It is no surprise, then, to learn of the anti-black actions mentioned above and to realize that the relation of blacks to Populists was not the harmonious arrangement some people today would have us believe.

It is true that black people in St. Louis and Kansas backed the Populists in the election of 1892, and North Carolina blacks supported them in 1896. But it is also true that the Populists in South Carolina, under the leadership of "Pitchfork" Ben Tillman, race-baited the black man. In some places—like Georgia—the Populists "fused" with the lily-white wing of the Republican Party, not with the so-called black-and-tan wing.

Or take the case of Tom Watson. This Populist from Georgia was at one time a staunch advocate of a united front between Negro and white farmers. In 1892, he wrote: "You are kept apart that you may be separately fleeced of your earnings. You are made to hate each other because upon that hatred is rested the keystone of the arch of financial despotism which enslaves you both. You are deceived and blinded that you may not see how this race antagonism perpetuates a monetary system which beggars both."[4]

But this is the same Tom Watson who, only a few years later and because the *political* tide was flowing against such an alliance, did a complete turnabout. At that time, Democrats were disfranchising black people in state after state. But, as John Hope Franklin recorded in *From Slavery to Freedom,* "Where the Populists were unable to control the Negro vote, as in Georgia in 1894, they believed that the Democrats had never completely disfranchised the Negroes because their votes were needed if the Democrats were to stay in power. This belief led the defeated and disappointed Tom

---

[4] Tom Watson, "The Negro Question in the South," *Arena,* Vol. 6 (1892), p. 548.

Watson to support a constitutional amendment excluding the Negro from the franchise—a complete reversal of his position in denouncing South Carolina for adopting such an amendment in 1895" (p. 218).

Watson was willing to ally with white candidates who were anti-Democratic-machine Democrats. With the black vote eliminated, the Populists stood to hold the balance of power between warring factions of the Democratic Party. Again C. Vann Woodward spells it out in his book, *Tom Watson, Agrarian Rebel:*

> He [Watson] . . . pledged his support, and the support of the Populists, to any anti-machine, Democratic candidate running upon a suitable platform that included a pledge to "a change in our Constitution which will perpetuate white supremacy in Georgia."
>
> How Watson managed to reconcile his radical democratic doctrine with a proposal to disfranchise a million citizens of his native state is not quite clear.
>
> "The white people dare not revolt so long as they can be intimidated by the fear of the Negro vote," he explained. Once the "bugaboo of Negro domination" was removed, however, "every white man would act according to his own conscience and judgment in deciding how he shall vote." With these words, Watson abandoned his old dream of uniting both races against the enemy, and took his first step toward the opposite extreme in racial views [pp. 371–72].

At all times, the Populists and Watson emerge as politically motivated. The history of the period tells us that the whites—whether Populists, Republicans or Democrats—always had their own interests in mind. The black man was little more than a political football, to be tossed and kicked around at the convenience of others whose position was more secure.

We can learn the same lesson from the politics of the city of Atlanta, Georgia today. It is generally recognized that the black vote there is crucial to the election of a mayor. This was true in the case of William B. Hartsfield, and it is no less true for the present mayor, Ivan Allen, Jr. The coalition which dominates Atlanta politics has been described thus by Professor Edward Banfield in *Big City Politics:*

The alliance between the business-led white middle class and the Negro is the main fact of local politics and government; only within the limits that it allows can anything be done, and much of what is done is for the purpose of holding it together [p. 35].

Mayor Hartsfield put together a "three-legged stool" as a base of power. The business power structure, together with "good government"-minded middle class that takes its lead from that power structure is one leg. The Atlanta press is another. The third leg is the black community. But something is wrong with this stool. In the first place, of course, the third leg is a hollow one. The black community of Atlanta is dominated by a black power structure of such "leaders" . . . concerned primarily with protecting their own vested interests and their supposed influence with the white power structure, unresponsive to and unrepresentative of the black masses. But even this privileged group is economically and politically insecure by comparison with the other two forces with whom they have coalesced. Note this description by Banfield:

Three associations of businessmen, *the leadership of which overlaps greatly,* play important parts in civic affairs. The Chamber of Commerce launches ideas which are often taken up as official city policy, and it is always much involved in efforts to get bond issues approved. The Central Atlanta Association is particularly concerned with the downtown business district and has taken the lead in efforts to improve expressways, mass transit, and urban renewal. Its weekly newsletter is widely read and respected. *The Uptown Association is a vehicle used by banks and other property owners to maintain a boundary line against expansion of the Negro district. To achieve this purpose it supports nonresidential urban renewal projects* [pp. 31–32, authors' italics].

Atlanta's substantial black bourgeoisie cannot compete with that line-up.

The political and economic interests causing the white leaders to enter the coalition are clear. So is the fact that those interests are often diametrically opposed to the interests of black people. We need only look at what the black man has received for his faithful support of politically and economically secure "alliance partners." Banfield puts it succinctly: "Hartsfield gave the Negro practically nothing in return for his vote" (p. 30). That vote, in 1957, was nine-tenths of the 20,000 votes cast by black people.

In 1963, a group of civic leaders from the black community of Southeast Atlanta documented the injustices suffered by that community's 60,000 black people. The lengthy list of grievances included faults in the sewerage system, sidewalks needed, streets which should be paved, deficient bus service and traffic control, substandard housing areas, inadequate parks and recreation facilities, continuing school segregation and inadequate black schools. Their report stated:

> Atlanta city officials have striven to create an image of Atlanta as a rapidly growing, modern, progressive city where all citizens can live in decent, healthful surroundings. This image is a blatant lie so long as the city provides no health clinics for its citizens but relies entirely upon inadequate county facilities. It is a lie so long as these health clinics are segregated and the city takes no action to end this segregation. Because of segregation, only one of the four health clinics in the South side area is available to over 60,000 Negroes. This clinic . . . is small, its equipment inadequate and outdated, and its service dangerously slow due to general overcrowding.

In 1962, the city employed 5,663 workers, 1,647 of them black, but only 200 of those did other than menial work. The document lists twenty-two departments in which, of 175 equipment operators in the Construction Department, not one was black. The city did not even make a pretense of belief in "getting ahead by burning the midnight oil": there was only one public library in the community, a single room with 12,000 volumes (mostly children's books) for 60,000 people.[5]

This is what "coalition politics" won for the black citizens of one sizeable community. Nor had the situation in Atlanta's ghettos improved much by 1966. When a so-called riot broke out in the Summerhill community, local civic groups pointed out that they had deplored conditions and called the area "ripe for riot" many months earlier.

---

[5] "The City Must Provide. South Atlanta: The Forgotten Community," Atlanta Civic Council, 1963.

Black people must ultimately come to realize that such coalitions, such alliances have *not* been in their interest. They are "allying" with forces clearly not consistent with the long-term progress of blacks; in fact, the whites enter the alliance in many cases precisely to impede that progress.

. . .

The third myth proceeds from the premise that political coalitions can be sustained on a moral, friendly or sentimental basis, or on appeals to conscience. We view this as a myth because we believe that political relations are based on self-interest: benefits to be gained and losses to be avoided. For the most part, man's politics is determined by his evaluation of material good and evil. Politics results from a conflict of interests, not of consciences.

We frequently hear of the great moral value of the pressure by various church groups to bring about passage of the Civil Rights Laws of 1964 and 1965. There is no question that significant numbers of clergy and lay groups participated in the successful lobbying of those bills, but we should be careful not to overemphasize the value of this. To begin with, many of those religious groups were available only until the bills were passed; their sustained moral force is not on hand for the all-important process of ensuring federal implementation of these laws, particularly with respect to the appointment of more federal voting registrars and the setting of guidelines for school desegregation.

It should also be pointed out that many of those same people did not feel so morally obliged when the issues struck closer to home—in the North, with housing, as an example. They could be morally self-righteous about passing a law to desegregate southern lunch counters or even a law guaranteeing southern black people the right to vote. But laws against employment and housing discrimination—which would affect the North as much as the South —are something else again. After all, ministers—North and South —are often forced out of their pulpits if they speak or act too forcefully in favor of civil rights. Their parishioners do not lose sleep at night worrying about the oppressed status of black Americans; they are not morally torn inside themselves. As Silberman said, they simply do not want their peace disrupted and their businesses hurt.

We do not want to belabor the church in particular; what we have said applies to all the other "allies" of black people. Furthermore, we do not seek to condemn these groups for being what they are so much as we seek to emphasize a fact of life: they are unre-

liable allies when a conflict of interest arises. Morality and sentiment cannot weather such conflicts, and black people must realize
this. No group should go into an alliance or a coalition relying on
the "good will" of the ally. If the ally chooses to withdraw that
"good will," he can do so usually without the other being able to
impose sanctions upon him of any kind.

Thus we reject the last myth. . . . Some believe that there
is a conflict between the so-called American Creed and American
practices. The Creed is supposed to contain considerations of equality and liberty, at least certainly equal opportunity, and justice. The
fact is, of course, that these are simply words which *were not even
originally intended* to have applicability to black people: Article I of
the Constitution affirms that the black man is three-fifths of a person.[6] The fact is that people live their daily lives making practical
day-to-day decisions about their jobs, homes, children. And in a
profit-oriented, materialistic society, there is little time to reflect
on creeds, especially if it could mean more job competition, "lower
property values," and the "daughter marrying a Negro." There is no
"American dilemma," no moral hang-up, and black people should
not base decisions on the assumption that a dilemma exists. It may
be useful to articulate such assumptions in order to embarrass, to
create international pressure, to educate. But they cannot form the
basis for viable coalitions.

What, then, are the grounds for viable coalitions?

Before one begins to talk coalition, one should establish
clearly the premises on which that coalition will be based. All
parties to the coalition must perceive a *mutually* beneficial goal
based on the conception of *each* party of his *own* self-interest. One
party must not blindly assume that what is good for one is automatically—without question—good for the other. Black people must
first ask themselves what is good *for them,* and then they can determine if the "liberal" is willing to coalesce. They must recognize
that institutions and political organizations have no consciences
outside their own special interests.

Secondly, there is a clear need for genuine power bases
before black people can enter into coalitions. Civil rights leaders
who, in the past or at present, rely essentially on "national sentiment" to obtain passage of civil rights legislation reveal the fact
that they are operating from a powerless base. They must appeal

[6] "Representatives and direct Taxes shall be apportioned among
the several States which may be included within this Union, according to
their respective Numbers, which shall be determined by adding to the whole
Number of free Persons, including those bound to Service for a Term of
Years, and excluding Indians not taxed, three-fifths of all other Persons."

to the conscience, the good graces of the society; they are, as noted earlier, cast in a beggar's role, hoping to strike a responsive chord. It is very significant that the two oldest civil rights organizations, the National Association for the Advancement of Colored People and the Urban League, have constitutions which specifically prohibit partisan political activity. (The Congress of Racial Equality once did, but it changed that clause when it changed its orientation in favor of Black Power.) This is perfectly understandable in terms of the strategy and goals of the older organizations, the concept of the civil rights movement as a kind of liaison between the powerful white community and the dependent black community. The dependent status of the black community apparently was unimportant since, if the movement proved successful, that community was going to blend into the white society anyway. No pretense was made of organizing and developing institutions of community power within the black community. No attempt was made to create any base of organized political strength; such activity was even prohibited, in the cases mentioned above. All problems would be solved by forming coalitions with labor, churches, reform clubs, and especially liberal Democrats.

. . . It should, however, already be clear that the building of an independent force is necessary; that Black Power is necessary. If we do not learn from history, we are doomed to repeat it, and that is precisely the lesson of the Reconstruction era. Black people were allowed to register, to vote and to participate in politics, because it was to the advantage of powerful white "allies" to permit this. But at all times such advances flowed from white decisions. That era of black participation in politics was ended by another set of white decisions. There was no powerful independent political base in the southern black community to challenge the curtailment of political rights. At this point in the struggle, black people have no assurance—save a kind of idiot optimism and faith in a society whose history is one of racism—that if it became necessary, even the painfully limited gains thrown to the civil rights movement by the Congress would not be revoked as soon as a shift in political sentiments occurs. (A vivid example of this emerged in 1967 with Congressional moves to undercut and eviscerate the school desegregation provisions of the 1964 Civil Rights Act.) We must build that assurance and build it on solid ground.

We also recognize the potential for limited, short-term coalitions on relatively minor issues. But we must note that such approaches seldom come to terms with the roots of institutional racism. In fact, one might well argue that such coalitions on subordinate issues are, in the long run, harmful. They could lead whites and blacks into thinking either that their long-term interests do *not* conflict when in fact they do, or that such lesser issues are the *only* issues which can be solved. With these limitations in mind, and a spirit of caution, black people can approach possibilities of coalition for specific goals.

Viable coalitions therefore stem from four preconditions: (a) the recognition by the parties involved of their respective self-interests; (b) the mutual belief that each party stands to benefit in terms of that self-interest from allying with the other or others; (c) the acceptance of the fact that each party has its own independent base of power and does not depend for ultimate decision-making on a force outside itself; and (d) the realization that the coalition deals with specific and identifiable—as opposed to general and vague goals.

The heart of the matter lies in this admonition from Machiavelli, writing in *The Prince:*

> And here it should be noted that a prince ought never to make common cause with one more powerful than himself to injure another, unless necessity forces him to it. . . . for if he wins you rest in his power, and princes must avoid as much as possible being under the will and pleasure of others.[7]

Machiavelli recognized that "necessity" might at times force the weaker to ally with the stronger. Our view is that those who advocate Black Power should work to minimize that necessity. It is crystal clear that such alliances can seldom, if ever, be meaningful to the weaker partner. They cannot offer the optimum conditions of a political *modus operandi.* Therefore, if and when such alliances are unavoidable, we must not be sanguine about the possibility of their leading to ultimate, substantial benefit for the weaker force.

Let black people organize themselves *first,* define their interests and goals, and then see what kinds of allies are available. Let any ghetto group contemplating coalition be so tightly organized, so strong, that—in the words of Saul Alinsky—it is an "indigestible body" which cannot be absorbed or swallowed up.[8] The advocates of Black Power are not opposed to coalitions per se. But we are *not* interested in coalitions based on myths. To the extent to which

[7] Niccolo Machiavelli, *The Prince and the Discourses,* New York: Random House (Modern Library), 1950, p. 84.

[8] Saul Alinsky speaking at the 1967 Legal Defense Fund Convocation in New York City, May 18, 1967.

black people can form *viable* coalitions will the end results of those alliances be lasting and meaningful. There will be clearer understanding of what is sought; there will be greater impetus on all sides to deliver, because there will be *mutual* respect of the power of the other to reward or punish; there will be much less likelihood of leaders selling out their followers. Black Power therefore has no connotation of "go it alone." Black Power simply says: enter coalitions only *after* you are able to "stand on your own." Black Power seeks to correct the approach to dependency, to remove that dependency, and to establish a viable psychological, political and social base upon which the black community can function to meet its needs. . . .

Until the mid-1950s, black attempts to gain equality with whites were confined to conventional legal and political channels. However, the Montgomery bus boycotts of 1955 inaugurated a decade in which growing numbers of Negroes took to the streets to demonstrate against segregation and racial discrimination. These demonstrations became most widespread in the early 1960s when the term "Negro Revolution" was applied to this militant stage of the civil rights movement. Civil rights demonstrations were instrumental in building the momentum necessary to achieve passage of the 1964 Civil Rights Act and the 1965 Voting Rights Act. But the very success of the civil rights movement contributed to its decline. The movement's premise was that blacks should ally themselves with liberal whites in nonviolent demonstrations which would appeal to the consciences of white Americans. These whites, in turn, would bring about positive social change. However, with the passage of the 1964 and 1965 civil rights legislation, even sympathetic whites became convinced that the major problems facing Negroes had been solved. Black people, on the other hand, were aware that these victories had only marginally affected their lives. It was at this point that blacks and white liberals parted company. By the late 1960s, black aspirations were being channeled into open street rebellions or exclusively black organizations whose ideology and tactics differed dramatically from those of the civil rights movement.

The first selection which follows is from James Q. Wilson's study of Negro politics in Chicago in the late 1950s, *Negro Politics*. When Wilson wrote, the NAACP monopolized organized Negro protest; but as Wilson demonstrates, it was primarily a middle-class organization with little real power. In this selection, Wilson examines the nature of the leadership of the NAACP and the many constraints on these leaders.

The second selection is a concise but comprehensive history of the civil rights movement by Kenneth B. Clark. In it, Clark discusses the many differences between the numerous civil rights organizations, but he concludes that they all share integrationist, basically conservative, goals: "All civil rights organizations are committed to full inclusion of the Negro in the economic and political life of America, without restrictions based on race or color." Clark wrote this article soon after the passage of the 1964 and 1965 civil rights acts, when the influence of the civil rights organizations was at its zenith. Nevertheless, Clark was concerned that the movement had failed to come to grips with the problems of the black ghettos of America.

The selection by Andrew Kopkind was written in August of 1967 after the "hottest" summer of black rebellions of the 1960s. Although this selection was taken from a review of Martin Luther King's book, *Where Do We Go from Here: Chaos or Community?*,[1] it can be read as a commentary on the civil rights movement in the late 1960s. Kopkind argues that the civil rights movement has become irrelevant to the ghetto: "The 'civil rights' organizations of last year's headlines are observers like the rest of us, no matter how loud their preachings or insistent their press releases." Kopkind suggests that the authentic political voice of the ghetto has become that of the urban guerrilla.

In the final selection, Joseph Boskin analyzes the urban revolts of the 1960s. Boskin shows that these riots were a massive, spontaneous reaction to the malaise of the black ghettos. After the occurrence of widespread rebellions in the summer of 1967, the frequency and scale of these riots subsided; black unrest began to express itself in the more organized channels of the Black Power movement. The ideology of that movement is examined in Part Six.

[1] New York, Harper & Row, 1967.

13
The Character
of Negro
Civic Action

James Q. Wilson

The NAACP has come to have a virtual monopoly of national Negro protest activity. Today it is the pre-eminent race organization, almost unchallenged within its field of competence. This has not always been the case. In earlier years, the NAACP was compelled to share its prestige with other, similar organizations, such as the March on Washington Movement. Doubts were expressed in the past as to the value of the NAACP's legalistic approach to race problems. It was criticized for not having a mass base, for ignoring economic and political problems in favor of legal problems, for having a "snobbish" leadership, and for failing to form an effective alliance with liberal forces in the American labor movement.[1] Membership in local NAACP branches was generally small and the amounts of money raised were not large.

These criticisms, while still heard in some quarters, have largely been muted today. In part this has been due to the ability of the NAACP to persist and to consolidate its reputation with numerous victories. For the most part, however, the enhanced prestige of the organization seems to be a direct result of its role in the 1954 school desegregation decision of the United States Supreme Court. The NAACP was hailed as the architect of the greatest single Negro victory of this century. The legal approach of the association was seen to have some merit. The NAACP quickly became a symbol of Negro protest. Negroes who had doubted its efficacy rushed to climb aboard the bandwagon. This process was accelerated by the

Reprinted with permission of The Macmillan Company from James Q. Wilson, *Negro Politics: The Search for Leadership,* pp. 281–294 and p. 332. Copyright © by The Free Press.

attack launched against the organization by whites in the South. By accusing it of radical and subversive tendencies, by elevating it to the position of the principal threat to white supremacy, the South immeasurably increased the standing of the NAACP among Negroes. For a Negro to criticize, much less oppose, the NAACP today is in effect to give aid and comfort to the enemy.

Although Southern opposition has made it difficult for the NAACP to recruit Negroes in the South, membership drives in the North have met with increasing success. In 1953, the year before the Supreme Court decision, the Chicago branch had about 4,000 members. In 1958, it had increased that figure to over 18,500. Since the bulk of the organization's money comes, at the local level, from membership dues (a minimum of $2 per person), this has meant a corresponding improvement in the NAACP's financial position.[2]

In the past, the local NAACP branches, such as the one in Chicago, have been regarded as a "tax base" which simply support the program of the national office by fund-raising campaigns. The national office firmly controls national policy for the organization. The association is not a federal structure, with power decentralized to local units; it is a unitary structure with support, but not policy-direction, coming from the base. Moreover, the national office has usually taken a "hands off" attitude toward factional quarrels in the local branches so long as fund-raising was not seriously impeded. The NAACP branches can be characterized as organizations with local memberships but a national constituency. The national program has been the overriding goal, and members are attracted, not on the basis of what the local branch is doing, but on the basis of what the national office has done.

The growing resources and prestige of the NAACP have, however, begun to alter this pattern somewhat. As the NAACP has come to monopolize the Negro protest, it has come to have greater significance for local leaders. It has risen in value as a source of status, and competition for its local control has become intense. In part because local leaders need to justify their tenure as officers of the organization, NAACP branches have attempted to develop a local program beyond simply dues-collecting. This programmatic emphasis has served to add fuel to the factional fires, for it causes principle as well as prestige to be at stake. Further, new groups in the Negro community have arisen which are demanding recognition and are asserting their claims to civic leadership. Foremost among these are certain Negro labor leaders. The Chicago branch has been gripped by a protracted controversy which has in part centered on the question of which segment of the Negro community will provide its leadership. On the one hand are the Negro lawyers and businessmen who, with certain ministers, have most often held the higher offices. On the other hand are some labor leaders and their allies who have in recent years been able to capture the executive committee and the presidency. Annual elections are typically a struggle between these groups in an organized form.

The intensity of this struggle seems, to the observer, to be completely out of proportion to what is actually at stake. No tangible rewards accrue to the victor. Neither group can usually attribute any significantly longer list of civic achievements to its tenure in office. Occasionally the NAACP becomes involved in an economic conflict between member groups, as it once did when certain labor leaders accused the lawyer-president of the association of supporting management in an all-Negro labor relations dispute. But typically Chicago remains the same no matter which Negro group controls the NAACP. These appearances are deceptive, however. Simply because the stakes are intangible does not make them insignificant. The NAACP is the most important and the best-known organization in the Negro community. Its president automatically becomes prominent. The values and goals of the race are intimately bound up with, if not actually embodied in, the association. The NAACP is not a mass organization in the sense that it organizes the Negro rank-and-file for any purpose; it is rather, an organization composed of and responsive to a relatively small but vocal and attentive group.[3] The game of NAACP control is played out almost entirely within this group and its component factions. When one faction gains control, it often alienates the volunteer support of another faction, but it almost never alienates the masses of Negroes. At the height of recent factional warfare, the NAACP was able to sell a record number of memberships in the community. The response of the community seems to depend, not on the achievements of the local NAACP, but on the state of race relations nationally. A brutal lynching or the closure of southern public schools will make donations easier to secure; a quiet year will make them harder to secure.

The game of civic leadership as a whole generally takes place in a relatively small group of persons. This group formulates its own rules of procedure, enforces its own penalties by manipulating reputations, and has its own rivalries. A Negro who was himself a member of this small universe described the elements of which it is composed and noted the consequences for each element of the incentives which attract it:

> There are three classes of people . . . active in it.
> . . . First, there are those who are quite common,

the ones that are temperamentally joiners. . . . They
want to believe in its purposes and they get all
wrapped up in it. They are hard to deal with. They
get all upset over little things. It is easy to insult
them. . . . They get a satisfaction out of it. They get
to be somebody and do something which is *good*.
But you can't work with them. They won't compromise.

Second, there are the professional groups—the
lawyers, doctors, and all. I am one of these. They
get a reputation out of work in the NAACP. Lawyers
pick up a few cases and they get some publicity.
. . . What the professional ethics prohibit you can
accomplish indirectly by this sort of thing. They differ from the first group in that they have no emotional problems. . . . They aren't easily offended.
You can work with them. They are in it for a crass
reason, and they don't mind doing a little trading.

The third group is the ordinary workers, the run-
of-the-mill type, who do want to make a contribution
and plug away at it. . . . The more serious Negroes
think that supporting the NAACP is something they
have to do; it is important; it is a duty. So they
work at it.

Both the fact that the incentives for Negro civic action are
largely intangible and the fact that the most important Negro civic
organization—the NAACP—has come to be invested with moral and
ideological significance contribute to an understanding of the character of Negro public life in Chicago. These two factors are important in explaining why there seem to be so few leaders and why
the leaders that exist act as they do. Leaders are recruited and
civic action occurs among white businessmen-civic leaders in a
manner rather different from that in the Negro community, and one
important reason for this difference is a frequent difference in incentives. White leaders, more than Negroes, act because for them
or for the firms which they represent, something is at stake. Land
holdings will be affected in value by urban renewal or railroad
terminal consolidation or institutional construction. Tax rates will be
affected by plans to subsidize public transportation systems. Private
hospitals might have part of their more unremunerative patient load
eased if a new branch of the county hospital is built. More customers may be induced to shop in the Loop department stores if
high-density apartment projects are built near those stores. Mem-

bership on welfare and social service agency boards can, it is felt, help the firm by improving its public relations.

Fewer such incentives exist for Negro volunteer civic action. Negro leaders will rarely benefit as persons or as members of a business if an FEPC law is passed or if an open occupancy ordinance is adopted. Where tangible stakes are involved at all, they often dispose a person to act against the race end for fear of its implications for their own position. Few Negro businesses as yet have the resources to afford or the inclination to value the kind of public image that comes from civic service. Several Negro life insurance companies operate in Chicago, but only one is conspicuously active in encouraging its officers to take part in civic work. Where Negro businesses and professions do supply civic leaders, they are usually supplied for the less controversial forms of civic life where public relations will be enhanced at minimum cost. The most important race ends are hardly lacking in controversy, and correspondingly the incentives they contain for even those Negro businesses which are willing to act civically are considerably reduced. In an important sense, what is surprising is not that there are so few Negro civic leaders but that, given the situation, there are as many as there are.

The intangible incentives to civic action are many and varied, and no one can pretend to know in any given case which one attracts what civic leader. Men may act to seek personal prestige, to acquire power, to gain an audience, to pursue strongly-held convictions, to prevent others from acquiring a certain reputation, or simply because they feel they "ought to." The kinds of persons attracted by intangible incentives are not always the easiest to work with; indeed, it seems to be a general rule that no competition is fiercer or more bitter than competition for intangible stakes.* Negro civic life attracts ideologues; this can make compromises hard and dispassionate discussion difficult. The role of "interest-balancer"—the man who reconciles factions by arranging a solution in which everyone gains a little and no one loses a great deal—is a role which is almost impossible to play when the issue at stake is one of principle. Little can be offered a person motivated by an attachment to a moral cause that will induce him to alter his position to any great extent, and the man who attempts to make such an offer quickly becomes morally suspect. Organizations created to

---

* The struggle for intangible rewards—prestige or status, for example—makes the internal politics of university faculties, church hierarchies, and Negro organizations among the most bitter to be found. When one seeks money as a reward, it can be sought impersonally; when one seeks prestige, it only can be sought in the realm of personalities.

seek ends which reflect such principles, and which have acquired enough prestige in the community to permit them to confer status on those who actively lead the quest for these principled ends, often become the objects of hot competition. There is a competition for office and a competition for issues where desires for prestige and commitment to principle are inextricably linked in a manner that imparts an astonishing intensity to the annual elections and internal politics of the NAACP.

The character of Negro civic action cannot be accounted for simply on the basis of the nature of the incentives for such action, however. Civic activity even among white Chicago businessmen is often a result of inducements equally as intangible as those which exist for Negroes. Another equally important factor which conditions Negro public life is the problem of powerlessness—the inability, in the most critical issues, to influence markedly the course of public affairs. This absence of power and the sense of frustration and futility which often are its result not only reduce the attractiveness of civic action but also shape the conduct of such civic activity as is pursued.

Negro civic leaders stand on the periphery of power. They hope to prod or needle or anger or humiliate those who can direct the course of affairs into granting concessions to Negro demands. The Negroes themselves are remote from the centers of influence, and this distance gives a certain logic to their views of the public interest and appropriate strategies for action. But those whom they seek to influence are often powerless also, if by power we mean the ability to establish binding public policy. The white civic leaders and politicians are either complacent or caught up in their own conflicts of interest, and are severely constrained by their opinions and fears as to the consequences of any radical change in the racial patterns of the city. Real power seems to lie at the front lines, not at the command post; the whites who resist, often with violence and always with protest, the incursions of Negroes into their neighborhoods are the real influentials who seem to set the bounds of action for the civic leaders and politicians. Negroes are thus twice removed from power: they are not influential in the civic and political circles of the city, and these circles are in turn the willing or unwilling agents of their constituents in the racially tense neighborhoods.

This clear lack of power has implications for Negro leaders that relate to their attitudes on civic issues. Lacking the kind of access and influence which seems—not always correctly—to characterize the white businessman-civic leader, the Negro leader is more easily persuaded of the plausibility of protest as the appropriate political style. It becomes hard to deny the logic of the frontal assault when efforts to negotiate fail. If one cannot "talk" to influential persons and induce them to make "decisions," then one is hard pressed to refute the claim of the militants that only an attack on these men with a mass campaign aimed at legislative remedies can hope to gain concessions. This appeal of protest leaders gains added plausibility when it is heard in the perspective of what is frequently an incorrect assessment of the position of the white businessman-civic leader. These men, the so-called "lords of the Loop," are seen by the Negroes to have almost palpable power which they concert to use against Negro interests out of either prejudice or desire for economic gain. Meeting obstacles with a call for new laws and legal action is a lure that can easily attract even Negroes who are not protest leaders, like a businessman who has hoped for a negotiated settlement of the housing problem:

> I stood out against legislation for many years, feeling that it wasn't the best way to handle it. But I'm fast coming to believe that legislation is the only way it will ever be solved. . . . The industry could solve it because they cause the problem, but they won't. . . .

The absence of power has its consequences for the internal problems of Negro organizations which attempt to act in race relations. The NAACP, for example, is beset with internal conflicts. These conflicts are partly, but not wholly, a form of competition for status. They are also a response to the experienced powerlessness of the organization.[4] An atmosphere of uncertainty surrounds its activities. No one knows the details in full of the public issues with which the organization must deal. Past experience provides few reliable guides for action. The problems are complex and difficult, and only certain kinds of leaders are able to see simple answers for them. Plausible courses of action are scarce; there seems to be no "solution." The aspirations which most members hold for the organization are very high; possible levels of achievement are seen to be low. The environment of the organization is hostile and unyielding. In such conditions, conflict within the NAACP—or within any organization placed in a comparable situation—tends to be high. The resources for action are few—the organization seems to be powerless—and controversy begins with how best to simply exist as an organization. The disagreement and conflict over ends, which in one sense arises out of the powerless state of the organization, ends by denying that state. Factional lines harden, and soon accusations are heard that certain leaders are failing to exercise what power they have. Militant leaders charge that the organization is not really powerless, but only appears to be in that state because "soft" leaders have willed it by refusing to *be* powerful. Soon the controversy becomes cast in the form of a debate as to whether the strategic or limiting factor on effective civic action is to be found in the environment of the organization (the insuperable obstacles which make the organization powerless) or within the organization itself (the ineffectual character of the organization's leadership). The powerlessness of Negro leaders produces contradictory effects because it creates a sense of frustration to which people respond in different ways—some by resignation and hopelessness, others by anger and chagrin. Negro leaders vacillate between an awareness and a denial of their relatively powerless state.

The sense of powerlessness, and the concomitant imputation of power to another elite, produces a sense of defeatism among Negroes. Those who do not respond to this situation by becoming protest leaders often respond by acting simply for individual ends without reference to collective goals. If nothing one can do will aid the Negro community, then one is justified in trying to better himself. The argument is often heard that this self-improvement in the long run benefits the race as well, because a successful Negro businessman gains the respect of whites and reflects credit on his race.

The problem of powerlessness cannot be fully understood unless it is seen in the light of the character of the ends being sought. For some ends—particularly ends related to housing and real estate—the Negro can do nothing to remedy his powerlessness. At best he can hope for a crisis which will compel others to act in an area where they have, until now, been afraid or unwilling to act. The Negro has difficulty in acquiring the power to act in this area because, for the most part, the power to act simply does not exist anywhere. When seeking ends that elicit less irreconcilable passions, scraps of power can be collected and assembled. Certain things can be done: more police protection can be demanded; less discriminatory insurance rates can be pressed for; firms can be induced to hire Negroes. Here, when Negroes fail to act effectively, it is more often a case of failures internal to the Negro community than of constraints imposed by the larger community. Briefly stated, constraints exist and are enforced by the city on Negro action, but in many areas those constraints are not really tested by Negro action. The problem of power is not simply a function of one or the other. Many obstacles exist only because they have not been probed. Hiring Negroes in the Loop banks seemed for years to be an impossible goal; but when a picket line appeared, the banks began to give way with surprising suddenness. Similarly, no one can say in advance what style of political action will be the most efficacious; the appropriate type and style of leadership depends largely on the character of the end sought.

If there is, as has been argued here, a "Negro problem," it cannot be completely explained on the basis of end conflicts, disagreements over appropriate styles, an absence of incentives, influence relations, or the sense of powerlessness. In short, it cannot be satisfactorily explained by an inquiry into Negro leadership alone, but would have to include an investigation of nonleaders and followers as well.

With this limitation clearly understood, certain important relationships among the themes developed in this study can be brought together. First, leaders acting in situations where large formal organizations must be maintained by intangible inducements tend to employ the militant style; while leaders acting in situations where access or position must be maintained tend to employ the moderate or bargaining style. This distinction cannot be driven too far, for many leaders called upon to head formal organizations (such as the NAACP) are, for a variety of reasons, unable to act with the militancy that others expect of them. But the maintenance needs of the organization—the need to attract and hold members and fend off challenges from other factions—will inevitably serve to heighten the militancy of even temperamentally moderate civic leaders. Even militant leaders often do not go far enough to meet the expectations of their followers. One remarked, after failing to join a picket line around the City Hall some years earlier:

> I was criticized and still am for not joining that picket line. Some people said that they weren't going to support me for president this last year because I hadn't been in the picket line. You have got to toe the mark with these people.

Second, the distinction between welfare and status ends tends (with important exceptions) to correspond to the distinction between the militant and moderate styles. The broadest, most inclusive, most ideological, most "advanced" ends are typically sought by the militants; more tangible, specific, and immediate ends are sought by the moderates. This is related to the utility of broad, general programs as means to attract and hold followers, when *followers* (rather than access or personal influence or prestige) are the usual resource of the militant leader. A leader heading such an organization as the NAACP can set less venturesome goals and pursue them in a less militant manner only when he has established himself in a position where he can reasonably afford to dispense with the small group of active, attentive, volunteer workers who in most instances operate the organization. This has been the case when the leader could depend on organized forms of support apart from these activists, for normally the activists have opposed the moderate and favored the militant leader.

Third, many of the problems of civic leadership might be avoided by avoiding the constraints of formal organizations. Formal organizations make civic action possible by mobilizing resources and creating a corporate identity which can be used by those desiring to influence others. But these advantages are purchased at a cost. That cost includes the need to retain the support of members, the problem of earning funds to meet payrolls and rent bills, the limitations imposed by the requirement that one must always act as the "representative" of the organization, and the intensification of disagreement over ends and means when such disagreement is linked to a desire for office and power in the organization. The maintenance of the organization often supersedes or modifies the substantive ends which are being sought.

Fourth, the most consistent single set of distinctions that can be detected among Chicago Negro civic leaders are distinctions based on class and status. Militants are more often (but not always) of a lower economic class and of a different social stratum than moderates. So, too, are prestige leaders on the one hand and organizers on the other. The important fact to be noted here is that although the two groups are different in terms of status, they are not necessarily different within a common status system. Negro militant-organizers do not act as civic leaders in order to raise themselves to the status level of the moderate-prestige leaders. On the contrary, the very act of civic leadership of the former type and style precludes the possibility that they will be able to move into the latter category. To account for the different status systems in which different kinds of leaders move and in which they find their rewards, we must introduce the notion of "audience." Each leader plays to a different audience. Often that audience is a formal organization; sometimes it is simply a loose grouping of associates and friends. The audiences of various leaders are often mutually exclusive.

The audience to which the militant plays is frequently one which is not a part of the world of Negro men's social clubs and fraternities. He seeks out and joins interracial activities, notably interracial social activities. Whites at these functions are often identified with liberal causes, but occasionally not. There are strong links with whites who act on behalf of Negroes and race ends. These Negroes have endeavored to leave the ghetto in either a psychological or a social sense or both. In Chicago, few have managed to leave it physically.

Moderate and prestige leaders move in an entirely different world. In Chicago, it is almost entirely a Negro world. There are social, professional and business links between almost all of them. Many of these people are uncomfortable in interracial social gatherings. Militant and organizer leaders outside this circle are acutely conscious of their exclusion and in turn are often the objects of suspicion because of that exclusion. As one militant remarked:

> A strong current of nationalism runs through the Negro community. It is thinly disguised as racial patriotism and it looks with definite suspicion upon the Negro who speaks for the "race" but is not "one of us" in his personal associations. He is never harshly condemned but it is quite bruited about that he is not a "race man." Thus he is not to be fully trusted. [I encounter] this attitude in varying degrees in all strata of Negro society.

The militant-organizer in most cases will have far more regularized social contacts with whites than other kinds of Negro civic leaders. This has the interesting implication that those seeking status or integration goals most vigorously are those with the highest relative level of personal integration; while those who are more attracted to welfare ends have a lower level of personal integration. There are, of course, many exceptions to both tendencies—some militants are bound up with "black nationalist" movements and some moderates have a large number of routinized contacts with white businessmen. Again, the nature of the audience (conservative or liberal, social or business) as well as the character of the formal organization within which civic action occurs (business or labor, church or voluntary association) are important conditioners of leadership type and style.

Although we have no detailed data on the social background and position of Negro civic leaders in cities other than Chicago, interviews with such leaders offer at least some suggestion as to the relationship between personal position, race ends, and leadership style. In New York, for example, more Negro civic leaders are integrated as persons into much of the life of the city as a whole. Negro leaders, both in and out of public office, move in the active world of liberal voluntary associations and civic causes. They have, in a real degree, "left the ghetto" in a civic, social, and often physical sense. Many of them are members of or are associated with the national board of the NAACP and are bound up with the liberal civic movements—often, again, at the national board level—in the city as a whole. These individuals seek status or integration goals, resist efforts to concentrate on welfare goals, and are militant in their leadership style. One leader of considerable stature who had experience in civic life in both New York and Chicago noted much less "ghetto-mindedness" among Negro business and professional men in the former city than in the latter. He felt more civic, business and even social contacts between Negroes and whites take place in New York and that this in part accounted for some differences in attitude and behavior. In Chicago, more frequent cases of Negro "self-segregation" were to be found. Many Negro informants in both cities agreed that this was true.

Such contacts, such an audience, provide a kind of stimulus and reinforcement pattern that encourages more Negroes to take positions backing the most advanced race causes and to pursue them with vigor. One important difference, then, between the quality of Negro leadership in Chicago and New York may be partially accounted for by the differing character and frequency of the contacts and audience which the more prestigious Negro leaders seek out.

Finally, many of the factors which have been discussed in this study—powerlessness, the lack of real progress, the cleavages which weaken the belief in race unity and race pride—have profound consequences for Negroes as persons, apart from their implications for civic action. Suggestions can be found in many interviews of a deep sense of personal inadequacy, perhaps even a feeling of inferiority, which is the product of so many frustrations and denials. This cannot here be illustrated, much less demonstrated, but it would be remarkable indeed if the forces which have been touched upon in this inquiry did not affect the lives of these people as individuals. For many Negroes, these doubts are heightened by an uneasiness over their economic position. The marginal nature of so many Negro business enterprises, the precarious state of the Negro in the economy, the awareness that so many of the gains of recent years could be wiped out by forces over which one has no control—all of these factors undoubtedly increase the sense of uncertainty and magnify the self-concern of many Negroes, leaders and led alike. An investigation into the ethos of the urban Negro might very well begin with this sense of limitation, of inadequacy, of an absent or uncertain future, as the central theme.

Footnotes

[1] Cf. Gunnar Myrdal, *An American Dilemma* (New York: Harper & Bros., 1944), pp. 831ff.

[2] The income for the Chicago branch of the NAACP during the year 1958–59 was approximately as follows: From the sale of memberships, $40,000; Freedom Fund Dinner, $20,000; Tag Day, $4,000; Annual Tea, $7,000. Of the $71,000 total, over half was sent to the national office. This total was an all-time high.

[3] In Philip Selznick, *Leadership in Administration* (Evanston, Ill.: Row, Peterson & Co., 1957), pp. 52–53, there is an interesting discussion of the "distinctive competence" of the NAACP as an organization which fits it for legal action but not for mass action. The inability of the NAACP to lead mass action is suggested in Martin Luther King, *Stride Toward Freedom: The Montgomery Story* (New York; Harper & Bros., 1958), pp. 34–35, and brought out explicitly in a discussion of the conflict between the NAACP and Rev. King contained in Paul Jacobs, "The NAACP's New Direction," *New Republic,* July 16, 1956, pp. 9–11. All these sources note the fact that local NAACP organizations are largely "dues-collecting stations" for the national headquarters, are supported mostly by middle-class Negroes, and have lost most of their initially heavy white membership. The Chicago branch of the NAACP has been struggling to solve its internal difficulties and at the same time define a role for itself in community civic action, but it has been unsuccessful so far in both areas. Meanwhile, the initiative has passed to the staff of the Chicago Urban League which, of course, has a different "distinctive competence"—one which fits it for research, persuasion, community liaison, and public relations work.

[4] March and Simon make this point explicitly in a discussion of the sources of intraorganizational conflict. I have used several of their phrases here, although they state the proposition much more formally than I: "We can predict directly that organizational conflict of the intraindividual type is most likely to occur when the conditions surrounding the organizational decision involve widespread uncertainty or a scarcity of acceptable alternatives of action." James G. March and Herbert A. Simon, *Organizations* (New York: John Wiley & Sons, 1958), p. 119.

14
The Civil Rights Movement: Momentum and Organization

Kenneth B. Clark

THE HISTORY OF THE CIVIL RIGHTS MOVEMENT

The American civil rights movement in its most important sense is as old as the introduction of human slavery in the New World. From the beginning, the essential conflict of the civil rights movement was inherent in the contradiction between the practical economic and status advantages associated with slavery and racial oppression, and the Judaeo-Christian ideals of love and brotherhood and their translation into the democratic ideology of equality and justice. The presence of African slaves visibly different in culture and color of skin intensified this conflict which demanded resolution.

One could read the early history of America as an attempt to resolve this conflict by combining both, that is, by continuing slavery while making grudging concessions to religious and democratic ideology. The decision to convert some of the African slaves to Christianity and to teach some to read could be interpreted as the first "victory" of the civil rights movement, but at the same time it paradoxically intensified the conflict. It would have been more consistent logically to leave the African slave heathen and ignorant if he were to be kept in slavery. Yet the economic demands of slavery required that the slaves be skilled, adaptable, and efficient. The fact that such skill could be developed was evidence of the humanity of the African and the beginning of the end of human slavery in a society committed to social and political democracy. The dynamics

Reprinted by permission from Kenneth B. Clark, "The Civil Rights Movement: Momentum and Organization," *Daedalus,* Journal of the American Academy of Arts and Sciences, 95, no. 1 (Winter, 1966), pp. 239–267.

of the contemporary civil rights movement continues to reflect this same struggle between the desire to deny the Negro full and un-qualified status as a human being and the unquestioned evidence that such denial cannot be based upon fact.

Signs of a civil rights renaissance in the North emerged in the 1940's when Negro resentment mounted against segregation in the armed services and discrimination in employment. A new period of overt and sustained protest had begun. In 1941, A. Philip Randolph threatened a march on Washington to force President Roosevelt to issue the first executive order compelling fair employment of Negroes. Testimony to the depth of the ambivalence of the American nation on civil rights was the fact that Roosevelt, himself generally considered one of the most liberal and far-seeing Presidents in American history, only reluctantly issued this order. His noted charm was brought into play in an attempt to persuade Randolph to compromise his demands. He appealed to Randolph's patriotism and his unwillingness to embarrass the nation at a time of dire emergency; only when all of these appeals failed did he accede to Randolph's demand. This conflict between Roosevelt and Randolph marked the beginning of a new militance and assertiveness on the part of the Northern Negro. It has been sustained ever since.

Since World War II, the Negro had succeeded in eliminating segregation in the armed forces, and, unsatisfied with less in peace than he had won in war, he gained a series of victories in the federal courts, culminating in the historic May 17, 1954 *Brown vs. Board of Education* decision of the United States Supreme Court. He developed and refined techniques for nonviolent direct-action boycotts in the South, resulting in the elimination of the more flagrant forms and symbols of racial segregation. The massive legislative commitment to racial reform, codified by the passage of the 1964 and 1965 Civil Rights Acts, had begun. The American press justified and validated the claims of its freedom and responsibility in its generally objective recording of racial injustices, while television brought into American living rooms the stark mob faces of primitive race hatred. The importance of television must eventually be evaluated by historians, but to this observer it appears to have played a most crucial role in intensifying the commitment of both Negroes and whites and increasing the momentum of the civil rights movement.

International politics also played a strong role in the struggle for justice. With the overthrow of colonial domination in the postwar decade, white Europeans and Americans could no longer sustain their political dominance over the nonwhite peoples of Asia and Africa. The increasing dignity associated with the independence of these colored peoples provided a new source of strength for the American Negro. And one should not underestimate the role of the Communist ideology as an aggressive world adversary of the American and Western concept of democracy. American Communists had never been successful in exploiting the grievances of the American Negro and attracting any significant numbers of Negroes to the Communist cause—probably because their dogmatic inability to understand the subtle but important psychological aspects of the Negro's aspirations and struggles had led them to advocate *segregation* under the guise of self-determination in the Black Belt. Nevertheless, the competitive struggle between world Communism and the American concept of democracy demanded an American response to this embarrassing and easily exploited violation of democratic ideals. America risked standing before the world as a hypocrite or resting its claims for leadership on might alone, subordinating any democratic ideological basis of appeal. The international struggle for the first time clearly placed racists on the defensive, in grave danger of being classed as subversives in their threat to America's ideological power.

One could define the civil rights movement in terms of organized and sustained activity directed toward the attainment of specific racial goals or the alleviation or elimination of certain racial problems. Such a definition, with its emphasis upon organization as the basis for changes in the status of Negroes in America, would suggest that the civil rights movement was synonymous with civil rights organizations. But this definition would obscure the important fact that the civil rights movement had its own historic and impersonal momentum, responsive to deep and powerful economic and international events and political and ideological forces beyond the control of individuals, agencies, or perhaps even individual governments. In fact, the uncontrollable power and momentum of the civil rights movement impelled it to create the necessary machinery, organizations, and leaders.[1]

THE HISTORY AND CHARACTER OF THE CIVIL RIGHTS ORGANIZATIONS

There is an understandable tendency to think of the civil rights movement, organizations, and leaders as if they were interchangeable or as if they were only parts of the same historic and social phenomenon. But, while there are similarities and overlaps among them, they are not identical, and their important historical and contemporary dynamic differences need clarification if one is to understand the present nature and force of the civil rights movement, or if one is to assess accurately the role and power of the various civil rights organizations and the actual extent of personal decision-making power held by their recognized leaders. Confusion on these questions can lead only to dangerous miscalculations. Specifically, political and governmental leaders may make demands upon civil rights leaders, demands which they genuinely believe can be fulfilled in the normal course of social bargaining and negotiation. The parties to these discussions may enter into such agreements in good faith only to find themselves unable to fulfill them. Those who view the civil rights movement in terms of the model of the American labor movement, with elected labor leaders holding responsibility for negotiating and bargaining for a disciplined rank and file, misjudge the nature of the movement. One obvious difference is that civil rights leaders have not been elected by any substantial number of Negroes. Either they are essentially hired executives, holding their office at the pleasure of a board of directors, or else they emerge as leaders by charismatic power, later creating an organization which, in effect, they control. Whitney Young is an example of the one, Martin Luther King of the other. So far, no machinery exists to enable the masses of Negroes to select a leader, but, if an individual strikes a responsive chord in the masses of Negroes, they will identify with him and "choose" him. So, too, an organizational leader may be accepted as spokesman by default, by the mere fact that he has been able to avoid overt repudiation.

One cannot understand the nature and the problems of contemporary civil rights organizations without understanding some of their individual histories. The *National Association for the Advancement of Colored People* and the *Urban League,* the two oldest, were founded in the first decade of this century in 1909 and 1910 respectively.

THE NATIONAL ASSOCIATION FOR THE ADVANCEMENT OF COLORED PEOPLE

The NAACP emerged from the Niagara Movement of W. E. B. Du Bois and other Negro and white liberals during that period when Negroes were moving North.

A meeting of some of the members of the Niagara movement was held in 1908, and it was agreed that a call should be issued by whites and Negroes for a conference on the centennial of the birth of Abraham Lincoln to discuss the status of the Negro in the United

States. Oswald Garrison Villard wrote the Call for the Conference which was held in New York City on February 12 and 13, 1909. It read in part:

> In many states today Lincoln would find justice enforced, if at all, by judges elected by one element in a community to pass upon the liberties and lives of another. He would see the black men and women, for whose freedom a hundred thousand of soldiers gave their lives, set apart in trains, in which they pay first-class fares for third class service, and segregated in railway stations and in places of entertainment; he would observe that State after State declines to do its elementary duty in preparing the Negro through education for the best exercise of citizenship. . . . Added to this, the spread of lawless attacks upon the Negro, North, South, and West—even in Springfield made famous by Lincoln —often accompanied by revolting brutalities, sparing neither sex nor age nor youth, could but shock the author of the sentiment that "government of the people, by the people, for the people, shall not perish from the earth." . . . Silence under these conditions means tacit approval. The indifference of the North is already responsible for more than one assault upon democracy, and every such attack reacts as unfavorably upon the whites as upon the blacks. Discrimination once permitted cannot be bridled; recent history in the South shows that in forging chains for the Negroes the white voters are forging chains for themselves. "A house divided against itself cannot stand;" this government cannot exist half-slave and half-free any better today than it could in 1861. . . . Hence we call upon all the believers in democracy to join in a national conference for the discussion of present evils, the voicing of protests, and the renewal of the struggle for civil and political liberty.[2]

The Call clearly indicates that, at its founding, the NAACP sensed that the status of the Negro in the North would not be significantly better than his status in the South. The founding of the NAACP anticipated the race riots of 1917, following the clues of the New York City riot of 1900. It was an attempt by the more perceptive and sensitive Negroes and whites to recapture the fervor, the purpose, and the concern of the pre-Civil War abolitionists.

The NAACP, from its beginning, took a more direct and militant stance, in spite of the fact that its founders and its Board of Directors were always interracial. The top staff tended to address itself to legislation and litigation. It pioneered in the use of direct action demonstrations. The more militant approach of the NAACP reflected, among other things, the role of W. E. B. Du Bois, paradoxically both a detached scholar and poet and an intense actionist. The direction and approach of the NAACP, to the extent that they can be attributed to a single person, were determined by his power and personality. In the tradition of a nineteenth-century New England aristocratic poet-actionist-crusader, Du Bois was a dignified intellectual, Harvard-educated, detached, aloof, and cold, but also intensely concerned and committed to the attainment of unqualified justice and equality for Negroes. He may well have been the most important figure in the American civil rights movement in the twentieth century. His importance lies not only in his role in setting the direction and the methods of the NAACP, but in his capacity to understand and predict the larger dimensions of the American racial problem. Like Frederick Douglass, he was a prophet and leader of the movement, but, unlike Douglass, he was a founder and leader of an organization within the movement, capable of articulating the purposes of that organization. Du Bois the scholar gave Du Bois the leader of the NAACP a deeper human understanding, and to the NAACP he gave a significance which a mere organization could not have had without him. Yet his temperament, facing the contradictions and the turmoil necessary to organizational struggle, determined that his role in the organization itself would be limited. One could speculate that the ardor, the intensity, the militance of Du Bois, his inability to tolerate anything other than acceptance of his complete humanity were viewed as a handicap to those willing to make the "necessary" compromises for the survival of the institution. He was a proud and uncompromising man.

The essence of the controversy between Du Bois and Booker T. Washington was that Washington could accommodate and adjust, while Du Bois could not. If the NAACP had been run by Washington, it would have been pragmatic and practical, but not militant or crusading. The clash between Washington and Du Bois was a clash of temperament and principle. Washington was willing to accept qualifications of his humanity; Du Bois was not. Du Bois' dignity and his inability to settle for anything less than total human acceptance set the tone for the approach, methods, and early militant stance of the NAACP.

The Du Bois-Washington controversy could be illustrated by their conflicting views on education for Negroes. Washington's support for a special kind of education "appropriate" to the caste status of the Negro—vocational education, the acceptance of separation (in a sense the acceptance of segregation itself)—was consistent with his pragmatic accommodation. Du Bois' insistence on academic education, his belief that, if the Negro were to progress in America, he would need to assume the same stance as whites, his belief that one could not make judgments about a person's role in terms of his color, his slogan of the "talented tenth," all were consistent with his refusal to allow color to qualify the rights of persons. He took seriously the American ideology. Washington was the realist, the moderate, yet he never founded a civil rights organization, but operated from the institutional base of Tuskegee Institute. He had gained acceptance from the white power controllers without an "organization." It is indeed doubtful that he could have mobilized a civil rights agency. It may be that his power and his usefulness to the equally pragmatic white political and economic structure would have been curtailed by even the semblance of a functioning civil rights organization. That Washington was not a particularly significant influence in the movement during its earliest stages may be due to the fact that his domain by this time was clearly the Southern Negro. The civil rights movement was then becoming Northern-oriented. One could speculate that the doctrine of accommodation preached by Washington and reinforced by white power effectively curtailed the growth of a Negro civil rights movement in the South until the mid-twentieth century.

THE NATIONAL URBAN LEAGUE

The Urban League was founded a year later than the NAACP, in 1910, for the specific purpose of easing the transition of the Southern rural Negro into an urban way of life. It stated clearly that its role was to help these people, who were essentially rural agrarian serf-peasants, adjust to Northern city life. Until the termination of Lester Granger's tenure as director in September 1961, the League announced in its fund-raising appeals and to both business and government that it was essentially a social service agency with a staff of social workers. Its implicit assumption was that the problems of the Negro were primarily those of adjustment and that their need was for training and help. The League summoned whites to demonstrate their good will, relying upon negotiation and persuasion to show white business leaders that it was in their "enlightened self interest," to use Lester Granger's term, to ease the movement of Negroes into middle-class status. The Urban League played down the more primitive and irrational components of racial hostility, depending on the conviction that white leadership, particularly in the North, could be dealt with in terms of rational economic appeals. The League courted the white community through its national and local boards, considering itself an effective bridge between the Negro community and the white decision-makers; to this end, it recruited a staff skilled not only in social work but also in negotiation procedure and style. During the early 1950's, one member of the top national staff of the Urban League described the role of the League as "the State Department of race relations," in contrast to the NAACP, which was characterized as "the War Department." This was more than an analogy; the style of speech and dress and manner of the League tended to be a stereotype of the style of the staff of the American State Department.

NAACP AND URBAN LEAGUE: DEMOCRATIC, NONPARTISAN, CONSERVATIVE

These two civil rights organizations, the NAACP and the Urban League, had in common their Northern base and their interracial character. They also shared a basic assumption that major changes in the status of the Negro could be obtained within the framework of the American democratic system. They sought to manipulate the machinery of government and to influence other institutions. The Urban League's primary emphasis was placed upon the economic, industrial, and social-service clusters of power, while the NAACP's primary interest was in political and legal power, with a major emphasis upon propaganda which sought to reach the conscience of the American people, both white and Negro. The League's appeal was to self-interest—employ Negroes, or you will spawn large numbers of dependent people. The NAACP's appeal was to public and judicial conscience; their argument was that America is intended to be a democratic nation with justice for all.

From the very beginning, both organizations were politically nonpartisan and therefore in some measure effective in flexibility of appeal and action. They could not afford identification with a particular political group, for they faced an always imminent prospect of political changes in government and the possibility of retaliation. Their decision on its face, seemed quite wise; but it limited the extent to which the civil rights organizations could, in any meaningful sense, be politically or socially revolutionary. They could not or did not identify with labor, and their sense of alienation was stimulated by the political immaturity of the American labor movement itself. The rank-and-file members of organized labor, if not its leaders, were contaminated by racism; thus, the civil rights organizations and American labor could not form a political coalition or develop a significant labor party. It would, however, be inaccurate to say these civil rights groups ever "sought" an alliance with a political labor movement. The mere fact that civil rights organizations were necessary made a civil rights-labor coalition impossible since one of the major sources of racial exclusion has been and remains the organized American labor movement.

The civil rights organizations were never revolutionary. Their assumptions and strategy and tactics were essentially conservative, in that they did not seek to change and certainly made no attempt to overthrow the basic political and economic structure. The social changes they sought were limited to the inclusion of the Negro in the existing society; the Negro wanted his own status raised to that of other American citizens. The NAACP and Urban League staked their strategies on a belief in the resilience, flexibility, and eventual inclusiveness of the American democratic system—in an ultimate sense, perhaps in a pathetic sense, upon acceptance and identification with the articulated American concept of democracy. They took literally the ideology and promises of the system and shared unquestioningly American democratic optimism. They believed in the words of Jefferson, the Declaration of Independence, the Constitution, and the Bill of Rights and asked only that these rights—and nothing less—be extended to Negroes. This was their main source of power. They could be considered revolutionary only if one tortures the meaning of the term to imply a demand to include other human beings in a system which promises fulfillment to others.

To call such modest requests disruptive or radical or extremist is to misunderstand and misjudge the logic of the original American revolution, and reflects the sickness of racism. In effect, a Marxist could justifiably accuse the civil rights movement from its beginning to the present, as well as the American labor movement, of being unrealistic and superficial in its belief that fundamental change for oppressed peoples was possible under a system within which the oppression occurred and was sustained.

The purpose of the civil rights movement has always been to counteract and destroy the lie that the Negro is subhuman, a lie that no one ever really believed, yet one that was reinforced by those with power. The fact that the Negro *is* human made him susceptible to and influenced by the same forces that influence other human beings in his society. Although the Negro's indoctrination in democracy was contaminated by the obvious reality of his rejection and exclusion by that democracy, he did not, astonishingly, respond by rejection of democracy itself. He seemed to show a sophisticated wisdom in understanding that the ideal of democracy itself was not to blame merely because democracy, as practiced, had not, for the Negro, advanced beyond verbal commitments. He sought a continuation of a revolution that had already begun. He desired only to join it and share its benefits.

Probably even more important is the compelling reality that the civil rights organizations could not have afforded to behave in a revolutionary manner. Even if a racial revolution were psychologically possible, it was not statistically possible. Negro slaves in the United States, unlike Negro slaves in the Caribbean or South America, remained a numerical minority. Attempts at rebellion during and after the period of slavery were ruthlessly suppressed and tended to introduce not the alleviation of oppression but a new period of intensified cruelty. The stark fact is that the Negro in the United States was never in a position to entertain seriously any notions of major disruption or changes in the existing economic or political system. If his condition were to improve, it would have to improve within the framework of the existing realities, realities which he could not modify in a fundamental way because he lacked the necessary power.

It may be that the strategies and techniques of the civil rights organizations could have been only more systematic and organizational forms of the very kinds of accommodations that individual Negroes were required to make in the face of the superior power of the white system. As the material economic, political, and military power of the United States increased during the twentieth century, the validity of this strategy of assertive accommodation on the part of the civil rights organizations became even more justifiable, practical, and realistic. It is important, however, to understand that these accommodations were never acquiescence in or acceptance of injustice, but rather tactical maneuvers, strategic retreats, or temporary delays, and the effective timing of demands for specific changes.

NAACP AND URBAN LEAGUE: LEADERSHIP AND STRATEGY

What were the effects of this strategy? There is no question that the rationale and techniques of the NAACP led to notable successes in the field of legislation and litigation. Civil rights victories in the federal courts, including equalization of salaries for teachers, the Gaines, Sweatt, and McLaurin cases, the restrictive covenant cases, and, finally, the *Brown vs. Board of Education* school-desegregation decision of 1954, are examples of the extent to which the NAACP has removed almost every legal support for racial segregation in all aspects of American life. Probably the only exception to this is the remaining laws dealing with intermarriage, and these laws may soon be declared unconstitutional.

The techniques, methods, and organizational structure of the NAACP in 1965 are essentially the same as they were in the 1920's. If one were to examine the NAACP today and compare it with the NAACP twenty or thirty years ago, the only significant difference one would find is an increase in the number of staff, particularly in the Legal Defense and Education Fund, Inc., staff.

This important legal arm of the NAACP has been officially separated as an independent corporation from the rest of the NAACP since 1939. But by the early 1950's this technical separation had increased in fact. The Legal Defense and Education Fund, Inc., has its own offices, budget, fund-raising program, and Board of Directors and staff. While there has remained a close working relationship with the NAACP itself, this increasing independence of the Legal Defense and Education Fund has made it possible for it to work closely and provide legal services to the newer more activist civil rights organizations such as CORE and SNCC.

The NAACP itself has added some staff for specialized work in such problem areas as labor and housing. The newer and more direct-actionist civil rights groups have forced the NAACP to initiate more concrete measures, but there is reason to believe that this advance was reluctant and that, left to its own devices, the NAACP would have continued to put its major emphasis on its traditional concerns. Ironically, ten, fifteen, or twenty years ago, such concerns seemed to be extreme militance. Today, in the view of the development of more activist civil rights groups, such as the Congress of Racial Equality (CORE), the Southern Christian Leadership Conference (SCLC), and the Student Nonviolent Coordinating Committee (SNCC), the NAACP is seen as a rather moderate, even conservative, organization.

As leaders of the NAACP, Walter White and, later, Roy Wilkins continued the tradition of Du Bois, but they stopped short where he had only begun. There is every reason to believe that Du Bois would have taken the NAACP to the front lines where CORE, SCLC, and SNCC are now. Walter White developed the method of personal contact and friendship with top public officials, and during his administration an effective NAACP lobby was begun and the legal staff strengthened. Nevertheless this program and his predilection for a "first name" approach to power figures necessarily supplanted direct-action confrontation. It approached the methods of the Urban League and transformed the Du Bois style of militance into one of personal diplomacy. On the death of Walter White in 1955, Roy Wilkins became executive director of the NAACP, after serving as editor of *The Crisis,* the NAACP's official journal. His approach differs little from Walter White's, in spite of the counter pressure of the more militant groups and more activist and impatient forces within the Board and staff of the NAACP. His style, manner, background, and personality are not consistent with a mass appeal. He seems more comfortable in rational discussions with key decision-makers in economic and governmental centers of power than before a mass meeting of his "followers." Wilkins is the personification of responsible, statesmanlike leadership. He jealously guards his belief in the rational and intellectual approach to significant social change and refuses to be pushed even temporarily into the stance of the fiery leader. The value of this approach is clear; its dangers are more obscure but nonetheless real. Its chief danger is that a primary and understandable concern of civil rights leaders for a posture of respectability might make them more vulnerable to the shrewd, psychological exploitation of skillful political leaders. The power of civil rights leaders could probably be more effectively controlled by affability than by racial brutality.

The NAACP either was not able or did not desire to modify its program in response to new demands. It believed it should continue its important work by using those techniques it had already perfected. It may, of course, have been impossible for an old-line organization to alter its course dramatically, and thus it may have been inevitable that new programs would have to stem from the apparently more militant, assertive, and aggressive civil rights organizations.

The Urban League, contrary to popular opinion, has by no means been so visibly successful as the NAACP in attaining its stated goals. Certainly its desire and efforts to aid the smooth adjustment of the Southern Negro who moved to Northern cities, while quite laudable, have not prevented the massive pathology which dominates the expanding ghettos of such cities as New York, Chicago, Philadelphia, Detroit, and Cleveland. The fascinating paradox is that the very areas in which the Urban League program has been most active—the blight of segregated housing, segregated and inferior education, and persistent and pernicious discrimination in employment—have been those areas in which the virulence of racism has increased in the North. Obviously, one cannot blame the program and activities of the Urban League for this blight. It remains a fact, however, that the approach used by the Urban League has not effectively stemmed the tide nor obscured the symptoms of Northern racism. The goals of the NAACP, resting on the vision and courage of the federal courts, were far more concrete and limited and hence more easily achieved. The ghettos of Northern cities and the forces which perpetuate such ghettos are clearly beyond the scope of an agency such as the Urban League or indeed any private agency. In response to this, there are indications that the League's present leadership is moving closer to direct involvement with governmental power.

It is clear also that the victories of the NAACP in the federal courts, the victories of all the combined forces of the civil rights organizations, leading to the Civil Rights Act of 1964 and the Voting Rights Act of 1965 do not appear to be relevant to the peculiar cancerous growth of racism in American ghettos now spreading from the North back to more "liberal" Southern cities like Atlanta and New Orleans. The difficult truth civil rights agencies must eventually face is that so far no technique has been developed which seems relevant to this problem which now has emerged as the key civil rights issue. Protest demonstrations, litigation, and legislation do not seem to be specific remedies for this pattern of social pathology.

Within recent years, under the guidance of its new executive director, Whitney Young, the Urban League has indicated its awareness of the complexities of the present civil rights problem. The Urban League has joined with more "militant" civil rights groups, associating itself with mass protest movements, acknowledging that a social-service approach is not adequate to deal with the more flagrant predicaments of Negroes in the North and South. It has joined in demands for effective legislation. Whitney Young, probably by force of his personality, his background as an academician and administrative social worker, and his diplomatic skill, has managed to combine the traditional approach with a more dramatic and seemingly more militant stance without major disruption to the Urban League. He has not alienated white supporters; indeed, he has convinced them to increase their contributions. He has demonstrated beyond question that a more assertive insistence upon the inclusion of Negroes in the main stream of American life (his "fair share" hiring plan) and the willingness of the Urban League to identify itself with more "militant" direct-action dramatization of the plight of the Negro have not been at a financial sacrifice. Whitney Young demonstrated in the Urban League a degree of flexibility not yet so clearly apparent in the NAACP.

THE CONGRESS OF RACIAL EQUALITY

The Congress of Racial Equality (CORE), like the Urban League and NAACP, began in the North. It was founded in Chicago in 1942 and became a national organization in 1943. From its inception it emphasized direct action and the dramatization of special forms of racial segregation. The founders of CORE were associated in some of their activities with a pacifist-oriented group, the Fellowship of Reconciliation, and the organization was interracial. In the initial stages of CORE, the evolution of a civil rights organization with a larger political commitment seemed possible. The pacifist aura and direct-action orientation of early CORE founders and members suggested a significant divergence from the politically nonpartisan policies and programs of the NAACP and the Urban League. In fact, one of the rationales for the founding of CORE was that it felt that legalism alone could not win the war against segregation.[3]

It is significant that CORE did not become a major civil rights organization until the civil rights movement reached a crescendo after the Brown decision of 1954. Before that, CORE seemed to be a rather constricted, dedicated, almost cult-like group of racial protesters who addressed themselves to fairly specific forms of racial abuse which could be dramatized by their particular method of direct action and personal protest. In 1943, they sat-in at a segregated Chicago restaurant, successfully desegregating it; in 1947 they co-sponsored with the Fellowship of Reconciliation a two-week freedom-ride to test discrimination in buses engaged in interstate travel; and through nonviolent stand-ins, they successfully desegregated the Palisades Amusement Park's pool in 1947–48.[4] These techniques could be viewed as the harbingers of the more extensive use of direct action, nonviolent techniques, which, since the Montgomery bus boycott, have become almost the symbol of the civil rights protest movement. Whether or not Martin Luther King, Jr., was aware of his debt to the CORE precedent, CORE set the pattern for Montgomery. The sit-in technique was initially CORE's, and CORE was also the first civil rights organization to rely upon nonviolent political pacifism.

James Farmer, executive director of CORE, was formerly a Methodist minister. He combines the appearance of personal calm and tolerant objectivity with a surprising forthrightness and fervent commitment. He makes no diplomatic accommodation to power figures, but demands uncompromising equality. In CORE's loose confederation of militant and seemingly undisciplined local chapters under a permissive national board, Farmer is a stabilizing influence, a convergence point; he holds power by virtue of his personal example of commitment. But while he is a symbol of the integrity of CORE and is generally accepted as such by the public and by CORE members, so far he does not seem able to control the activities of some of the more zealous and activistic CORE chapters.

When local CORE groups in Brooklyn threatened to use a dramatic, but seemingly ineffective tactic—the abortive stall-in to keep people from getting to the New York World's Fair in April of 1964—Farmer was forced to intervene in an unaccustomed show of discipline to save the national organization. He allowed himself to be arrested at the Fair partly to demonstrate his own commitment to the cause but also to divert the spotlight from his unruly locals. Yet, whatever the anarchism of these locals and the inadvisability of demonstrations not directly related to concrete grievances, there is something to be said for the observation that, when multitudes are inconvenienced or threatened with discomfort, the very random quality of the action reflects the desperation of the demonstrators and has some impact, even if only irritation, upon the white majority. To the Negro, white irritation and anger is at least a *response.* And where chaos threatens, more responsible leaders of society intervene. The danger of disruptive demonstration, of course, is that the intervention may be repressive and the repressiveness may seem justifiable in the name of public order. But thus far CORE has not demonstrated that its tactics and methods are relevant to the problems and the pervasive pathology of the Negro in urban ghettos.

THE SOUTHERN CHRISTIAN LEADERSHIP CONFERENCE

The Southern Christian Leadership Conference, which Martin Luther King, Jr., heads, has the distinction of being the first civil rights organization to start in the South. It began in Atlanta in 1957, primarily as an expression of the commitment of nearly one hundred men throughout the South to the idea of a Southern movement to implement through nonviolent means the Supreme Court's decision against bus segregation. This commitment was made concrete by formation of a permanent organization, the SCLC, and Martin Luther King, Jr., was elected its president.

In order to understand SCLC and King, one must understand that this movement would probably not have existed at all were it not for the 1954 Supreme Court school-desegregation decision which provided a tremendous boost to the morale of Negroes by its clear affirmation that color is irrelevant to the rights of American citizens. Until this time, the Southern Negro generally had accommodated himself to the separation of the black from the white society. In spite of the fact that Southern rural Negroes in Clarendon County, South Carolina, were the original plaintiffs in the school-desegregation cases, one could speculate that if the United States Supreme Court had ruled against them, the Southern Negro would probably have retreated into stagnation or inner rebellion or protest by indirection. The leadership of King came immediately, however, as a consequence of a Negro woman's refusal, in 1955, to make the kinds of adjustments to racial humiliation that Negro women had been making in the South throughout the twentieth century. Rosa Parks' defiance was publicized in *The Montgomery Advertiser,* which also revealed the fact that Negroes were organizing. Ironically, the chief boost to the boycott came from the white press. Scores of Negroes, who would not have known about the boycott, learned of it in the Montgomery newspaper and offered help to King and other ministers.

The bus boycott catapulted King first into local leadership as head of the Montgomery Improvement Association, formed for the purpose of coordinating the bus boycott, and then by virtue of the drama and success of that boycott into national leadership. He had responded to forces beyond his control, forces let loose by the early work of the NAACP in clearing away the legal support for segregation, by the urbanization and industrialization of society, and by the pressures of America's role in a predominantly nonwhite world. Here was a man who, by virtue of his personality and his role as minister, did not excite an overt competitive reaction from others. He could and did provide the symbol of unified protest and defiance. As a minister trained not only in theology, but in philosophy and history as well, sensitive and jealous of his understanding of world events and world history, King could develop and articulate a philosophical rationale for the movement, an ideology to support his strategy. Associating his role in Montgomery with the Gandhian philosophy of passive resistance and nonviolence, he emphasized another dimension of the civil rights movement in America, systematically articulating and developing the form of racial protest first used by CORE more than ten years before. The question has been raised whether or not this philosophy and the commitment to love one's oppressor is relevant to the effectiveness of the method itself. What happened in Montgomery was not a consequence of King's philosophy. The Montgomery affair demonstrated rather the ability of King and others to exploit the errors of the whites and to unify the Negroes for an effective boycott. There is no evidence that whites react to philosophy, but they do react to what happens. King's philosophy did not exist before the fact; rather, it was adopted after it was found to be working.

The development of philosophical and religious support for the method did, however, help to gather support for future action by focusing and refining a tactic and by an appeal to the conscience of Negro and white. King effectively turned the main weakness of the Negro, his numerical, economic, and political impotence, into a working strategy. Practically speaking, he could not seek redress by violence, but he did have available resources of nonviolence. Nietzsche said that Christ developed a philosophy of love because the Jews were weak; and that only when Christianity becomes strong can love become powerful. King's philosophy is actually a response to the behavior of others, effective directly in terms of the ferocity of the resistance it meets. It is not only nonviolent; it is also assertive. It depends on the reactions of others for its own strength. King and SCLC sometimes appear, indeed, to be satisfied, as in the case of Birmingham, with negotiations leading to minimal concessions. King does not insist upon total change in the status of Negroes in a community but considers partial change temporarily satisfactory. What he settles for can be questioned in terms of the energy expended and the risks taken.

One cannot understand SCLC solely in terms of its organization, which is amorphous and more symbolic than functional, even though the national headquarters in Atlanta, Georgia, has sixty-five affiliates throughout the South. To understand this organization, one has to understand King, because SCLC *is* Martin Luther King, Jr. King is a national hero, a charismatic leader, portrayed in America and through the world as a man of quiet dignity, a personification of courage in the face of racial danger. He has the ability to articulate a philosophy and ideology of race relations clearly acceptable to the larger society. As far as the general public is concerned, the civil rights movement has converged in his personality. His ability to portray selflessness and to understand other civil rights leaders has made him a suitable person for his role. In the complexities, tensions, and frustrations of the civil rights movement, King fills an important function of simplification through personalization.

The presence of King and SCLC indicates something about the inadequacy or the inappropriateness of the methods and techniques used by the NAACP and the Urban League in the South today. If either the NAACP or the Urban League had been sufficient, King could not have been so successful as he is. King moved into a vacuum that existing civil rights groups did not fill. He mobilized people not in protest against the entire system but against specific injustices. Concrete successes, in turn, raised Negro morale. But SCLC's program, as a means to transform society, is more apparently than actually successful. The dramatization of the direct-action, SCLC-King technique over the mass media leads to the impression that the civil rights movement in the South is in fact a mass movement. In those situations in which white police and political officers do not exacerbate the resentment of Negroes by acts of cruelty and hostility, even King's appeal does not actively involve more than a fraction of the Negro population. It can, of course, be said of any "mass" movement that it rarely involves more than a small minority in direct action, at least in its initial stages.

King himself seems to realize the limitations of his method as shown by his unsuccessful attempt to encourage a less concrete strategy, a general boycott of the state of Alabama. In his plans to extend his program into Northern cities he seems likely to be less successful. In the future phase of the civil rights movement where Negroes confront not direct tyranny but pervasive oppression, King's strategy and charisma may be less effective. Furthermore, it would probably be all too easy to abort and to make impotent the whole King-SCLC approach, if white society could control the flagrant idiocy of some of its own leaders, suppress the more vulgar, atavistic tyrants like Sheriff Jim Clark, and create instead a quiet, if not genteel, intransigence. Such intransigence presents a quite different problem to the civil rights movement. A philosophy of love or techniques which seem compatible with such a philosophy would seem effective only in a situation of flagrant hate or cruelty. When love meets either indifference or passive refusal to change, it does not seem to have the power to mobilize the reactions of potential allies. Nor does it seem to affect the enemy—it appears irrelevant to fundamental social change.

Gandhi, of course, whose philosophy was one of nonviolent resistance, was the leader of a *majority* in the fight for Indian independence, King of a *minority;* this fact, important in an analysis of power, may be the decisive one in determining whether King can achieve a transformation of American society as deep and real as the Gandhian victory in India. The willingness of an oppressed people to protest and suffer, passively or assertively, without bitterness or with "love for the oppressors" seems to have influence only where the conscience of the majority of the society can be reached. In Hitler's Germany the Jews suffered nonviolently without stirring Nazi repentance; the early Christians who were eaten by lions seem to have stimulated not guilt but greed in the watching multitudes. King's strategy depends therefore for its success not only upon the presence of flagrant cruelty in a society but also upon the inherent good will, the latent conscience of the majority of the American people, as Gandhi's did upon the British commitment to justice.

In a situation of benign intransigence—like New York City— or a society of gentlemen—North Carolina, for example—a philosophy of love for the oppressor may be less effective than in Alabama. There Negroes do not face overt cruelty but rather the refusal to alter their status. What do you do in a situation in which you have laws on your side, where whites smile and say to you that they are your friends, but where your white "friends" move to the suburbs leaving you confronted with segregation and inferior education in schools, ghetto housing, and a quiet and tacit discrimination in jobs? How can you demonstrate a philosophy of love in response to this? What is the appropriate form of protest? One can "sit-in" in the Board of Education building, and not a single child will come back from the suburbs or from the private and parochial schools. One can link arms with the Mayor of Boston and march on the Commons, but it will not affect the housing conditions of Negroes in Roxbury. One can be hailed justifiably as a Nobel Prize hero by the Mayor of New York City, but this will not in itself change a single aspect of the total pattern of pathology which dominates the lives of the prisoners of the ghettos of New York.

THE STUDENT NONVIOLENT COORDINATING COMMITTEE

The rise of the Student Nonviolent Coordinating Committee intensified and sharpened the dramatic confrontation begun by CORE in the 1940's and developed by Martin Luther King, Jr., in the late 1950's. The restless young students who originally led the movement used direct assertive defiance and resistance, nonviolent in tactic and yet militant in spirit. They had gone beyond the quiet, stubborn, passive resistance of the bus boycott in Montgomery to a new stage of challenge—no less stubborn but considerably less passive. The first demonstrations in Greensboro, North Carolina, and Nashville, Tennessee, were appropriately in college towns. It was as a result of these that the Student Nonviolent Coordinating Committee was formed.[5] SNCC was organized in April 1960 at a meeting at Shaw University in Raleigh, North Carolina. It took as its original function the coordination of the protest work of the many student groups conducting sit-ins.[6]

This program, representing the impatience of a younger generation, came at a time when more established civil rights groups seemed ready to settle for post-Little Rock tokenism and moderation. During the years since 1954 and up to that time, the letter and spirit of the Brown decision had been effectively eroded. "All deliberate speed" had been translated into "any perceptible movement," or mere verbalization of movement. The presence of a single Negro child in a previously white school was considered a famous victory. But the SNCC "kids" in their worn denims brought new verve, drive, daring, and enthusiasm—as well as the brashness and chaos of youth—to sustain the dynamism of direct-action civil rights tactics. They propelled more orderly and stable groups like the NAACP and Urban League toward increasing acceptance of direct-action methods not only because some of the older leaders found the ardor of youth contagious but also because, after the manner of experienced leaders, they sensed that bolder programs would be necessary if their own role were not to be undermined. The intervention of youth revitalized CORE and sustained the intensity of the direct involvement of King and SCLC. It has helped make possible—indeed it may have played a vital part in—the continuation of King's role as charismatic leader by arousing weary and apathetic Negroes to the imminence of justice, thereby stimulating an atmosphere sympathetic to crusade and sacrifice.

The SNCC uniform of blue denims and the manner of defiance were far removed from the neat white shirt and tie and Ivy League jacket of Urban League workers and the courteous, Biblical eloquence of King. After SNCC's initial stage of urban protest, it decided to move into the deep South and consciously attempted to express through dress, manner, and method a direct identification with working-class Southern Negroes. Nonetheless, many of the SNCC leaders were actually even closer than the SCLC, NAACP, and Urban League leadership to sophisticated Northern campuses where militance previously had been less action-oriented than intellectual.

SNCC seems restless with long-term negotiation and the methods of persuasion of the Urban League, and it assumes that the legislative and litigation approach of the NAACP has practically attained its goals. SNCC has not overtly repudiated King's philosophy of nonviolence, but it does not root its own acceptance of this strategy in love of the enemy. Rather SNCC leaders seem almost nationalistic in spirit, in the sense of pride that they hold, not so much in *being* black (an appreciable number of SNCC workers are white) as in their conviction that justice and the future are on their side. SNCC welcomes dedicated whites and others who presumably share its concern for total justice. The style and manner of the SNCC leaders and workers are not consistent with any overt display of gratitude even to those whites who share their dangers and daily risks. The underlying assumption of the SNCC approach appears to be that the struggle for political and social democracy in the South is the responsibility of all Americans. They approach their programs and tasks with pride, courage, and flexibility and with an absence of sentimentality which those seeking gratitude or deference might view as disdain. They do not seem to be so concerned with the careful political screening of co-workers and exclusion of "radicals" as are the more experienced and "respectable" civil rights organizations. But it would be a mistake to interpret the SNCC style and method of challenge to the racial hypocrisies of the South as evidence of "left-wing" or Communist domination. SNCC is flexible and inclusive—not doctrinaire and dogmatic. Being loosely organized, SNCC has practically no hierarchy or clear lines of authority. The discipline of its workers seems to be determined by each individual's identification with the "cause" and the direct confrontation approach rather than by external controls or organizational structure.

Instead of a single leader, SNCC has many "leaders." Nominally, John Lewis is president of the Board of Directors and James Forman is executive director of SNCC. Actually "policy" and "operational" leadership is not only shared by Lewis and Forman but must be shared with others. Robert Moses, who plays a key role in the SNCC leadership team, directed the activities of the Council of Federated Organizations (COFO) in Mississippi during the summer of 1964. The individuals who coordinate SNCC activities for such Southern states as Georgia, Louisiana, and South Carolina also insist upon being heard in the leadership councils of SNCC. So far no single personality has emerged to speak for SNCC. John Lewis and Bob Moses seem deceptively retiring and soft-spoken in manner, but each is doggedly determined, assertive, and courageous in pursuit of the goals of unqualified equality. James Forman and Donald Harris, formerly SNCC coordinator in Georgia, are more overtly assertive and articulate but are no less likely to assume personal risks. The essence of SNCC leadership appears to be this willingness to assume personal risks, to expose oneself to imprisonment and brutality, and thereby to dramatize the nature of American racism before the nation and the world. Its members play the important role of commando raiders on the more dangerous and exposed fronts of the present racial struggle. This is not to be understood as mere adolescent bravado or defiance. It must be understood as an insistence upon total honesty, unwillingness to settle for anything less than uncompromised equality. It is an impatience with the verbalizations and euphemisms of "the accommodations" of more "realistic" or "strategic" leaders and organizations. This stance could be and has been described as "unrealistic" and "radical."

A VARIETY OF METHODS, THE SAME GOALS, AND CONTEMPORARY RELEVANCE

There are obvious and subtle problems in any social movement when a variety of organizations with different philosophies, strategies, tactics, organizational structure, and leadership all seek the same broad goals. All civil rights organizations are committed to full inclusion of the Negro in the economic and political life of America, without restrictions based on race or color. But each differs from the other in its conception of how this commitment can best be fulfilled.

There is general agreement that the successes of the civil rights movement and organizations have catapulted the civil rights struggle into a new stage with more complex and difficult problems and goals. Martin Luther King, Jr., in an interview with this observer which included other civil rights leaders, sought to verbalize this growing awareness of the fact that the civil rights movement must now address itself to the problem of bringing about observable changes in the actual living conditions of the masses of Negroes. He said:

> Well, aren't we saying, gentlemen, that a program
> has not yet been worked out to grapple with the
> magnitude of this problem in the United States,
> both North and South? Isn't there a need now, be-
> cause of the urgency and the seriousness of the
> situation, to develop a sort of crash program to lift
> the standards of the Negro and to get rid of the
> underlying conditions that produce so many social
> evils and develop so many social problems?
> I think this is what we face at this time, and I
> know it leads to the whole question of discrimination
> in reverse, and all of that. But I think we've got to
> face the fact in this country, that because of the
> legacy of slavery and segregation, and the seeds of
> injustice planted in the past, we have this harvest
> of confusion now, and we're going to continue to
> have it until we get to the root of the problem.[7]

The disturbing question which must be faced is whether or not the present civil rights organizations are equipped in terms of perspective, staff, and organizational structure to deal effectively with the present level of civil rights problems. And, if not, whether they are flexible enough to make the necessary changes in order to be relevant.

An examination of some of the concrete deficiencies in the organizations themselves shows that the NAACP and Urban League are under the handicap of experience. Committed to a method and a goal, they have not altered either in major ways since their founding. The sweep of the civil rights movement in the past two decades has not significantly affected these two elders of the movement. They still appear to function primarily in terms of personal leadership rather than staff competence. An exception is the expansion of the NAACP's legal and educational fund staff, which still remains largely legal and pays little attention to education. A serious analysis of the way in which the NAACP has attempted to modify its structure to meet the current civil rights struggle would force one to conclude that it has done so to a minimal degree. For example, the staff concerned with the problems of housing is, practically speaking, nonexistent. As of June 1965, and for the previous two years, the position of housing secretary was unfilled. The NAACP staff concerned with labor consists of a director and a secretary. This is true also for education. The staff responsible for public relations, promotion, and propaganda has increased from five to seven persons within the past crucial decade of civil rights activity. These facts suggest that the NAACP has made virtually no organizational response to meet the present increased civil rights demands. The local branches are archaic and generally ineffective, with barely adequate communication and coordination of policy and procedures between the national organization and the local branches. Probably the NAACP's most glaring inadequacy in light of the present and future demands of the civil rights revolution is the lack of a fact-gathering and research staff.

The Urban League seems more modern and efficient in its fund raising, promotion, and public relations and in its relationship with its local groups. It also, however, seems weak in research.

One could speculate that this weakness—which is shared by the newer organizations as well—reflects the difficulty of moving from reliance on personal leadership to the more demanding, less dramatic, less ego-satisfying but imperative staff approach. Now that the maximum gains have been obtained through legislation, litigation, and appeals to conscience, the difficult problem of implementation, of translating these gains into actual changes in the lives of Negroes, remains. This cannot be achieved by charisma alone. It requires adequate and efficient staffs, working, of course, under inspired and creative leadership.

In spite of these objective limitations, the NAACP and the Urban League are flourishing. In 1962, the NAACP was said to have a membership of 370,000 in 1,200 local branches in forty-four states and the District of Columbia.[8] By the end of 1964, its membership was given as 455,839 in 1,845 branches in forty-eight states and the District of Columbia. An unaudited budget indicates that income for 1964 was $1,116,565.68.

The picture for the Urban League is even more dramatic. Until Whitney Young became executive director of the organization in 1961, the largest fund-raising total in any one year was $325,000. In 1962, contributions were $700,000; in 1963, $1,441,000; and in 1964, $1,650,000. Of particular note is the fact that, prior to 1962, no corporate body had made a contribution of more than $5,000 to the Urban League. In 1964, several donations of $50,000 were received from corporations, and foundations have given as much as $150,000. These impressive accretions are, no doubt, a testament not only to the skill and eloquence of Young but also, as in the case of the NAACP's growth, to the dynamic momentum and strength of the entire civil rights movement. The success of both might be a reflection, at least in part, also of their relative respectability.

CORE's chief deficiencies are its weak organizational structure, the fact that its executive does not have sufficient power, and the problem that it has seemed at various times to be endangered by lack of discipline. However weak in discipline, it is nevertheless strong in enthusiasm and dedication among its members and its locals. It appears to be weak also in its fiscal arrangements, its fund-raising and systematic promotion. CORE is in serious financial difficulties. There is a serious question whether CORE's lack of organizational discipline and structure is an asset or liability in terms of the flexibility necessary for it to be relevant to the present civil rights problems.

Behind SCLC's inspiring reality lie some very real difficulties, many of them quite human. Financially, however, it seems strong; it seems relatively easy for SCLC, through King, to attract a majority of the nonselective contributions to the civil rights movement, despite the minimal organization of SCLC itself. It is reasonable to conclude that if King were not its leader there would be no SCLC. Indeed, it is difficult to understand the role of SCLC's Board of Directors. It and the organization seem to be dominated by the magnetic appeal of King, by the personal loyalty and reverence of his top aides and of the masses who respond to his leadership. It is reasonable to assume that most of those who respond most enthusiastically to King's and SCLC's leadership are not members of his organization. The burdens of this special type of personal leadership are great if not intolerable. Probably the most desperate need of King and SCLC is for an effective supporting working staff to provide King with the type of background information and program planning which are necessary if this organization is to be relevant and if the type of leadership held by King is to continue to be effective.

SNCC is probably the least organized of all the civil rights organizations, suggesting that the degree of organization is not necessarily related to effectiveness or to the appearance of effectiveness.

As movements become more structured, they fall prey to the problems that plague most organizations, namely, red tape, bureaucracy, hierarchical discipline restricting spontaneous and imaginative experimentation, fear of change and, therefore, of growth. In large industrial, economic, financial, and governmental bureaucracies, and in political parties, major decisions are not personal, in spite of the existence of a charismatic leader. Similarly in the civil rights movement, major decisions must now reflect painstaking difficult staff work based on fact-finding, intelligence, continuing critical analyses of data and strategies. Institutions tend to repress the rebel and to elevate the businessman-diplomat, yet the civil rights movement is full of rebels and its goal is independence. It is possible that the vitality of all of the civil rights organizations will depend on sustaining certain respectable organizations like the NAACP and the Urban League while stimulating them to pursue new programs and encouraging the fluid realignment of younger, more restless forces from whom the momentum for change must certainly come.

WHO SPEAKS FOR THE NEGRO?

It would be understandable to succumb to the temptation to rank the civil rights organizations in terms of their degree of militance and effectiveness. And it has been argued persuasively that for maximum effectiveness the civil rights organizations should develop an efficient and disciplined machinery for coordination and genuine cooperation. This tendency and these suggestions, while understandable, would reduce the complexities of the present civil rights movement and the role of the organizations and leaders to a convenient oversimplification. The civil rights problems—the American racial problem—are historically and currently complex and multidimensional. Each approach has some validity and no one now knows which is more valid than others. The ultimate test of a given approach or pattern of approaches will be in the demonstration of observable and sustained changes in the status of Negroes—

the evidence that the Negroes are included in all aspects of American life with the equal protection of laws and governmental power. This goal is not likely to be obtained by a single agency, method or leader. Certain approaches will be more compatible with the temperament of some individuals, Negro and white, than with others.

The civil rights groups vary in organizational efficiency as well as in philosophy, approach, and methods. The rank and file of liberal or religious whites might be more responsive to the seemingly nonthreatening, Christian approach of Martin Luther King, Jr. More tough-minded and pragmatic business and governmental leaders might find a greater point of contact with the appeals and approaches of the NAACP and the Urban League. The more passionate Negroes and whites who seek immediate and concrete forms of justice will probably gravitate toward CORE and SNCC. Obviously one would not offer financial or other support to an organization whose philosophy and methods made one uncomfortable or threatened one's status. Therefore, while the extent of financial support for a given organization may be seen as an index of the degree of the general acceptability of that organization's approach, it is not necessarily an index of the relevance or effectiveness of its program. One is tempted to hypothesize from these data that the financial success of an organization engaged in the civil rights confrontation is directly related to the *perceived* respectability of the organization and its nominal head. Correlative to this would be the hypothesis that the relative financial success of a civil rights group is inversely related to the *perceived* degree of radicalism of the organization and its nominal head.

The question "Who speaks for the Negro?" is real; perhaps no one group can speak for all Negroes just as no one political party can speak for all citizens of a democracy or no one religion can satisfy the needs of all individuals. The variety of organizations and "leaders" among Negroes may be viewed as a sign of democracy, health, and the present strength of the movement rather than as a symptom of weakness. This variety and loose coordination can help revitalize each through dynamic competition. Each organization influences the momentum and pace of the others. The inevitable interaction among them demands from each a level of effectiveness and relevance above the minimum possible for any single organization.

As Roy Wilkins said in response to a question from this observer:

> We cannot promise you . . . that there will be a
> co-ordinated, organized structural, formalized attack

on these matters and that each will be apportioned a part of this task. But we will say this: like Martin (Luther King, Jr.) said, there is more unity than there ever has been before, there's more division of work, and there's more co-ordination and backing up of each other than there has been before. Maybe in 1975, or some other time, there will come an over-all organization, but no other group has managed that, and why should we?[9]

Direct observation and analysis of relevent data and events lead to the conclusion that the stresses and strains within the civil rights movement and within and among the various organizations are real and cannot be denied; and a great deal of energy is expended in preventing these difficulties from becoming overt and thus destroying the public image of unity. But these problems can be seen as symptoms of the irresistible strength of the civil rights movement rather than as signs of inherent flaws or fatal weaknesses of the organizations and their leaders. Furthermore, the power and the momentum of the movement itself seem able to compensate for the present deficiencies in the organizations and leadership. Probably, and paradoxically, the clearest indication of the solidity and rapidity of movement toward the goal of unqualified rights for America's Negro citizens is the fact that civil rights agencies not only have mobilized and organized some of the latent power of committed whites and Negroes necessary for social change, but, in so doing, have now achieved sufficient strength to risk the beginnings of public debate over philosophy, strategy, and tactics. The lie which supports racism is being supplanted by more forthright dialogue and honest confrontation between whites and Negroes, among various classes of Negroes, between Negro "leaders" and their white and Negro co-workers, and within the civil rights movement itself.

References

[1] For a thoughtful discussion of the Negro revolt, see Lerone Bennett, Jr., *Confrontation: Black and White* (Chicago, 1965).

[2] E. Franklin Frazier, *The Negro in the United States* (rev. ed.; New York, 1957), pp. 524–525.

[3] Louis Lomax, *The Negro Revolt* (New York, 1963), p. 145.

[4] James Peck, *Freedom Ride* (New York, 1962), *passim.*

[5] For an excellent study of SNCC, see Howard Zinn, *SNCC, The New Abolitionists* (Boston, 1964).

⁶ W. Haywood Burns, *The Voices of Negro Protest in America* (London, 1963), p. 44.

⁷ Kenneth Clark, Roy Wilkins, Whitney Young, Jr., James Farmer, Martin Luther King, Jr., and James Forman, "The Management of the Civil-Rights Struggle," in Alan F. Westin (ed.), *Freedom Now! The Civil Rights Struggle in America* (New York, 1964).

⁸ W. Haywood Burns, *op. cit.,* p. 19.

⁹ Kenneth Clark, *et al.,* in Alan F. Westin (ed.), *op.cit.*

15
Soul
Power
Andrew Kopkind

The Movement is dead; the Revolution is unborn. The streets are bloody and ablaze, but it is difficult to see why, and impossible to know for what end. Government on every level is ineffectual, helpless to act either in the short term or the long. The force of Army and police seems not to suppress violence, but incite it. Mediators have no space to work; they command neither resources nor respect, and their rhetoric is discredited in all councils, by all classes. The old words are meaningless, the old explanations irrelevant, the old remedies useless. It is the worst of times.

It is the best of times. The wretched of this American earth are together as they have never been before, in motion if not in movement. No march, no sit-in, no boycott ever touched so many. The social cloth which binds and suffocates them is tearing at its seamiest places. The subtle methods of co-optation work no better to keep it intact than the brutal methods of repression; if it is any comfort, liberalism proves hardly more effective than fascism. Above all, there is a sense that the continuity of an age has been cut, that we have arrived at an infrequent fulcrum of history, and that what comes now will be vastly different from what went before.

It is not a time for reflection, but for evocation. The responsibility of the intellectual is the same as that of the street organizer, the draft resister, the Digger: to talk *to* people, not *about* them. The important literature now is the underground press, the speeches of Malcolm, the works of Fanon, the songs of the Rolling Stones and Aretha Franklin. The rest all sounds like the Moynihan Report

Reprinted by permission from Andrew Kopkind, "Soul Power," *The New York Review of Books,* 9, no. 3 (August 24, 1967), pp. 3–6.

and *Time*-Essay, explaining everything, understanding nothing, changing no one.

Martin Luther King once had the ability to talk to people, the power to change them by evoking images of revolution. But the duty of a revolutionary is to make revolutions (say those who have done it), and King made none. By his own admission, things are worse in the US today—for white people and black—than when he began the bus boycott in Montgomery eleven years ago. Last summer, in Chicago, he was booed at a mass meeting, and later, as he lay in bed unsleeping, he understood why:

> For twelve years I, and others like me, had held out radiant promises of progress. I had preached to them about my dream. I had lectured to them about the not too distant day when they would have freedom, "all, here and now." I had urged them to have faith in America and in white society. Their hopes had soared. They were now booing because they felt we were unable to deliver on our promises. They were booing because we had urged them to have faith in people who had too often proved to be unfaithful. They were now hostile because they were watching the dream that they had so readily accepted turn into a nightmare.

The fault is no more King's than it is ours, though no less, either. He has been outstripped by his times, overtaken by the events which he may have obliquely helped to produce but could not predict. He is not likely to regain command. Both his philosophy and his techniques of leadership were products of a different world, of relationships which no longer obtain and expectations which are no longer valid. King assumed that the political economy of America was able to allow the integration of the mass of poor Negroes into the mainstream of society, with only minor pushing and shoving. White liberals would be the thin edge of the wedge, the Democratic Party the effective agency of change, a marching army of blacks the sting to conscience. The trick lay in finding the best tactics, presenting the most feasible programs, and putting on the most idealistic faces.

It worked well for a while. Southern feudalism began to disintegrate (it was already unsupportable), voters were registered and lunch counters integrated, and civil-rights acts were passed. But there were stonier walls behind the first defenses of segregation. A

society infused with racism would not easily discard the arrangements by which it confers status. Unlike anachronistic feudalism
in the deep South, the national system of industrial and technological capitalism was practically invulnerable. Marches and freedom
songs were unavailing. The "power structures" of the Mississippi
Delta may have trembled when they heard "Ain't Gonna Let Nobody
Turn Me 'Round," but the one in Cook County was unmoved. It had
better weapons: an anti-poverty program, an Uncle Tom congressman, available jobs, and huge stores of tolerance. When that failed,
as it did, there were armies of police and soldiers prepared for
final solutions.

King may have first realized his predicament as he sat,
silently, in the caucus of Mississippi Freedom Democrats in Atlantic
City. The National Democratic Party in which he had placed his
faith for change denied their petition for representation; it had no
intention of altering the balance of power between blacks and
whites in Mississippi. Worst of all, the liberal vanguard of that Party,
Hubert Humphrey and Walter Reuther, were wielding the heaviest
hatchets, to protect their own skins and secure their own
interests.

If that lesson was unclear, King could have seen a half year
later how the party of peace embarked on the most barbaric imperialistic war of this century. At best, he might have understood that
the institutional demands that induced the war—the politics and
economics of anti-communism—were parallel to the ones that kept
the underclass in its place—the politics and economics of racism.
At least, he began to realize that social destruction in Vietnam was
somehow incompatible with social advancement at home.

When the going was good, King still had his white liberals
and his black marchers. But then the going was bad and getting
worse. The white liberals had apparently misunderstood or had
been misinformed. They were willing supporters when the goals of
the Movement were integration and the *embourgeoisement* of poor
Negroes. When the goal was liberation, the slogan "power" instead
of "freedom," and the consequences were convulsions in the society
they wanted desperately to preserve, the liberals dropped back, with
their marching feet and then their checks. At the same time, and for
the same reasons, King's black base began to thin. With no agents
for change responsive to his demands, there would be no goods
to deliver. It was not that King had chosen the wrong tactics, or
picked the wrong allies. He had simply, and disastrously, arrived
at the wrong conclusions about the world. No coalitions available
and no programs imaginable could "succeed" even in his own

terms. Insofar as his objectives were revolutionary, they could not come out of status-quo institutions; insofar as they were not, his followers were not interested.

King's response was to fly out in all directions in search of a new constituency. He arrived in Chicago last summer with fanfares in the national press, the commensurate ballyhoo in the streets. The thrust of his attack was the formation of community organizations to "End the Slums." His strategy had three phases: tenants' councils would harass landlords, mass (integrated) marches would arouse the country, and the Democratic Administration in Washington would push an open-housing bill through Congress.

Within a few months, he had failed in all three endeavors. The local councils were haphazardly organized by staff workers with no understanding of the problems of building a solid base of local people. The marches were premature—the community was not ready to support them to the end—and King had to surrender to Mayor Daley and his friends for a worthless list of promises that would never be fulfilled. The national Democratic Party was unable to pass a housing bill, although it was theoretically in charge of the most "liberal" congress in thirty years.

King retired in defeat to write a book, surfacing only a few months ago to condemn the war in which his movement had been drowned. As always, his speeches were fluent and moving, but as always, again, they never quite got to the heart of the problem. For like his formulation of the race conflict, his conception of the war is devoid of historical perspective and a sense of the processes of society. He seems to believe that progress is inevitable because compelled by an abstract moral force. Reality is seen as a series of episodes: "every revolutionary movement has its peaks of united activity and its valleys of debate and internal confusion." Life is just one damn thing after another.

It is not easy to reconcile King's morality and his history— or the lack of it. Conventional commentators these days like to speak of King's "nobility" and the purity of his humanism, and then they sigh that the world is not ready for him. But it is more accurate to say that King is not ready for the world. His morality derives from where *he* is, not from where his followers are. The black people of America are at the losing ends of shotguns, outweighed by thumb-heavy scales, on the outermost margins of power. King's invocation of love and integration and non-violence may embody what he likes to call the "Judaeo-Christian tradition," but in the U.S. in this generation those are basically the demands of the boss, the preacher, the publisher, and the politician. Turn-the-other-cheek was always a personal standard, not a general rule; people can commit suicide but peoples cannot. Morality, like politics, starts at the barrel of a gun. . . .

What is hardest now to comprehend—remembering the *Time* covers and the Nobel award—is King's irrelevancy. Almost seven years ago, in *Harper's,* James Baldwin wrote that King had "succeeded, in a way no Negro before him has managed to do, to carry the battle into the individual heart and make its resolution the province of the individual will. . . . He has incurred, therefore, the grave responsibility of continuing to lead in the path he has encouraged so many people to follow. How he will do this I do not know, but I do not see how he can possibly avoid a break, at last, with the habits and attitudes, stratagems and fears of the past."

Baldwin's skepticism was wise. The break has not come, and the heart is no longer the battleground. Nearly Jeremiah in 1960, King now seems a black Joshua Loth Liebman:

> Our most fruitful course is to stand firm, move forward nonviolently, accept disappointments and cling to hope. Our determined refusal not to be stopped will eventually open the door to fulfillment. By recognizing the necessity of suffering in a righteous cause, we may achieve our humanity's full stature. To guard ourselves from bitterness, we need the vision to see in this generation's ordeals the opportunity to transfigure both ourselves and American society.

This summer, King is shuffling between Chicago and Cleveland. He has all but abandoned the "End the Slums" campaign in Chicago, and instead is pushing "Operation Breadbasket," a program of economic pressure against large food-marketing corporations in an effort to get more jobs for Negroes. A similar tactic had some limited success in Philadelphia many years ago, but its gains have not been significant anywhere else. From a Chicago base, King hopes to get ministers across the country who are affiliated with his Southern Christian Leadership Conference to start local "Breadbaskets"—against National Dairy Products, Kellogg, and California Packing Company goods. The theory is that the ministers will negotiate for jobs with company representatives; if no progress is made, congregations will be mobilized to picket, and, if necessary, boycott proscribed products. At the same time, King's staff in Chicago has a federal HEW grant to do vocational education, so that some untrained Negroes off the streets may be able to fill the new jobs if they appear.

There is no reason to believe that the national "Breadbasket" will make more headway than the local ones. The organization is crude, and, more than that, many of the assumptions are questionable. The few jobs that may open will not noticeably change the character of ghettos; at best, a few more black people will pop out into the middle class, like overheated molecules in a brimming beaker of water. Many of the jobs would go to Negroes who are either skilled already (and may leave slightly less desirable employment) or at the very top of the underclass—those few who are ready to jump. Local groups backing up the demands for jobs will be thoroughly controlled by SCLC staff workers, in consultation with the odd black businessman in town. There is little implication for permanent organization or real movement. "Breadbasket" amounts to an escalation of rhetoric, but a diminution of power over a broad base. More than anything King has attempted so far, it assumes the permanence and even the desirability of present economic relationships. The only change would be the imposition of a few black faces behind desks and counters.

In Cleveland, King's staff is working on a larger scale, but his campaign there is new, and it is likely to suffer from the same deficiencies found in the Chicago experience: top-heavy organization, premature action, orientation toward small goals (instead of movements). If there is violence there, King's position will be all the more precarious. He has maneuvered for several years now between white anxieties and black anger. On one side, he tells whites that he alone can control the ghettos, if they support his work and give him goods to deliver; on the other, he tells the black people presumably under his influence that rioting will get them nowhere, and that he alone can give them what they want. It is a complicated game requiring consummate political skill and, although King abides by the rules, he has not been winning many points. Whites have ceased to believe him, or really to care; the blacks hardly listen.

It is not that the ghetto listens to anyone else. No black "leaders" with national reputations speak in understandable accents. The only authentic black hero of this revolutionary generation was Malcolm; Stockely Carmichael comes closer to that standard than most, but he is somehow unscarred, not deeply cynical enough to evoke the radical funkiness of Black America. Carmichael, like the rest of the brilliant SNCC organizers of his early Sixties era, is still hung-up on white culture. What happens when a child of Camus grows up? There is something stagey about his public performances; each is too much a *tour de force.* "Stokely Carmichael, the tee vee starmichael," his SNCC friends called him in Mississippi in 1964. Until now, at least, he has had too good a time. His successor, Rap Brown, lacks Carmichael's smile and brittle brilliance, but he seems more at ease with the slowly moving black poor. He may well sound too dangerous to be tolerated. "We' going to burn this town to the ground," he says. Apocalypse is the normal mood of ghetto talk, but on the outside it sounds like criminal anarchy. Brown must choose between understanding from his audience or tolerance from the enemy.

SNCC decided last winter to move into Northern urban centers and begin the kind of organizing there that it had once done in Southern black belt counties. The stated political objectives of the Southern campaign—politicians elected, schools desegregated, economic improvement—have not been fulfilled. But SNCC had been able to devise radical new models for the organization of communities. The projects in Mississippi and Alabama had suddenly given people a sense of themselves and their power.

It worked so well for the wrong reasons as well as the right ones. SNCC's black and white intellectuals charmed the rural "folks" as much as they organized them. When the SNCC kids left, the local communities often slid back—if not into the lives that they had led, then to a less sophisticated kind of political organization than SNCC had envisioned. A rough kind of black tammanyism began to arise in the counties where SNCC and the Freedom Democrats had worked hardest. SNCC became largely irrelevant, and its staff members more or less uninterested in hanging around to see the after-effects.

The Northern campaign never really happened. A few workers in a small number of cities are still at it, but their total effort is small, and its effect diffuse. A Harlem SNCC staffer works with a school parents' committee; a Newark team tries to turn people on to radical ways of dealing with whatever problems most concern them. Since the spring, SNCC has been most actively involved in energizing Negro college campuses, for, after all, Carmichael and most of the other SNCC breed relate best to people like themselves. SNCC started at Southern black colleges, and its return is both logical and useful.

Of the other "national" organizations, only CORE is attempting to reach the bottom layers of blackness. Floyd McKissick may not know exactly where he is, but in his year as director he has at least had a good try at finding out where he should be. He quite quickly saw that his base was not in the black and white middle class which had formed the organization. It was deep in the ghetto, and in successive meetings, speeches, and programs, McKissick has been trying to get there. Still, there are few cities where CORE is more than a journalistic reference point.

We have been accustomed—trained, even—to think of social change as the work of visible political organizations. That perception is produced by reliance on the "media," which respond mindlessly to the sheer size and solidity of the institutions that are to be changed. The Lowndes County (Alabama) Freedom Party, the "Black Panther," was considered unimportant because it could not effectively take power in the state. It could not quickly and decisively shatter the existing social arrangement over a wide area. Parties— traditional or revolutionary—are assumed to be the only agencies of social movement, and their size is of crucial importance. The significance of a political party, a demonstration, a publication, or an organization is thought to be directly related to its weight in raw numbers.

But somehow that perception lies. In the past few years, dislocations have taken place that utterly destroy the numbers theory. Political parties did not cause tanks to rumble through the heart of the nation's biggest cities in July, they did not bring out soldiers by the thousands, nor destroy billions of dollars' worth of property. Something much more subtle is happening, much more difficult to locate in time or place. The "civil rights" organizations of last year's headlines are observers like the rest of us, no matter how loud their preachings or insistent their press releases. Black politicians, from Tom to militant, have all they can do just to stay on camera. Rep. John Conyers in Detroit—heralded as the model of the new breed—is as irrelevant to his war zone as Rep. William Dawson is to Chicago's. History moves at breakneck speed. Adam Powell had better stay on Bimini.

Even the Black Power Conference in Newark . . . was two weeks too late. It was always to be a rather pointless convention of hustlers, all scrambling for coalitions when they could not win constituencies in the streets. Much of the emphasis on blackness was a charade. The conference met at the white man's hotels and in the white man's churches, and huge white-owned corporations (Bell Telephone, for example) provided presents and facilities. Most of the participants were supported by white payrolls. If they wanted to be where the action was, they could have walked eight blocks from the Military Park Hotel into the Newark ghetto, all burnt and looted and crumbling from five nights of violence. Late in the conference, a few paid a perfunctory visit; many went as sightseers. None had come when they should have, in the days when "black power" was incarnate in the streets. By the time the conference took place, it had no bearing on the black revolution which the delegates so eloquently hymned.

So all that has come until now is prologue—not the first steps in a long flight of equal gradations, but preliminaries of a different order from the main event. The maneuverings of the last half-decade have been predicated on King's assumption that the American system can somehow absorb the demands of its under-class and its alienated. Now this summer we all know that it can-not. Those who speak in seats of power seem not to have the slightest idea what those demands are, much less know how to meet them. Jerome Cavanaugh of Detroit is the most "progressive" mayor in the country; his battleground is bloodier than Sam Yorty's was. The United Auto Workers tried in Detroit to integrate Negroes into the economic community; no other big union will be nearly so helpful. Anti-poverty programs, swimming pools, free trips to the ballpark, aid to education: if that was riot control, it failed.

Martin Luther King, and the "leaders" who appealed for non-violence, CORE, the black politicians, the old SNCC *are all* beside the point. Where the point is is in the streets of Detroit and Plainfield, Newark and Cambridge, Maryland. There has been no response by government because there can be no adequate answers, save suppression and investigation, to people who by their actions indict the very legitimacy of that government. "The name of the game," a movement operative in San Francisco said recently, "is chaos."

But not quite. There was more method in the uprisings than the press and the public outside could see. Looting was pur-poseful: the best merchandise went first, and often the least prized goods were left untouched. What observers called indiscriminate "rampage" was the deliberate and selective destruction by thou-sands of people of white-owned stores. In Newark, for example, not one "Soul Brother" was attacked, except by police. That kind of unanimity of purpose (any one or two looters could have invaded a black merchant's store, but they did not) suggests that the rebel-lions have an authenticity beyond chaotic mob action.

Both Governor Hughes of New Jersey and Mayor Cavanaugh said they were "appalled" at the carnival spirit of their respective ghettos. They watched in horror as the looters hauled out television sets and furniture. But in a strange way, those reactions may be exactly what the looters meant to inspire. Ghetto life has always been a mean caricature of middle-class values: the pink Cadillac bought on credit, the TVs in every crowded flat, the boozing on Saturday nights just as they do in the country clubs. The riots, too, mocked the materialism of the suburbs and the legal violence committed in the name of government. The man tells black people to amass goods and to kill enemies of the state; the people comply in the way they know how. Seen from afar, the riots were scenes in a vast, spontaneous morality play, staged by guerrilla actors in the only real theater.

There was some sense in the riots, and from them a primitive new kind of politics has come out of the ghettos this summer. There are tough black street leaders who have emerged as local heroes, and although they are not interviewed on Huntley-Brinkley nor appeal to the suburban fund-raisers, they are legitimate and powerful. The first wave came out of Watts—Tommy Jacquette, Brother Crook, and a dozen others. They were street rumblers before the summer of 1965; now they are the new political organizers in the L.A. ghetto. More like them are spinning out of Newark and Detroit. They are half guerrilla, half ward heeler. They work between organization and revolution, groping for a way in which a bitter and mobilized minority can change a system they know will never accept them as they are. They disdain the numbers game, they avoid the "visibility" hang-up. They are told it is hopeless, but they are beyond hoping. The strategy is to keep people moving and working, to make noise and trouble, and always to disrupt. Slowly, others in the ghetto learn how to do the same. There is no talk yet of revolutionary institutions; there cannot be, for there is no revolutionary context, and now there can only be approximations. At best, there may be new ghetto organizations: community schools, block councils, tenant unions, police patrols, labor groups. The point now is to extend democracy radically, and that task will involve whites as well as blacks.

The insurrections of July have done what everyone in America for thirty years has thought impossible: mass action has convulsed the society and brought smooth government to a halt. Poor blacks have stolen the center stage from the liberal elites, which is to say that the old order has been shattered. It is at once obvious that the period of greatest danger is just beginning. The political establishment will swing wide to the right and "buffers"— the Committees of Concerned Citizens, the defenders of dissent, the liberal politicians who give cover to the Left—may be obliterated. Those who are working in the streets need to have a new coalition behind them to absorb the inevitable calls for repression.

The civil war and the foreign one have contrived this summer to murder liberalism—in its official robes. There are few mourners. The urgent business now is for imaginations freed from the old myths to see what kind of a society might be reconstructed that would have no need for imperialism and no cause for revolt. At least we know now that even if all Martin Luther King's programs were enacted, and all Jerome Cavanaugh's reforms were adopted, and the Great Society as it is described materialized before our very eyes, there would still be the guerrillas.

16

The Revolt of the Urban Ghettos, 1964-1967

Joseph Boskin

Alternating extremes of elation and despair have characterized black protest in the 1960's. Vacillating between the studied nonviolent and the spontaneous violent approaches to the entrapments of ghetto life, Negro behavior has mirrored the dilemma of the exploited, dark-skinned person: whether to withstand the rejection of the majority in the hope that ameliorative actions would bring rewards within the system or to lash out and destroy the hated environment, thus bringing the abrupt awareness to the majority and release for oneself. Over one hundred major revolts in as many cities in the incredibly short space of three years have demonstrated that for those blacks outside of the civil rights and other allied protest movements of the mid-1950's and early 1960's, the course of protest was to be disruptive and violent. Clearly, the behavior of blacks in the large and small ghettos connoted a consensus of attitude toward their own communities, one another, and the larger society. Their actions signified the most important underclass revolt[1] in recent American history.

THE CONTINUING CONFLICT OF RACE

The urban protest riots proved to be the pivotal black response. The riots affected the course of the civil rights movement;

Reprinted by permission from Joseph Boskin, "The Revolt of the Urban Ghettos, 1964–1967," *Annals* of the American Academy of Political and Social Science, 381 (March, 1969), pp. 1–14.
[1] The terms "riot" and "revolt" are used interchangeably in this study. They describe acts of assault on the status quo and its tangible legitimate authorities, in this instance, the police and business establishments.

they coalesced the young, lower- and middle-class Negroes in the cities; they marked the growing conflict between the generations and the classes in Negro communities throughout the nation. Further, they symbolized the inability of American democracy to cope effectively with the historical-psychological problem of racism. The riots, in fact, split the nation in the 1960's and prompted the period of polarization. The clashes of the summer of 1967, however, marked an end to the spontaneous outbursts of the previous period of urban violence. A new stance was effected, as militant groups fashioned a framework of sociopolitical objectives essentially absent in the earlier period of protest.

As the incidence of riots marked the departure from the civil rights period, this new expression of protest in the 1960's can be differentiated from the more characteristic form of urban racial violence which prevailed in the past. With the exception of the Harlem riots of 1935 and 1943, which seemed more clearly to be the consequence of economic and wartime conditions, the riots of the past two centuries were initiated by Caucasians and were motivated by racist attitudes.

In these racial episodes, Negroes suffered the bulk of personal and property damage, with little restitution offered from civil authorities. Between 1900 and 1949, there were thirty-three major interracial clashes. Of these, eighteen occurred during the period of World War I and its aftermath, whereas five occurred during World War II. Obviously, the majority of these occurrences reflected situations of a critical nature.

From the end of World War II until 1964, there were several large-scale urban disturbances which reflected the underlying potential for social violence. None of these conflicts expanded into major urban conflagrations. Rather, most of the clashes were manifestations of what Allen Grimshaw has called "assaults upon the accommodative structure," that is, Negro challenges to the socioeconomic structure of a community. The most intense violence occurred when minority groups attempted to change residential patterns or when a number of Caucasians defined the situation as one in which such an attempt was being made.

The volatility of these situations was constantly reflected in the years following the termination of the war. Resentment against Negroes who moved into all-white neighborhoods resulted in more than a hundred incidents: the Airport Homes violence in Chicago in November 1945; the Fernwood Project violence, also in Chicago, August 1947; the Georgia house-bombings in May 1947; and the highly publicized violence of 1951 in Cicero, Illinois. Some of the weapons employed by white assaulters—bricks, guns, sniping, Molotov cocktails—were those which were utilized by blacks in the 1960's. Racial violence also occurred when Negroes attempted to use public recreational facilities traditionally reserved for Caucasians in northern and midwestern cities. In sum, the race riots which raged in American society from the turn of the century until the mid-1960's reflected extensions of white racism. The rebellions which began in 1964 represented a major response to that racism.

The explosion of the blacks in the urban ghettos from 1964 to 1967 was presaged three decades ago in the lines of poet Langston Hughes:

> Negroes,
> Sweet and docile,
> Meek, humble, and kind:
> Beware the day
> They change their minds![2]

As late as the year of the first riots came the powerful words of Kenneth Clark, the eminent psychologist, in his work *Dark Ghetto:*

> The poor are always alienated from normal society,
> and when the poor are Negro, as they increasingly
> are in the American cities, a double trauma exists—
> rejection on the basis of class and race is a danger
> to the stability of the society as a whole.[3]

And, in 1965, a shocked but largely lethargic suburban society was admonished by Mayor Robert Wagner of New York:

> There are lions in the streets, angry lions, aggrieved
> lions, lions who have been caged until the cages
> crumbled. We had better do something about those
> lions, and when I speak of lions I do not mean indi-
> viduals. I mean the spirit of the people. Those who
> have been neglected and oppressed and discrimin-
> ated against and misunderstood and forgotten.[4]

[2] Langston Hughes, "Roland Hayes Beaten," *One-Way Ticket* (New York: Alfred A. Knopf, 1949), p. 86. Copyright © 1948 by Alfred A. Knopf, Inc. Reprinted from *Selected Poems,* by Langston Hughes, by permission of the publisher.
[3] Kenneth Clark, *Dark Ghetto* (New York: Harper and Row, 1964), p. 21.
[4] Quoted in Gurston D. Goldin, "Violence: The Integration of Psy- chiatric and Sociological Concepts," *Notre Dame Lawyer,* Vol. XL, No. 5, 1965, p. 513.

Yet, despite a year of violent urban disruptions and countless admonitions from leaders in the Caucasian and black communities, the disturbances were ascribed to a minority of disgruntled blacks. Few were prepared—even after studies had demonstrated that a sizable proportion of Negroes were actively involved in the rebellions—to accept the fact that Negroes were indeed alienated from American society and angry enough to destroy the environments immediately surrounding them which represented the outside repressive world.

That blacks vented their antagonism on the buildings, streets, and businesses within their immediate reach and avoided these same places in exclusively white areas is crucial to an understanding of their motivations. Central to the development of the *zeitgeist* of the revolts were the attitudes of the Caucasian not only regarding the Negro—which, to understate the situation, is well understood as being antagonistic—but regarding the Negro's environment, that is, the city itself. The experience of the blacks in their mass migration into the core cities was inextricably related to the attitudes of whites toward the cities. For it is not merely the fact of high-density populations living in slum conditions which brought blacks to convulsive actions but, more importantly, the approach which predominates in relation to those enclaves which we call the city. The riot was a response to the interaction of both majority and minority in their respective attitudes toward the ghetto and the city. An essential component of its origin was the majority's rejection of the city as a viable and creative environment within which to live. Thus, an ecological malaise was one of the primary causes of the violent protest.

THE CITY: NEVER THE PROMISED LAND

One of the most poignant and enduring conflicts in our national life, frequently subtle, yet constantly gnawing, has been the antagonism between rural and urban America. This has been far more than a conflict between the political and power interests of divergent human locales; it has been a conflict in the American consciousness, and is implicit in the American value system. Since the early nineteenth century, millions of Americans have yielded to a seemingly fatal attraction to make the great migration from farm and village to the city. Whatever may have been the harsh imperatives which guided them, there was a persistent tendency to look back, with a degree of nostalgia and with a sense of irreparable loss, to an idyllic rural setting. In a nation in which the forces of urbanization were unrelenting, where urban living was clearly the shape of the future, there was a deep conviction, as Walter Lippmann wrote, that the city should not be acknowledged as the American ideal. This mood was not limited merely to those who had strayed from the intended ways, but was shared by those who were born in the city environs. The city has never been conceived as being the preferred place to inhabit permanently, nor has it been romanticized in the arts and mass media. It has rarely been regarded as a focus for creative living.

The burgeoning of industry, and the expansion of the middle class, with its increased financial and physical mobility, enabled the nostalgic rural life to be transplanted into suburbia and exurbia. Thus, for this group of urban dwellers, alternatives of living were possible. The actuality of choice, however, gave rise to an ambivalence in which the best and worst of feelings conjoined: the desire for the idealized rural life-style and a strong desire to partake in the activities of the city.

The movement into the cities in the past two centuries, then, was not accomplished without the creation of a basic paradox. The economic means to achieve a fuller life, though associated with the city, was not fulfilled within the city. The compromise of the suburban community seemed to provide a solution to the uncomfortable dilemma of rural versus urban life. Seemingly, one could have the best of both styles. Several difficulties, however, prevented the suburb from becoming the American middle-class nirvana. The magnitude of the march to the suburbs necessitated mass transportation to and from the central cities. The city administrators' choice, the freeway, soon became a strangulated contact with the city, bringing it not close enough, yet too far away. Yet, many who lived in suburbia were economically dependent upon the city, so that contact with the core city was never physically far removed. Ironically, too, transportation arteries made possible the invisibility of the ghettos.

The development of a sophisticated mass communications system, in the form of television, in the early 1950's reinforced the ambivalent antagonisms towards the city. Throughout the 1950's and 1960's, television portrayed the city as a violent, unhealthy, dirty, corrupt, lonely, unseemly place for people to live, develop, and grow. Survival appeared to be the main component dramatized in series after series. With the exceptions of such productions as were borrowed from earlier successful radio shows, the bulk of television performances were antiurban in substance. In such medical series as "Ben Casey," "The Young Interns," and "The Nurses," psychological maladies or life and death were constant themes. The decade of the 1920's, depicted in such series as "The Roaring Twenties" and "The Untouchables," consistently associated the city with gang violence. In such outstanding series as "Naked City," which dealt with some realistic problems of life in New York, and "East Side, West Side," a series based on the experiences of a social worker, the promise and potential of the city were lacking. Television largely reinforced the image of the city earlier perpetuated by literature and the movies. As Herbert Kosower has correctly noted: "Almost all of Hollywood's films deal with contemporary urban life on a superficial fantasy plane."[5] Even *Street Scene, On the Waterfront, The Naked City, The Pawnbroker,* and *A Thousand Clowns* tended to reflect the harsh aspects of urban life.

Resistance to city living grew from several sources. The organization of the city was felt to be antagonistic to basic American values. It bred impersonality, detachment, and unhealthy conditions. Criticism stemmed from the conception of the city as being anti-individualistic. Groups of people were herded together in living and working conditions which placed a premium on co-operative and collectivistic solutions to social problems.

The city was further indicted for altering the landscape of America for denying its past and playing havoc with its future. As Anselm Strauss has accurately written, the United States managed to develop an industrial economy without developing a thoroughly urbanized citizenry. Americans, he noted, entered upon the great urbanization of the nineteenth century "protestingly, metaphorically walking backward."[6]

The image of the city was capped in the catch phrase originally ascribed to New York City: "It's a nice place to visit but I wouldn't want to live there." Living was to be done in the suburbs, away from the source of corruptions. The "Promised Land," then, was to be sought outside the city.

Aided by affluence, millions fled from the city into the landscaped suburbs—leaving the core cities to the newer migrant and immigrant groups. Negro-, Puerto Rican-, Mexican-, and Japanese-Americans, and other smaller American minority groups with dark or nonwhite skins, filled the central cities. By the 1960's, all major and most smaller cities had sizable numbers of various ethnic groups in the downtown areas, living in slum ghettos, breathing the increasingly foul urban air, and becoming increasingly alienated.

[5] Herbert Kosower, King Vidor, and Joseph Boskin, "The Arts," *Psychology Today,* Vol. II, No. 3 (August 1968), p. 16.
[6] Anselm Strauss, *Images of the American City* (New York: Free Press, 1961), p. 123.

They gradually developed an urban consciousness—a consciousness of the entrapped underclass.

The sense of entrapment stemmed from the inability of the ethnic groups to break out of the urban ghetto and become part of the burgeoning middle classes. Alienation grew out of the anger of betrayal, a betrayal that began when the inner-city dwellers were made the inheritors of decaying cities. That they were being deserted, that the promised land in the North and West was drying up, as Langston Hughes caustically expressed it, "like a raisin in the sun," became increasingly clear in the decades of the 1950's and 1960's. Claude Brown, in his *Manchild in the Promised Land,* an affectionate portrayal of Harlem, began his sketch with this denial of the promise:

> I want to talk about the first Northern urban generation of Negroes. I want to talk about the experiences of a misplaced generation, of a misplaced people in an extremely complex, confused society. This is a story of their searching, their dreams, their sorrows, their small and futile rebellions, and their endless battle to establish their own place in America's greatest metropolis—and in America itself.
>
> The characters are sons and daughters of former Southern sharecroppers. These were the poorest people of the South, who poured into New York City during the decade following the Great Depression. These migrants were told that unlimited opportunities for prosperity existed in New York and that there was no "color problem" there. They were told that Negroes lived in houses with bathrooms, electricity, running water, and indoor toilets. To them, this was the "promised land" that Mammy had been singing about in the cotton fields for many years. . . . It seems that Cousin Willie, in his lying haste, had neglected to tell the folks down home about one of the most important aspects of the promised land: it was a slum ghetto. There was a tremendous difference in the way life was lived up North. There were too many people full of hate and bitterness crowded into a dirty, stinky, uncared-for closet-size section of a great city.
>
> Before the soreness of the cotton fields had left Mama's back, her knees were getting sore from scrubbing "Goldberg's" floor. Nevertheless, she was

better off; she had gone from the fire into the frying pan.

The children of these disillusioned colored pioneers inherited the total lot of their parents—the disappointments, the anger. To add to their misery, they had little hope of deliverance. For where does one run to when he's already in the promised land?[7]

One runs to one's soul brother.

The significant consequences of the great migration along the hallelujah trail was the development of an urban consciousness in the ghettos of the industrial cities. Alain Locke, in his important book in the 1920's, *The New Negro,* took cognizance of the ecological forces at work in Harlem. Proscription and prejudice, he noted, had thrown dissimilar black elements into a common area of contact and interaction. Prior to the movement into Harlem, the Negro was "a race more in name than in fact, or to be exact, more in sentiment than in experience." The central experience between these groups, he continued, was that of "a common condition rather than a life in common. In Harlem, Negro life is seizing upon its first chances for group expression and self-determination."[8] The fusing of sentiment and experience in Harlem was repeated over and again in ghettos across the country. Indeed, ghetto experience became a common denominator, its lifestyle and language and conditions a similarity of experiences.

Had the ghetto become a viable environment within a dynamic city existence, the level of grievance-consciousness shared by Negroes would have been muted. But the opposite occurred. Instead, the ghetto became a dead-end to those who lived in it. It became an object of loathing, a mirror of a squalid existence. Feelings of hopelessness and isolation were recurrent themes in the testimony of the slum residents, wrote the United States Commission on Civil Rights in 1967. When asked what she would do if she had sufficient income, one resident declared, "The first thing I would do myself is move out of the neighborhood. I feel the entire neighborhood is more or less a trap."[9]

Compounding these antagonisms were, of course, the intensifying antiurban attitudes of whites. "The people in Harlem," wrote

---

[7] Claude Brown, *Manchild in the Promised Land* (New York: New American Library, 1965), pp. vii–viii. Reprinted by permission of The Macmillan Company.

[8] Alain Locke, *The New Negro* (New York: Albert and Charles Boni, 1925), pp. 6–7.

[9] U.S., Commission on Civil Rights, *A Time to Listen . . . A Time to Act* (Washington, D.C.: U.S. Government Printing Office, 1967), p. 6.

James Baldwin in *Nobody Knows My Name,* two years before the first protest riot, "know they are living there because white people do not think they are good enough to live elsewhere. No amount of 'improvement' can sweeten this fact. . . . A ghetto can be improved in one way only: out of existence."[10] These resentments were further exacerbated by the obvious disparity between the Caucasian and black neighborhoods. Said a young man to Budd Schulberg in the Watts Happening Coffee House immediately after the riots:

> The contrast: the spectacular growth of central and
> west L.A. vs. the stagnation of Watts. . . . You've
> conquered it, baby. You've got it made. Some nights
> on the roof of our rotten falling down buildings we
> can actually see your lights shining in the distance.
> So near and yet so far. We want to reach out and
> grab it and punch it on the nose.[11]

The mythical urban melting pot began to simmer and finally boiled over.

The protest riots which occurred in massive profusion were thus the consequence of a myriad of historical and ecological factors which fused in the 1960's. Their outstanding feature was a collective mode of attitude, behavior, and sense of power.

THE CRY: BURN, BABY, BURN

The sudden burst of rage which rent Harlem in July 1964 was the third mass outburst in that community in the twentieth century. On two previous occasions, the first time during the Great Depression and the second during World War II, blacks in one of the most highly concentrated, racially, ethnic ghettos in the nation signified their protest in spontaneous rioting. Unlike the earlier uprisings which were confined to Harlem, however, the actions in 1964 proved to be the beginning of an urban black protest throughout the country. In city after city, summer after summer, blacks took vengeance by wrecking the hated symbols within their own ghetto areas.

The violent protest in Harlem was rapidly repeated in seven other urban Negro ghettos in the next two months: Bedford-

[10] James Baldwin, *Nobody Knows My Name* (New York: Delta Books, 1962), p. 65.
[11] "Watts—End or Beginning," *Los Angeles Times,* Calendar, May 15, 1966, p. 3, col. 2.

Stuyvesant (Brooklyn), Rochester, Paterson, Jersey City, Elizabeth, Philadelphia, and Dixmoor (Chicago). In 1965, eruptions occurred in five cities, the major conflagrations taking place in Chicago and especially in Los Angeles. Large-scale rioting increased in intensity in the following year, when blacks took to the streets in twenty cities, including Cleveland, Chicago, Omaha, East Oakland, and San Francisco. The year 1967 began on a volatile note as disturbances occurred in the spring in the Southern cities of Nashville, Jackson, and Houston. As the heat of the summer increased, so did the temper for violence. There were mass assaults in Roxbury (Boston), Tampa, Dayton, Atlanta, Buffalo, and Cincinnati in the month of June. Within the next two months, Negroes swarmed through the ghettos of twenty-two cities in the North, Midwest, and South, with the largest riots taking place in Toledo, Grand Rapids, Plainfield (New Jersey), Milwaukee, and especially in Newark and Detroit. By 1968 the rioting had subsided, suggesting that the anger had been channeled into aggressive community programs.

The toll of the rioting over the four-year period was devastating. Between 1964 and 1967, approximately 130 civilians, mainly Negroes, and 12 civil personnel, mainly Caucasian, were killed. Approximately 4,700 Negroes and civil personnel were injured. Over 20,000 persons were arrested during the melees; property damages mounted into the hundreds of millions of dollars; many cities resembled the hollowed remnants of war-torn cities.[12]

Despite the disparity of distance, there was a consensus of attitudes and a similarity of actions among those urban blacks who revolted and those who supported the violent protest.[13] Significantly, the riots were largely unplanned, unorganized, and unscheduled. Ray Lewis, a Cleveland youth worker, explained the origins of the outbreak in that city:

> It wasn't that people planned our riot so consciously. But take a Negro ghetto where men sit around for years saying, "we gonna get whitey," and you build up a group knowledge of what to do.[14]

[12] The rioting which occurred following the assassination of Dr. Martin Luther King in April 1968 is not covered in this paper. These actions were not specifically related to the origins and spread of the urban revolt.

[13] For a further analysis of the 'consensus of attitudes and behavior,' see Joseph Boskin, "Violence in the Ghettos: A Consensus of Attitudes," in *Violence in Contemporary Society,* ed. Joseph Frank, *New Mexico Quarterly,* Vol. XXXVII, No. 4 (Winter 1968), pp. 317–334.

[14] John Allan Long, "After the Midwest Riots," *Christian Science Monitor,* November 10, 1966, p. 11.

Taken together, the riots were the actions of a people, poor and dispossessed and crushed in huge numbers into large slum ghettos, who rose up in wrath against a society committed to democratic ideals. Their outburst was an expression of class antagonism, resentment against racial prejudice, anger at the unreachable affluence around them, and frustration at their sociopolitical powerlessness. "What are these people riotin' about in other cities?" exclaimed Efelka Brown, of the "Sons of Watts," an organization set up to train young males in trade skills. "They want *recognition* and the only way they goin' get it is to riot. We don't want to overthrow the country—we just want what we ain't got."[15]

The sense of betrayal of expectations brought about a focus on the grievances of the past and present. The visibility of an affluent, comfortable, middle-class life, made possible by a powerful mass communications system, was in itself enough to induce dual feelings of resentment and emulation. Pronouncements by the political establishment, however, served only to increase these emotions. Thus, enticed by advertising of the leisure life, excited by legislative programs such as the Civil Rights Acts and the War on Poverty, lured by television programs depicting middle-class life, and hopeful of change in their environment, the poor anticipated an imminent improvement in their socioeconomic position. The failure of society effectively to raise the status of those trapped in the cities contributed immensely to the smoldering resentments.

The urge to retaliate, to return the hurts and the injustices, played an integral part of the protest. By itself, the riot was not "a major thing," stated James Richards to the United States Commission on Civil Rights after the Hunter's Point riot in San Francisco in 1966:

> It was just an idea to strike out at something and someone. Even if you don't do anything but break a window or a chair or something like this, you feel that you are hurting a white man or something like this because the white man is the one that is doing everything to you that causes you to have all these problems on you now.[16]

Similar expressions of deep-welled anger were heard from Puerto Ricans in Spanish Harlem. Piri Thomas, author of *Down*

---

[15] "The Hard-Core Ghetto Mood," *Newsweek*, Vol. LXX, No. 8, August 21, 1967, p. 21.
[16] *A Time to Listen . . . A Time to Act*, p. 5.

These Mean Streets, in testimony before the National Advisory Commission on Civil Disorders, described the origins of the explosion in that area:

> Did you ever stand on street corners and look the other way, at the world of muchos ricos and think, I ain't got a damn? Did you ever count the garbage that flowed down dirty streets, or dig in the back yards who in their glory were a garbage dumps dream? Did you ever stand on rooftops and watch night time cover the bad below? Did you ever put your hand around your throat and feel your pulse beat say, "I do belong and there's not gonna be nobody can tell me, I'm wrong?"[17]

Intense grievances vis-à-vis their inability to achieve even the basic promises of American life of work, status, and housing combined with other minor factors to make the cities highly combustible. The National Advisory Commission found in almost all the cities surveyed "the same major grievance topic among Negro communities."[18] The Commission ranked three levels of grievances among Negroes:

First Level of Intensity:
1. Police practices
2. Unemployment and underemployment
3. Inadequate housing

Second Level of Intensity:
1. Inadequate education
2. Poor recreational facilities and programs
3. Ineffectiveness of the political structure and grievance mechanisms

Third Level of Intensity:
1. Disrespectful white attitudes
2. Discriminatory administration of justice
3. Inadequacy of federal programs
4. Inadequacy of municipal services
5. Discriminatory consumer and credit practices
6. Inadequate welfare programs[19]

[17] Piri Thomas, in testimony before the National Advisory Commission on Civil Disorders, September 21, 1967.

[18] U.S. Riot Commission, *Report of the National Advisory Commission on Civil Disorders* (New York: Bantam Books, 1968), p. 143.

[19] *Ibid.,* pp. 143–144.

To strike out against the visible symbols of white society became a sign of brotherhood. In more than one instance, rock-throwing blacks placed missiles into the hands of residents of the community, saying, "You're either with us or against us, man." In the Watts riot, Mervin Dymally, a Negro assemblyman, was asked by one of the rioters to prove his loyalty by heaving an object at a police car. Dymally refused, saying, "No, man, I'm for peace." The boy quickly replied, "No, you're with the man."[20] Many residents of ghetto areas who did not participate in the actions shouted their approval to those on the streets.

That a general approval, a collective behavior, pervaded the ghettos can be borne out by analysis of the actions of blacks. The two groups singled out for attack were the police and Caucasian-owned businesses. Relations between the police and the minorities, particularly members of the dark-skinned ethnic groups, have always been volatile. As an institution, the police have reflected the attitudes of the majority. To have expected the police to act as a social agency oriented towards reform or conflict-amelioration is to misconstrue their primary function as they view it: namely, the maintenance of law and order. Thus, the police have practiced physical attacks and verbal harassment on minority-group members without interference. Though the public was generally unaware of the treatment accorded minority-ethnic-group members, a prejudicial attitude on its part sanctioned police actions. The language of the police vis-à-vis Negroes—"nigger," "monkey," "them," "boy"— were terms in general use in American culture. For many years, blacks have attempted to bring to light the ample evidence of discriminatory beatings and humiliations. One such attempt in 1965, by furious blacks in the South-Central area of Los Angeles, compiled a listing of the discriminatory remarks of the then Los Angeles Chief of Police William H. Parker—which resulted in a fifteen-page report entitled "Police Chief William H. Parker Speaks"—and distributed it in the community.[21]

Yet, the police became a main focal point for attack not only because of their attitude toward and behavior with minority groups, but primarily because they came to symbolize the despised invisible white power structure. Of the institutional contacts with which ghetto-dwellers have intimate contact—schools, social welfare and employment agencies, medical facilities, business owners

[20] *Report of the Governor's Commission on the Los Angeles Riot,* Vol. II (Sacramento, 1966), pp. 88–89.
[21] William H. Parker, "Police Chief William H. Parker Speaks" (Los Angeles: Community Relations Conference of Southern California, 1965).

—the police embody the most crushing authority. For many blacks, the police had come to represent more than enforcement of law; they were viewed as members of an occupying army and as an oppressive force acting on behalf of those who rule their environment but who fled it for the greener pastures. "A policeman is an object of contempt," Ernie W. Chambers of Omaha bitterly stated in testimony given before the National Advisory Commission on Civil Disorders.[22] The system represented by the police has been oppressive, the method of rule has been heavy with force, and the phrase "maintain law and order" has been directed basically towards the control of Negroes. "Like why, man, should I get home?" angrily inquired a young black during the Watts riot. "These cops have been pushin' me 'round all my life. Kickin' my —— and things like that. Whitey ain't no damn good, he talks 'bout law and order, it's his law and order, it ain't mine [word deleted by the Commission]."[23]

That a collective wrath directed against the police goaded ghetto residents is evident from an analysis of the early stages of the riots. It is significant that most revolts began as a consequence of an incident in which the police were, in some manner, involved. In several instances, the initiating episode was in the line of routine activity. In the Watts situation, for instance, police stopped two men who were driving in an intoxicated condition. Nevertheless, the significance of the specific event bore no relation to the more serious undercurrent of animosity which had been previously created. In other cases, verbal and physical actions by the police were instrumental in increasing a tense situation by inflaming the ghetto people, as happened in the Newark riot of 1967, which really began when the police charged out of the station house towards a large group of demonstrating and jeering Negroes.

Equally instructive is the fact that snipers, despite their numbers, hit extremely few policemen and firemen during the three years of rioting. The low number of deaths of law officials could hardly be ascribed to poor marksmanship. By 1967, especially in Detroit, the incidence of sniper fire had increased considerably; yet, only four law officers were killed, as compared to thirty-nine civilians. Indeed, of the eighty-three persons who died in seventy-five disorders analyzed by the Permanent Sub-committee on Investigations of the Senate Committee on Government Operations in 1967,

[22] Ernie W. Chambers, in testimony before the National Advisory Commission on Civil Disorders, September 23, 1967. The Commission described Chambers as a "grass-roots leader."
[23] *Report of the Governor's Commission on the Los Angeles Riot*, Vol. I (Sacramento, 1966), p. 43.

approximately ten persons were public officials, primarily law officers and firemen, whereas the remainder were civilians, primarily
Negroes.[24]

White businessmen were the second most exposed group
singled out for attack. Resentment against the practices of exploitation, in the form of hidden and higher interest rates, shoddy goods
and lower quality, higher prices and questionable service, had likewise been building for many years. The communications system in
the community had long isolated such business establishments.
Consequently, the majority of stores damaged and looted were
those against which ill-feelings had developed. Negro stores frequently were protected by identifying signs: "Blood Brother," "Soul
Brother," "Negro-owned." Not only were black businesses generally
left untouched, but so, too, were libraries, schools, hospitals, clinics,
and, surprisingly, governmental agencies. There were instances of
bricks and sniper fire hitting these various buildings: however, no
concerted attack was conducted. Many places burned down because
of the refusal of the rioters to permit fire engines into the area.

Nevertheless, retail businesses suffered a much greater proportion of the damage during the violence than public institutions,
industrial properties, or private residences. In Newark in 1967,
1,029 establishments listed damage to buildings or loss of inventory
or both.[25] Those businesses which were hardest hit by rioters were
those which were felt to be the most exploitative in their business
practices: liquor, clothing, food, and furniture stores. Indeed, in at
least nine of the riots studied by the President's National Advisory
Commission on Civil Disorders, the damage was, in part, the result
of "deliberate attacks on white-owned businesses characterized in
the Negro community as unfair or disrespectful toward Negroes."[26]

The riot brought a sense of exultation in the community.
It served as a release of frustration, anger, and helplessness. Even
those participants who afterwards regretted their actions admitted
to the joy that they had personally experienced. In testimony before
the McCone Commission, conducted after the riot in central Los
Angeles, Winston Slaughter, age twenty, a junior college student,
responded to the question: "Do you think the riot helped or hurt
the Negro cause?"

> Well, you can say regret and then you can say
> there are some who are glad it happened. Now,

[24] *Report of the National Advisory Commission on Civil Disorders,*
pp. 115–116.

[25] *Ibid.*

[26] *Ibid.*

me personally, I feel that I regret it, yes. But, deep down inside I know I was feeling some joy while it was going on, simply because I am a Negro.[27]

Others felt no regret, but a sense of pride. As the riots spread to other ghetto areas, those communities which experienced no turmoil felt the need to emulate their brothers. An exchange between three young blacks after the Detroit riot indicated the fulfilling exuberance of the historical moment:

"Those buildings goin' up was a pretty sight," a long-legged kid said. "I sat right here and watched them go. And there wasn't nothin' them honkies could do but sweat and strain to put it out."
"Yeah, man," a pal chimed in, "it's about time those honkies started earnin' their money in this neighborhood."
"You know," said Long Legs, "we made big news. They called this the country's worst race riot in history."
"Yeah," said another gangly kid, straddling the railing. "My kids goin' to study about that in school, and they'll know their old man was part of it."
"We got the record man," exulted another youth.
. . . "They can forget all about Watts and Newark and Harlem. This is where the riot to end all riots was held."[28]

Further, the protest riot assumed certain features of conventional warfare. The weapons and tactics employed were those standardized in the past thirty years: Molotov cocktails, selected targets, visible enemies, harassing tactics, sniping, mobility, and a capitulation to a more powerful military force in the form of national guardsmen or federal troops. Parallels between war as a means of confronting an enemy and the protest riot could also be observed in the attitudes of ghetto residents. Although the term "riot" was used by blacks, it became clear that they meant to describe their actions in a larger sense. "We in a war," a black youth told a reporter. "Or hasn't anybody told you that?"[29]

The attitude of immediacy was heard from many persons.

[27] *Report of the Governor's Commission on the Los Angeles Riot,* Vol. XIII (Sacramento, 1966), pp. 28–29.
[28] "The Hard-Core Ghetto Mood," p. 20.
[29] *Ibid.*

"Many Negroes would rather die than live under conditions as they are now," exclaimed a male at a youth symposium. "For these people, riots present the only chance of ever achieving equality."[30] An absence of fear was notable among those who actively participated in the streets. "The cops think we are scared of them because they got guns," stated a male in testimony before the McCone Commission, "but you can only die once: if I get a few of them I don't mind dying."[31] Thus, the riots were emotionally liberating. The joy in retaliating and the fun in looting reinforced the feelings of communal action. The individual acts fused with the collective act. The term "we" was used with frequency among the protesting rioters: "We put ourselves on the map." "We were whole again." During the civil violences, there was a partial suspension of conscience. "This liberation from conscience and from conscientiousness made possible for the rioters an involvement and an extreme commitment usually denied them."[32] Moreover, the pride in action played an integral role in the historical consciousness of the community. Two years after the Watts riot, black and brown high school students, selected to participate in an upward-bound educational project, were asked to complete a form which contained the question: "What kinds of civil rights activities have you participated in?" One student answered: "Watts Riot." Such statements and actions indicate a high degree of participation in the protest disturbances.

Several significant studies have pointedly noted a high degree of community participation in the violence of the small and large riots in the 1960's. The Los Angeles Riot Study (LARS), initiated immediately after the 1965 riot, collated the interviews of 2,070 persons living within the curfew area.[33] The group of Negroes interviewed was a random sample, stratified by age, sex, and income. Interviews were approximately two hours in length; the interview covered questions of attitude toward the riot, activity in the riot, general social and political attitudes, and background information. The LARS survey noted that the majority of Negroes had spent their childhood in the South but that over 60 per cent of the sample had matured in urban areas. Significantly, about the same percentage

---

[30] California, Alameda County, Human Relations Commission, "Youth Discuss Racial Problems," *Human Relations News*, Vol. I, No. 2 (September 1967), p. 1.

[31] *Report of the Governor's Commission on the Los Angeles Riot,* Vol. I, p. 16.

[32] Frederick J. Hacker and Aljean Harmetz, "What the McCone Commission Didn't See," *Frontier*, Vol. XVII, No. 5 (March 1966), p. 13.

[33] Institute of Government and Public Affairs, University of California, Los Angeles, 1967.

had lived in Los Angeles ten years or longer at the time of the riot. Contrary to reports about the low educational level of the rioters, the study indicated that over half of the sample had completed high school. Contrary to popular assumption as well, the study indicated that 72 per cent of the males and 35 per cent of the females were employed in August 1965.

With regard to participation in the riot, the LARS survey demonstrated that up to 15 per cent of the Negro adult population, or about 22,000 persons, were active at some point during the rioting; that an additional 35 or 40 per cent, or 51,000 persons, were active spectators. Support for the violence was greater among the younger persons, was greater among men than women, and was as great among relatively longtime residents of South-Central Los Angeles as it was among the more recent migrants from the South. The latter point is of particular importance, inasmuch as it undercut the notion that the riot was largely the work of the unacculturated and of the recent influx of migrants from the South.

A high percentage of the community supported the violence, in attitude if not in action. Approximately 34 per cent of the sample were favorably disposed toward the actions, and 38 per cent of the population in the curfew area felt that the revolt would help in their quest to improve their positions. Only 20 per cent indicated that the riot hurt the community. In sum, a high proportion of persons in the riot area participated in, or gave support to, the action of fellow residents.

Studies undertaken after the LARS report substantially corroborated its conclusions. The National Advisory Commission on Civil Disorders conducted 1,200 interviews in approximately twenty cities, studied arrest records in twenty-two cities, and elicited additional reports from participants. According to the Report of the Commission, the typical rioter was an unmarried male, between the ages of fifteen and twenty-four, born in the state, and a lifelong resident of the city in which the riot occurred. His education was substantially good, having attended high school, and, economically, his position was approximately the same as his counterpart who did not actively participate in the riot. Nonetheless, he was more likely to be working in a menial or low-status job as an unskilled laborer. In special surveys taken after the Newark and Detroit revolts, interviewers noted strong feelings of racial pride, "if not racial superiority."[34] The riot experience was a definite factor in increased self- and communal pride:

[34] Report of the National Advisory Commission on Civil Disorders, p. 133.

Interviewer: *You said you were feeling good when you followed the crowd?*
Respondent: *I was feeling proud, man, at the fact that I was a Negro. I felt like I was a first-class citizen. I didn't feel ashamed of my race because of what they did* [Detroit, 1967].[35]

The nature of the rioting which marked the mid-1960's appeared to undergo serious change by the end of the decade. Two indications of this change were, firstly, the Detroit riot of 1967 in which a sizable proportion of Caucasians joined with the Negroes in burning and looting, thus indicating a meshing of an economic underclass; and, secondly, the development and intensity of the Black Power movement. The activists have been concerned with developing cultural, economic, and political programs within the community. These activist organizations have, on more than one occasion, prevented violent outbreaks by ghetto residents who were angered by representatives of the power structure, particularly the police. Within the broad Black Power movement, moreover, militant groups have counseled for the termination of nonviolence as a technique of bringing about necessary change. "We know that we cannot change violent people by nonviolence," read a mimeographed sheet handed out by the Black Student Union at the University of California, San Diego, immediately after the assassination of Dr. Martin Luther King in April 1968. "We must build mass armed self-defense groups. We must unite to get rid of the government and people that oppress and murder Black People." Thus, by the end of the decade, the energies of the younger blacks were oriented towards more specific, militant goals.

In sum, the revolts in the mid-1960's—more than the non-violent movement of Dr. Martin Luther King and the extraordinary powerful civil rights movement of the early 1960's—directed attention to the anguished plights of millions of Negroes, Puerto Ricans, and Mexican-Americans living in the urban centers of the country. The spontaneous outbursts, the collective actions, and the consensual attitudes of blacks and browns highlighted the failure of American society to recognize the problems of the racial minority groups in the cities. The events stemmed not only from the tradition of racist mentality but also from the ambiguous attitudes towards the city itself. The enormity of the failure led to one of the most intense social crises in American society in the twentieth century.

[35] *Ibid.*

Part
Six
The Evolving Ideology
of the Black Revolution

The strength of the black revolutionary movement lies not in its numbers or organizational structure, but in its ideological appeal. There are relatively few hard-core black revolutionaries in America, and most black radical groups lack any national structure. But despite these weaknesses, growing numbers of black Americans have become sympathetic to many of the goals of the black revolutionary movement. While a majority of Negroes reject tactics of violence, it is probable that most blacks share the social analysis of the black radicals. The latent power of the movement for black liberation lies in the fact that if the problems facing black people are not solved within the context of the status quo, support for black revolution may swell to significant proportions.

At present, the struggle for black liberation is primarily an ideological one. Charismatic black leaders have convinced countless Negroes that they should reexamine their attitudes and behavior and face squarely the realities of black deprivation. One reason why black leaders have acted as teachers rather than organizers is that their careers have been brief. Martin Luther King and Malcolm X are dead; Huey Newton is in prison; and Stokely Carmichael and Eldridge Cleaver are in exile. But ideas have an existence independent of their authors, and the ideas of black revolution continue to spread.

Martin Luther King was clearly not a black revolutionary in the current sense of that term. But he did influence the development of black radicalism in a number of ways. First, he emphasized black pride and self-respect. Second, he condoned civil disobedience and in so doing questioned the legitimacy of the American political system. Finally, he stressed the need for blacks to organize themselves in order to achieve their goals. Nevertheless, King was a devout Christian who believed that change should be achieved only through nonviolent means. His famous letter from Birmingham jail is perhaps the most eloquent statement of his philosophy.

King's assassination seemed to verify the belief of many blacks that it is futile to try to achieve social change through nonviolent means. In addition, many black people have long despaired of gaining equality within the context of American society. The movement for black liberation has been a response to this situation. The second and third selections are by an early exponent of black liberation, Malcolm X, whose influence on contemporary black radical thought has been immense.

Malcolm X was a man of unique leadership skills. Like Lenin, Malcolm played a variety of political roles; he was an administrator, an agitator, and a theorist. Again, like Lenin, he was skilled at adapting radical theory to the historical situation. Before he died, Malcolm had abandoned the ideological dead-end which was the Black Muslim movement, and in a creative marriage of black nationalism and Trotskyite Marxism laid the intellectual foundation for the current black revolutionary movement. His oratorical skill not only drew a personal following, but he could express the most sophisticated—and revolutionary—ideas in parable language which all could understand. Two of Malcolm's speeches are included here. The first, "Message to the Grass Roots," was given in Detroit in November, 1963. It was one of Malcolm's last speeches as a member of the Black Muslims. The second speech, "Prospects for Freedom in 1965," was given to a predominantly white audience in New York on January 7, 1965, less than two months before his death.

The ideology of the Black Panther Party owes much to Malcolm X. Founded in Oakland in 1966, the Black Panthers have become the leading organization of the black revolutionary movement. The fourth selection is an interview with Huey Newton, the founder of the Black Panthers, by the radical magazine, *The Movement*. In this interview, Newton gives a lucid explanation of the tactics and goals of the Black Panthers. Based in the San Francisco Bay area, the Panthers have branches in many of the ghettos of the North.

Another strategy for black liberation is presented in the final selection of this part. The authors of "A Second Civil War" argue that the rural South, not the urban North, is the logical terrain for a movement for black independence. They believe that "the question of Black Liberation/American Revolution is still (and more so than ever today) a Southern states question. . . ."

Martin Luther King, Jr.

April 16, 1963

My Dear Fellow Clergymen:

While confined here in the Birmingham city jail, I came across your recent statement calling my present activities "unwise and untimely." Seldom do I pause to answer criticism of my work and ideas. If I sought to answer all the criticisms that cross my desk, my secretaries would have little time for anything other than such correspondence in the course of the day, and I would have no time for constructive work. But since I feel that you are men of genuine good will and that your criticisms are sincerely set forth, I want to try to answer your statement in what I hope will be patient and reasonable terms.

I think I should indicate why I am here in Birmingham, since you have been influenced by the view which argues against

Reprinted by permission of Harper & Row from Martin Luther King, Jr., "Letter from Birmingham Jail—April 16, 1963" in *Why We Can't Wait.* Copyright © 1963 by Martin Luther King, Jr.

Author's Note: This response to a published statement by eight fellow clergymen from Alabama (Bishop C. C. J. Carpenter, Bishop Joseph A. Durick, Rabbi Hilton L. Grafman, Bishop Paul Hardin, Bishop Holan B. Harmon, the Reverend George M. Murray, the Reverend Edward V. Ramage and the Reverend Earl Stallings) was composed under somewhat constricting circumstances. Begun on the margins of the newspaper in which the statement appeared while I was in jail, the letter was continued on scraps of writing paper supplied by a friendly Negro trusty, and concluded on a pad my attorneys were eventually permitted to leave me. Although the text remains in substance unaltered, I have indulged in the author's prerogative of polishing it for publication.

"outsiders coming in." I have the honor of serving as president of the Southern Christian Leadership Conference, an organization operating in every southern state, with headquarters in Atlanta, Georgia. We have some eighty-five affiliated organizations across the South, and one of them is the Alabama Christian Movement for Human Rights. Frequently we share staff, educational and financial resources with our affiliates. Several months ago the affiliate here in Birmingham asked us to be on call to engage in a nonviolent direct-action program if such were deemed necessary. We readily consented, and when the hour came we lived up to our promise. So I, along with several members of my staff, am here because I was invited here. I am here because I have organizational ties here.

But more basically, I am in Birmingham because injustice is here. Just as the prophets of the eighth century B.C. left their villages and carried their "thus saith the Lord" far beyond the boundaries of their home towns, and just as the Apostle Paul left his village of Tarsus and carried the gospel of Jesus Christ to the far corners of the Greco-Roman world, so am I compelled to carry the gospel of freedom beyond my own home town. Like Paul, I must constantly respond to the Macedonian call for aid.

Moreover, I am cognizant of the interrelatedness of all communities and states. I cannot sit idly by in Atlanta and not be concerned about what happens in Birmingham. Injustice anywhere is a threat to justice everywhere. We are caught in an inescapable network of mutuality, tied in a single garment of destiny. Whatever affects one directly, affects all indirectly. Never again can we afford to live with the narrow, provincial "outside agitator" idea. Anyone who lives inside the United States can never be considered an outsider anywhere within its bounds.

You deplore the demonstrations taking place in Birmingham. But your statement, I am sorry to say, fails to express a similar concern for the conditions that brought about the demonstrations. I am sure that none of you would want to rest content with the superficial kind of social analysis that deals merely with the effects and does not grapple with underlying causes. It is unfortunate that demonstrations are taking place in Birmingham, but it is even more unfortuate that the city's white power structure left the Negro community with no alternative.

In any nonviolent campaign there are four basic steps: collection of the facts to determine whether injustices exist; negotiation; self-purification; and direct action. We have gone through all these steps in Birmingham. There can be no gainsaying the fact that racial injustice engulfs this community. Birmingham is probably the most thoroughly segregated city in the United States. Its ugly record of brutality is widely known. Negroes have experienced grossly unjust treatment in the courts. There have been more unsolved bombings of Negro homes and churches in Birmingham than in any other city in the nation. These are the hard, brutal facts of the case. On the basis of these conditions, Negro leaders sought to negotiate with the city fathers. But the latter consistently refused to engage in good-faith negotiation.

Then, last September, came the opportunity to talk with leaders of Birmingham's economic community. In the course of the negotiations, certain promises were made by the merchants—for example, to remove the stores' humiliating racial signs. On the basis of these promises, the Reverend Fred Shuttlesworth and the leaders of the Alabama Christian Movement for Human Rights agreed to a moratorium on all demonstrations. As the weeks and months went by, we realized that we were the victims of a broken promise. A few signs, briefly removed, returned; the others remained.

As in so many past experiences, our hopes had been blasted, and the shadow of deep disappointment settled upon us. We had no alternative except to prepare for direct action, whereby we would present our very bodies as a means of laying our case before the conscience of the local and the national community. Mindful of the difficulties involved, we decided to undertake a process of self-purification. We began a series of workshops on nonviolence, and we repeatedly asked ourselves: "Are you able to accept blows without retaliating?" "Are you able to endure the ordeal of jail?" We decided to schedule our direct-action program for the Easter season, realizing that except for Christmas, this is the main shopping period of the year. Knowing that a strong economic-withdrawal program would be the by-product of direct action, we felt that this would be the best time to bring pressure to bear on the merchants for the needed change.

Then it occurred to us that Birmingham's mayoralty election was coming up in March, and we speedily decided to postpone action until after election day. When we discovered that the Commissioner of Public Safety, Eugene "Bull" Connor, had piled up enough votes to be in the run-off, we decided again to postpone action until the day after the run-off so that the demonstrations could not be used to cloud the issues. Like many others, we waited to see Mr. Connor defeated, and to this end we endured postponement after postponement. Having aided in this community need, we felt that our direct-action program could be delayed no longer.

You may well ask: "Why direct action? Why sit-ins, marches and so forth? Isn't negotiation a better path?" You are quite right in calling for negotiation. Indeed, this is the very purpose of direct action. Nonviolent direct action seeks to create such a crisis and foster such a tension that a community which has constantly refused to negotiate is forced to confront the issue. It seeks so to dramatize the issue that it can no longer be ignored. My citing the creation of tension as part of the work of the nonviolent-resister may sound rather shocking. But I must confess that I am not afraid of the word "tension." I have earnestly opposed violent tension, but there is a type of constructive, nonviolent tension which is necessary for growth. Just as Socrates felt that it was necessary to create a tension in the mind so that individuals could rise from the bondage of myths and half-truths to the unfettered realm of creative analysis and objective appraisal, so must we see the need for nonviolent gadflies to create the kind of tension in society that will help men rise from the dark depths of prejudice and racism to the majestic heights of understanding and brotherhood.

The purpose of our direct-action program is to create a situation so crisis-packed that it will inevitably open the door to negotiation. I therefore concur with you in your call for negotiation. Too long has our beloved Southland been bogged down in a tragic effort to live in monologue rather than dialogue.

One of the basic points in your statement is that the action that I and my associates have taken in Birmingham is untimely. Some have asked: "Why didn't you give the new city administration time to act?" The only answer that I can give to this query is that the new Birmingham administration must be prodded about as much as the outgoing one, before it will act. We are sadly mistaken if we feel that the election of Albert Boutwell as mayor will bring the millennium to Birmingham. While Mr. Boutwell is a much more gentle person than Mr. Connor, they are both segregationists, dedicated to maintenance of the status quo. I have hope that Mr. Boutwell will be reasonable enough to see the futility of massive resistance to desegregation. But he will not see this without pressure from devotees of civil rights. My friends, I must say to you that we have not made a single gain in civil rights without determined legal and nonviolent pressure. Lamentably, it is an historical fact that privileged groups seldom give up their privileges voluntarily. Individuals may see the moral light and voluntarily give up their unjust posture; but, as Reinhold Niebuhr has reminded us, groups tend to be more immoral than individuals.

We know through painful experience that freedom is never voluntarily given by the oppressor; it must be demanded by the oppressed. Frankly, I have yet to engage in a direct-action campaign that was "well timed" in the view of those who have not suffered unduly from the disease of segregation. For years now I have heard the word "Wait!" It rings in the ear of every Negro with piercing familiarity. This "Wait" has almost always meant "Never." We must come to see, with one of our distinguished jurists, that "justice too long delayed is justice denied."

We have waited for more than 340 years for our constitutional and God-given rights. The nations of Asia and Africa are moving with jetlike speed toward gaining political independence, but we still creep at horse-and-buggy pace toward gaining a cup of coffee at a lunch counter. Perhaps it is easy for those who have never felt the stinging darts of segregation to say, "Wait." But when you have seen vicious mobs lynch your mothers and fathers at will and drown your sisters and brothers at whim; when you have seen hate-filled policemen curse, kick and even kill your black brothers and sisters; when you see the vast majority of your twenty million Negro brothers smothering in an airtight cage of poverty in the midst of an affluent society; when you suddenly find your tongue twisted and your speech stammering as you seek to explain to your six-year-old daughter why she can't go to the public amusement park that has just been advertised on television, and see tears welling up in her eyes when she is told that Funtown is closed to colored children, and see ominous clouds of inferiority beginning to form in her little mental sky, and see her beginning to distort her personality by developing an unconscious bitterness toward white people; when you have to concoct an answer for a five-year-old son who is asking: "Daddy, why do white people treat colored people so mean?"; when you take a cross-country drive and find it necessary to sleep night after night in the uncomfortable corners of your automobile because no motel will accept you; when you are humiliated day in and day out by nagging signs reading "white" and "colored"; when your first name becomes "nigger," your middle name becomes "boy" (however old you are) and your last name becomes "John," and your wife and mother are never given the respected title "Mrs."; when you are harried by day and haunted by night by the fact that you are a Negro, living constantly at tiptoe stance, never quite knowing what to expect next, and are plagued with inner fears and outer resentments; when you are forever fighting a degenerating sense of "nobodiness"—then you will understand why we find it difficult to wait. There comes a time when the cup of endurance runs over, and men are no longer willing to be plunged into the abyss of despair. I hope, sirs, you can understand our legitimate and unavoidable impatience.

You express a great deal of anxiety over our willingness to break laws. This is certainly a legitimate concern. Since we so diligently urge people to obey the Supreme Court's decision of 1954 outlawing segregation in the public schools, at first glance it may seem rather paradoxical for us consciously to break laws. One may well ask: "How can you advocate breaking some laws and obeying others?" The answer lies in the fact that there are two types of laws: just and unjust. I would be the first to advocate obeying just laws. One has not only a legal but a moral responsibility to obey just laws. Conversely, one has a moral responsibility to disobey unjust laws. I would agree with St. Augustine that "an unjust law is no law at all."

Now, what is the difference between the two? How does one determine whether a law is just or unjust? A just law is a man-made code that squares with the moral law or the law of God. An unjust law is a code that is out of harmony with the moral law. To put it in the terms of St. Thomas Aquinas: An unjust law is a human law that is not rooted in eternal law and natural law. Any law that uplifts human personality is just. Any law that degrades human personality is unjust. All segregation statutes are unjust because segregation distorts the soul and damages the personality. It gives the segregator a false sense of superiority and the segregated a false sense of inferiority. Segregation, to use the terminology of the Jewish philosopher Martin Buber, substitutes an "I–it" relationship for an "I–thou" relationship and ends up relegating persons to the status of things. Hence segregation is not only politically, economically and sociologically unsound, it is morally wrong and sinful. Paul Tillich has said that sin is separation. Is not segregation an existential expression of man's tragic separation, his awful estrangement, his terrible sinfulness? Thus it is that I can urge men to obey the 1954 decision of the Supreme Court, for it is morally right; and I can urge them to disobey segregation ordinances, for they are morally wrong.

Let us consider a more concrete example of just and unjust laws. An unjust law is a code that a numerical or power majority group compels a minority group to obey but does not make binding on itself. This is *difference* made legal. By the same token, a just law is a code that a majority compels a minority to follow and that it is willing to follow itself. This is *sameness* made legal.

Let me give another explanation. A law is unjust if it is inflicted on a minority that, as a result of being denied the right to vote, had no part in enacting or devising the law. Who can say that the legislature of Alabama which set up that state's segregation laws was democratically elected? Throughout Alabama all sorts of devious methods are used to prevent Negroes from becoming registered voters, and there are some counties in which, even though Negroes constitute a majority of the population, not a single Negro is registered. Can any law enacted under such circumstances be considered democratically structured?

Sometimes a law is just on its face and unjust in its application. For instance, I have been arrested on a charge of parading without a permit. Now, there is nothing wrong in having an ordinance which requires a permit for a parade. But such an ordinance becomes unjust when it is used to maintain segregation and to deny citizens the First-Amendment privilege of peaceful assembly and protest.

I hope you are able to see the distinction I am trying to point out. In no sense do I advocate evading or defying the law, as would the rabid segregationist. That would lead to anarchy. One who breaks an unjust law must do so openly, lovingly, and with a willingness to accept the penalty. I submit that an individual who breaks a law that conscience tells him is unjust, and who willingly accepts the penalty of imprisonment in order to arouse the conscience of the community over its injustice, is in reality expressing the highest respect for law.

Of course, there is nothing new about this kind of civil disobedience. It was evidenced sublimely in the refusal of Shadrach, Meshach and Abednego to obey the laws of Nebuchadnezzar, on the ground that a higher moral law was at stake. It was practiced superbly by the early Christians, who were willing to face hungry lions and the excruciating pain of chopping blocks rather than submit to certain unjust laws of the Roman Empire. To a degree, academic freedom is a reality today because Socrates practiced civil disobedience. In our own nation, the Boston Tea Party represented a massive act of civil disobedience.

We should never forget that everything Adolf Hitler did in Germany was "legal" and everything the Hungarian freedom fighters did in Hungary was "illegal." It was "illegal" to aid and comfort a Jew in Hitler's Germany. Even so, I am sure that, had I lived in Germany at the time, I would have aided and comforted my Jewish brothers. If today I lived in a Communist country where certain principles dear to the Christian faith are suppressed, I would openly advocate disobeying that country's antireligious laws.

I must make two honest confessions to you, my Christian and Jewish brothers. First, I must confess that over the past few years I have been gravely disappointed with the white moderate. I have almost reached the regrettable conclusion that the Negro's great stumbling block in his stride toward freedom is not the White Citizen's Counciler or the Ku Klux Klanner, but the white moderate, who is more devoted to "order" than to justice; who prefers a negative peace which is the absence of tension to a positive peace which is the presence of justice; who constantly says: "I agree with you in the goal you seek, but I cannot agree with your methods of direct action"; who paternalistically believes he can set the timetable for another man's freedom; who lives by a mythical concept of time and who constantly advises the Negro to wait for a "more convenient season." Shallow understanding from people of good will is more frustrating than absolute misunderstanding from people of ill will. Lukewarm acceptance is much more bewildering than outright rejection.

I had hoped that the white moderate would understand that law and order exist for the purpose of establishing justice and that when they fail in this purpose they become the dangerously structured dams that block the flow of social progress. I had hoped that the white moderate would understand that the present tension in the South is a necessary phase of the transition from an obnoxious negative peace, in which the Negro passively accepted his unjust plight, to a substantive and positive peace, in which all men will respect the dignity and worth of human personality. Actually, we who engage in nonviolent direct action are not the creators of tension. We merely bring to the surface the hidden tension that is already alive. We bring it out in the open, where it can be seen and dealt with. Like a boil that can never be cured so long as it is covered up but must be opened with all its ugliness to the natural medicines of air and light, injustice must be exposed, with all the tension its exposure creates, to the light of human conscience and the air of national opinion before it can be cured.

In your statement you assert that our actions, even though peaceful, must be condemned because they precipitate violence. But is this a logical assertion? Isn't this like condemning a robbed man because his possession of money precipitated the evil act of robbery? Isn't this like condemning Socrates because his unswerving commitment to truth and his philosophical inquiries precipitated the act by the misguided populace in which they made him drink hemlock? Isn't this like condemning Jesus because his unique God-consciousness and never-ceasing devotion to God's will precipitated the evil act of crucifixion? We must come to see that, as the federal courts have consistently affirmed, it is wrong to urge an individual to cease his efforts to gain his basic constitutional rights because the quest may precipitate violence. Society must protect the robbed and punish the robber.

I had also hoped that the white moderate would reject the myth concerning time in relation to the struggle for freedom. I have just received a letter from a white brother in Texas. He writes: "All Christians know that the colored people will receive equal rights eventually, but it is possible that you are in too great a religious hurry. It has taken Christianity almost two thousand years to accomplish what it has. The teachings of Christ take time to come to earth." Such an attitude stems from a tragic misconception of time, from the strangely irrational notion that there is something in the very flow of time that will inevitably cure all ills. Actually, time itself is neutral; it can be used either destructively or constructively. More and more I feel that the people of ill will have used time much more effectively than have the people of good will. We will have to repent in this generation not merely for the hateful words and actions of the bad people but for the appalling silence of the good people. Human progress never rolls in on wheels of inevitability; it comes through the tireless efforts of men willing to be co-workers with God, and without this hard work, time itself becomes an ally of the forces of social stagnation. We must use time creatively, in the knowledge that the time is always ripe to do right. Now is the time to make real the promise of democracy and transform our pending national elegy into a creative psalm of brotherhood. Now is the time to lift our national policy from the quicksand of racial injustice to the solid rock of human dignity.

You speak of our activity in Birmingham as extreme. At first I was rather disappointed that fellow clergymen would see my nonviolent efforts as those of an extremist. I began thinking about the fact that I stand in the middle of two opposing forces in the Negro community. One is a force of complacency, made up in part of Negroes who, as a result of long years of oppression, are so drained of self-respect and a sense of "somebodiness" that they have adjusted to segregation; and in part of a few middle-class Negroes who, because of a degree of academic and economic security and because in some ways they profit by segregation, have become insensitive to the problems of the masses. The other force is one of bitterness and hatred, and it comes perilously close to advocating violence. It is expressed in the various black nationalist groups that are springing up across the nation, the largest and best-known being Elijah Muhammad's Muslim movement. Nourished by the Negro's frustration over the continued existence of racial discrimination, this movement is made up of people who have lost faith in America, who have absolutely repudiated Christianity, and who have concluded that the white man is an incorrigible "devil."

I have tried to stand between these two forces, saying that we need emulate neither the "do-nothingism" of the complacent nor the hatred and despair of the black nationalist. For there is the more excellent way of love and nonviolent protest. I am grateful to God that, through the influence of the Negro church, the way of nonviolence became an integral part of our struggle.

If this philosophy had not emerged, by now many streets of the South would, I am convinced, be flowing with blood. And I am further convinced that if our white brothers dismiss as "rabble-rousers" and "outside agitators" those of us who employ nonviolent direct action, and if they refuse to support our nonviolent efforts, millions of Negroes will, out of frustration and despair, seek solace and security in black-nationalist ideologies—a development that would inevitably lead to a frightening racial nightmare.

Oppressed people cannot remain oppressed forever. The yearning for freedom eventually manifests itself, and that is what has happened to the American Negro. Something within has reminded him of his birthright of freedom, and something without has reminded him that it can be gained. Consciously or unconsciously, he has been caught up by the *Zeitgeist,* and with his black brothers of Africa and his brown and yellow brothers of Asia, South America and the Caribbean, the United States Negro is moving with a sense of great urgency toward the promised land of racial justice. If one recognizes this vital urge that has engulfed the Negro community, one should readily understand why public demonstrations are taking place. The Negro has many pent-up resentments and latent frustrations, and he must release them. So let him march; let him make prayer pilgrimages to the city hall; let him go on freedom rides—and try to understand why he must do so. If his repressed emotions are not released in nonviolent ways, they will seek expression through violence; this is not a threat but a fact of history. So I have not said to my people: "Get rid of your discontent." Rather, I have tried to say that this normal and healthy discontent can be channeled into the creative outlet of nonviolent direct action. And now this approach is being termed extremist.

But though I was initially disappointed at being categorized as an extremist, as I continued to think about the matter I gradually gained a measure of satisfaction from the label. Was not Jesus an extremist for love: "Love your enemies, bless them that curse you, do good to them that hate you, and pray for them which despitefully use you, and persecute you." Was not Amos an extremist for justice: "Let justice roll down like waters and righteousness like an ever-flowing stream." Was not Paul an extremist for the Christian gospel: "I bear in my body the marks of the Lord Jesus." Was not Martin Luther an extremist: "Here I stand; I cannot do otherwise, so help me God." And John Bunyan: "I will stay in jail to the end of my days before I make a butchery of my conscience." And Abraham Lincoln: "This nation cannot survive half slave and half free." And Thomas Jefferson: "We hold these truths to be self-evident, that all men are created equal. . . ." So the question is not whether we will be extremists, but what kind of extremists we will be. Will we be extremists for hate or for love? Will we be extremists for the preservation of injustice or for the extension of justice? In that dramatic scene on Calvary's hill three men were crucified. We must never forget that all three were crucified for the same crime—the crime of extremism. Two were extremists for immorality, and thus fell below their environment. The other, Jesus Christ, was an extremist for love, truth and goodness, and thereby rose above his environment. Perhaps the South, the nation and the world are in dire need of creative extremists.

I had hoped that the white moderate would see this need. Perhaps I was too optimistic; perhaps I expected too much. I suppose I should have realized that few members of the oppressor race can understand the deep groans and passionate yearnings of the oppressed race, and still fewer have the vision to see that injustice must be rooted out by strong, persistent and determined action. I am thankful, however, that some of our white brothers in the South have grasped the meaning of this social revolution and committed themselves to it. They are still all too few in quantity, but they are big in quality. Some—such as Ralph McGill, Lillian Smith, Harry Golden, James McBride Dabbs, Ann Braden and Sarah Patton Boyle—have written about our struggle in eloquent and prophetic terms. Others have marched with us down nameless streets of the South. They have languished in filthy, roach-infested jails, suffering the abuse and brutality of policemen who view them as "dirty nigger-lovers." Unlike so many of their moderate brothers and sisters, they have recognized the urgency of the moment and sensed the need for powerful "action" antidotes to combat the disease of segregation.

Let me take note of my other major disappointment. I have been so greatly disappointed with the white church and its leadership. Of course, there are some notable exceptions. I am not unmindful of the fact that each of you has taken some significant stands on this issue. I commend you, Reverend Stallings, for your Christian stand on this past Sunday, in welcoming Negroes to your worship service on a nonsegregated basis. I commend the Catholic leaders of this state for integrating Spring Hill College several years ago.

But despite these notable exceptions, I must honestly reiterate that I have been disappointed with the church. I do not say this as one of those negative critics who can always find something wrong with the church. I say this as a minister of the gospel, who loves the church; who was nurtured in its bosom; who has been sustained by its spiritual blessings and who will remain true to it as long as the cord of life shall lengthen.

When I was suddenly catapulted into the leadership of the bus protest in Montgomery, Alabama, a few years ago, I felt we would be supported by the white church. I felt that the white ministers, priests and rabbis of the South would be among our strongest allies. Instead, some have been outright opponents, refusing to understand the freedom movement and misrepresenting its leaders; all too many others have been more cautious than courageous and have remained silent behind the anesthetizing security of stained-glass windows.

In spite of my shattered dreams, I came to Birmingham with the hope that the white religious leadership of this community would see the justice of our cause and, with deep moral concern, would serve as the channel through which our just grievances could reach the power structure. I had hoped that each of you would understand. But again I have been disappointed.

I have heard numerous southern religious leaders admonish their worshipers to comply with a desegregation decision because it is the law, but I have longed to hear white ministers declare: "Follow this decree because integration is morally right and because the Negro is your brother." In the midst of blatant injustices inflicted upon the Negro, I have watched white churchmen stand on the sideline and mouth pious irrelevancies and sanctimonious trivialities. In the midst of a mighty struggle to rid our nation of racial and economic injustice, I have heard many ministers say: "Those are social issues, with which the gospel has no real concern." And I have watched many churches commit themselves to a completely other-wordly religion which makes a strange, un-Biblical distinction between body and soul, between the sacred and the secular.

I have traveled the length and breadth of Alabama, Mississippi and all the other southern states. On sweltering summer days and crisp autumn mornings I have looked at the South's beautiful churches with their lofty spires pointing heavenward. I have beheld the impressive outlines of her massive religious-education buildings. Over and over I have found myself asking: "What kind of people worship here? Who is their God? Where were their voices when the lips of Governor Barnett dripped with words of interposition and nullification? Where were they when Governor Wallace gave a clarion call for defiance and hatred? Where were their voices of support when bruised and weary Negro men and women decided to rise from the dark dungeons of complacency to the bright hills of creative protest?"

Yes, these questions are still in my mind. In deep disappointment I have wept over the laxity of the church. But be assured that my tears have been tears of love. There can be no deep disappointment where there is not deep love. Yes, I love the church. How could I do otherwise? I am in the rather unique position of being the son, the grandson and the great-grandson of preachers. Yes, I see the church as the body of Christ. But, oh! How we have blemished and scarred that body through social neglect and through fear of being nonconformists.

There was a time when the church was very powerful—in the time when the early Christians rejoiced at being deemed worthy to suffer for what they believed. In those days the church was not merely a thermometer that recorded the ideas and principles of popular opinion; it was a thermostat that transformed the mores of society. Whenever the early Christians entered a town, the people in power became disturbed and immediately sought to convict the Christians for being "disturbers of the peace" and "outside agitators." But the Christians pressed on, in the conviction that they were "a colony of heaven," called to obey God rather than man. Small in number, they were big in commitment. They were too God-intoxicated to be "astronomically intimidated." By their effort and example they brought an end to such ancient evils as infanticide and gladiatorial contests.

Things are different now. So often the contemporary church is a weak, ineffectual voice with an uncertain sound. So often it is an archdefender of the status quo. Far from being disturbed by the presence of the church, the power structure of the average community is consoled by the church's silent—and often even vocal—sanction of things as they are.

But the judgment of God is upon the church as never before. If today's church does not recapture the sacrificial spirit of the early church, it will lose its authenticity, forfeit the loyalty of millions, and be dismissed as an irrelevant social club with no meaning for the twentieth century. Every day I meet young people whose disappointment with the church has turned into outright disgust.

Perhaps I have once again been too optimistic. Is organized religion too inextricably bound to the status quo to save our nation and the world? Perhaps I must turn my faith to the inner spiritual church, the church within the church, as the true *ekklesia* and the hope of the world. But again I am thankful to God that some noble souls from the ranks of organized religion have broken loose from the paralyzing chains of conformity and joined us as active partners in the struggle for freedom. They have left their secure congregations and walked the streets of Albany, Georgia, with us. They have gone down the highways of the South on tortuous rides for freedom. Yes, they have gone to jail with us. Some have been dismissed from their churches, have lost the support of their bishops and fellow ministers. But they have acted in the faith that right defeated is stronger than evil triumphant. Their witness has been the spiritual salt that has preserved the true meaning of the gospel in these troubled times. They have carved a tunnel of hope through the dark mountain of disappointment.

I hope the church as a whole will meet the challenge of this decisive hour. But even if the church does not come to the aid of justice, I have no despair about the future. I have no fear about the outcome of our struggle in Birmingham, even if our motives are at present misunderstood. We will reach the goal of freedom in Birmingham and all over the nation, because the goal of America is freedom. Abused and scorned though we may be, our destiny is tied up with America's destiny. Before the pilgrims landed at Plymouth, we were here. Before the pen of Jefferson etched the majestic words of the Declaration of Independence across the pages of history, we were here. For more than two centuries our forebears labored in this country without wages; they made cotton king; they built the homes of their masters while suffering gross injustice and shameful humiliation—and yet out of a bottomless vitality they continued to thrive and develop. If the inexpressible cruelties of slavery could not stop us, the opposition we now face will surely fail. We will win our freedom because the sacred heritage of our nation and the eternal will of God are embodied in our echoing demands.

Before closing I feel impelled to mention one other point in your statement that has troubled me profoundly. You warmly commended the Birmingham police force for keeping "order" and "preventing violence." I doubt that you would have so warmly commended the police force if you had seen its dogs sinking their teeth into unarmed, nonviolent Negroes. I doubt that you would so quickly commend the policemen if you were to observe their ugly and inhumane treatment of Negroes here in the city jail; if you were to watch them push and curse old Negro women and young Negro girls; if you were to see them slap and kick old Negro men and young boys; if you were to observe them, as they did on two occasions, refuse to give us food because we wanted to sing our grace together. I cannot join you in your praise of the Birmingham police department.

It is true that the police have exercised a degree of discipline in handling the demonstrators. In this sense they have conducted themselves rather "nonviolently" in public. But for what purpose? To preserve the evil system of segregation. Over the past few years I have consistently preached that nonviolence demands that the means we use must be as pure as the ends we seek. I have tried to make clear that it is wrong to use immoral means to attain moral ends. But now I must affirm that it is just as wrong, or perhaps even more so, to use moral means to preserve immoral ends. Perhaps Mr. Connor and his policemen have been rather nonviolent in public, as was Chief Pritchett in Albany, Georgia, but they have used the moral means of nonviolence to maintain the immoral end of racial injustice. As T. S. Eliot has said: "The last temptation is the greatest treason: To do the right deed for the wrong reason."

I wish you had commended the Negro sit-inners and demonstrators of Birmingham for their sublime courage, their willingness to suffer and their amazing discipline in the midst of great provocation. One day the South will recognize its real heroes. They will be the James Merediths, with the noble sense of purpose that enables them to face jeering and hostile mobs, and with the agonizing loneliness that characterizes the life of the pioneer. They will be old, oppressed, battered Negro women, symbolized in a seventy-two-year-old woman in Montgomery, Alabama, who rose up with a sense of dignity and with her people decided not to ride segregated buses, and who responded with ungrammatical profundity to one who inquired about her weariness: "My feets is tired, but my soul is at rest." They will be the young high school and college students, the young ministers of the gospel and a host of their elders, courageously and nonviolently sitting in at lunch counters and willingly going to jail for conscience' sake. One day the South will know that when these disinherited children of God sat down at lunch counters, they were in reality standing for what is best in the American dream and for the most sacred values in our Judaeo-Christian heritage, thereby bringing our nation back to those great wells of democracy which were dug deep by the founding fathers in their formulation of the Constitution and the Declaration of Independence.

Never before have I written so long a letter. I'm afraid it is much too long to take your precious time. I can assure you that it would have been much shorter if I had been writing from a comfortable desk, but what else can one do when he is alone in a narrow jail cell, other than write long letters, think long thoughts and pray long prayers?

If I have said anything in this letter that overstates the truth and indicates an unreasonable impatience, I beg you to forgive me.

If I have said anything that understates the truth and indicates my having a patience that allows me to settle for anything less than brotherhood, I beg God to forgive me.

I hope this letter finds you strong in the faith. I also hope that circumstances will soon make it possible for me to meet each of you, not as an integrationist or a civil-rights leader but as a fellow clergyman and a Christian brother. Let us all hope that the dark clouds of racial prejudice will soon pass away and the deep fog of misunderstanding will be lifted from our fear-drenched communities, and in some not too distant tomorrow the radiant stars of love and brotherhood will shine over our great nation with all their scintillating beauty.

Yours for the cause of Peace and Brotherhood,

Martin Luther King, Jr.

18

Message to the Grass Roots

Malcolm X

We want to have just an off-the-cuff chat between you and me, us. We want to talk right down to earth in a language that everybody here can easily understand. We all agree tonight, all of the speakers have agreed, that America has a very serious problem. Not only does America have a very serious problem, but our people have a very serious problem. America's problem is us. We're her problem. The only reason she has a problem is she doesn't want us here. And every time you look at yourself, be you black, brown, red or yellow, a so-called Negro, you represent a person who poses such a serious problem for America because you're not wanted. Once you face this as a fact, then you can start plotting a course that will make you appear intelligent, instead of unintelligent.

What you and I need to do is learn to forget our differences. When we come together, we don't come together as Baptists or Methodists. You don't catch hell because you're a Baptist, and you don't catch hell because you're a Methodist. You don't catch hell because you're a Methodist or Baptist, you don't catch hell because you're a Democrat or a Republican, you don't catch hell because you're a Mason or an Elk, and you sure don't catch hell because you're an American; because if you were an American, you wouldn't catch hell. You catch hell because you're a black man. You catch hell, all of us catch hell, for the same reason.

So we're all black people, so-called Negroes, second-class citizens, ex-slaves. You're nothing but an ex-slave. You don't like to be told that. But what else are you? You are ex-slaves. You didn't come here on the "Mayflower." You came here on a slave ship. In chains, like a horse, or a cow, or a chicken. And you were brought here by the people who came here on the "Mayflower," you were brought here by the so-called Pilgrims, or Founding Fathers. They were the ones who brought you here.

We have a common enemy. We have this in common: We have a common oppressor, a common exploiter, and a common discriminator. But once we all realize that we have a common enemy, then we unite—on the basis of what we have in common. And what we have foremost in common is that enemy—the white man. He's an enemy to all of us. I know some of you all think that some of them aren't enemies. Time will tell.

In Bandung back in, I think, 1954, was the first unity meeting in centuries of black people. And once you study what happened at the Bandung conference, and the results of the Bandung conference, it actually serves as a model for the same procedure you and I can use to get our problems solved. At Bandung all the nations came together, the dark nations from Africa and Asia. Some of them were Buddhists, some of them were Muslims, some of them were Christians, some were Confucianists, some were atheists. Despite their religious differences, they came together. Some were communists, some were socialists, some were capitalists—despite their economic and political differences, they came together. All of them were black, brown, red or yellow.

The number-one thing that was not allowed to attend the Bandung conference was the white man. He couldn't come. Once they excluded the white man, they found that they could get together. Once they kept him out, everybody else fell right in and fell in line. This is the thing that you and I have to understand. And these people who came together didn't have nuclear weapons, they didn't have jet planes, they didn't have all the heavy armaments that the white man has. But they had unity.

They were able to submerge their little petty differences and agree on one thing: That one African there came from Kenya and was being colonized by the Englishman, and another African came from the Congo and was being colonized by the Belgian, and another African came from Guinea and was being colonized by the French, and another came from Angola and was being colonized by the Portuguese. When they came to the Bandung conference, they looked at the Portuguese, and at the Frenchman, and at the Englishman, and at the Dutchman, and learned or realized the one thing that all of them had in common—they were all from Europe, they were all Europeans, blond, blue-eyed and white skins. They began to recognize who their enemy was. The same man that was colonizing our people in Kenya was colonizing our people in the Congo. The same one in the Congo was colonizing our people in South Africa, and in Southern Rhodesia, and in Burma, and in India, and in Afghanistan, and in Pakistan. They realized all over the world where the dark man was being oppressed, he was being oppressed by the white man; where the dark man was being exploited, he was being exploited by the white man. So they got together on this basis—that they had a common enemy.

And when you and I here in Detroit and in Michigan and in America who have been awakened today look around us, we too realize here in America we all have a common enemy, whether he's in Georgia or Michigan, whether he's in California or New York. He's the same man—blue eyes and blond hair and pale skin—the same man. So what we have to do is what they did. They agreed to stop quarreling among themselves. Any little spat that they had, they'd settle it among themselves, go into a huddle—don't let the enemy know that you've got a disagreement.

Instead of airing our differences in public, we have to realize we're all the same family. And when you have a family squabble, you don't get out on the sidewalk. If you do, everybody calls you uncouth, unrefined, uncivilized, savage. If you don't make it at home, you settle it at home; you get in the closet, argue it out behind closed doors, and then when you come out on the street, you pose a common front, a united front. And this is what we need to do in the community, and in the city, and in the state. We need to stop airing our differences in front of the white man, put the white man out of our meetings, and then sit down and talk shop with each other. That's what we've got to do.

I would like to make a few comments concerning the difference between the black revolution and the Negro revolution. Are they both the same? And if they're not, what is the difference? What is the difference between a black revolution and a Negro revolution? First, what is a revolution? Sometimes I'm inclined to believe that many of our people are using this word "revolution" loosely, without taking careful consideration of what this word actually means, and what its historic characteristics are. When you study the historic nature of revolutions, the motive of a revolution, the objective of a revolution, the result of a revolution, and the methods used in a revolution, you may change words. You may devise another program, you may change your goal and you may change your mind.

Look at the American Revolution in 1776. That revolution was for what? For land. Why did they want land? Independence. How was it carried out? Bloodshed. Number one, it was based on land, the basis of independence. And the only way they could get it was bloodshed. The French Revolution—what was it based on? The landless against the landlord. What was it for? Land. How did they get it? Bloodshed. Was no love lost, was no compromise, was no negotiation. I'm telling you—you don't know what a revolution is. Because when you find out what it is, you'll get back in the alley, you'll get out of the way.

The Russian Revolution—what was it based on? Land; the landless against the landlord. How did they bring it about? Bloodshed. You haven't got a revolution that doesn't involve bloodshed. And you're afraid to bleed. I said, you're afraid to bleed.

As long as the white man sent you to Korea, you bled. He sent you to Germany, you bled. He sent you to the South Pacific to fight the Japanese, you bled. You bleed for white people, but when it comes to seeing your own churches being bombed and little black girls murdered, you haven't got any blood. You bleed when the white man says bleed; you bite when the white man says bite; and you bark when the white man says bark. I hate to say this about us, but it's true. How are you going to be nonviolent in Mississippi, as violent as you were in Korea? How can you justify being nonviolent in Mississippi and Alabama, when your churches are being bombed, and your little girls are being murdered, and at the same time you are going to get violent with Hitler, and Tojo, and somebody else you don't even know?

If violence is wrong in America, violence is wrong abroad. If it is wrong to be violent defending black women and black children and black babies and black men, then it is wrong for America to draft us and make us violent abroad in defense of her. And if it is right for America to draft us, and teach us how to be violent in defense of her, then it is right for you and me to do whatever is necessary to defend our own people right here in this country.

The Chinese Revolution—they wanted land. They threw the British out, along with the Uncle Tom Chinese. Yes, they did. They set a good example. When I was in prison, I read an article—don't be shocked when I say that I was in prison. You're still in prison. That's what America means: prison. When I was in prison, I read an article in *Life* magazine showing a little Chinese girl, nine years old; her father was on his hands and knees and she was pulling the trigger because he was an Uncle Tom Chinaman. When they had the revolution over there, they took a whole generation of Uncle Toms and just wiped them out. And within ten years that little girl became a full-grown woman. No more Toms in China. And today it's one of the toughest, roughest, most feared countries on this earth— by the white man. Because there are no Uncle Toms over there.

Of all our studies, history is best qualified to reward our research. And when you see that you've got problems, all you have to do is examine the historic method used all over the world by others who have problems similar to yours. Once you see how they got theirs straight, then you know how you can get yours straight. There's been a revolution, a black revolution, going on in Africa. In Kenya, the Mau Mau were revolutionary; they were the ones who brought the word "Uhuru" to the fore. The Mau Mau, they were revolutionary, they believed in scorched earth, they knocked everything aside that got in their way, and their revolution also was based on land, a desire for land. In Algeria, the northern part of Africa, a revolution took place. The Algerians were revolutionists, they wanted land. France offered to let them be integrated into France. They told France, to hell with France, they wanted some land, not some France. And they engaged in a bloody battle.

So I cite these various revolutions, brothers and sisters, to show you that you don't have a peaceful revolution. You don't have a turn-the-other-cheek revolution. There's no such thing as a non-violent revolution. The only kind of revolution that is nonviolent is the Negro revolution. The only revolution in which the goal is loving your enemy is the Negro revolution. It's the only revolution in which the goal is a desegregated lunch counter, a desegregated theater, a desegregated park, and a desegregated public toilet; you can sit down next to white folks—on the toilet. That's no revolution. Revolution is based on land. Land is the basis of all independence. Land is the basis of freedom, justice, and equality.

The white man knows what a revolution is. He knows that the black revolution is world-wide in scope and in nature. The black revolution is sweeping Asia, is sweeping Africa, is rearing its head in Latin America. The Cuban Revolution—that's a revolution. They overturned the system. Revolution is in Asia, revolution is in Africa, and the white man is screaming because he sees revolution in Latin America. How do you think he'll react to you when you learn what a real revolution is? You don't know what a revolution is. If you did, you wouldn't use that word.

Revolution is bloody, revolution is hostile, revolution knows no compromise, revolution overturns and destroys everything that gets in its way. And you, sitting around here like a knot on the wall, saying, "I'm going to love these folks no matter how much they hate me." No, you need a revolution. Whoever heard of a revolution where they lock arms . . . singing "We Shall Overcome"? You don't do that in a revolution. You don't do any singing, you're too busy swinging. It's based on land. A revolutionary wants land so he can set up his own nation, an independent nation. These Negroes aren't asking for any nation—they're trying to crawl back on the plantation.

When you want a nation, that's called nationalism. When the white man became involved in a revolution in this country against England, what was it for? He wanted this land so he could set up another white nation. That's white nationalism. The American Revolution was white nationalism. The French Revolution was white nationalism. The Russian Revolution too—yes, it was—white nationalism. You don't think so? Why do you think Khrushchev and Mao can't get their heads together? White nationalism. All the revolutions that are going on in Asia and Africa today are based on what? —black nationalism. A revolutionary is a black nationalist. He wants a nation. . . . If you're afraid of black nationalism, you're afraid of revolution. And if you love revolution, you love black nationalism.

To understand this, you have to go back to what the young brother here referred to as the house Negro and the field Negro back during slavery. There were two kinds of slaves, the house Negro and the field Negro. The house Negroes—they lived in the house with master, they dressed pretty good, they ate good because they ate his food—what he left. They lived in the attic or the basement, but still they lived near the master; and they loved the master more than the master loved himself. They would give their life to save the master's house—quicker than the master would. If the master said, "We got a good house here," the house Negro would say, "Yeah, we got a good house here." Whenever the master said "we," he said "we." That's how you can tell a house Negro.

If the master's house caught on fire, the house Negro would fight harder to put the blaze out than the master would. If the master got sick, the house Negro would say, "What's the matter, boss, *we* sick?" *We* sick! He identified himself with his master, more than his master identified with himself. And if you came to the house Negro and said, "Let's run away, let's escape, let's separate," the house Negro would look at you and say, "Man, you crazy. What you mean, separate? Where is there a better house than this? Where can I wear better clothes than this? Where can I eat better food than this?" That was that house Negro. In those days he was called a "house nigger." And that's what we call them today, because we've still got some house niggers running around here.

This modern house Negro loves his master. He wants to live near him. He'll pay three times as much as the house is worth just to live near his master, and then brag about "I'm the only Negro out here." "I'm the only one on my job." "I'm the only one in this school." You're nothing but a house Negro. And if someone comes to you right now and says, "Let's separate," you say the same thing that the house Negro said on the plantation. "What you mean, separate? From America, this good white man? Where you going to get a better job than you get here?" I mean, this is what you say. "I ain't left nothing in Africa," that's what you say. Why, you left your mind in Africa.

On that same plantation, there was the field Negro. The field Negroes—those were the masses. There were always more Negroes in the field than there were Negroes in the house. The Negro in the field caught hell. He ate leftovers. In the house they ate high up on the hog. The Negro in the field didn't get anything but what was left of the insides of the hog. They call it "chitt'lings" nowadays. In those days they called them what they were—guts. That's what you were—gut-eaters. And some of you are still gut-eaters.

The field Negro was beaten from morning to night; he lived in a shack, in a hut; he wore old, castoff clothes. He hated his master. I say he hated his master. He was intelligent. That house Negro loved his master, but that field Negro—remember, they were in the majority, and they hated the master. When the house caught on fire, he didn't try to put it out; that field Negro prayed for a wind, for a breeze. When the master got sick, the field Negro prayed that he'd die. If someone came to the field Negro and said, "Let's separate, let's run," he didn't say "Where we going?" He'd say, "Any place is better than here." You've got field Negroes in America today. I'm a field Negro. The masses are the field Negroes. When they see this man's house on fire, you don't hear the little Negroes talking about *"our* government is in trouble." They say, *"The* government is in trouble." Imagine a Negro: *"Our* government"! I even heard one say *"our* astronauts." They won't even let him near the plant and *"our* astronauts"! *"our* Navy"—that's a Negro that is out of his mind, a Negro that is out of his mind.

Just as the slavemaster of that day used Tom, the house Negro, to keep the field Negroes in check, the same old slavemaster today has Negroes who are nothing but modern Uncle Toms, twentieth-century Uncle Toms, to keep you and me in check, to keep us under control, keep us passive and peaceful and nonviolent. That's Tom making you nonviolent. It's like when you go to the dentist, and the man's going to take your tooth. You're going to fight him when he starts pulling. So he squirts some stuff in your jaw called novocaine, to make you think they're not doing anything to you. So you sit there and because you've got all that novocaine in your jaw, you suffer—peacefully. Blood running all down your jaw, and you don't know what's happening. Because someone has taught you to suffer—peacefully.

The white man does the same thing to you in the street, when he wants to put knots on your head and take advantage of you and not have to be afraid of your fighting back. To keep you from fighting back, he gets these old religious Uncle Toms to teach you and me, just like novocaine, to suffer peacefully. Don't stop suffering—just suffer peacefully. As Rev. Cleage pointed out, they say you should let your blood flow in the streets. This is a shame. You know he's a Christian preacher. If it's a shame to him, you know what it is to me.

There is nothing in our book, the Koran, that teaches us to suffer peacefully. Our religion teaches us to be intelligent. Be peaceful, be courteous, obey the law, respect everyone; but if someone puts his hand on you, send him to the cemetery. That's a good religion. In fact, that's that old-time religion. That's the one that Ma and Pa used to talk about: an eye for an eye, and a tooth for a tooth, and a head for a head, and a life for a life. That's a good religion. And nobody resents that kind of religion being taught but a wolf, who intends to make you his meal.

This is the way it is with the white man in America. He's a wolf—and you're sheep. Any time a shepherd, a pastor, teaches you and me not to run from the white man and, at the same time, teaches us not to fight the white man, he's a traitor to you and me. Don't lay down a life all by itself. No, preserve your life, it's the best thing you've got. And if you've got to give it up, let it be even-steven.

The slavemaster took Tom and dressed him well, fed him well and even gave him a little education—a *little* education; gave him a long coat and a top hat and made all the other slaves look up to him. Then he used Tom to control them. The same strategy that was used in those days is used today, by the same white man. He takes a Negro, a so-called Negro, and makes him prominent, builds him up, publicizes him, makes him a celebrity. And then he becomes a spokesman for Negroes—and a Negro leader.

I would like to mention just one other thing quickly, and that is the method that the white man uses, how the white man uses the "big guns," or Negro leaders, against the Negro revolution. They are not a part of the Negro revolution. They are used against the Negro revolution.

When Martin Luther King failed to desegregate Albany, Georgia, the civil-rights struggle in America reached its low point. King became bankrupt almost, as a leader. The Southern Christian Leadership Conference was in financial trouble; and it was in trouble, period, with the people when they failed to desegregate Albany, Georgia. Other Negro civil-rights leaders of so-called national stature became fallen idols. As they became fallen idols, began to lose their prestige and influence, local Negro leaders began to stir up the masses. In Cambridge, Maryland, Gloria Richardson;

in Danville, Virginia, and other parts of the country, local leaders began to stir up our people at the grass-roots level. This was never done by these Negroes of national stature. They control you, but they have never incited you or excited you. They control you, they contain you, they have kept you on the plantation.

As soon as King failed in Birmingham, Negroes took to the streets. King went out to California to a big rally and raised I don't know how many thousands of dollars. He came to Detroit and had a march and raised some more thousands of dollars. And recall, right after that Roy Wilkins attacked King. He accused King and CORE [Congress Of Racial Equality] of starting trouble everywhere and then making the NAACP [National Association for the Advancement of Colored People] get them out of jail and spend a lot of money; they accused King and CORE of raising all the money and not paying it back. This happened; I've got it in documented evidence in the newspaper. Roy started attacking King, and King started attacking Roy, and Farmer started attacking both of them. And as these Negroes of national stature began to attack each other, they began to lose their control of the Negro masses.

The Negroes were out there in the streets. They were talking about how they were going to march on Washington. Right at that time Birmingham had exploded, and the Negroes in Birmingham—remember, they also exploded. They began to stab the crackers in the back and bust them up 'side their head—yes, they did. That's when Kennedy sent in the troops, down in Birmingham. After that, Kennedy got on the television and said "this is a moral issue." That's when he said he was going to put out a civil-rights bill. And when he mentioned civil-rights bill and the Southern crackers started talking about how they were going to boycott or filibuster it, then the Negroes started talking—about what? That they were going to march on Washington, march on the Senate, march on the White House, march on the Congress, and tie it up, bring it to a halt, not let the government proceed. They even said they were going out to the airport and lay down on the runway and not let any airplanes land. I'm telling you what they said. That was revolution. That was revolution. That was the black revolution.

It was the grass roots out there in the street. It scared the white man to death, scared the white power structure in Washington, D.C., to death; I was there. When they found out that this black steamroller was going to come down on the capital, they called in Wilkins, they called in Randolph, they called in these national Negro leaders that you respect and told them, "Call it off." Kennedy said, "Look, you all are letting this thing go too far." And Old Tom said, "Boss, I can't stop it, because I didn't start it." I'm telling you what they said. They said, "I'm not even in it, much less at the head of it." They said, "These Negroes are doing things on their own. They're running ahead of us." And that old shrewd fox, he said, "If you all aren't in it, I'll put you in it. I'll put you at the head of it. I'll endorse it. I'll welcome it. I'll help it. I'll join it."

A matter of hours went by. They had a meeting at the Carlyle Hotel in New York City. The Carlyle Hotel is owned by the Kennedy family; that's the hotel Kennedy spent the night at, two nights ago; it belongs to his family. A philanthropic society headed by a white man named Stephen Currier called all the top civil-rights leaders together at the Carlyle Hotel. And he told them, "By you all fighting each other, you are destroying the civil-rights movement. And since you're fighting over money from white liberals, let us set up what is known as the Council for United Civil Rights Leadership. Let's form this council, and all the civil-rights organizations will belong to it, and we'll use it for fund-raising purposes." Let me show you how tricky the white man is. As soon as they got it formed, they elected Whitney Young as its chairman, and who do you think became the co-chairman? Stephen Currier, the white man, a millionaire. Powell was talking about it down at Cobo Hall today. This is what he was talking about. Powell knows it happened. Randolph knows it happened. Wilkins knows it happened. King knows it happened. Every one of that Big Six—they know it happened.

Once they formed it, with the white man over it, he promised them and gave them $800,000 to split up among the Big Six; and told them that after the march was over they'd give them $700,000 more. A million and a half dollars—split up between leaders that you have been following, going to jail for, crying crocodile tears for. And they're nothing but Frank James and Jesse James and the what-do-you-call-'em brothers.

As soon as they got the setup organized, the white man made available to them top public-relations experts; opened the news media across the country at their disposal, which then began to project these Big Six as the leaders of the march. Originally they weren't even in the march. You were talking this march talk on Hastings Street, you were talking march talk on Lenox Avenue, and on Fillmore Street, and on Central Avenue, and 32nd Street and 63rd Street. That's where the march talk was being talked. But the white man put the Big Six at the head of it; made them the march. They became the march. They took it over. And the first move they made after they took it over, they invited Walter Reuther, a white man; they invited a priest, a rabbi, and an old white preacher, yes, an old white preacher. The same white element that put Kennedy into power—labor, the Catholics, the Jews, and liberal Protestants;

the same clique that put Kennedy in power, joined the march on Washington.

It's just like when you've got some coffee that's too black, which means it's too strong. What do you do? You integrate it with cream, you make it weak. But if you pour too much cream in it, you won't even know you ever had coffee. It used to be hot, it becomes cool. It used to be strong, it becomes weak. It used to wake you up, now it puts you to sleep. This is what they did with the march on Washington. They joined it. They didn't integrate it, they infiltrated it. They joined it, became a part of it, took it over. And as they took it over, it lost its militancy. It ceased to be angry, it ceased to be hot, it ceased to be uncompromising. Why, it even ceased to be a march. It became a picnic, a circus. Nothing but a circus, with clowns and all. You had one right here in Detroit—I saw it on television—with clowns leading it, white clowns and black clowns. I know you don't like what I'm saying, but I'm going to tell you anyway. Because I can prove what I'm saying. If you think I'm telling you wrong, you bring me Martin Luther King and A. Philip Randolph and James Farmer and those other three, and see if they'll deny it over a microphone.

No, it was a sellout. It was a takeover. When James Baldwin came in from Paris, they wouldn't let him talk, because they couldn't make him go by the script. Burt Lancaster read the speech that Baldwin was supposed to make; they wouldn't let Baldwin get up there, because they know Baldwin is liable to say anything. They controlled it so tight, they told those Negroes what time to hit town, how to come, where to stop, what signs to carry, what song to sing, what speech they could make, and what speech they couldn't make; and then told them to get out of town by sundown. And every one of those Toms was out of town by sundown. Now I know you don't like my saying this. But I can back it up. It was a circus, a performance that beat anything Hollywood could ever do, the performance of the year. Reuther and those other three devils should get an Academy Award for the best actors because they acted like they really loved Negroes and fooled a whole lot of Negroes. And the six Negro leaders should get an award too, for the best supporting cast.

19
Prospects for Freedom in 1965

Malcolm X

Mr. Chairman (who's one of my brothers), ladies and gentlemen, brothers and sisters:

It is an honor to me to come back to the Militant Labor Forum again this evening. It's my third time here. I was just telling my brother up here that probably tomorrow morning the press will try to make it appear that this little chat that we're having here this evening took place in Peking or someplace else . . .

But it's the third time that I've had the opportunity to be a guest of the Militant Labor Forum. I always feel that it is an honor and every time that they open the door for me to do so, I will be right here.

The *Militant* newspaper is one of the best in New York City. In fact, it is one of the best anywhere you go today because everywhere I go I see it. I saw it even in Paris about a month ago. They were reading it over there, and I saw it in some parts of Africa where I was during the summer. I don't know how it gets there. But if you put the right things in it, what you put in it will see that it gets around.

Tonight, during the few moments that we have, we're going to have a little chat, like brothers and sisters and friends, and probably enemies too, about the prospects for peace—or the prospects for freedom in 1965. As you notice, I almost slipped and said peace and freedom. Actually you can't separate peace from freedom because no one can be at peace unless he has his freedom. You can't separate the two—and this is the thing that makes 1965 so explosive and so dangerous.

DEFINE FREEDOM

The people in this country who in the past have been at peace and have been peaceful were that way only because they didn't know what freedom was. They let somebody else define it for them, but today, 1965, you find those who have not had freedom, and are not in a position to define freedom, are beginning to define it for themselves. And as they get in a position intellectually to define freedom for themselves, they see that they don't have it, and it makes them less peaceful, or less inclined towards peace.

So, in discussing this topic tonight, prospects for freedom in 1965, I think we have to go back at least 12 years, or ten years, to the time when the struggle of the black man in America began to be projected into the limelight, not only in this country but throughout the world.

It started primarily with the Supreme Court decision, so-called desegregation decision, and I should say so-called desegregation so-called decision, because there has been some doubt as to what they really handed down.

One of the main ingredients of the struggle of the black man in America for the past 12 years has been the Black Muslim movement. No one can deny that the role that the Black Muslim movement has played in America during the past 12 years has been one of the main ingredients in the stepped-up militancy on the part of black people throughout this country.

No matter what direction the Black Muslim movement itself was headed in, no matter what its own organizational philosophy was, and no matter what other people thought about it, no matter what their personal opinions were of the Black Muslim movement, still it cannot be denied that that movement, because of its uncompromising stand, and because of its uncompromisingly militant approach to things, forced other civil-rights organizations to be more militant than they normally would have been, and forced many of the civil-rights leaders definitely to be more militant than they ever would have thought of being.

So the militancy of the black man in America during the past ten years can be traced largely to the existence and presence of the movement which I'm referring to now for purposes of identification as the Black Muslim movement. Its contribution to the black struggle for freedom in this country was militancy. It made many of our people dare to get loud for the first time in 400 years. It made many of the black leaders of the civil-rights movement dare to get loud for the first time—I mean really loud—for the first time in nearly 400 years in our country . . .

The leaders themselves never intended, and they never do intend, for our people to go too far. Their primary purpose has always been to contain our struggle, not to lead our struggle. Proof of this is that seldom are they seen until the "irresponsible" elements in the black community begin to explode. And then they go all the way around the country to grab one of them from wherever he's traveling and bring him in to cool things down, to tell us to be cool, or to tell us to take it easy—don't rock the boat. This is their function. This is their role—at least it has been until recent times . . .

But the existence of some of the Muslim groups and the black nationalist groups that couldn't be controlled by the power structure downtown (and I only use the expression "power structure downtown" to keep from calling it what it actually is) actually served their purpose in the sense that they gave respectability to the civil-rights groups and gave acceptability to the civil-rights groups. Ten years ago or more, the NAACP was looked upon as a radical leftist, almost subversive, movement, and then when the Black Muslim movement came along, the power structure said thank the Lord for Roy Wilkins and the NAACP . . .

WILKINS, FARMER, KING

When they looked around one day and found someone talking about, "all of them are devils," they were all night looking up Roy Wilkins and James Farmer and the right reverend Dr. King and some of the others to soothe them and keep them thinking that all of our people didn't think like that . . .

One of the things I noticed, when I was in Africa traveling around, was many Africans who were still colonized, still exploited, still oppressed. And one of the things all of them had in common was they seemed sad. They would discuss their sad plight, but they weren't ready to really do anything to change it. They seemed to be waiting for a miracle.

But the contrasting difference between them and what happened in Kenya was that the Kikuyu got mad. They just didn't care what the consequences were. They cared nothing about legality, morality, or anything. All they knew was that they were being oppressed unjustly, illegally, immorally. And because of this unjust, illegal, immoral oppression they were suffering, they came to the conclusion that they would be within their rights to bring it to a halt by any means necessary. And they adopted those means. And when they began to use these means in their struggle for freedom, the press of the West began to project them in a very negative image . . .

NOT IMAGE CONSCIOUS

But the Mau-Mau weren't image conscious. They weren't status seekers. They weren't social climbers. They wanted freedom, and they came to a conclusion in a point in their journey that the only way there was to get it was the way they did it. And they got it. I admire them for that. I respect them for that . . .

I say and I must say—because a reporter was asking me a few moments ago either to confirm or deny the statement that the *Times* had mentioned when I said we needed a Mau-Mau in the United States—I never would deny that we need more than a Mau-Mau in the U.S. I mean, actually a person has a lot of nerve to ask me that in a society (I'm deviating now because they put me off the track) where in 1964 three civil-rights workers can be murdered in cold blood and—not the Mississippi government—but the federal government can't do anything about it.

I say we need a Mau-Mau when a Negro educator can be murdered in Georgia and they know who murdered him and the government can do nothing about it. I say we need a Mau-Mau and I'll be the first to join it. A lot of people that you don't think go for it will line right up behind me.

So getting back to the Black Muslim movement. You have to understand it to understand what has taken place in the civil-rights movement in this country during the past ten years and in order to understand what might take place in 1965. The Black Muslim movement attracted the most militant young black people in this country. The most restless, the most impatient and the most uncompromising black men and women were attracted to the Black Muslim movement.

But the movement itself, as it began to grow, actually was maneuvered into a vacuum, in that it represented itself as a religious movement and the religion with which it identified itself was Islam, and the people in the part of the world who also identified that as their religion did not accept the Black Muslim movement as a *bonafide* Islamic or Moslem movement. They never did accept it as that. So it was put in the position of going by a religion that rejected it, which put it into a vacuum or made it a religious hybrid.

On the other hand, the government in Washington (I guess that's where it is) tried to label the Black Muslim movement as political. It used the press, it maneuvered the press to project the Black Muslim movement in an image that would enable the government itself to list it as political and therefore to label it seditious and subversive and step in and stomp it out . . .

So the Black Muslim movement was not only a religious hybrid but it became a political hybrid in that it was more political than religious, but at the same time it didn't take part in politics. It didn't take part in the civil-rights struggle. It took part in nothing that black people in this country were doing to correct conditions that existed in our community, other than it had a moral force— it stopped our people from getting drunk and taking drugs and things of that sort, which is not enough. After you sober up, you're still poor.

So it became in a vacuum. It actually developed, it grew, it became powerful—but it was in a vacuum. And it was filled with extremely militant young people who weren't willing to compromise with anything and wanted action. More action, actually, than the organization itself could produce. More constructive action, and more positive action, than the hierarchy of the organization was qualified, actually, to produce.

The main objective of the movement was land. But those in the movement were told that God would come and take them to that land. Well, for a time this was all right. But, as no visible means were ever detected by anyone in the movement that would enable us to see that a plan was afoot to make this objective materialize, it caused dissatisfaction. It caused dissension—which eventually developed division. And . . . out of that division or out of those who left was formed an authentic religious group, known as Muslim Mosque, Inc., which practiced the religion of Islam as it is practiced and taught in Mecca and Cairo and Lahore and other parts of the Moslem world.

MUSLIM MOSQUE, INC.

But those who went into the orthodox practice of the Islam religion in the Muslim Mosque, Inc., at the same time we realized that we were black people in a white society. We were black people in a racist society. We were black people in a society whose very political system was based and nourished upon racism, whose social system was a racist system, whose economic system was nourished with racism. We were black people who wanted to be religious, who wanted to practice brotherhood and all of that, who wanted to love everybody, and all of that, too; but, at the same time, that was a dream—you know, as my good friend, the doctor, said.

So, wanting brotherhood and wanting peace and wanting all these other beautiful things, we had to also face reality and realize that we were in a racist society that was controlled by racists from the federal government right on down to the local governments—from the White House right on down to City Hall. Racism was what we were confronted by. So we knew that this was a problem that was beyond religion and we formed another organization that was non-religious. And this organization was called the Organization of Afro-American Unity or the OAAU.

We got the idea for it from travels and observations of the success that our brothers on the African continent were having in their struggle for freedom. They were getting free faster than we. They were getting their independence faster than we. They were getting recognition and respect, *even when they came to this country,* faster than we. We had to find out what was happening, how were they doing it, and what were they doing, so we could try a little bit of it.

On the African continent, the imperialists, the colonial powers had always divided and conquered. They had practiced "divide and conquer," and this had kept the people of Africa, and Asia, from ever coming together. So on the African continent had appeared an organization known as the OAU, or Organization of African Unity, and this had been put together by a group of people—a highly skilled group of African intellectuals and politicians . . .

And since we in America were confronted with the same divisive tactics from *our* enemy, we decided to call ours the Organization of Afro-American Unity—which would be designed after the letter and spirit of the Organization of African Unity. In fact, we considered ourselves an offspring of our parent organization on our mother continent.

After it was formed, I spent five months in the Middle East and Africa, primarily for the purpose of getting better acquainted with them and making them better acquainted with us, giving them a first-hand account of our problems and what our problems actually consist of. When I first got there in July, I found some of them difficult to talk to. But by the time I left, in November, I didn't find anybody difficult to talk to . . .

By the time I had returned last month, the Muslim Mosque, Inc., had received official recognition and support by all of the official religious bodies in the Moslem world and the Organization of Afro-American Unity had also received official recognition and support from all of the African countries I visited and from most of those I didn't visit.

The first thing when I returned . . . I kept being asked the question by some reporters, "We heard you changed" . . . I smiled and all. But I would say to myself: How in the world can a white man expect a black man to change before *he* has changed? How do you expect us to change when you haven't changed? How do you expect us to change when the causes that made us as we are have not been removed? . . .

It's true I'm a Moslem and I believe in brotherhood. And I believe in the brotherhood of all men. But my religion doesn't make me a fool. My religion makes me be against all forms of racism. It keeps me from judging any man by the color of his skin. It teaches me to judge him by his deeds and his conscious behavior. And it teaches me to be for the rights of all human beings, but especially the Afro-American human being, because my religion is a natural religion, and the first law of nature is self-preservation . . .

In 1964, oppressed people all over the world, in Africa, in Asia and Latin America, in the Caribbean, made some progress. Northern Rhodesia threw off the yoke of colonialism and became Zambia, and was accepted into the United Nations, the society of independent governments. Nyasaland became Malawi and was also accepted into the UN, into the family of independent governments. Zanzibar had a revolution, threw out the colonialists and their lackeys and then united with Tanganyika into what is now known as the Republic of Tanzania—which is progress, indeed . . .

Also in 1964 the oppressed people of South Vietnam, and in that entire Southeast Asia area, were successful in fighting off the legions of imperialism . . . And with all the highly-mechanized weapons of warfare—jets, napalm, battleships, everything else, and they can't put those rice farmers back where they want them . . .

In 1964 this government, subsidizing Tshombe, the murderer of Lumumba, and Tshombe's mercenaries, hired killers from South Africa, along with the former colonial power, Belgium, dropped paratroopers on the people of the Congo, used Cubans, that they had trained, to drop bombs on the people of the Congo with American-made planes—to no avail. The struggle is still going on, and America's man, Tshombe, is still losing.

All of this in 1964. Now, in speaking like this, it doesn't mean that I am anti-American. I am not. I'm not anti-American, or un-American. And I'm not saying that to defend myself. Because if I was that I'd have a right to be that—after what America has done to us. This government should feel lucky that our people aren't anti-American . . . And the whole world would side with us, if we became anti-American. You know, that's something to think about.

But we are not anti-American. We are anti or against what America is doing wrong in other parts of the world as well as here, and what she did in the Congo in 1964 is wrong. It's criminal, criminal. And what she did to the American public, to get the American public to go along with it, is criminal. What she's doing in South Vietnam is criminal. She's causing American soldiers to be murdered every day, killed every day, die every day, for no reason at all. That's wrong. Now, you're not supposed to be so blind with patriotism that you can't face reality. Wrong is wrong, no matter who does it or who says it . . .

Also in 1964, China exploded her bomb, which was a scientific breakthrough for the oppressed people of China who suffered for a long time. I, for one, was very happy to hear that the great people of China were able to display their scientific advancement, their advanced knowledge of science, to the point where a country which is as backward as *this* country keeps saying China is, and so behind everybody, and so poor, could come up with an atomic bomb. Why, I had to marvel at that. It made me realize that poor people can do it as well as rich people.

So all these little advances were made by oppressed people in other parts of the world during 1964. These were tangible gains, and the reason that they were able to make these gains—they realized that power was the magic word—power against power. Power in defense of freedom is greater than power in behalf of tyranny and oppression, because power, real power, comes from conviction which produces action, uncompromising action. It also produces insurrection against oppression. This is the only way you end oppression—with power.

Power never takes a back step—only in the face of more power. Power doesn't back up in the face of a smile, or in the face of a threat, or in the face of some kind of non-violent loving action. It's not the nature of power to back up in the face of anything but some more power. And this is what the people have realized in Southeast Asia, in the Congo, in Cuba, in other parts of the world. Power recognizes only power, and all of them who realize this have made gains.

Now here in America it's different. When you compare our strides in 1964 with strides that have been made forward by people elsewhere all over the world, only then can you appreciate the great doublecross experienced by black people here in America. In 1964, the power structure started out the new year the same way they started it out in Washington the other day. Only now they call

it—what's that?—"The Great Society." Last year, 1964, was supposed to be the "Year of Promise." They opened up the new year
in Washington D.C., and in the City Hall and in Albany talking about
the Year of Promise . . .

MARCH ON WASHINGTON

But by the end of 1964 we had to agree that instead of the
year of promise, instead of these promises materializing, they substituted devices to create the illusion of progress and 1964 was the
Year of Illusion and Delusion. We received nothing but a promise . . .
In 1963 they had used the trick, one of their devices to let off the
steam across the nation, was the March on Washington. They used
that to make us think we were making progress. Imagine marching
to Washington and getting nothing for it whatsoever . . .

In '63 it was the March on Washington. In '64, what was it?
The Civil Rights Bill. Right after they passed the Civil Rights Bill
they murdered a Negro in Georgia and did nothing about it, murdered two whites and a Negro in Mississippi and did nothing about
it. So that the Civil Rights Bill has produced nothing where we're
concerned. It was only a valve, a vent, that was designed to enable
us to let off our frustrations. But the Bill, itself, was not designed
to solve our problems.

Since we see what they did in 1963, and we saw what they
did in 1964, what will they do now, in 1965? If the March on Washington was supposed to lessen the explosion, and the Civil Rights
Bill was designed to lessen the explosion—that's all it was designed
to do—it wasn't designed to solve the problems. It was designed to
lessen the explosion, because everyone in his right mind knows
there should have been an explosion. You can't have all those ingredients, those explosive ingredients that exist in Harlem and elsewhere where our people suffer and not have an explosion. So these
are devices to lessen the danger of the explosion, but not designed
to remove the material that's going to explode.

What will they give us in 1965? I just read where they
planned to make a black cabinet member. Yes, they have a new
gimmick every year. They're going to take one of their boys, black
boys, and put him in the cabinet so he can walk around Washington
with a cigar—fire on one end and fool on the other.

And because his immediate personal problem will have
been solved, he will be the one to tell our people how much progress
we're making: "I'm in Washington, D.C. I can have tea in the White
House. I'm your spokesman, I'm your, you know, your leader" . . . But

will it work? Can that one, whom they are going to put down there, step into the fire and put it out when the flames begin to leap up? When people take to the streets in their explosive mood? Will that one that they're going to put in the cabinet, be able to go among those people? Why, they'll burn him faster than they burn the ones who sent him.

ATLANTIC CITY

On the national scale during 1964, as I just mentioned, politically, the Mississippi Freedom Democratic Party had its face slapped at Atlantic City, at a convention over which Lyndon B. Johnson was the boss, and Hubert Humphrey was the next boss and Mayor Wagner had a lot of influence himself; still none of that influence was shown in any way whatsoever when the hopes and aspirations of the people, the black people of Mississippi, were at stake.

Though at the beginning of '64 we were told that our political life would be broadened, it was in 1964 that the two white civil-rights workers, working with the black civil-rights worker, were murdered . . . They were trying to show our people in Mississippi how to become registered voters. This is their crime. This was the reason for which they were murdered.

And the most pitiful part about them being murdered was the civil-rights organizations themselves being so chicken when it comes to reacting in the way that they should have reacted to the murder of these three civil-rights workers. The civil-rights groups sold those three brothers out—sold them out—sold them right down the river. Because they died and what has been done about it? And what voice is being raised every day today in regards to the murder of those three civil-rights workers? . . .

So this is why I say if we get involved in the civil-rights movement and go to Mississippi, or anyplace else, to help our people get registered to vote, we intend to go prepared. We don't intend to break the law but when you're trying to register to vote you're upholding the law. It's the one who tries to prevent you from registering to vote who's breaking the law and you got a right to protect yourself by any means necessary. Then if the government doesn't want civil-rights groups going equipped, the government should do its job.

Concerning the Harlem incident that took place during the summer when the citizens of Harlem were attacked in a pogrom (I can't pronounce it 'cause it's not my word) . . . We had gotten the word that there were elements in the power structure that were going to incite a riot—something in Harlem that they could call a riot—in order that they could step in and be justified in using whatever measures necessary to crush the militant groups which were still considered in the embryonic stage.

And realizing that there was a plan afoot to instigate something in Harlem so they could step in and crush it, there were elements in Harlem who were prepared and qualified and equipped to retaliate in situations like that, who purposely did not get involved. And the real miracle of the Harlem explosion was the restraint exercised by the people of Harlem. The miracle of 1964, I'll tell it to you straight, the miracle of 1964, during the incidents that took place in Harlem was the restraint exercised by the people in Harlem who are qualified and equipped and whatever else there is to protect themselves when they are being illegally and immorally and unjustly attacked.

An illegal attack, an unjust attack and an immoral attack can be made against you by anyone. Just because a person has on a uniform does not give him the right to come and shoot up your neighborhood. No, this is not right and my suggestions would be that as long as the police department doesn't use those methods in white neighborhoods, they shouldn't come to Harlem and use it in our neighborhood . . .

And it all started when a little boy was shot by a policeman and he was turned loose the same as the sheriff was turned loose in Mississippi when he killed the three civil-rights workers . . .

So that I point out that 1964 was not a pie-in-the-sky year of promise as was promised in January of that year. Blood did flow in the streets of Harlem, Philadelphia, Rochester, some places over here in Jersey and elsewhere. In 1965 even more blood will flow. More than you ever dreamed. It'll flow downtown as well as uptown. Why? Why will it flow? Have the causes that forced it to flow in '64 been removed? Have the causes that made it flow in '63 been removed? The causes are still there . . .

In 1964, 97 per cent of the black American voters supported Lyndon B. Johnson, Hubert Humphrey and the Democratic Party. Ninety-seven per cent! No one minority group in the history of the world has ever given so much of its uncompromising support to one candidate and one party. No one people, no one group has ever gone all the way to support a party and its candidate as did the people, the black people, in America in 1964 . . .

And the first act of the Democratic Party, Lyndon B. included, in 1965, when the representatives from the state of Mississippi who *refused* to support Johnson came to Washington, D.C., and the black people of Mississippi sent representatives there to challenge the legality of these people being seated, what did Johnson say? Nothing! What did Humphrey say? Nothing! What did Robert Pretty-Boy Kennedy say? Nothing! Nothing! Not one thing! These are the people that black people have supported. This is the party that they have supported . . .

The frustration of these black representatives from Mississippi when they arrived in Washington, D.C., the other day, thinking, you know, that the Great Society was going to include them—only to see the door close in their face like that. That's what makes them think. That's what makes them realize what they're up against. It is this type of frustration that produced the Mau-Mau. They reached the point where they saw that it takes power to talk to power. It takes power to make power respect you. It takes madness almost to deal with a power structure that's so corrupt—so corrupt.

So 1965 should see a lot of action. Since the old methods haven't worked, they'll be forced to try new methods . . .

The Movement: *The question of nationalism is a vital one in the black movement today. Some have made a distinction between cultural nationalism and revolutionary nationalism. Would you comment on the differences and give us your views?*

Huey P. Newton: *There are two kinds of nationalism, revolutionary nationalism and reactionary nationalism. Revolutionary nationalism is first dependent upon a people's revolution with the end goal being the people in power. Therefore to be a revolutionary nationalist you would by necessity have to be a socialist. If you are a reactionary nationalist you are not a socialist and your end goal is the oppression of the people.*

Cultural nationalism, or pork chop nationalism, as I sometimes call it, is basically a problem of having the wrong political perspective. It seems to be a reaction instead of responding to political oppression. The cultural nationalists are concerned with returning to the old African culture and thereby regaining their identity and freedom. In other words, they feel that the African culture will automatically bring political freedom. Many times cultural nationalists fall into line as reactionary nationalists.

Papa Doc in Haiti is an excellent example of reactionary nationalism. He oppresses the people but he does promote the African culture. He's against anything other than black,

Reprinted by permission from "Huey Newton Talks to *The Movement*," *The Movement*, August, 1968.

which on the surface seems very good, but for him it
is only to mislead the people. He merely kicked out the
racists and replaced them with himself as the oppressor.
Many of the nationalists in this country seem to desire
the same ends.

The Black Panther Party, which is a revolutionary
group of black people, realizes that we have to have an
identity. We have to realize our black heritage in order
to give us strength to move on and progress. But as far
as returning to the old African culture, it's unnecessary
and it's not advantageous in many respects. We believe
that culture itself will not liberate us. We're going to need
some stronger stuff.

REVOLUTIONARY NATIONALISM

A good example of revolutionary nationalism was the
revolution in Algeria when Ben Bella took over. The
French were kicked out but it was a people's revolution
because the people ended up in power. The leaders that
took over were not interested in the profit motive where
they could exploit the people and keep them in a state
of slavery. They nationalized the industry and plowed
the would-be profits into the community. That's what
socialism is all about in a nutshell. The people's
representatives are in office strictly on the leave of
the people. The wealth of the country is controlled by the
people and they are considered whenever modifications
in the industries are made.

The Black Panther Party is a revolutionary Nationalist
group and we see a major contradiction between capitalism
in this country and our interests. We realize that this
country became very rich upon slavery and that slavery
is capitalism in the extreme. We have two evils to fight,
capitalism and racism. We must destroy both racism and
capitalism.

Movement: *Directly related to the question of nationalism is the
question of unity within the black community. There has
been some question about this since the Black Panther
Party has run candidates against other black candidates
in recent California elections. What is your position on
this matter?*

Huey: *Well a very peculiar thing has happened. Historically you got what Malcolm X calls the field nigger and the house nigger. The house nigger had some privileges, a little more. He got the worn-out clothes of the master and he didn't have to work as hard as the field black. He came to respect the master to such an extent until he identified with the master because he got a few of the leftovers that the field blacks did not get. And through this identity with him, he saw the slavemaster's interest as being his interest. Sometimes he would even protect the slavemaster more than the slavemaster would protect himself. Malcolm makes the point that if the master's house happened to catch on fire the house Negro will work harder than the master to put the fire out and save the master's house. While the field Negro, the field black was praying that the house burned down. The house black identified with the master so much that when the master would get sick the house Negro would say, "Master, we's sick!"*

BLACK BOURGEOISIE

The Black Panther Party are the field blacks, we're hoping the master dies if he gets sick. The Black bourgeoisie seem to be acting in the role of the house Negro. They are pro-administration. They would like a few concessions made, but as far as the overall setup, they have a little more material goods, a little more advantage, a few more privileges than the black have-nots; the lower class. And so they identify with the power structure and they see their interests as the power structure's interest. In fact, it's against their interest.

The Black Panther Party was forced to draw a line of demarcation. We are for all of those who are for the promotion of the interests of the black have-nots, which represents about 98% of blacks here in America. We're not controlled by the white mother country radicals nor are we controlled by the black bourgeoisie. We have a mind of our own and if the black bourgeoisie cannot align itself with our complete program, then the black bourgeoisie sets itself up as our enemy. And they will be attacked and treated as such.

Movement: *The Black Panther Party has had considerable contact*

with white radicals since its earliest days. What do you
see as the role of these white radicals?

Huey: The white mother country radical is the off-spring of the
children of the beast that has plundered the world
exploiting all people, concentrating on the people of
color. These are children of the beast that seek now to
be redeemed because they realize that their former
heroes, who were slave masters and murderers, put forth
ideas that were only facades to hide the treachery they
inflicted upon the world. They are turning their backs on
their fathers.

The white mother country radical, in resisting the system,
becomes somewhat of an abstract thing because he's not
oppressed as much as black people are. As a matter of
fact his oppression is somewhat abstract simply because
he doesn't have to live in a reality of oppression.

Black people in America and colored people throughout
the world suffer not only from exploitation, but they suffer
from racism. Black people here in America, in the black
colony, are oppressed because we're black and we're
exploited. The whites are rebels, many of them from the
middle class and as far as any overt oppression this is
not the case. So therefore I call their rejection of the
system somewhat of an abstract thing. They're looking
for new heroes. They're looking to wash away the
hypocrisy that their fathers have presented to the world.
In doing this they see the people who are really fighting
for freedom. They see the people who are really standing
for justice and equality and peace throughout the world.
They are the people of Vietnam, the people of Latin
America, the people of Asia, the people of Africa, and
the black people in the black colony here in America.

WHITE REVOLUTIONARIES

This presents somewhat of a problem in many ways
to the black revolutionary, especially to the cultural
nationalist. The cultural nationalist doesn't understand
the white revolutionaries because he can't see why anyone
white would turn on the system. So they think that maybe
this is some more hypocrisy being planted by white people.
I personally think that there are many young white

revolutionaries who are sincere in attempting to realign themselves with mankind, and to make a reality out of the high moral standards that their fathers and forefathers only expressed. In pressing for new heroes the young white revolutionaries found the heroes in the black colony at home and in the colonies throughout the world.

The young white revolutionaries raised the cry for the troops to withdraw from Vietnam, hands off Latin America, withdraw from the Dominican Republic and also to withdraw from the black community or the black colony. So you have a situation in which the young white revolutionaries are attempting to identify with the oppressed people of the colonies and against the exploiter.

The problem arises then in what part they can play. How can they aid the colony? How can they aid the Black Panther Party or any other black revolutionary group? They can aid the black revolutionaries first by simply turning away from the establishment, and secondly by choosing their friends. For instance, they have a choice between whether they will be a friend of Lyndon Baines Johnson or a friend of Fidel Castro. A friend of Robert Kennedy or a friend of Ho Chi Minh. And these are direct opposites. A friend of mine or a friend of Johnson's. After they make this choice then the white revolutionaries have a duty and a responsibility to act.

The imperialistic or capitalistic system occupies areas. It occupies Vietnam now. They occupy them by sending soldiers there, by sending policemen there. The policemen or soldiers are only a gun in the establishment's hand. They make the racist secure in his racism. The gun in the establishment's hand makes the establishment secure in its exploitation. The first problem it seems is to remove the gun from the establishment's hand. Until lately the white radical has seen no reason to come into conflict with the policemen in his own community. The reason I said until recently is because there is friction now in the mother country between the young white revolutionaries and the police. Because now the white revolutionaries are attempting to put some of their ideas into action, and there's the rub. We say that it should be a permanent thing.

Black people are being oppressed in the colony by white policemen, by white racists. We are saying they must withdraw. We realize that it is not only the Oakland

*police department but rather the security forces in general.
On April 6 it wasn't just the Oakland police department
who ambushed the Panthers. It was the Oakland police
department, the Emeryville police department and I
wouldn't be surprised if there were others. When the
white revolutionaries went down to close up the Army
terminal in October 1965, it wasn't the Oakland police by
themselves who tried to stop them, it was the Oakland
police, the Berkeley police, the Highway Patrol, the
Sheriff's Department and the national guard was standing
by. So we see that they're all part of one organization.
They're all a part of the security force to protect the status
quo; to make sure that the institutions carry out their
goals. They're here to protect the system.*

*As far as I'm concerned the only reasonable conclusion
would be to first realize the enemy, realize the plan, and
then when something happens in the black colony—
when we're attacked and ambushed in the black colony—
then the white revolutionary students and intellectuals
and all the other whites who support the colony should
respond by defending us, by attacking the enemy in their
community. Every time that we're attacked in our
community there should be a reaction by the white
revolutionaries; they should respond by defending us, by
attacking part of the security force. Part of that security
force is determined to carry out the racist ends of the
American institutions.*

*As far as our party is concerned, the Black Panther
Party is an all black party, because we feel as Malcolm X
felt that there can be no black-white unity until there is
first black unity. We have a problem in the black colony
that is particular to the colony, but we're willing to accept
aid from the mother country as long as the mother country
radicals realize that we have, as Eldridge Cleaver says in
SOUL ON ICE, a mind of our own. We've regained our
mind that was taken away from us and we will decide the
political as well as the practical stand that we'll take.
We'll make the theory and we'll carry out the practice. It's
the duty of the white revolutionary to aid us in this.*

*So the role of the mother country radical, and he does
have a role, is to first choose his friend and his enemy
and after doing this, which it seems he's already done,
then to not only articulate his desires to regain his moral
standard and align himself with humanity, but also to put*

this into practice by attacking the protectors of the
institutions.

Movement: *You have spoken a lot about dealing with the
protectors of the system, the armed forces. Would you
like to elaborate on why you place so much emphasis on
this?*

Huey: *The reasons that I feel very strongly about dealing with
the protectors of the system is simply because without
this protection from the army, the police and the military,
the institutions could not go on in their racism and
exploitation. For instance, as the Vietnamese are driving
the American imperialist troops out of Vietnam, it
automatically stops the racist imperialist institutions of
America from oppressing that particular country. The
country cannot implement its racist program without the
guns. And the guns are the military and the police. If the
military were disarmed in Vietnam, then the Vietnamese
would be victorious.*

*We are in the same situation here in America. Whenever
we attack the system the first thing the administrators do
is to send out their strongarm men. If it's a rent strike,
because of the indecent housing we have, they will send
out the police to throw the furniture out the window. They
don't come themselves. They send their protectors. So to
deal with the corrupt exploiter you are going to have to
deal with his protector, which is the police who take orders
from him. This is a must.*

Movement: *Would you like to be more specific on the conditions
which must exist before an alliance or coalition can be
formed with predominantly white groups? Would you
comment specifically on your alliance with the California
Peace and Freedom Party?*

Huey: *We have an alliance with the Peace and Freedom Party.
The Peace and Freedom Party has supported our program
in full and this is the criterion for a coalition with the black
revolutionary group. If they had not supported our program
in full, then we would not have seen any reason to make
an alliance with them, because we are the reality of the
oppression. They are not. They are only oppressed in an
abstract way; we are oppressed in the real way. We
are the real slaves! So it's a problem that we
suffer from more than anyone else and its our
problem of liberation. Therefore we should decide what
measures and what tools and what programs to use to*

become liberated. Many of the young white revolutionaries realize this and I see no reason not to have a coalition with them.

Movement: *Other black groups seem to feel that from past experience it is impossible for them to work with whites and impossible for them to form alliances. What do you see as the reasons for this and do you think that the history of the Black Panther Party makes this less of a problem?*

SNCC AND LIBERALS

Huey: *There was somewhat of an unhealthy relationship in the past with the white liberals supporting the black people who were trying to gain their freedom. I think that a good example of this would be the relationship that SNCC had with its white liberals. I call them white liberals because they differ strictly from the white radicals. The relationship was that the whites controlled SNCC for a very long time. From the very start of SNCC until here recently whites were the mind of SNCC. They controlled the program of SNCC with money and they controlled the ideology, or the stands SNCC would take. The blacks in SNCC were completely controlled program-wise; they couldn't do any more than these white liberals wanted them to do, which wasn't very much. So the white liberals were not working for self-determination for the black community. They were interested in a few concessions from the power structure. They undermined SNCC's program.*

Stokely Carmichael came along and realizing this started to follow Malcolm X's program of Black Power. This frightened many of the white liberals who were supporting SNCC. Whites were afraid when Stokely came along with Black Power and said that black people have a mind of their own and that SNCC would be an all-black organization and that SNCC would seek self-determination for the black community. The white liberals withdrew their support leaving the organization financially bankrupt. The blacks who were in the organization, Stokely and H. Rap Brown, were left very angry with the white liberals who had been aiding them under the disguise of being sincere. They weren't sincere.

The result was that the leadership of SNCC turned away from the white liberal, which was very good. I don't think they distinguished between the white liberal and the white revolutionary, because the white revolutionary is white also and they are very much afraid to have any contact whatsoever with white people. Even to the point of denying that the white revolutionaries could give support, by supporting the programs of SNCC in the mother country. Not by making any programs, not by being a member of the organization, but simply by resisting. Just as the Vietnamese people realize that they are supported whenever other oppressed people throughout the world resist. Because it helps divide the troops. It drains the country militarily and economically. If the mother country radicals are sincere then this will definitely add to the attack that we are making on the power structure. The Black Panther Party's program is a program where we recognize that the revolution in the mother country will definitely aid us in our freedom and has everything to do with our struggle!

HATE THE OPPRESSOR

I think that one of SNCC's great problems is that they were controlled by the traditional administrator: the omnipotent administrator, the white person. He was the mind of SNCC. And so SNCC regained its mind, but I believe that it lost its political perspective. I think that this was a reaction rather than a response. The Black Panther Party has NEVER been controlled by white people. The Black Panther Party has always been a black group. We have always had an integration of mind and body. We have never been controlled by whites and therefore we don't fear the white mother country radicals. Our alliance is one of organized black groups with organized white groups. As soon as the organized white groups do not do the things that would benefit us in our struggle for liberation, that will be our departure point. So we don't suffer in the hangup of a skin color. We don't hate white people; we hate the oppressor. And if the oppressor happens to be white then we hate him. When he stops oppressing us then we no longer hate him. And right now in America you have the slave-master being a white group. We are pushing him out of office through revolution in this country. I think the responsibility of the white revolutionary will be

*to aid us in this. And when we are attacked by the police
or by the military then it will be up to the white mother
country radicals to attack the murderers and to respond
as we respond, to follow our program.*

SLAVE MASTERS

Movement: *You indicate that there is a psychological process that
has historically existed in white-black relations in the U.S.
that must change in the course of revolutionary struggle.
Would you like to comment on this?*

Huey: *Yes. The historical relationship between black and white
here in America has been the relationship between the
slave and the master; the master being the mind and the
slave the body. The slave would carry out the orders that
the mind demanded him to carry out. By doing this the
master took the manhood from the slave because he
stripped him of a mind. He stripped black people of their
minds. In the process the slave-master stripped himself
of a body. As Eldridge puts it, the slave master.
became the omnipotent administrator and the slave
became the supermasculine menial. This puts the omnipotent administrator into the controlling position or the
front office and the supermasculine menial into the field.*

*The whole relationship developed so that the omnipotent
administrator and the supermasculine menial became
opposites. The slave being a very strong body doing all
the practical things, all of the work becomes very
masculine. The omnipotent administrator in the process
of removing himself from all body functions realizes later
that he has emasculated himself. And this is very disturbing
to him. So the slave lost his mind and the slave-master
his body.*

PENIS ENVY

*This caused the slave-master to become very envious
of the slave because he pictured the slave as being more
of a man, being superior sexually, because the penis is
part of the body. The omnipotent administrator laid down
a decree when he realized that his plan to enslave the
black man had a flaw, when he discovered that he had*

emasculated himself. He attempted to bind the penis of the slave. He attempted to show that his penis could reach further than the supermasculine menial's penis. He said "I, the omnipotent administrator can have access to the black woman." The supermasculine menial then had a psychological attraction to the white woman (the ultra feminine freak) for the simple reason that it was forbidden fruit. The omnipotent administrator decreed that this kind of contact would be punished by death. At the same time in order to reinforce his sexual desire, to confirm, to assert his manhood, he would go into the slave quarters and have sexual relations with the black women (the self-reliant Amazon). Not to be satisfied but simply to confirm his manhood. Because if he can only satisfy the self-reliant Amazon then he would be sure that he was a man. Because he doesn't have a body, he doesn't have a penis, he psychologically wants to castrate the black man. The slave was constantly seeking unity within himself: a mind and a body. He always wanted to be able to decide, to gain respect from his woman. Because women want one who can control. I give this outline to fit into a framework of what is happening now. The white power structure today in America defines itself as the mind. They want to control the world. They go off and plunder the world. They are the policemen of the world exercising control especially over people of color.

RE-CAPTURE THE MIND

The white man cannot gain his manhood, cannot unite with the body because the body is black. The body is symbolic of slavery and strength. It's a biological thing as he views it. The slave is in a much better situation because his not being a full man has always been viewed psychologically. And it's always easier to make a psychological transition than a biological one. If he can only recapture his mind, recapture his balls, then he will lose all fear and will be free to determine his destiny. This is what is happening at this time with the rebellion of the world's oppressed people against the controller. They are regaining their mind and they're saying that we have a mind of our own. They're saying that we want freedom to determine the destiny of the people, thereby uniting the mind with their bodies. They are taking the mind back from the omnipotent administrator, the controller, the exploiter.

In America black people are also chanting that we have a mind of our own. We must have freedom to determine our destiny. It's almost a spiritual thing, this unity, this harmony. This unity of the mind and of the body, this unity of man within himself. Certain slogans of Chairman Mao I think demonstrate this theory of uniting the mind with the body within the man. An example is his call to the intellectuals to go to the countryside. The peasants in the countryside are all bodies; they're the workers. And he sent the intellectuals there because the dictatorship of the proletariat has no room for the omnipotent administrator; there's no room for the exploiter. So therefore he must go to the countryside to regain his body; he must work. He is really done a favor, because the people force him to unite his mind with his body by putting them both to work. At the same time the intellectual teaches the people political ideology, he educates them, thus uniting the mind and the body in the peasant. Their minds and bodies are united and they control their country. I think this is a very good example of this unity and it is my idea of the perfect man.

THE GUERRILLA

Movement: *You mentioned at another point that the guerrilla was was the perfect man and this kind of formulation seems to fit in directly with the guerrilla as a political man. Would you like to comment on this?*

Huey: *Yes, the guerrilla is a very unique man. This is in contrast to Marxist-Leninist orthodox theories where the party controls the military. The guerrilla is not only the warrior, the military fighter; he is also the military commander as well as the political theoretician. Debray says "poor the pen without the guns, poor the gun without the pen." The pen being just an extension of the mind, a tool to write down concepts, ideas. The gun is only an extension of the body, the extension of our fanged teeth that we lost through evolution. It's the weapon, it's the claws that we lost, it's the body. The guerrilla is the military commander and the political theoretician all in one.*

In Bolivia Che said that he got very little help from the

Communist Party there. The Communist Party wanted to be the mind, the Communist Party wanted to have full control of the guerrilla activity. But yet weren't taking part in the practical work of the guerrillas. The guerrilla on the other hand is not only united within himself, but he also attempts to spread this to the people by educating the villagers, giving them political perspective, pointing out things, educating them politically, and arming the people. Therefore the guerrilla is giving the peasants and workers a mind. Because they've already got the body you get a unity of the mind and the body. Black people here in America, who have long been the workers, have regained our minds and we now have a unity of mind and body.

Movement: Would you be willing to extend this formula in terms of white radicals; to say that one of their struggles today is to get back their bodies.

Huey: Yes. I thought I made that clear. The white mother country radical by becoming an activist is attempting to regain his body. By being an activist and not the traditional theoretician who outlines the plan, as the Communist Party has been trying to do for ever so long, the white mother country radical is regaining his body. The resistance by white radicals in Berkeley during the past three nights is a good indication that the white radicals are on the way home. They have identified their enemies. The white radicals have integrated theory with practice. They realize the American system is the real enemy but in order to attack the American system they must attack the ordinary cop. In order to attack the educational system they must attack the ordinary teacher. Just as the Vietnamese people to attack the American system must attack the ordinary soldier. The white mother country radicals now are regaining their bodies and they're also recognizing that the black man has a mind and that he is a man.

Movement: Would you comment on how this psychological understanding aids in the revolutionary struggle?

Huey: You can see that in statements until recently black people who haven't been enlightened have defined the white man by calling him "the MAN." "The Man" is making this decision, "The Man" this and "The Man" that. The black woman found it difficult to respect the black man because he didn't even define himself as a man! Because he didn't have a mind, because the decision maker was outside of himself. But the vanguard group, the Black Panther Party, *along with all revolutionary black groups, have regained our mind and our manhood. Therefore we no longer define the omnipotent administrator as "the Man" . . . or the authority as "the Man." Matter of fact the omnipotent administrator along with his security agents are less than a man because WE define them as pigs! I think that this is a revolutionary thing in itself. That's political power. That's power itself. Matter of fact what is power other than the ability to define phenomenon and then make it act in a desired manner? When black people start defining things and making it act in a desired manner, then we call this Black Power!*

Movement: *Would you comment further on what you mean by Black Power?*

Huey: *Black Power is really people's power. The Black Panther Program, Panther Power as we call it, will implement this people's power. We have respect for all of humanity and we realize that the people should rule and determine their destiny. Wipe out the controller. To have Black Power doesn't humble or subjugate anyone to slavery or oppression. Black Power is giving power to people who have not had power to determine their destiny. We advocate and we aid any people who are struggling to determine their destiny. This is regardless of color. The Vietnamese say Vietnam should be able to determine its own destiny. Power of the Vietnamese people. We also chant power of the Vietnamese people. The Latins are talking about Latin America for the Latin Americans. Cuba, Si and Yanqui, Non. It's not that they don't want the Yankees to have any power, they just don't want them to have the power over them. They can have power over themselves. We in the black colony in America want to be able to have power over our destiny and that's black power.*

Movement: *A lot of white radicals are romantic about what Che said: "In a revolution one wins or dies . . ." For most of us it is really an abstract or theoretical question. It's a real question for you and we'd like you to rap about how you feel about it.*

Huey: *Yes. The revolutionary sees no compromise. We will not compromise because the issue is so basic. If we compromise one iota we will be selling our freedom out. We will be selling the revolution out. And we refuse to remain slaves. As Eldridge says in SOUL ON ICE, "a slave who dies of natural causes will not balance two dead flies on* *the scales of eternity." As far as we're concerned we would rather be dead than to go on with the slavery that we're in. Once we compromise we will be compromising not only our freedom, but also our manhood. We realize that we're going up against a highly technical country, and we realize that they are not only paper tigers, as Mao says, but real tigers too because they have the ability to slaughter many people. But in the long run, they will prove themselves paper tigers because they're not in line with humanity; they are divorced from the people. We know that the enemy is very powerful and that our manhood is at stake, but we feel it necessary to be victorious in regaining ourselves, regaining our manhood. And this is the basic point. So either we will do this or we won't have any freedom. Either we will win or we will die trying to win.*

MOOD OF BLACK PEOPLE

Movement: *How would you characterize the mood of black people in America today? Are they disenchanted, wanting a larger slice of the pie, or alienated, not wanting to integrate into a burning house, not wanting to integrate into Babylon? What do you think it will take for them to become alienated and revolutionary?*

Huey: *I was going to say disillusioned, but I don't think we were ever under the illusion that we had freedom in this country. This society is definitely a decadent one and we realize it. Black people are realizing it more and more. We cannot gain our freedom under the present system; the system that is carrying out its plans of institutionalized racism. Your question is what will have to be done to stimulate them to revolution. I think it's already being done. It's a matter of time now for us to educate them to a program and show them the way to liberation. The Black Panther Party is the beacon light to show black people the way to liberation.*

You notice the insurrections that have been going on throughout the country, in Watts, in Newark, in Detroit. They were all responses of the people demanding that they have freedom to determine their destiny, rejecting exploitation. Now the Black Panther Party does not think that the traditional riots, or insurrections that have

taken place are the answer. It is true they have been
against the Establishment, they have been against authority
and oppression within their community, but they have
been unorganized. However, black people learned from
each of these insurrections.

They learned from Watts. I'm sure the people in Detroit
were educated by what happened in Watts. Perhaps this
was wrong education. It sort of missed the mark. It
wasn't quite the correct activity, but the people were
educated through the activity. The people of Detroit
followed the example of the people in Watts, only they
added a little scrutiny to it. The people in Detroit learned
that the way to put a hurt on the administration is to make
Molotov cocktails and to go into the street in mass
numbers. So this was a matter of learning. The slogan
went up "Burn, baby, burn." People were educated
through the activity and it spread throughout the country.
The people were educated on how to resist, but perhaps
incorrectly.

EDUCATE THROUGH ACTIVITY

What we have to do as a vanguard of the revolution
is to correct this through activity. The large majority of
black people are either illiterate or semiliterate. They
don't read. They need activity to follow. This is true of
any colonized people. The same thing happened in Cuba
where it was necessary for twelve men with a leadership
of Che and Fidel to take to the hills and then attack the
corrupt administration; to attack the army who were the
protectors of the exploiters in Cuba. They could have
leafleted the community and they could have written books,
but the people would not respond. They had to act and
the people could see and hear about it and therefore
become educated on how to respond to oppression.

In this country black revolutionaries have to set an
example. We can't do the same things that were done in
Cuba because Cuba is Cuba and the U.S. is the U.S.
Cuba has many terrains to protect the guerrilla. This
country is mainly urban. We have to work out new solutions
to offset the power of the country's technology and
communication; its ability to communicate very rapidly
by telephone and teletype and so forth. We do have

*solutions to these problems and they will be put into
effect. I wouldn't want to go into the ways and means of
this, but we will educate through action. We have to engage
in action to make the people want to read our literature.
Because they are not attracted to all the writing in this
country; there's too much writing. Many books make one
weary.*

THREAT FROM REFORMERS

Movement: *Kennedy before his death, and to a lesser extent
Rockefeller and Lindsay and other establishment liberals
have been talking about making reforms to give black
people a greater share in the pie and thus stop any
developing revolutionary movement. Would you comment
on this?*

Huey: *I would say this: If a Kennedy or Lindsay or anyone else
can give decent housing to all of our people; if they can
give full employment to our people with a high standard;
if they can give full control to black people to determine
the destiny of their community; if they can give fair trials
in the court systems by turning over the structure to the
community; if they can end their exploitation of people
throughout the world; if they can do all of these things they
would have solved the problems. But I don't believe that
under this present system, under capitalism, that they
will be able to solve these problems.*

PEOPLE MUST CONTROL

*I don't think black people should be fooled by their
come-ons because every one who gets in office promises
the same thing. They promise full employment and decent
housing; the Great Society, the New Frontier. All of these
names, but no real benefits. No effects are felt in the black
community, and black people are tired of being deceived
and duped. The people must have full control of the
means of production. Small black businesses cannot
compete with General Motors. That's just out of the
question. General Motors robbed us and worked us for
nothing for a couple hundred years and took our money
and set up factories and became fat and rich and then*

talks about giving us some of the crumbs. We want full control. We're not interested in anyone promising that the private owners are going to all of a sudden become human beings and give these things to our community. It hasn't ever happened and, based on empirical evidence, we don't expect them to become Buddhists over night.

Movement: *We raised this question not because we feel that these reforms are possible, but rather to get your ideas on what effects such attempted reforms might have on the development of a revolutionary struggle.*

Huey: *I think that reforms pose no real threat. The revolution has always been in the hands of the young. The young always inherit the revolution. The young population is growing at a very rapid rate and they are very displeased with the authorities. They want control. I doubt that under the present system any kind of program can be launched that will be able to buy off all these young people. They have not been able to do it with the poverty program, the great society, etc. This country has never been able to employ all of its people simply because it's too interested in private property and the profit motive. A bigger poverty program is just what it says it is, a program to keep people in poverty. So I don't think that there is any real threat from the reforms.*

Movement: *Would you like to say something about the Panther's organizing especially in terms of the youth?*

Huey: *The Panthers represent a cross section of the black community. We have older people as well as younger people. The younger people of course are the ones who are seen on the streets. They are the activists. They are the real vanguard of change because they haven't been indoctrinated and they haven't submitted. They haven't been beaten into line as some of the older people have. But many of the older people realize that we're waging a just fight against the oppressor. They are aiding us and they are taking a part in the program.*

JAIL

Movement: *Tell us something about your relations with the prisoners in the jail.*

Huey: *The black prisoners as well as many of the white prisoners identify with the program of the Panthers. Of course by the* very nature of their being prisoners they can see the oppression and they've suffered at the hands of the Gestapo. They have reacted to it. The black prisoners have all joined the Panthers, about 95% of them. Now the jail is all Panther and the police are very worried about this. The white prisoners can identify with us because they realize that they are not in control. They realize there's someone controlling them and the rest of the world with guns. They want some control over their lives also. The Panthers in jail have been educating them and so we are going along with the revolution inside of the jail.

Movement: What has been the effect of the demonstrations outside the jail calling for "Free Huey"?

Huey: Very positive reactions. One demonstration, I don't remember which one, a couple of trustees, white trustees, held a cardboard sign out the laundry window reading "Free Huey." They say people saw it and responded to it. They were very enthusiastic about the demonstrators because they too suffer from being treated unfairly by the parole authorities and by the police here in the jail.

OPEN OR UNDERGROUND

Movement: The Panthers organizing efforts have been very open up until this point. Would you like to comment about the question of an underground political organization versus an open organization at this point in the struggle?

Huey: Yeah. Some of the black nationalist groups feel that they have to be underground because they'll be attacked. But we don't feel that you can romanticize being underground. They say we're romantic because we're trying to live revolutionary lives, and we are not taking precautions. But we say that the only way we would go underground is if we're driven underground. All real revolutionary movements are driven underground. Take the revolution in Cuba. The agitation that was going on while Fidel was in law school was very much above ground. Even his existence in the hills was, so to speak, an above the ground affair because he was letting it be known who was doing the damage and why he was doing the damage. To catch him was a different story. The only way we can educate the people is by setting an example for them. We feel that this is very necessary.

This is a pre-revolutionary period and we feel it is very

necessary to educate the people while we can. So we're very open about this education. We have been attacked and we will be attacked even more in the future but we're not going to go underground until we get ready to go underground because we have a mind of our own. We're not going to let anyone force us to do anything. We're going to go underground after we educate all of the black people and not before that time. Then it won't really be necessary for us to go underground because you can see black anywhere. We will just have the stuff to protect ourselves and the strategy to offset the great power that the strong-arm men of the establishment have and are planning to use against us.

WHITE ORGANIZING

Movement: *Your comments about the white prisoners seemed encouraging. Do you see the possibility of organizing a white Panther Party in opposition to the establishment possibly among poor and working whites?*

Huey: *Well, as I put it before, Black Power is people's power and as far as organizing white people we give white people the privilege of having a mind and we want them to get a body. They can organize themselves. We can tell them what they should do, what their responsibility is if they're going to claim to be white revolutionaries or white mother country radicals, and that is to arm themselves and support the colonies around the world in their just struggle against imperialism. But anything more than that they will have to do on their own.*

21
The
Second
Civil War

Casey Mann
Melvin Mitchell
Robert Jayson
Harry Quintana

Perhaps a more appropriate title would be "The Second Wave," meaning the second phase in the struggle of Black people to regain the precise *land* in which the blood, sweat, tears and bones of our ancestors are invested and which is the only possible base from which we might be able to meet the needs of the masses of Black people while at the same time precipitating national confrontations of such an order as to either destroy or revolutionize existing American political, economic and social systems.

It was primarily through the sacrifices and efforts of the First Wave that the objective conditions of such a move are now logical. That wave was composed basically of dedicated, idealistic people armed with no more than the perverted courage to practice non-violence and the vague knowledge that something was dreadfully wrong and merely needed exposing. Needless to say, both the non-violent and exposure theories were tactical errors. Just as it is true now, it was also true then that the question of Black control and liberation of the Southern region of the U.S. would be resolved in open warfare. It is not so clear at this time as to whom the battle will be waged between, e.g., Federal guns against Black fighters, or Southern police and militia against Black fighters, or a combination of both against Black fighters. This question is solely dependent upon the ability, quality and political astuteness of our Black leadership. Unfortunately, no such qualified leadership appears to be available upon the national scene today. We can only hope that it is simply lying dormant at present.

Reprinted by permission of *Liberator* from Casey Mann, Melvin Mitchell, Robert Jayson, and Harry Quintana, "The Second Civil War," *Liberator,* November, 1968, pp. 4–9.

It has been observed time and time again by exasperated liberals that the Wallace crowd and the Black Nationalist crowd are in the same bag vis-à-vis their opposition to the federal government apparatus. And the liberals are right as far as they have taken their analysis. From that point, however, all similarities end.

Both the Wallacites and the Black Nationalists would like the federal political apparatus to do something which that apparatus is not about to do at this time. Wallace would like the Feds to exterminate Black liberationists and dissenters. The reality is that they won't, not yet anyway. That is a task which Wallace and his crowd must take upon themselves. But they lack the courage. Therefore, the Wallacites arrive at the conclusion that they must decentralize power from the Feds so that their people can then "legally" exterminate Black people through political rape, economic strangulation and educational castration (States' rights).

On the other hand, the Black Nationalists would like the Feds to immediately eliminate the Wallacites' ability to control Black people by using any means necessary. The Feds aren't about to do that either—now or later. And again, the Nationalists do not seem to possess the courage to do this themselves. Hence, the Nationalist, like the Wallacite, has concluded that he must decentralize federal power into his own hands so that he may "legally" deal with his "enemy."

Thus, once past the shared *immediate* goal of decentralization, similarities between the two groups' objectives break down. The Wallacites' objectives are reactionary and repressive, leading to the continued political, economic and social suppression of a minority group, and the Nationalists' objectives are revolutionary and liberational.

Our own opinion is that the Feds will back whichever group has the courage and organizational ability to move on the other first, and this brings us squarely into the Second Wave theory.

For whatever reasons the Black Nationalists and revolutionary organizers left the South and turned North, we can only logically assume that they were in fact not Nationalists and revolutionaries while down South but became so in the Northern urban centers. What else could we possibly conclude when we see that the Black liberation question in the South is still as far away from resolution now as it was ten years after the institution of the Post-Reconstruction Black Codes. In fact, considering that half of the Black constituency is now scattered across the U.S. in isolated Northern and Western urban colony pockets, resolution might well be further away.

And so it is that we see the participants of the First Wave—

which have evolved from advocates of civil rights, integration and nonviolence into revolutionary nationalists willing (or so they say) to tactically utilize force and violence—regrouping as the political vanguard of the Second Wave. And this time, the ranks of the bloodied political vanguard will be joined by two additional subgroups: at least half of the do-rag guerrillas of the urban ghettos who, while totally dependent economically upon whitey, have nonetheless broken the psychological slave bond they formerly had with whites and are ready to fight (in fact have already) to attain their manhood; and the young bourgeois Nationalist technicians and administrators—i.e., educators, chemists, engineers, architect-planners, physicists, doctors, lawyers, etc.—who are capable of implementing the revolutionary objectives of the seizure of state and county farm boards, legislative houses, state public works departments, welfare departments, hospitals, schools, colleges, industrial complexes, agricultural research facilities and planning commissions.

Our thesis that the question of Black Liberation/American Revolution is still (and more so than ever today) a Southern states question as opposed to the vague theory of "urban Northern cities" is rooted within our own analysis of the fundamental difference between "city" power and "state" (or even more accurately, "region") power.

We believe that the tragedy of our time is the fact that Black Power has, for a host of reasons, come to rest upon the theoretical base of white-theorized, white-projected, white-stimulated and white-implemented south to north demographic and migration patterns of Black people.

How many times, oh Lord, how many times have we heard some Black Nationalist theoretician grandly announce that migration and population projections show that by 1975 Black people will constitute electorate majorities in many urban cities, and that therefore, the city is the political power base which Black people must seek to capture?

The syllogistic reasoning in such thinking is unmistakable. The ridiculous major premise is that there has been (for the past 100 years) a complete lack of coordination, a major communications breakdown and absolutely no analysis at the national level on the part of the corporate-monopoly-capitalist sector and the Department of Housing and Urban Development on the question of the disposition of Black people.

The equally preposterous minor premise is that there has been planning, coordination, strategy, and geo-political objectives worked out at a national level by Black people around their past and future projected migratory patterns.

The rancid conclusion then derived from all of this is that Black people will somehow effect their liberation by continuing to be objects, rather than makers and shapers, of the national forces, pressures and strategies affecting their lives.

Meanwhile, the Nationalist theoretician sits around partying and pontificating in the city waiting for his "power base" to be driven off the land in Southern states.

It should be obvious to even the most naive observer that cities have long since, in substance if not in fact, become politically and economically absorbed into metropolitan regions, regions within which that city is no more than a subordinate part. How many times does one have to observe Carl Stokes begging the surrounding white suburbs to "share fiscal responsibility" (share power) with him so that he might then be able to meet the material and social needs in terms of revenue and services for the masses of "Black controlled" Cleveland? How many times does Richard Hatcher have to tell us that the social and welfare powers necessary for relief of the housing, medical and educational needs of the Black masses of "Black controlled" Gary, Indiana, rest in the intransigent Indiana State House and county machineries (not even to mention U.S. Steel)?

The city-metro region relationship was resolved long before contemporary Black Power broke upon the scene. For every Black person COFO registered in the South, ten were disenfranchised in the urban centers of the North through some variation of the urban planning/metropolitan region game.

A good number of Black people, including some of the most intellectually violent and revolutionary, are in substantial agreement about at least one historical fact: that Black people did possess the substantive semblances of Black Power over their own lives in the U.S. during the Reconstruction period just prior to the Hayes-Tilden betrayal, the acquiescence of the Northern capitalists to the subdued Southern racists on the "States' rights" issue. What may not be agreed upon is that this Black Power, as manifested in our political control over our lives, was not due to white racism having been eliminated. Quite the contrary—Southern whites were just as racist as ever. But they were prevented from effectively exercising that racism, and we not only possessed individual rights such as the franchise but also a numerical superiority. We were, in addition, a very political people, and even though we had been betrayed earlier in terms of a revolutionary solution to the land question by the bourgeois Northern radicals, we were still "getting our thing together."

It therefore seems to us that given the history between that period prior to the Hayes-Tilden affair and today, 1968, Black people lack control in the Southern slaves states not because of white racism per se, but rather because of our inability to numerically, politically and para-militarily overwhelm the white racists in power.

In other words, it is not enough simply to voice the over-worked cliche about Black people having been driven off the land in the South. We must analyze the deeper implications of the fact that the Southern Black Power is now languishing in isolated Northern slum pockets.

The great dream of Black Nationalists and white radical liberals of Black-controlled urban centers in the North is clearly a dangerous myth whose political and economic naivete all but staggers the imagination. The American city of today is the worst political-geographical unit which Black people could desire to capture. Such a victory would be at best pyrrhic, turning into ashes before our very eyes. For by the time Black people will have succeeded in controlling the votes of just ten major cities, that unit will have become totally impotent. What little power is now left in cities is very rapidly being converted into the hands of a new polity: the planner, who fronts for corporate and real estate interests organized on a metro level.

The ultimate irony is that this animal will probably be Black! He will have spent several years at the MIT or Harvard Graduate Planning Schools learning how to convert neo-colonialism and corporate imperialism into the most innocuous nonpolitical and technical terms.

The question is how do we take the reality of our being half in and half out of the South and consciously plan and structure that into a national strategy which would lead not only to our existential survival, but to our acquisition of the substance and not just the illusion of power.

The strategy which we are developing will be anathema to urban-based integrationists and American dreamers, particularly those with dashikis, natural hair-dos and copies of Fanon under their arm. Only the true Nationalist will be able to give us at least the courtesy of nonhysterical consideration.

Che Guevera conceded (from analysis as opposed to intuition) that offensive violence preceding the exhaustion of all available political alternatives was questionable—i.e., the governments of the original slave states still maintain some semblance of constitutional legitimacy even in an international context. It is without question that this quasi-legitimacy is based purely upon numbers. Thus, we will only have a truly colonialist-nationalist situation on our hands similar to South Africa, Rhodesia, etc., at precisely that point when

Black people have engineered a restoration of a Black political majority and are still not able to seize the governmental apparatus of those states.

With this in mind, we propose that all Black communities outside the South be organized to secede from their metropolitan context through land reform as opposed to electoral politics, model cities, etc. The term land means all the real estate, whether developed, undeveloped, streets, alleys, structures, schools or other institutions. The Black community must buy these areas outright at prices which they can afford. The question of whether or not landlords are to be compensated over and above the resources which the community can afford would be a matter strictly between the landlords and the federal government.

Given the implementation of local community secession through land reform (merely a quasi-nationalist issue at this level), no development should take place which is not a part of the local community prepared plan as effected through Black technicians (who would, in some cases, have to be borrowed from a national pool). Even more important, no development should take place that Black people are not themselves able to finance, so that the Black local communities will be primarily responsible for meeting their most immediate needs in terms of food and shelter. The important thing is that the aggregate sum of these local communities would be in control of the two most important items—*the land and the human resources necessary to develop it*—once planning, national strategy and capital reorganization has been effected.

The result, not to be confused with an end in itself, of the Northern urban aspect of the concept is simply this: Black-owned territories adjacent to major urban centers throughout the country will only need enough Black people in and on them for maintenance, development and to provide the protection against governmental intervention (based upon our retaliatory potential against urban central business districts) of the evolving Southern Black regions.

This slave state political recapture coupled with Northern urban territorial acquisition and retention offers the following inherent advantages:
(1) Given the national level of Cultural Black Nationalism among our people, especially the young, and our present possession of administrative, technical, social and cultural-educational skills, there will be no need for the Black states to rely on imported white nationalist personnel for developmental needs as has always been the case in African countries. (One should not be unaware that it is primarily through technical assistance and only incidentally through military power that the U.S. holds its world-wide empire together.) And the

Southern Black schools, with certain structural changes at the internal level coupled with the structural changes at the state government level, will allow us to keep abreast of this need for engineers, architects, planners, etc., to man the massive state public works departments charged with building houses and hospitals.

(2) The concepts of self-determination, Black Power, nonexploitive economic relationships and political power to plan, shape and determine the form of our own lives and give aid and substance internationally to others in a similar plight are simply not attainable in terms of our present haphazard geographical relationship to each other or the rest of the country.

While we are not as poor as we think, in that we take 40 billion dollars annually out of the white economy in wages and immediately dump it right back in, we are certainly not wealthy or in the possession of surplus capital. The fact is that we don't even possess the economic forms necessary for the collective accumulation of the capital we need to meet our social needs. Presently, the logistics in terms of communications/transportation alone preclude the immediate future evolution of such forms, but geography and geographic relationships within the framework of actual power can go a long way towards alleviating some of these obstacles.

(3) Not one single "integrated" Northern Black would be required to give up whatever position, power, influence, wealth, civil right or what have you in his present location. Even the thoroughly "integrated" Black bourgeoisie would be capable, in conjunction with the do-rag brother who chooses to remain North, of creatively utilizing their considerable skills and abilities from their "integrated" position to assist and protect the struggling Black region against overt hostilities and constitutional double-dealing by the rest of the country.

(4) This concept offers the only meaningful alternative synthesis of individual civil rights and ethnic group economic, political, social and cultural needs to the uncounted legions of the "unintegrated"; the teeming Black masses packed like sardines in the rat-infested crumbling Northern slums and who face the imminent threat of being at best re-housed in more vertical filing cabinets or, at worst, dispersed to the suburbs; the young Black Power educators, administrators and technicians who now can only choose between being stooges for outside controlled poverty programs or private industry.

There are those who will dismiss our thesis by simply saying that "the Man would never let us get away with it." Then there are those who criticize it as being non- or anti-revolutionary. We maintain that both these reactions are based upon the assimilationist-integrationist ideology which has led us to the untenable position we are in now.

Unfortunately, the first question Black Power intellectuals and Nationalist organizers do ask themselves is "What will the Man let Black people do?" The Man did not "let" the Cuban, Vietnamese, Algerian, Chinese or Tanzanian Republics take place. Those events were the result of the *will* of the respective peoples. The Man does not "let" anybody do anything that he did not plan for them in his own interest. A far more serious question is whether or not Black people can be mobilized and *organized* to decide nationally, *plan* their objectives and be prepared to die to see them fulfilled.

And as for the criticism around the issue of "revolution," too often we as a people have deluded ourselves with our international and third world rhetoric. So many of us seem to be laboring under the conception that because we are inside the belly of the whale, the whole third world is depending on us for their liberation—on our final act of nihilistic and frenzied collective suicide in a confrontation with the local offices of the U.S. world empire. In the first place, even if we did offer ourselves up on such a noble sacrificial altar, who do we suppose would pick up the pieces and start putting them back together? *The Rockefellers, Mellons and Fords, et al., in conjunction with the Brezhnevs, Soslovs and Kosygins.*

The reality is that Africa and Asia, not to mention Cuba, have not, are not and will not sit around waiting for us to effect their liberation. They're taking care of business. (Or perhaps we're waiting for the situation to occur the other way around—which sounds just like us!)

We talk a beautiful third-world game, but there has not been a single nonwhite colonial revolution of late to which we have been able to offer anything outside of lip service and vicarious identification.

To those of us who would like to fight no matter what, let us remind ourselves that that opportunity will come in due time no matter what *we* plan for ourselves. But first, let us at least *plan.* We could be of far more value to the rest of the third world by taking an action which has truly magnificent potential for the weakening and final breakup of the empire, while letting us survive to build the kind of society worthy of man.

Each of the following selections presents a commentary on contemporary American race relations as well as a vision of the future. The initial selection is a powerful essay by the black writer, LeRoi Jones. To Jones, "these are the Last Days of The American Empire. Understand that Lyndon Johnson is a war criminal of the not so distant future." Jones believes "there is *no chance* that the American white man will change;" he sees "a war of liberation going on now in America . . ."

The National Advisory Commission on Civil Disorders was appointed by President Johnson to determine the causes of the black rebellions of the mid-1960s. The second selection is taken from its final report. It describes the continuing growth of the nation's black ghettos and predicts that if the present ways of dealing with black poverty and powerlessness continue, America will become permanently divided into "two societies, separate and unequal." The Commission rejects the concept that aid should be channeled exclusively into the ghetto. Instead, it argues that programs of aid to the black community must be combined "with programs designed to encourage integration of substantial numbers of Negroes into the society outside the ghetto."

Nathan Glazer presents a different view. He argues in the third selection that "things *are* getting better" for black Americans. (The selections in Part Two provide a contrasting picture of black socioeconomic progress.) Glazer sees black militancy as an unnecessary barrier to black entry into America's pluralist society. He feels "there is a failure to understand, on the part of black militants and their too-complaisant white allies, that there *is* an American society with a tremendous power to incorporate and make part of itself new groups, to their advantage and not to the advantage of the larger society, and that this is not a *white* society."

Another sociologist, Lewis M. Killian, is less optimistic about the likelihood that American society can successfully incorporate black people. In the final selection, Killian discusses the conditions which may eventually lead to a black revolution in the United States. His analysis leads him to the somber conclusion that such an "impossible revolution" will be hopeless, but may be inevitable. In Killian's words, "the United States is engaged in a dangerous race against time."

22
The Last Days of the American Empire
(Including Some Instructions for Black People)

LeRoi Jones

NEWS PICTURES

information

Death throes of the empire. UGLY CRACKERS! Negro policemen with sad-twisted eyes. Strong faces (big Mammas with their arms folded, lonely children whose future lives you wonder about), black faces set into America. There is no America without those whites of eyes against black skin. . . .

ALL KINDS OF VICTIMS. People being burned.

What does America mean to you? Does it mean what these pictures say? Well it do. It sure do. It surely definitely absolutely does. This is world-America. You are in the trance of the White People. You will be escorted to your cell. In fact you will be pre-born into your cell. "And there you can be quaint in our lighter moments. Now, for christ sakes, you have to admit that Mantan Moreland was funny." (This man I was talking to meant "amusing.")

Is there anyone in the realworldAmerica who thinks Slavery Has Been Abolished? Or for that matter, another irrelevance, would there be someone in the statesies so stoned, as would qualify America as being less sick than the invention of Lee Oswald? (Many oil men are inventors, and they have weird hobbies, like their freakish fakeman brothers, bombing churchchildren through the tobacco spit of their brains.)

These pictures should make anybody think. This is what America looks like now. Where is the hope? Why should this terrible place not fall? Who can *dare* defend it? Look at your LEADERS. What do they look like? Do they look like you, any of you??? If they do, then you have something to lose. And chances are you'll lose it.

It is the blackness of the sufferers, their absolute existence as a *different race,* that cheapens any further social description as to what, actually, is going on? Explanation is a selfish act. But The Man says, What's going on? What do you mean people are suffering? I didn't realize. . . . What? That it was real and really happening and real and really happening, but only to the niggers, and those white people too stupid to be rich in this last fat bastion of the white man, doomed now to go down hard, and eaten, smashed at, from its insides by its acquisitions, and the "holiness" of them. Black People will prove to be the most costly of those acquisitions.

The white eyes of those who say (and with them the brutal cuteness of the Negro middle class, who perhaps will never understand what's really going on till they reexamine the value of their social connections, *i.e.,* it is a scientific guess that the white man will not be El Hombre too much longer, *i.e.,* you cannot fail to recognize the difference between Boone, Daniel and Boone, Pat). How can these people live this way? Why don't they do something? No one ought to deny the validity of that question. Finally our enemies are right. Why don't they do something?

Maybe what a few of the white eyes saw, showing up in Bedford Stuyvesant, or St. Francesville, Louisiana—to catch a part of time-now, to be exposed to a reality, a basic truth of the world— filthy makeshift playgrounds, the children's eyes deep in their black skin, woodplank streets in parts of black Brooklyn, and summer, everybody outside, children playing on their knees, men sitting or walking slowly, or staring, or laid out in the street dying in sneakers —these are truths the television will not even use as news, except when the people out on those streets start moving, like they did "last summer," and being thrashed for at least assuming the dignity of an organism that will react when it is struck. This is the rest of the world. This is what the good white man cannot connect himself with; cannot or will not, it makes no real difference, the results are the same. Most white men I meet say they are not responsible. Perhaps it is best to be left there. To take them at their word, that I'm hip, you are not responsible to the world. But you will be held responsible, anyway, since you own it, you think.

But then, who demands these whippings and bombings? Is J. Edgar Hoover an intelligent man? Will Lyndon B. Johnson submit to an aptitude test? Why isn't automation a help to man? Who is H. L. Hunt? Is there any reason why all the world should be working and dying and growing hopeless with rage, just to feed fat white faces. What is this bullshit?

Black people, if you can steal this expensive book, at your liberal employer's, for instance, though he may even be "a friend of your people"—just remember the only reason you are there in the first place is *for the money, to stay alive, to survive*—steal this book, it will make you very very hot, but even so you will learn that your brothers and sisters are strong, strong, under all the horrors of The White Hell. And in seeing the horrors, and by becoming angry, but even beyond that anger realizing what strength you have —YOU BLACK PEOPLE ARE STRONG, remember that—then you will realize that it is now not even the time to be angry, I mean so angry that you will not remember that you are strong, much stronger than the white eyes. Then you will not need to be angry any longer, you will have gotten to that point, where you will be absolutely rational. Our singing is beautiful, but we can sing while we move. MOVE!

To be rational now in this insane asylum, where we are held prisoner by the inmates. They want us to be their keepers. Do you Negroes like being keepers for these sadists? But to be rational. Rational men would do something to stop the mad, before they destroy not only the asylum, but the rest of the world. There is no reason why we should allow the white man to destroy the world, just because he will not share it, will not share it with the *majority.* The nerve, the stupid arrogance, the ignorance, AND FEAR, in those cracker eyes, those firemen, state patrolmen, the dog holders, all that fear is in the bones of this society. Those mad white policemen are the soul of this society. And their technology has made them strong. We have accepted that technology, as fact, as useful to our dreams, etc., but its owners are mad, because they do not value reality, and therefore they are not real. Hollow Men, Paper Tigers, Closet Queens of the Universe.

Look at those weak fag faces on those patrolmen arresting that beautiful chick, and finally there is something in her face which is stronger than anything in white eyes' life. Because she has had to live in a world of extremes, which is the widening of the consciousness. And this is the "hip" syndrome, simple awareness— America will make you aware if you are black. So that, for instance, in any argument with a liberal white man, finally the black man must grow speechless with rage, because there is always a point beyond which no black-white argument can be pushed with reason. We know what has happened to us, to our mothers and fathers. What more can be said? The black man was brought to the West in chains, he is still in chains. He is still a captive, Negroes, a captive people. What can you say? Look at any pictures of America. They must show the final impasse between White America and Black America. Pictures like these should be used when the black man runs out of words. When the exasperation of explaining his life to justify his desires makes him silent with rage, in the face of *any* white man.

There is an absolute gulf that separates white from black. Slave/SlaveMaster are two different worlds. Segregation reinforces itself, spawns, continues, *separate* cultures. So the Beatles can make millions of dollars putting on a sophisticated coon show, which drives weak white girls into gism fits—all that energy and force, but even so transmuted and disguised. But it is still the Chuck Berrys, the Muddy Waters, etc., who first harnessed that energy. The Ornette Colemans. No matter the use such changed and weakened force might be put to in Winosha, Wisconsin, or by Lynda-Bird's fake Watusi, the real power remains where it naturally falls.

The force of the Negro's life in America has always been very evident in America, no matter the lengths to which white Americans have tried to hide and obfuscate it. But I mean you cannot, for instance, blame any white man for liking Andre Previn more than Cecil Taylor; it is his life that is reflected by his choices (is, in fact, those choices). Most white men in America are closer to Andre Previn than CT or Duke Ellington either, for that matter. White America reflects its energies by its choices. You think that the heroimage in American flicks is homosexual merely by *chance*?

Reality is only useful to people who have some use for it. Otherwise they get something else. But everybody's got to pay some kind of dues, one way or another. It won't even matter, finally, if the person happens to be "innocent"; there is no such thing. If you are alive, now, you are involved with now, even if only by default. You know what "Germans" still means. First of all, now, it means liar. No matter what the man can tell you, *e.g.,* "I was head of the anti-Nazi forces, etc., etc.," the word "German" is sufficient to give any story the shakes. What? you will say. What . . . are you talking about . . . aren't you a German? And that's the end of that. In a few years, "American" will have that connotation, for the rest of the world. (In most of the world it has that connotation already.) And, even more horrible, it will not even matter to the rest of the world that the Negro was "the victim," etc. People will simply ask, Why? And, given the plausibility of supposing that most men would rather not be victims, the fact will remain that any "answer" to that Why? will have to be shaky. The only answer could be, I was in the trance of the whitepeople. But that is a cop out, I'm afraid. Your questioner will not even bother to point out certain obvious alternatives. You will be listed simply as "Coward."

But there are many Negroes now, young and otherwise, who have no use for the role (of victim) the white man has cast him in. Again, look at the black faces. The young boys marching across the street with their signs, or the young fox wet and screaming her defiance, her hatred, but most of all her *will* to live, and to fight back. Look at the young Northern middle-class black lady sitting demurely on the pavement surrounded by cops. Look at her face and posture. You cannot lie to this woman. She knows you're lying. She reads *The Times.* She knows the *New York Times* lies. The poor black man will not even have had to read it to know it lies. "It's whitey's paper, ain't it? What you expect?" Right again. (I looked at a photograph of a black cop arresting a black woman.) Dig for a few seconds, the big spook cop's mouth. He's got his lips pinched together, staring at the lady. BLACK NEW YORK COP SGT. NUMBER 67, YOU KNOW YOU'RE WRONG! YOU ARE FIGHTING YOUR OWN PEOPLE!

Another sense gotten from any true picture of this society is the isolation of the black man in America. He is a different race from the white man. The poor white has been brainwashed into wanting to kill the black man, so that black man won't get his job or his little girl's drawers. All the immigrants to this country, the Italians, the Irish, the Jews, etc., where are they in this struggle? All the white people in America who have grounds for dissent, and will not dissent. They have had to pay a price for their shaky seat in this enterprise. The dues I spoke of, which even they have had to pay, is to be mistreated, used, duped, and still put out on the street to handle America's light work. Where are the Italian Anarchists? The Sacco-Vanzetti frame put them on the skids, and the Maffia takes up the wild strong ones whose lifeneeds still put them outside straightup WASP-AMERICA. The Jewish Radicals, Socialists, Communists, etc., of the 30's, what happened to them? Have they all disappeared into those sullen suburbs hoping Norman Podhoretz or Leslie Fiedler will say something real? The price the immigrants paid to get into America was that they had to become Americans. The black man *cannot* become an American (unless we get a different set of *rules*) because he is black. And even the hopeless CORE representative I met who claimed black men were as evil as white men can never become a white man. Though he might desire it more than anything in the universe. He cannot change the one thing about him that is most important in this place. He must remain, even deluded, a certain kind of black man. The black man's dissent cannot be gotten rid of. It just builds. And builds.

But the white man splits the black man into cadres, "classes," when there is none except blackness—which the white man is the first to realize. Against the filth of America (and with it, the white West—the British, the French, the Germans, the Belgians, the Portuguese, the Dutch, etc., and their ugly little roles in Asia, Africa, Latin America) the black man has to be absolutely *together* in order to survive. But too often, certainly most times in the past, the white man has been able to win out, maintain his stranglehold on us, merely because most of us were so busy looking out for ourselves, which is the "ME ONLY" syndrome, that we were willing to let the worst things in the world happen to our brothers. With black people all over the world dying the most horrible kinds of death imaginable some fools would still be walking around with their behinds in the air saying, "But I'm Cool." Well the word is No You're Not, not as long as one of your brothers and sisters is being messed over by "the man."

Get it together! We must lock arms, take each other's hand, and never stop working until the stone is rolled over the deep stinking hole even some of our "civil rights leaders" speak of as if it were paradise.

Since this book is so expensive, it will fall into the hands of more MC Negroes than people out on the block. (MC meaning middle class or master of ceremonies, and in America the ceremony is blood violence and hatred.)

MC Negroes, I know you can still be made angry too. Perhaps something in the faces of white terrorists will frighten you out from under your shaky cover stories; cover stories like "middle class" or "college trained" or "qualified Negro" or any other fake entrances into this crumbling Rome, which somehow cut off your testicles, usually with the hard cold edge of a dollar bill. ANYBODY CAN PRINT MONEY! BUT NOT EVERYBODY CAN LIVE IN THE WORLD WITH THE PEACEFUL STRENGTH OF THE TRULY VIRTUOUS MAN. (White Americans cannot.)

If you have made some "progress," or somehow got your hands on a good taste of white eyes' loot, keep it moving among your people; also your knowledge. We are in this *together,* let us help each other and begin rolling that huge black stone. *Most* of the world is with us.

I cannot repeat it too many times, nor can any of you black people repeat it too many times to one another. DO NOT ALLOW YOURSELF TO BE SEPARATED from your brothers and sisters, or your culture. This is what makes us think we are weak. But we are not weak. Remember the stories of your parents and grandparents. We have survived over three hundred years of the worst treatment possible, and still come up strong. All Charles has to show for those years is his loot, but the world changes each second, and Charles's hands grow more and more spastic, his lies more and more obvious. For instance, where would the US Olympic Team be without the black man??? This analogy can be extended into any meaningful level of American life. The black man should dig, for instance, that he is one of the chief reasons this society, these Mad American White People (. . . MAWPS . . .) can continue to exercise their will over the rest of the world. We black people, by our labor, are supporting these murderers. It is a paradox, but one no black man should fail to recognize. Even the isolated Negro who has gained "acceptance" into this Gomorrah or the hard-working black man in a "defense" plant or steel mill, must realize the vicious uses his entrance into the mainstream will be put to. All you Negroes making "good livings" now, do you know what the fruits of your labor are being used for? Usually your labors contribute heavily to the murders of nonwhite peoples all over the globe.

Where have all these "police actions" in which the U.S. has taken the major part since the Second World War been happening? And police action is a good phrase because that's what white eye is now—anywhere—a policeman working feverishly to keep the nonwhite peoples down, in colonial or semi-slave positions whether they are American Negroes, Africans, Asians, or Latin Americans. It's all the same. The same mad white people you see in any *Life Magazine* home are our real "ambassadors" all over the world; spiritual cops and cretins. (Do you think that the television series "Burke's Law," where the hero is a white millionaire who is also chief of police, is *accidental*? This is the way these folks think, and what they legitimately aspire to. Ditto, in the case of James Bond, the suave, unbeatable fascist. All these things merely prepare the American's psyche for his role in world domination.)

What I am saying is that there is *no chance* that the American white man will change. Why should he? Isn't this the richest nation in the world? The gross national product rose to $624 billion this year, the growth figure over last year's $584 billion is about $45 billion. This money is not being made because the white eye is ready to "understand" the needs of the world, but because he has been even more successful recently in suppressing those needs. Can there be even one American so out of it as not to realize that this money, this luxury, exists only at the expense of the rest of the world's peoples? Can there be a Negro so out of it as not to understand that the worst racists in South Africa are brothers to the men he sees in our newspapers daily being celebrated for their "humanity"? It is sickening, for instance, to see in our free newspapers accounts every day of how the white man is trying to save the world. This is true. He is trying to save the world—as his personal victory garden and commode. As for instance, in the Congo, where thousands of black people are slaughtered to make the world safe for the white man. The only difference between the Congo and, say, Philadelphia, Mississippi, is the method the white man employs to suppress and murder; essentially, it is the same scene, the same people dying for the same reasons. And of course, they are the same murderers who kill our people all over the globe.

But it sickens me to know that there are supposedly intelligent black people walking around who would actually believe that the Belgians and Americans flew those paratroopers into the Congo for humanitarian reasons. My God! You mean Charles would send planeloads of paratroopers (plus those divisions of white mercenaries) into the Congo to save . . . how many? twenty-one white hostages? and yet still be unable to send even one Vietnamese helicopter to Mississippi to find out who assassinated Medgar Evers, or maybe one Special Forces (anti-liberation "guerrillas") to Birmingham, so maybe just one shred of information might be turned up concerning the identities of the dynamite murderers of those four little church children.

Does it makes sense to any of you that Uncle Sap will spend millions to "put West Germany back on its feet," and yet have a place such as Harlem in the world's showplace, which they will not spend one honest nickel to alter or intelligently repair. And there are Harlems in every American city where there are great numbers of Negroes. But even more diabolical is this fact, that even the most liberal white man in America does not want to see the existing system really *changed*. What this liberal white man wants is for the black man somehow to be "elevated" Martin Luther King style so that he might be able to enter this society with some kind of general prosperity and join the white man in a truly democratic defense of this cancer, which would make the black man equally culpable for the evil done to the rest of the world. The liberal white man wants the black man to learn to love this America as much as he does, so that the black man will want to murder the world's peoples, his own brothers and sisters Moise Tshombe style. And let no black man forget all the black traitors all over the world, most of whom, like Tshombe or JaJa Wachuku of Nigeria, have been so brainwashed that they might even think what they are doing (*i.e.,* helping in the murder of thousands of black people) is right. One man, an American Negro, George Schuyler, has even come on the side of a straightup oppressor, Portugal, defending its actions in Angola where it murdered thousands of black Africans. Black people, do not forget Negroes like this, remember them and every detail of their treason. It will help us to be more scientific.

But these are the Last Days Of The American Empire. Understand that Lyndon Johnson is a war criminal of the not so distant future. Understand that the power structure that controls this country and the world has grown desperate . . . in the face of so much prosperity, but prosperity that is coupled with more unrest than ever before. There are wars of national liberation going on all over the world. The Second World War made emphatic America's newly won security as absolute world ruler, but it also shook up most of the other colonial empires of the world. The need to have that war seen as "A War Against Fascism" contributed dramatically to the organization of many of the world's colonial peoples into armed nationalistic liberation fronts who saw as their task, even after the war against fascism, the eradication of any form of colonialism or imperialism. British, French, and Dutch colonialism suffered almost irreparable losses, but these sorry people are still trying, by one ruse or another, to regain control of their subject peoples. But where before there were only cries of outrage, now these European white eyes are met with bullets and bombs.

There is a war of liberation going on now in America, although the black American has still not gotten hip enough to organize a National Liberation Front that would include all groups and aspirations, and sweep, by the increase of its power, right over this failing power structure, and push these sadists and perverts into the sea. That is the unity that is needed. When will we be strong enough and wise enough to commit ourselves to this kind of unity?

In one sense, when I speak of unity, I mean that seeing one young man being followed menacingly down a road by half the Crackers in Georgia, makes me wonder what it was, specifically, that moved him to do this. I want to know what was he thinking, sprawled in the dust, holding his head, knees pulled up against his chest? I want to know did this young black man really feel that by letting some subhuman superfools abuse and beat him, he was somehow accomplishing something. That is, I cannot yet understand what kind of mind shift I would have to undergo, for instance, so that I would be convinced, as these rednecks were working me over, that I was doing something to break Charlie's back. The unity I desire would be most apparent when most Black People realized that the murderous philosophies of the Western white man take many curious forms. And that one of the most bizarre methods the man has yet to utilize against black people is to instruct large masses of black people that they are to control their tempers, turn the other cheek, etc., in the presence of, but even more so under the feet and will of, the most brutal killers the world has yet produced.

The kind of unity I would want to see among black Americans would at least produce a huge WHY? when some gentle oppressor talked convincingly about pacifism and nonviolence. In the white West nonviolence means simply doing nothing to change this pitiful society, just do as you have been doing, *e.g.*, suffer, and by some beautiful future-type miracle the minds of the masses of white men will be changed, and they will finally come around to understanding that the majority of peoples in the world deserve to live in that world, no longer plagued by the white man's disgusting habits. But why, WHY, must anyone wait until these cretins . . . change . . . ha ha . . . their famous minds, before people are permitted to live with the simple dignity any man ought to know? Why indeed? The answer is that these askers for nonviolence, *i.e.*, virtuous stagnation, are usually people who would suffer, or at least think they would, if this society were changed with the suddenness of the next second. Even the black man who preaches nonviolence is essentially functioning under the trance of the white people. There are black men who love the white man so dearly, who love, I must suppose, the nice warm feeling of shoe sole on their woolly heads, that they would do nothing to see that the white man relinquishes his stranglehold in the world. But then, there are other black people in America and the rest of the world who will not rest until that stranglehold is broken. So poised against the image of the young man hugging his knees in the dust, there are also images of young men and old men silhouetted on their porches with their rifles, watchful all through long black Southern nights, men who have no desire to be masters or slaves, but who cannot live in the world as it is without at least attempting to defend what little of the world they know is theirs. I look at an old man sitting next to his gun, or a young man holding his like in a photo to be sent back to a girlfriend, and I wonder about the young man holding his head in the dust. I wonder also about Robert Williams, the ex-NAACP leader from Monroe, North Carolina, who was framed on a kidnapping charge by local officials with the help of the Federal Government simply because he had "advocated" that black men realize that they were living among savages and barbarians and that they must protect themselves and their families, because the Government was made up of these same savages and barbarians. Mr. Williams is in exile in Cuba now for that reason; that he made a few rational statements about the nature of the white American, and what possibly ought to be done when faced with one, and such reasoning is dangerous to the white man, and the white man will have none of it.

The kind of unity I would like to see among black Americans is a unity that would permit most of them to understand that the murder of Patrice Lumumba in the Congo and the murder of Medgar Evers were conducted by the same people. I want them also to realize that a man like Robert Williams faced the same fate, for the same reasons. I want them to realize that any attempt the black man makes to be seen or heard, clearly, honestly, from where he has been made to live during the three-hundred-odd year residency in the West, is always met with repression and violence. Or else such attempts will be subverted by the wills of the holiest of white men, the liberals, who do not want to be our bosses, but our guides. But listen, black men, these liberals are usually agents. That is, even though what these men say might seem to come freely out of an untroubled heart, chances are these words, *e.g.,* "moderation," pacifism, nonviolence, gradualism, etc., etc., seek merely to dim your passion and turn your most rational needs and desires into evil fantasies white (and black) schoolchildren condemn when they are learning to count. Ask the next white liberal you meet, would he be willing to let you, you black man, be his, this white man's, "spiritual guide." And also when the next white man comes up to you and describes the sparkling democratic utopias of the future, remember that he is asking you to pull your knees up against your chest, head hidden, and dream in the dust of never-never land. And when the next missionary comes on to you about nonviolence use his own bible as your lever, pointing out that the God of the Jews was not particularly interested in turning cheeks, *viz.,* all those drowned Egyptians.

But opposed to that image of dreaming in the dust, there is the image of one brother with the sign reading NOW. Look at his face—there's nothing any kind of missionary type could tell this man. He looks like he's beyond all the loads of buckrogers happiness bullshit, and is demanding simple truth. And the sign says NOW, which is clear enough. In news photos all over America there are many other signs of the times: LOVE THY NEIGHBOR (a sign maybe which ought to sit in huge letters in the White House and Pentagon and CIA); WHO NEEDS NIGGERS (from the self-confessed purest of whities); WHERE IS DEMOCRACY (a woman with a very good question): FREEDOM (the most ambiguous term known to man, if Barry Goldwater, the "half-Jewish" Uebermensch, can use it, to rally his 25,000,000, and Martin Luther King can use it, presumably with a different sense intended. But to BG freedom means, like they say, free enterprise, which means OPEN YOUR POCKETS 80 per cent of the world, big white meatface wants to get his rocks off!! That is the freedom to murder, rob, and lie to any people who stand in the way of your own holy luxury.) There is also a sign, on an old beatup Southern store that reads NEGRO KEEP OUT. There are signs like this all over America. And where there are no written signs, brains have been marked, so that the same sentiment leaps out of people's eyes. And finally, the paradox is that these people are right: NEGRO STAY OUT! Because now, when Charles is up tight all over the world, and will of course ask the black lackeys to help him out, it is high time the black man began to make use of the Tonto-syndrome, *i.e.,* leave The Lone Ranger to his own devices, and his own kind of death.

There are pictures of very old black men and women in the news too. Some of the faces look as if they were too old to be lied to. And there is an essential unity existing among these old faces that can no longer be put on by trinkets and fake wampum, and the face of the young man with the NOW sign, just above his eyes. Add to these images, the images of the black men standing on their porches with their rifles looking into a night made unfriendly by the hideousness of the white man's ego, and you will probably get a sense of the powerful emotions and will for release that is crackling in the psyches of the majority of black men today. But there are crucial American social paradoxes that the black man must also understand if he is really to understand the nature of his enemy. For instance, Negroes have been killed and beaten in Mississippi, Alabama, etc., for even attempting to register to vote. In the North, Negroes have long mustered a heavy voting bloc, and because of this have some degree of token political power. But the ugly paradox is to be seen everywhere in the North, the promised land. This token political power can do nothing to change the basic structure of the society. This society, for as long as it has functioned, was never meant to be equitable as far as black men were concerned. It was made for the white man, and the black man was brought here only to be *used,* to promote the luxury of the white man. That was the only reason. It still is the only reason the black man is alive in the West today, that continued exploitative use. But one day, and very soon, the white man might just look up, hip again, and see that the black man has outlived his usefulness. Then the murders will break out in earnest.

So it is a very grim spectacle to see all these Negroes beaten and brutalized for trying to vote, and some ofays must fall on the floor laughing every time they think of it. Because finally in those Southern states, or in the rest of America for that matter, who could you vote for, Negro? I mean, do you really think that by your getting a chance to vote on these criminals who run for political office in America, that somehow you'll be getting closer to peace and social justice? You cannot really think that! I cannot believe that you can still believe that, after so many years of lies and abuse. The choice on almost any level you care to name is roughly like that contest between Lyndon Johnson and Barry Goldwater, in the South most times even worse—and if there's any black man anywhere in the world who thinks that either one of those chumps is working for him, he is laboring under a hideous delusion, or else maybe he is in the Tshombe-bag, which will soon be converted into a shroud.

The main difference right now between the Northern and Southern Negro is that in the South the fight is still for equal rights, civil rights, etc., whereas in the North, the black man already has seen the bad faith of these terms, and has realized now for a long time that these rights we are asked to move toward, are less than abstract rhetoric. Last summer the Northern urban industrial towns popped like mean firecrackers hooked up from ghetto to ghetto. Perhaps next summer these firecrackers will grow even larger— and it was largely in the North, where presumably all these civil rights etc., have been attained, where these most recent demonstrations against white law have taken place. In the South the madness of the oppressors and their stupid henchmen, the poor whites, is completely out in the open, the lines already clearly drawn. In the North, because of the lies and chicanery of the Northern industrialist's social form the lines may seem less clearly drawn, the oppressor's hand more heavily veiled, but because of this veil, an even heavier sense of frustration incites the black man to anger. In the South, you know the landscape is for real, in the North they try to tell you it's not. It is the added weight of being lied to, on top of every other indignity, that makes it all so hard to take. And then some white man hearing about oppressed Negroes on television will ask you for a little rational conversation on the subject. This will be a man (this hypothetical questioner) who probably does not know that policemen are menacing subhumans, whose sociocultural conditioning—because they are usually grandsons of immigrants, *i.e.,* poor whites—has usually prepared them to hate niggers even before they get the official instructions (like James Bond) that they are "licensed to kill." The American policeman is the foulest social category in the world today, whether domestic, *e.g.,* "New York's Finest," or international (Humanitarians dropping out of the clouds, etc.).

You may see a barefoot South Carolina Negro, just grinning

quietly—you wonder what's in behind those tired eyes—or you see another man just walking along, outwardly desolate, hands jammed deep in his pockets, and again you wonder, knowing and not knowing. Or you see a scene in Harlem or Bedford Stuyvesant, and know, that even in the North, the ghettos (compounds) duplicate the South, and only add new frustrations not unlike the old. Sitting on garbage cans, thinking, or sleeping on benches, dreaming, or even pushing those "Jewish airplanes" in the garment center, grown men doing what they call a boy's job, but then still get sharp on weekends and go out hunting foxes. Blind anger sometimes in Georgia or the Bronx; staring at its image will set you off again, thinking of all these strong sweet people, their joy, even of those old hip black moles of men whose only conspicuous association with this century is a button that says, "I am registered, are you?"

What we would see in any realistic photo essay of America would be the image, pinpoints of light which show us the running sore called America. There is hope though, hope in some faces. Even the very young (the boys marching with their signs, the screaming little girls) know what it's all about. A sign says "Everybody wants Freedom." But what is the hope? What can it be? (America will not change because a few blacks and whites can kiss each other, or because Michael Schwerner or Andrew Goodman get themselves murdered. Most of the white kids who go into the South are only trying to save America or save themselves in America; there is more than enough guilt to go round. But there are people all over the world who don't want to see it saved.) Like I was asking, what is the hope? I say if your hope is for the survival of this society, this filthy order, no good. You lose. The hope is that young blacks will remember all of their lives what they are seeing, what they are witness to just by being alive and black in America, and that eventually they will use this knowledge scientifically, and erupt like Mt. Vesuvius to crush in hot lava these willful maniacs who call themselves white Americans.

23
The Future of the Cities

**National Advisory Commission
on Civil Disorders**

INTRODUCTION

We believe action of the kind outlined in preceding pages [of the U.S. Riot Commission Report] can contribute substantially to control of disorders in the near future. But there should be no mistake about the long run. The underlying forces continue to gain momentum.

The most basic of these is the accelerating segregation of low-income, disadvantaged Negroes within the ghettos of the largest American cities.

By 1985, the 12.1 million Negroes segregated within central cities today will have grown to approximately 20.3 million—an increase of 68 percent.

Prospects for domestic peace and for the quality of American life are linked directly to the future of these cities.

Two critical questions must be confronted: Where do present trends now lead? What choices are open to us?

I. THE KEY TRENDS

Negro Population Growth[1]

The size of the Negro population in central cities is closely related to total national Negro population growth. In the past 16

Reprinted from *Report of the National Advisory Commission on Civil Disorders,* Washington, D.C., 1968, pp. 215–227.

[1] Tables and explanations of the projections on which they are based appear at the end of the chapter.

years, about 98 percent of this growth has occurred within metropolitan areas, and 86 percent in the central cities of those areas.

A conservative projection of national Negro population growth indicates continued rapid increases. For the period 1966 to 1985, it will rise to a total of 30.7 million, gaining an average of 484,000 a year, or 7.6 percent more than the increase in each year from 1960 to 1966.

Central Cities: Further Negro population growth in central cities depends upon two key factors: in-migration from outside metropolitan areas, and patterns of Negro settlement within metropolitan areas.

From 1960 to 1966, the Negro population of all central cities rose 2.4 million, 88.9 percent of total national Negro population growth. We estimate that natural growth accounted for 1.4 million, or 58 percent of this increase, and in-migration accounted for 1 million, or 42 percent.

As of 1966, the Negro population in all central cities totaled 12.1 million. By 1985, we have estimated that it will rise 68 percent to 20.3 million. We believe that natural growth will account for 5.2 million of this increase and in-migration for 3.0 million.

Without significant Negro out-migration, then, the combined Negro populations of central cities will continue to grow by an average of 274,000 a year through 1985, even if no further in-migration occurs.

Growth projected on the basis of natural increase and in-migration would raise the proportion of Negroes to whites in central cities by 1985 from the present 20.7 percent to between an estimated 31 and 34.7 percent.

Largest Central Cities: These, however, are national figures. Much faster increases will occur in the largest central cities where Negro growth has been concentrated in the past two decades. Washington, D.C., Gary, and Newark are already over half Negro. A continuation of recent trends would cause the following 10 major cities to become over 50 percent Negro by the indicated dates:

New Orleans	1971	St. Louis	1978
Richmond	1971	Detroit	1979
Baltimore	1972	Philadelphia	1981
Jacksonville	1972	Oakland	1983
Cleveland	1975	Chicago	1984

These cities, plus Washington, D.C. (now over 66 percent Negro), and Newark, contained 12.6 million people in 1960, or 22 percent of the total population of all 224 American central cities. All 13 cities undoubtedly will have Negro majorities by 1985, and the suburbs ringing them will remain largely all white, unless there are major changes in Negro fertility rates,[2] in-migration, settlement patterns or public policy.

Experience indicates that Negro school enrollment in these and other cities will exceed 50 percent long before the total population reaches that mark. In fact, Negro students already comprise more than a majority in the public elementary schools of 12 of the 13 cities mentioned above. This occurs because the Negro population in central cities is much younger and because a much higher proportion of white children attend private schools. For example, St. Louis' population was about 36 percent Negro in 1965; its public elementary school enrollment was 63 percent Negro. If present trends continue, many cities in addition to those listed above will have Negro school majorities by 1985, probably including:

Dallas	Louisville
Pittsburgh	Indianapolis
Buffalo	Kansas City, Mo.
Cincinnati	Hartford
Harrisburg	New Haven

Thus, continued concentration of future Negro population growth in large central cities will produce significant changes in those cities over the next 20 years. Unless there are sharp changes in the factors influencing Negro settlement patterns within metropolitan areas, there is little doubt that the trend toward Negro majorities will continue. Even a complete cessation of net Negro in-migration to central cities would merely postpone this result for a few years.

Growth of the Young Negro Population

We estimate that the nation's white population will grow 16.6 million, or 9.6 percent, from 1966 to 1975, and the Negro population 3.8 million, or 17.7 percent, in the same period. The Negro age group from 15 to 24 years of age, however, will grow much faster than either the Negro population as a whole, or the white population in the same age group.

From 1966 to 1975, the number of Negroes in this age group will rise 1.6 million, or 40.1 percent. The white population aged 15 to 24 will rise 6.6 million, or 23.5 percent.

This rapid increase in the young Negro population has im-

[2] The fertility rate is the number of live births each year per 1,000 women aged 15 to 44.

portant implications for the country. This group has the highest unemployment rate in the nation, commits a relatively high proportion of all crimes, and plays the most significant role in civil disorders. By the same token, it is a great reservoir of underused human resources which are vital to the nation.

The Location of New Jobs

Most new employment opportunities do not occur in central cities, near all-Negro neighborhoods. They are being created in suburbs and outlying areas—and this trend is likely to continue indefinitely. New office buildings have risen in the downtowns of large cities, often near all-Negro areas. But the out-flow of manufacturing and retailing facilities normally offsets this addition significantly—and in many cases has caused a net loss of jobs in central cities while the new white collar jobs are often not available to ghetto residents.

Providing employment for the swelling Negro ghetto population will require society to link these potential workers more closely with job locations. This can be done in three ways: by developing incentives to industry to create new employment centers near Negro residential areas; by opening suburban residential areas to Negroes and encouraging them to move closer to industrial centers; or by creating better transportation between ghetto neighborhoods and new job locations.

All three involve large public outlays.

The first method—creating new industries in or near the ghetto—is not likely to occur without government subsidies on a scale which convinces private firms that it will pay them to face the problems involved.

The second method—opening up suburban areas to Negro occupancy—obviously requires effective fair housing laws. It will also require an extensive program of federally-aided, low-cost housing in many suburban areas.

The third approach—improved transportation linking ghettos and suburbs—has received little attention from city planners and municipal officials. A few demonstration projects show promise, but carrying them out on a large scale will be very costly.

Although a high proportion of new jobs will be located in suburbs, there are still millions of jobs in central cities. Turnover in those jobs alone can open up a great many potential positions for Negro central city residents—if employers cease racial discrimination in their hiring and promotion practices.

Nevertheless, as the total number of Negro central city job-seekers continues to rise, the need to link them with emerging new employment in the suburbs will become increasingly urgent.

The Increasing Cost of Municipal Services

Local governments have had to bear a particularly heavy financial burden in the two decades since the end of World War II. All United States cities are highly dependent upon property taxes that are relatively unresponsive to changes in income. Consequently, growing municipalities have been hard-pressed for adequate revenues to meet rising demands for services generated by population increase. On the other hand, stable or declining cities have not only been faced with steady cost increases but also with a slow-growing, or even declining, tax base.

As a result of the population shifts of the post-war period, concentrating the middle class in residential suburbs while leaving the poor in the central cities, the increasing burden of municipal taxes frequently falls upon that part of the urban population least able to pay them.

Increasing concentrations of urban growth have called forth greater expenditures for every kind of public service: education, health, police protection, fire protection, parks, sanitation, etc. These expenditures have strikingly outpaced tax revenues.

The story is summed up below:

Local Government Revenues, Expenditures and Debt (Billions of dollars)			
	1950	1966	Increase
Revenues	11.7	41.5	+29.8
Expenditures	17.0	60.7	+43.7
Debt outstanding	18.8	77.5	+58.7

Despite the growth of federal assistance to urban areas under various grant-in-aid programs, the fiscal plight of many cities is likely to grow even more serious in the future. Local expenditures inevitably will continue to rise steeply as a result of several factors, including the difficulty of increasing productivity in the predominantly service activities of local governments, and the rapid technologically-induced increases in productivity in other economic sectors.

Traditionally, individual productivity has risen faster in the manufacturing, mining, construction, and agricultural sectors than in those involving personal services.

However, all sectors compete with each other for talent and personnel. Wages and salaries in the service-dominated sectors generally must keep up, therefore, with those in the capital-dominated sectors. Since productivity in manufacturing has risen about 2.5 percent per year compounded over many decades, and even faster in agriculture, the basis for setting costs in the service-dominated sectors has gone up, too.

In the postwar period, costs of the same units of output have increased very rapidly in certain key activities of local government. For example, education is the single biggest form of expenditure by local governments (including school districts), accounting for about 40 percent of their outlays. From 1947 to 1967, costs per pupil-day in United States public schools rose at a rate of 6.7 percent per year compounded—only slightly less than doubling every ten years.[3] This major cost item is likely to keep on rising rapidly in the future, along with other government services like police, fire, and welfare activities.

Some increases in productivity may occur in these fields, and some economies may be achieved through use of assistants such as police and teachers' aides. Nevertheless, the need to keep pace with private sector wage scales will force local government costs to rise sharply.

This and other future cost increases are important to future relations between central cities and suburbs. Rising costs will inevitably force central cities to demand more and more assistance from the federal government. But the federal government can obtain such funds through the income tax only from other parts of the economy. Suburban governments are, meanwhile, experiencing the same cost increases along with the rising resentment of their constituents.

II. CHOICES FOR THE FUTURE

The complexity of American society offers many choices for the future of relations between central cities and suburbs and patterns of white and Negro settlement in metropolitan areas. For practical purposes, however, we see two fundamental questions:
• Should future Negro population growth be concentrated in central cities, as in the past 20 years, thereby forcing Negro and white populations to become even more residentially segregated?

[3] It is true that the average pupil-teacher ratio declined from 28 to about 25, and other improvements in teaching quality may have occurred. But they cannot account for anything approaching this rapid increase in costs.

• Should society provide greatly increased special assistance to Negroes and other relatively disadvantaged population groups?

For purposes of analysis, the Commission has defined three basic choices for the future embodying specific answers to these questions:

The Present Policies Choice

Under this course, the nation would maintain approximately the share of resources now being allocated to programs of assistance for the poor, unemployed and disadvantaged. These programs are likely to grow, given continuing economic growth and rising federal revenues, but they will not grow fast enough to stop, let alone reverse, the already deteriorating quality of life in central-city ghettos.

This choice carries the highest ultimate price, as we will point out.

The Enrichment Choice

Under this course, the nation would seek to offset the effects of continued Negro segregation and deprivation in large city ghettos. The Enrichment Choice would aim at creating dramatic improvements in the quality of life in disadvantaged central-city neighborhoods—both white and Negro. It would require marked increases in federal spending for education, housing, employment, job training, and social services.

The Enrichment Choice would seek to lift poor Negroes and whites above poverty status and thereby give them the capacity to enter the mainstream of American life. But it would not, at least for many years, appreciably affect either the increasing concentration of Negroes in the ghetto or racial segregation in residential areas outside the ghetto.

The Integration Choice

This choice would be aimed at reversing the movement of the country toward two societies, separate and unequal.

The Integration Choice—like the Enrichment Choice—would call for large-scale improvement in the quality of ghetto life. But it would also involve both creating strong incentives for Negro movement out of central-city ghettos and enlarging freedom of choice concerning housing, employment, and schools.

The result would fall considerably short of full integration. The experience of other ethnic groups indicates that some Negro households would be scattered in largely white residential areas. Others—probably a larger number—would voluntarily cluster together in largely Negro neighborhoods. The Integration Choice would thus produce both integration and segregation. But the segregation would be voluntary.

Articulating these three choices plainly oversimplifies the possibilities open to the country. We believe, however, that they encompass the basic issues—issues which the American public must face if it is serious in its concern not only about civil disorder, but the future of our democratic society.

III. THE PRESENT POLICIES CHOICE

Powerful forces of social and political inertia are moving the country steadily along the course of existing policies toward a divided country.

This course may well involve changes in many social and economic programs—but not enough to produce fundamental alterations in the key factors of Negro concentration, racial segregation, and the lack of sufficient enrichment to arrest the decay of deprived neighborhoods.

Some movement towards enrichment can be found in efforts to encourage industries to locate plants in central cities, in increased federal expenditures for education, in the important concepts embodied in the "War on Poverty," and in the Model Cities Program. But congressional appropriations for even present federal programs have been so small that they fall short of effective enrichment.

As for challenging concentration and segregation, a national commitment to this purpose has yet to develop.

Of the three future courses we have defined, the Present Policies Choice—the choice we are now making—is the course with the most ominous consequences for our society.

The Probability of Future Civil Disorders

We believe that the Present Policies Choice would lead to a larger number of violent incidents of the kind that have stimulated recent major disorders.

First, it does nothing to raise the hopes, absorb the energies, or constructively challenge the talents of the rapidly-growing number of young Negro men in central cities. The proportion of unemployed or underemployed among them will remain very high. These young men have contributed disproportionately to crime and violence in cities in the past, and there is danger, obviously, that they will continue to do so.

Second, under these conditions, a rising proportion of Negroes in disadvantaged city areas might come to look upon the deprivation and segregation they suffer as proper justification for violent protest or for extending support to now isolated extremists who advocate civil disruption by guerrilla tactics.

More incidents would not necessarily mean more or worse riots. For the near future, there is substantial likelihood that even an increased number of incidents could be controlled before becoming major disorders, if society undertakes to improve police and National Guard forces so that they can respond to potential disorders with more prompt and disciplined use of force.

In fact, the likelihood of incidents mushrooming into major disorders would be only slightly higher in the near future under the Present Policies Choice than under the other two possible choices. For no new policies or programs could possibly alter basic ghetto conditions immediately. And the announcement of new programs under the other choices would immediately generate new expectations. Expectations inevitably increase faster than performance: in the short run, they might even increase the level of frustration.

In the long run, however, the Present Policies Choice risks a seriously greater probability of major disorders, worse, possibly, than those already experienced.

If the Negro population as a whole developed even stronger feelings of being wrongly "penned in" and discriminated against, many of its members might come to support not only riots, but the rebellion now being preached by only a handful.

If large-scale violence resulted, white retaliation could follow. This spiral could quite conceivably lead to a kind of urban *apartheid* with semi-martial law in many major cities, enforced residence of Negroes in segregated areas, and a drastic reduction in personal freedom for all Americans, particularly Negroes.

The same distinction is applicable to the cost of the Present Policies Choice. In the short run, its costs—at least its direct cash outlays—would be far less than for the other choices.

Any social and economic programs likely to have significant lasting effect would require very substantial annual appropriations for many years. Their cost would far exceed the direct losses sustained in recent civil disorders. Property damage in all the disorders we investigated, including Detroit and Newark, totalled less than $100 million.

But it would be a tragic mistake to view the Present Policies Choice as cheap. Damage figures measure only a small part of the costs of civil disorder. They cannot measure the costs in terms of the lives lost, injuries suffered, minds and attitudes closed and frozen in prejudice, or the hidden costs of the profound disruption of entire cities.

Ultimately, moreover, the economic and social costs of the Present Policies Choice will far surpass the cost of the alternatives. The rising concentration of impoverished Negroes and other minorities within the urban ghettos will constantly expand public expenditures for welfare, law enforcement, unemployment and other existing programs without arresting the decay of older city neighborhoods and the breeding of frustration and discontent. But the most significant item on the balance of accounts will remain largely invisible and incalculable—the toll in human values taken by continued poverty, segregation and inequality of opportunity.

Polarization

Another and equally serious consequence is the fact that this course would lead to the permanent establishment of two societies: one predominantly white and located in the suburbs, in smaller cities, and in outlying areas, and one largely Negro located in central cities.

We are well on the way to just such a divided nation.

This division is veiled by the fact that Negroes do not now dominate many central cities. But they soon will, as we have shown, and the new Negro mayors will be facing even more difficult conditions than now exist.

As Negroes succeed whites in our largest cities, the proportion of low-income residents in those cities will probably increase. This is likely even if both white and Negro incomes continue to rise at recent rates, since Negroes have much lower incomes than whites. Moreover, many of the ills of large central cities spring from their age, their location, and their obsolete physical structures. The deterioration and economic decay stemming from these factors have been proceeding for decades and will continue to plague older cities regardless of who resides in them.

These facts underlie the fourfold dilemma of the American city:

- Fewer tax dollars come in, as large numbers of middle-income taxpayers move out of central cities and property values and business decline;
- More tax dollars are required to provide essential public services and facilities, and to meet the needs of expanding lower-income groups;

- Each tax dollar buys less, because of increasing costs;
- Citizen dissatisfaction with municipal services grows as needs, expectations and standards of living increase throughout the community.

These are the conditions that would greet the Negro-dominated municipal governments that will gradually come to power in many of our major cities. The Negro electorates in those cities probably would demand basic changes in present policies. Like the present white electorates there, they would have to look for assistance to two basic sources: the private sector and the federal government.

With respect to the private sector, major private capital investment in those cities might have ceased almost altogether if white-dominated firms and industries decided the risks and costs were too great. The withdrawal of private capital is already far advanced in most all-Negro areas of our large cities.

Even if private investment continued, it alone would not suffice. Big cities containing high proportions of low-income Negroes and block after block of deteriorating older property need very substantial assistance from the federal government to meet the demands of their electorates for improved services and living conditions.

By that time, however, it is probable that Congress will be more heavily influenced by representatives of the suburban and outlying city electorate. These areas will comprise 40 percent of our total population by 1985, compared with 31 percent in 1960. Central cities will decline from 32 percent to 27 percent.[4]

Yet even the suburbs will be feeling the squeeze of higher local government costs. Hence, Congress might resist providing the extensive assistance which central cities will desperately need.

Thus the Present Policies Choice, if pursued for any length of time, might force simultaneous political and economic polarization in many of our largest metropolitan areas. Such polarization would involve large central cities—mainly Negro, with many poor, and nearly bankrupt—on the one hand, and most suburbs—mainly white, generally affluent, but heavily taxed—on the other hand.

Some areas might avoid political confrontation by shifting to some form of metropolitan government designed to offer regional solutions for pressing urban problems such as property taxation, air and water pollution and refuse disposal, and commuter transport. Yet this would hardly eliminate the basic segregation and relative poverty of the urban Negro population. It might even

---

[4] Based on Census Bureau Series D projections.

increase the Negro's sense of frustration and alienation if it operated to prevent Negro political control of central cities.

The acquisition of power by Negro-dominated governments
in central cities is surely a legitimate and desirable exercise of
political power by a minority group. It is in an American political
tradition exemplified by the achievements of the Irish in New York
and Boston.

But such Negro political development would also involve
virtually complete racial segregation and virtually complete spatial
separation. By 1985, the separate Negro society in our central
cities would contain almost 21 million citizens. That is almost 68
percent larger than the present Negro population of central cities.
It is also larger than the current population of every Negro nation
in Africa except Nigeria.

If developing a racially integrated society is extraordinarily
difficult today when 12.1 million Negroes live in central cities, then
it is quite clearly going to be virtually impossible in 1985 when
almost 21 million Negroes—still much poorer and less educated than
most whites—will be living there.

Can Present Policies Avert Extreme Polarization?

There are at least two possible developments under the
Present Policies Choice which might avert such polarization. The
first is a faster increase of incomes among Negroes than has
occurred in the recent past. This might prevent central cities from
becoming even deeper "poverty traps" than they now are. It suggests the importance of effective job programs and higher levels
of welfare payments for dependent families.

The second possible development is migration of a growing
Negro middle class out of the central city. This would not prevent
competition for federal funds between central cities and outlying
areas, but it might diminish the racial undertones of that competition.

There is, however, no evidence that a continuation of present policies would be accompanied by any such movement. There
is already a significant Negro middle class. It grew rapidly from
1960 to 1966. Yet in these years, 88.9 percent of the total national
growth of Negro population was concentrated in central cities—the
highest in history. Indeed, from 1960 to 1966, there was actually a
net total in-migration of Negroes from the urban fringes of metropolitan areas into central cities.[5] The Commission believes it un-

---

[5] Although Negro population on the urban fringe of metropolitan
areas did increase slightly (0.2 million) from 1960 to 1966, it is safe to assume an actual net in-migration to central cities from these areas based
upon the rate of natural increase of the Negro population.

likely that this trend will suddenly reverse itself without significant changes in private attitudes and public policies.

IV. THE ENRICHMENT CHOICE

The Present Policies Choice plainly would involve continuation of efforts like Model Cities, manpower programs, and the War on Poverty. These are in fact enrichment programs, designed to improve the quality of life in the ghetto.

Because of their limited scope and funds, however, they constitute only very modest steps toward enrichment—and would continue to do so even if these programs were somewhat enlarged or supplemented.

The premise of the Enrichment Choice is performance. To adopt this choice would require a substantially greater share of national resources—sufficient to make a dramatic, visible impact on life in the urban Negro ghetto.

The Effect of Enrichment on Civil Disorders

Effective enrichment policies probably would have three immediate effects on civil disorders.

First, announcement of specific large-scale programs and the demonstration of a strong intent to carry them out might persuade ghetto residents that genuine remedies for their problems were forthcoming, thereby allaying tensions.

Second, such announcements would strongly stimulate the aspirations and hopes of members of these communities—possibly well beyond the capabilities of society to deliver and to do so promptly. This might increase frustration and discontent, to some extent cancelling the first effect.

Third, if there could be immediate action on meaningful job training and the creation of productive jobs for large numbers of unemployed young people, they would become much less likely to engage in civil disorders.

Such action is difficult now, when there are about 585,000 young Negro men aged 14 to 24 in the civilian labor force in central cities—of whom 81,000 or 13.8 percent, are unemployed and probably two or three times as many are underemployed. It will not become easier in the future. By 1975, this age group will have grown to nearly 700,000.

Given the size of the present problem, plus the large growth of this age group, creation of sufficient meaningful jobs will require extensive programs, begun rapidly. Even if the nation is willing to embark on such programs, there is no certainty that they can be made effective soon enough.

Consequently, there is no certainty that the Enrichment Choice would do much more in the near future to diminish violent incidents in central cities than would the Present Policies Choice. However, if enrichment programs can succeed in meeting the needs of residents of disadvantaged areas for jobs, education, housing and city services, then over the years this choice is almost certain to reduce both the level and frequency of urban disorder.

The Negro Middle Class

One objective of the Enrichment Choice would be to help as many disadvantaged Americans as possible—of all races—to enter the mainstream of American prosperity, to progress toward what is often called middle-class status. If the Enrichment Choice were adopted, it could certainly attain this objective to a far greater degree than would the Present Policies Choice. This could significantly change the quality of life in many central city areas.

It can be argued that a rapidly enlarging Negro middle class would also promote Negro out-migration, and thus the Enrichment Choice would open up an escape hatch from the ghetto. This argument, however, has two weaknesses.

The first is experience. Central cities already have sizeable and growing numbers of middle-class Negro families. Yet only a few have migrated from the central city. The past pattern of white ethnic groups gradually moving out of central-city areas to middle-class suburbs has not applied to Negroes. Effective open-housing laws will help make this possible. It is probable, however, that other more extensive changes in policies and attitudes will be required—and these would extend beyond the Enrichment Choice.

The second weakness in the argument is time. Even if enlargement of the Negro middle class succeeded in encouraging movement out of the central city, it could not do so fast enough to offset the rapid growth of the ghetto. To offset even *half* the growth estimated for the ghetto by 1975 would call for the out-migration from central cities of 217,000 persons a year. This is eight times the annual increase in suburban Negro population—including natural increase—which occurred from 1960 to 1966. Even the most effective enrichment program is not likely to accomplish this.

A corollary problem derives from the continuing migration of poor Negroes from the Southern to Northern and Western cities.

Adoption of the Enrichment Choice would require large-scale efforts to improve conditions in the South sufficiently to remove the pressure to migrate. Under present conditions, slightly over a third of the estimated increase in Negro central-city population by 1985 will result from in-migration—3.0 million out of a total increase of 8.2 million.

Negro Self-Development

The Enrichment Choice is in line with some of the currents of Negro protest thought that fall under the label of "Black Power." We do not refer to versions of Black Power ideology which promote violence, generate racial hatred, or advocate total separation of the races. Rather, we mean the view which asserts that the American Negro population can assume its proper role in society and overcome its feelings of powerlessness and lack of self-respect only by exerting power over decisions which directly affect its own members. A fully integrated society is not thought possible until the Negro minority within the ghetto has developed political strength—a strong bargaining position in dealing with the rest of society.

In short, this argument would regard predominantly Negro central cities and predominantly white outlying areas not as harmful, but as an advantageous future.

Proponents of these views also focus on the need for the Negro to organize economically as well as politically, thus tapping new energies and resources for self-development. One of the hardest tasks in improving disadvantaged areas is to discover how deeply deprived residents can develop their own capabilities by participating more fully in decisions and activities which affect them. Such learning-by-doing efforts are a vital part of the process of bringing deprived people into the social mainstream.

Separate But Equal Societies?

The Enrichment Choice by no means seeks to perpetuate racial segregation. In the end, however, its premise is that disadvantaged Negroes can achieve equality of opportunity with whites while continuing in conditions of nearly complete separation.

This premise has been vigorously advocated by Black Power proponents. While most Negroes originally desired racial integration, many are losing hope of ever achieving it because of seemingly implacable white resistance. Yet they cannot bring themselves to accept the conclusion that most of the millions of Negroes who are forced to live racially segregated lives must therefore be condemned to inferior lives—to inferior educations, or inferior housing, or inferior status.

Rather, they reason, there must be some way to make the

quality of life in the ghetto areas just as good—or better—than elsewhere. It is not surprising that some Black Power advocates are denouncing integration and claiming that, given the hypocrisy and racism that pervade white society, life in a black society is, in fact, morally superior. This argument is understandable, but there is a great deal of evidence that it is unrealistic.

The economy of the United States and particularly the sources of employment are preponderantly white. In this circumstance, a policy of separate but equal employment could only relegate Negroes permanently to inferior incomes and economic status.

The best evidence regarding education is contained in recent reports of the Office of Education and Civil Rights Commission which suggest that both racial and economic integration are essential to educational equality for Negroes. Yet critics point out that, certainly until integration is achieved, various types of enrichment programs must be tested, and that dramatically different results may be possible from intensive educational enrichment—such as far smaller classes, or greatly expanded pre-school programs, or changes in the home environment of Negro children resulting from steady jobs for fathers.

Still others advocate shifting control over ghetto schools from professional administrators to local residents. This, they say, would improve curricula, give students a greater sense of their own value, and thus raise their morale and educational achievement. These approaches have not yet been tested sufficiently. One conclusion, however, does seem reasonable: any real improvement in the quality of education in low-income, all-Negro areas will cost a great deal more money than is now being spent there—and perhaps more than is being spent per pupil anywhere. Racial and social class integration of schools may produce equal improvement in achievement at less total cost.

Whether or not enrichment in ghetto areas will really work is not yet known, but the Enrichment Choice is based on the yet-unproved premise that it will. Certainly, enrichment programs could significantly improve existing ghetto schools if they impelled major innovations. But "separate but equal" ghetto education cannot meet the long-run fundamental educational needs of the central-city Negro population.

The three basic educational choices are: providing Negro children with quality education in integrated schools; providing them with quality education by enriching ghetto schools; or continuing to provide many Negro children with inferior education in racially segregated school systems, severely limiting their life-time opportunities.

Consciously or not, it is the third choice that the nation is now making, and this choice the Commission rejects totally.

In the field of housing, it is obvious that "separate but equal" does not mean really equal. The Enrichment Choice could greatly improve the quantity, variety, and environment of decent housing available to the ghetto population. It could not provide Negroes with the same freedom and range of choice as whites with equal incomes. Smaller cities and suburban areas together with the central city provide a far greater variety of housing and environmental settings than the central city alone. Programs to provide housing outside central cities, however, extend beyond the bounds of the Enrichment Choice.

In the end, whatever its benefits, the Enrichment Choice might well invite a prospect similar to that of the Present Policies Choice: separate white and black societies.

If enrichment programs were effective, they could greatly narrow the gap in income, education, housing, jobs, and other qualities of life between the ghetto and the mainstream. Hence the chances of harsh polarization—or of disorder—in the next 20 years would be greatly reduced.

Whether they would be reduced far enough depends on the scope of the programs. Even if the gap were narrowed from the present, it still could remain as a strong source of tension. History teaches that men are not necessarily placated even by great absolute progress. The controlling factor is relative progress—whether they still perceive a significant gap, between themselves and others whom they regard as no more deserving. Widespread perception of such a gap—and consequent resentment—might well be precisely the situation 20 years from now under the Enrichment Choice, for it is essentially another way of choosing a permanently divided country.

V. THE INTEGRATION CHOICE

The third and last course open to the nation combines enrichment with programs designed to encourage integration of substantial numbers of Negroes into the society outside the ghetto.

Enrichment must be an important adjunct to any integration course. No matter how ambitious or energetic such a program may be, relatively few Negroes now living in central-city ghettos would be quickly integrated. In the meantime, significant improvement in their present environment is essential.

The enrichment aspect of this third choice should, however,

be recognized as interim action, during which time expanded and new programs can work to improve education and earning power. The length of the interim period surely would vary. For some it may be long. But in any event, what should be clearly recognized is that enrichment is only a means toward the goal; it is not the goal.

The goal must be achieving freedom for every citizen to live and work according to his capacities and desires, not his color.

We believe there are four important reasons why American society must give this course the most serious consideration. First, future jobs are being created primarily in the suburbs, while the chronically unemployed population is increasingly concentrated in the ghetto. This separation will make it more and more difficult for Negroes to achieve anything like full employment in decent jobs. But if, over time, these residents began to find housing outside central cities, they would be exposed to more knowledge of job opportunities. They would have to make much shorter trips to reach jobs. They would have a far better chance of securing employment on a self-sustaining basis.

Second, in the judgment of this Commission, racial and social-class integration is the most effective way of improving the education of ghetto children.

Third, developing an adequate housing supply for low-income and middle-income families and true freedom of choice in housing for Negroes of all income levels will require substantial out-movement. We do not believe that such an out-movement will occur spontaneously merely as a result of increasing prosperity among Negroes in central cities. A national fair housing law is essential to begin such movement. In many suburban areas, a program combining positive incentives with the building of new housing will be necessary to carry it out.

Fourth, and by far the most important, integration is the only course which explicitly seeks to achieve a single nation rather than accepting the present movement toward a dual society. This choice would enable us at least to begin reversing the profoundly divisive trend already so evident in our metropolitan areas—before it becomes irreversible.

VI. CONCLUSIONS

The future of our cities is neither something which will just happen nor something which will be imposed upon us by an inevitable destiny. That future will be shaped to an important degree by choices we make now.

We have attempted to set forth the major choices because we believe it is vital for Americans to understand the consequences of our present drift.

Three critical conclusions emerge from this analysis:

1. The nation is rapidly moving toward two increasingly separate Americas.

Within two decades, this division could be so deep that it would be almost impossible to unite:
• a white society principally located in suburbs, in smaller central cities, and in the peripheral parts of large central cities; and
• a Negro society largely concentrated within large central cities.

The Negro society will be permanently relegated to its current status, possibly even if we expend great amounts of money and effort in trying to "gild" the ghetto.

2. In the long run, continuation and expansion of such a permanent division threatens us with two perils.

The first is the danger of sustained violence in our cities. The timing, scale, nature, and repercussions of such violence cannot be foreseen. But if it occurred, it would further destroy our ability to achieve the basic American promises of liberty, justice, and equality.

The second is the danger of a conclusive repudiation of the traditional American ideals of individual dignity, freedom, and equality of opportunity. We will not be able to espouse these ideals meaningfully to the rest of the world, to ourselves, to our children. They may still recite the Pledge of Allegiance and say "one nation . . . indivisible." But they will be learning cynicism, not patriotism.

3. We cannot escape responsibility for choosing the future of our metropolitan areas and the human relations which develop within them. It is a responsibility so critical that even an unconscious choice to continue present policies has the gravest implications.

That we have delayed in choosing or, by delaying, may be making the wrong choice, does not sentence us either to separatism or despair. But we must choose. We will choose. Indeed, we are now choosing.

NOTE ON NEGRO POPULATION PROJECTIONS

1. The Census Bureau publishes four projections of future population growth based upon differing assumptions about future fertility rates (i.e., the rate is the annual number of live births per 1,000 women aged 15 to 44). Series A assumes fertility rates similar

to those prevalent from 1962 to 1966. Series B through D assume lower rates. Assuming that Negro fertility rates will continue to decline, we have used the average of Series C and D—which are based on the lowest assumptions about such rates. We have also converted the Census Bureau's nonwhite population projections into Negro projections by assuming Negroes will continue to comprise about 92 percent of all nonwhites. If, however, fertility rates remain at their present levels, then the total Negro population in 1985 would be 35.8 million rather than 30.7 million. The average annual rate of increase from 1966 to 1985 would be 753,000, rather than 484,000—56 percent higher.

The projection is as follows:

Date	Total U.S. Negro Population (in millions)	Negroes As % of Total U.S. Population	Total Increase Number (in millions)	Total Increase Percent	Annual Average
1960	18.8 (actual)	10.4%	—	—	—
1966	21.5 (actual)	10.9	2.7	14.4	450,000
1970	23.2	11.3	1.7	7.9	425,000
1975	25.3	11.6	2.1	9.1	420,000
1980	28.1	12.0	2.5	9.9	500,000
1985	30.7	12.4	2.9	10.9	580,000

2. The general concept of a metropolitan area is of an integrated, economic and social unit with a recognized large population nucleus. Statistically, it is called a Standard Metropolitan Statistical Area—one which contains at least one central city of at least 50,000 inhabitants. It covers the county of the central city and adjacent counties found to be economically and socially integrated with that county.

A Central City is the largest city of an SMSA and which gives the SMSA its name.

"Core city" or "inner city" is a popular expression sometimes meaning central city and sometimes meaning the central business district and densely populated downtown neighborhoods of generally poorer residents.

The array of statistical materials for metropolitan areas by "central city" and "outside central city" categories carries with it some dangers. The general proposition made in such displays is that the Negro population is concentrated in the central city and is kept out of the suburbs. Certainly this is true.

The danger arises from the inference which the reader may make about the character of "outside central city" and "suburb." "Outside central city" means the whole metropolitan area outside the city or cities whose names are given to the Standard Metropolitan Statistical Area. This is not a homogeneous, affluent, white-only collection of bedroom communities or housing developments. It is a wide-ranging assortment of these and more. Some are attractive communities with trees, grass and fresh air. Others are grimy, industrial towns with all the problems commonly associated with the central city. There are, in fact, 246 cities of over 25,000 "hidden" in the concept "outside central city." Seventy-seven of these had over 50,000 population in 1960. Many are white only or close to it. Many are not. Some even have higher proportions of Negroes to total population than the central cities of the metropolitan areas of which they are a part. Some of these cities are new. Some are old and have to fight the same battles against urban blight as the central cities of many metropolitan areas.

3. We have considered two projections of this population. The first projection assumes no further in-migration or out-migration of Negroes to or from central cities. This assumption is unrealistic, but it provides a measure of how much the central-city Negro population is likely to expand through natural increase alone. The second projection assumes that central cities will continue to contain 88.9 percent of all Negro population growth, as they did from 1960 to 1966.

Date	Total U.S. Central-City Negro Population (in millions)	
	Based on Natural Increase from the Existing Base Only	Based on 88.9% of All Future Negro Growth In Central Cities
1966 (actual)	12.1	12.1
1970	13.1	13.6
1975	14.2	15.5
1980	15.6	17.7
1985	17.3	20.3

Thus, even assuming no Negro migration into central cities, the total Negro population would increase six million, 43.0 percent, by 1985. Under the more realistic assumption of both continued in-migration (at present rates) and natural growth, total Negro population of central cities would increase by 8.2 million Negroes, 68 percent.

4. We have arrived at these estimates by making three different assumptions about future white central-city population shifts: (a) that it will remain constant at its 1966 level of 46.4 million; (b) that it will decline, as it did from 1960 to 1966, by an amount equal to half the increase in central-city Negro population; and (c) that it will decline by an absolute amount equal to the total gains in central-city Negro population. In all three cases, we assume that Negro central-city population will continue to account for 88.9 percent of all Negro population growth. The full projections are as follows:

		White Population Declines at an Absolute Annual Rate Equal to:	
Date	White Population Remains Constant at 1966 Level	One-Half Negro Population Gains	Total Negro Population Gains
1966 (actual)	20.7%	20.7%	20.7%
1975	25.0	25.7	26.5
1985	30.4	32.4	34.7

Proportion of Total Central City Population Negro if:

The first assumption requires a rise in total central-city population from 58.5 million in 1966 to 66.7 million in 1985. Since many of the largest central cities are already almost fully developed, so large an increase is probably unrealistic. On the other hand, the third assumption involves no change in the 1966 central-city population figure of 58.5 million. This may be unrealistically low. But in any event, it seems likely that continued concentration will cause the total proportion of Negroes in central cities to reach at least 25 percent by 1975 and 30 percent by 1985.

24
America's Race Paradox: The Gap Between Social Progress and Political Despair

Nathan Glazer

Something very strange is happening in the racial crisis in the United States. On the one hand, the concrete situation of Negro Americans is changing rapidly for the better. This is not only true when we look at economic measures of all kinds (although we all know that these are an inadequate measure of group progress, and that a people that feels oppressed will never be satisfied by the argument "you never had it so good"); but it is also true that things are better when we look at measures of political participation and power. It is even true when we look at the critical area of police behaviour and police attitudes. There is no question that police in city after city are becoming more careful in how they address Negro Americans, more restrained in the use of force, of fire-arms. The history of the riots alone, from 1964, demonstrates that.

But on the other hand, the political attitudes of Negroes have become more extreme and more desperate. The riots are called "rebellions," and hardly any Negro leader today bothers to deplore them. Militant groups become larger, and their language and demands more shocking. Cultural nationalism flourishes—and I think most people think that is good—but political separatism becomes an ever more popular demand, and hardly anyone can consider that without thinking again. (We all know what may happen when a country begins to break up. Look at Nigeria.)

This is an incredible dilemma for social policy. For the fact is that most of us—black and white, liberals and conservatives, socialists and free enterprisers—believe *(1)* that political and social attitudes reflect the concrete economic and social and political

Reprinted by permission from Nathan Glazer, "America's Race Paradox: The Gap between Social Progress and Political Despair," *Encounter,* October, 1968, pp. 9–18.

situation of people; *(2)* that we can affect those attitudes by changing the concrete conditions; and *(3)* that when things get better
people become more satisfied, less violent, the society becomes
more stable. When concrete conditions improve and political attitudes become at the same time more extreme and violent, we can
resort to two explanations.

There is the well-known "revolution of rising expectations,"
and the ease with which expectations can outstrip concrete positive
changes. And there is the theory of Alexis de Tocqueville, developed
in his study of the French Revolution, that the improvement of conditions increases the desire for greater change and for revolutionary
change, because people themselves feel stronger and more potent.
Both of these processes are undoubtedly taking place, but one's
attitude to them must depend on one's attitude to American society.
If one looks upon American society as Tocqueville and the French
people looked upon their Old Régime, that is, as a conservative,
sclerotic, repressive, irrational, and selfish régime which prevented
the free development of the people, then one of course will accept
favourably the rise of extreme opinion, and look forward to the
crash of the American Old Régime. But if one sees American society
and state as fundamentally democratic, as capable of change, as
responsive to people's wishes—then one will be deeply concerned
whether this society and state can survive. That expectations should
rise is good—that they should rise so fast that no policy of any
type carried out by anybody can satisfy them, is bad. That people
should feel potent and powerful and free to express their resentments and anger is encouraging—that that resentment and anger
should serve to overthrow a system that works, that is capable of
satisfying their needs and hopes, is deplorable.

A rapid rate of social change has improved the condition
of Negro Americans and has gone some way to closing gaps
between the condition of Negro and white Americans, but it has
not only *not* moderated the rise of extremism and violence—it has
been accompanied by it. At some point one must expect improvement and change to moderate extremism and violence, despite the
revolution of rising expectations and the Tocquevillean hypothesis.
If there is such a point, it is clear we are not only not arriving at
it: we are getting further and further away from it.

There is, of course, another possible explanation of what
is happening: that Negro Americans are no longer interested in
integration or even in educational, economic, and political advance
within the American social system. They have begun to see themselves as "a subject people" and, as in the case of every such
people, only independent political existence can satisfy them. This,

in any case, is the direction that militant Negro demands have now begun to take. And if most Negro Americans follow the militant leaders, then all the political skill, ingenuity, and creativity the American nation possesses will be necessary to keep it from being torn apart.

First, let me briefly document the fact that things *are* getting better. We must do this because so many liberal and progressive shapers of opinion, and the vast flock that follows them, are convinced (and *insist*) that the concrete situation of Negro Americans has *not* changed, or has indeed got worse. Sadly enough, social scientists, who should know the facts best, are often among the worst offenders. The writer of that fine study of Negro street-corner men, *Tally's Corner,* for example, states casually that "the number of the poor and their problems have grown steadily since World War II. . . ." Social scientists who contend that the economic situation of Negroes is getting worse will point to the rising *absolute* gap between Negro and white incomes and ignore the fact that Negro incomes have come closer to white incomes as a *percentage* of white incomes. By this logic, if we come to a fortunate time when white median incomes are $10,000 and the non-white median-incomes are $8,000, it could be argued that Negroes are "worse off" than when whites made $5,000 and Negroes $3,500!

In October 1967, the Bureau of Labor Statistics and the Bureau of the Census put out a compendium of statistics on the *Social and Economic Conditions of Negroes in the United States.* Here are some of the major findings:

Income: In 1966, 23% of non-white families had incomes of more than $7,000, against 53% of white families. Ten years before, using dollars of the same value, only 9% of the non-white families had incomes at this level, against 31% of white families.

If we look at the U.S. outside the South, where the Negro situation on all measures is worst, we find in 1966 38% of non-white families with income above $7,000, against 59% of white families at that level.

Occupation: Between 1960 and 1966, the number of non-whites in the better-paying and more secure occupational categories increased faster than whites: a 50% increase for non-whites in professional, technical and managerial work, against a 13% increase for whites; a 48% increase in clerical occupations, against a 19% increase for whites; a 32% increase in sales workers, against a 7% increase for whites; a 45% increase in craftsmen and foremen, against a 10% increase for whites. And during the same time, the proportions of non-whites working as private household workers and labourers dropped.

Education: In 1960 there was a 1.9 years gap in median years of school completed between non-white and white males from 25 to 29 years of age; by 1966 there was only a .5 years gap.

In 1960, 36% of non-white males from 25 to 29 had completed high school, against 63% of white males; by 1966, 53% of non-white males had completed high school, against 73% of white males.

In 1960, 3.9% of Negro males from 25 to 34 had completed college, against 15.7% of white males; in 1966, 7.4% of Negro males had completed college, against 17.9% of white males—a 90% increase among non-white college graduates, against a 14% increase in white college graduates.

Housing: Between 1960 and 1966, there was a 25% drop in the number of substandard housing units occupied by non-whites (from 2,263,000 to 1,691,000 units), and a 44% increase in the number of standard units occupied by non-whites—from 2,881,000 to 4,135,000 units.

If we look at political participation—voting, offices held, in effect, political power—we find an equally striking increase. Thus, Negro voter registration in the South increased from 2,164,000 in March 1964 to 3,072,000 in May 1968, while Negro population remained stable. The National Commission on Civil Disorders surveyed twenty cities to find out the extent of Negro political representation. The cities averaged 16% in Negro population; 10% in proportion of elected Negro political representatives. We have to interpret such a figure in the light of the fact that Negroes of voting age are generally a smaller proportion of the total Negro population in most cities than whites of voting age of the white population, since Negroes in cities have a higher proportion of young families and children, whites a higher proportion of the aged.

Even on that sorest point of black-white relations, the police, the Kerner Commission reports progress in one significant respect: there are now substantial numbers of Negroes on many city police forces—Washington 21%, Phialdelphia 20, Chicago 17, St. Louis 11, Hartford 11, Newark 10, Atlanta 10, Cleveland 7, New York 5, Detroit 5.

These are simply overall measures. When one considers the large number of programmes devoted to getting Negroes into colleges, into graduate and professional schools, into various corporations, to raise their grades in the Federal Civil Service, to moderate police attitudes—and when one considers the incentives to do all these things to be found in riot and threat of riot, boycott and threat of boycott, one cannot help conclude that the situation of Negroes is changing . . . for "the better."

To be sure, all the figures I have quoted can be disputed. Thus 14% of Negro males as against only 2% of white males (we have recently become aware) never get counted by the census; and if they were counted, they would undoubtedly depress the Negro figures on income, education, occupation, housing. But as against this, it must be pointed out that we have probably not been counting similar proportions of Negro males of working age in earlier censuses; so the change from one census to another represents real change.

It can be argued that the quality of jobs held by Negroes, even if they are in white-collar and skilled labour categories, is worse than that held by whites; and this too is true. But the changes over time are real, and the quality of jobs has certainly not on the whole decreased. Indeed, it has probably improved. Less Negro professionals today are preachers, more are engineers.

It can be argued that the improvement in the economic and educational and housing condition of the Negro is largely an effect of their migration from the South, and from small town and rural areas, to the North and West, and to big cities; if we were to look at Negroes in the North and West alone, we would not find such marked changes. But the statistics show improvement in every section.

It has been argued that while these overall measures of improvement truly reflect improvement for the Negro middle classes and stable working classes, the lower working classes have relatively declined, and have shown no progress. But an unpublished analysis of income statistics by Dr. Albert Wohlstetter (of the University of Chicago) reveals that the *lower* Negro income groups have improved their position relative to white low-income groups more in recent years than the Negro upper-income groups have improved their position relative to white upper-income groups. In other words, the gap between poor Negroes and poor whites in terms of income is narrower now than in the 1950s. At the same time it is true that other social indicators—*e.g.,* the proportion of broken families and of illegitimacy—continue to reveal worsening conditions.

Finally, one may argue that much of the advance to which I have pointed has taken place since the Viet Nam War expanded in 1965, just as the previous economic advances of the Negro took place during the Korean War, and came to an end when that war came to an end. Between the wars there was relative decline and stagnation.

There is much truth in these last two arguments with the gross statistics of recent improvement. But it is also true that the advances made during wars have not been fully wiped out in the past—it is rather that the rate of change has not kept up. By now the build-up of Negro political power and of national programmes and commitments that guarantee advance is so great and the scale of the advances that have taken place in recent years is so massive, that I cannot believe they will not continue after the war—if, that is, there is not a radical change in the political situation to reverse the social and economic trends of the last eight years.

More striking, however, than the advance itself is the fact that on the basis of our present social statistics we can not single out the Negro as a group in the United States which suffers unique deprivation, *i.e.,* as compared to other ethnic and racial groups which suffer from the effects of poor education, depressed rural backgrounds, and recent migration to urban areas. There has been a division among American social scientists as to how to view Negro Americans in the context of the ethnic and racial history of the United States. One tendency is to emphasise everything that is "unique"—and a great deal is unique: the manner of their arrival (by force, and in chains); the conditions under which they lived for two hundred years (slavery); the conditions under which they have lived for the last hundred years (legal inferiority in a good part of the country); finally, the special role of the Negro Americans in American imagination and in culture (as central participants in shaping it, and as the subjects of some of its major themes). But it is also possible to see Negro Americans as part of a sequence of ethnic and racial groups that have moved into American society and become a part of it.

A new illusion is now abroad in the land. It asserts that all white ethnic groups have rapidly moved into American society, achieving respectable levels of income, good conditions of living, and political power. All racially distinct groups, suffering from the racism of American society, have been held back; and the Negro American, suffering from the special character of chattel slavery, is furthest back. The truth is nothing like this. Some white ethnic groups—such as the Jews—have shown a rapid economic mobility. Others have been much slower to achieve economically. One of these economically-backward white ethnic groups, the Irish, has been politically gifted, and members of the group are to be found disproportionately among elected officials of every level and in almost every part of the country. Others, such as Italians and Poles, have done poorly both economically *and* politically. Some racially distinct groups—such as the Japanese—have done remarkably well in education and occupation. Most others have done badly.

The range in experience is enormous, and the cause of this difference is not only degree of discrimination and prejudice, though that is an important factor. Equally important is a whole range of elements we vaguely group under the term "culture"—attitudes and behaviour in connection with School, Work, Family. (These have their origin in history and it may well be that the discrimination and prejudice of the past creates the cultural attributes of the present.) Nor is it true that these grossly different patterns of achievement among different groups are to be found in the U.S.A. alone. They are to be found wherever different ethnic and racial groups live together, whether it is Malays, Chinese, and Indians in Malaya, or Indians and Africans in Kenya, or Chinese and Indonesians in Indonesia, or Maharashtrians and Gujaratis and South Indians in Bombay, *etc.* Indeed, it is often the case that when a group is politically favoured in terms of educational and job opportunities—*e.g.,* the Malays in Malaya—these powerful cultural factors prevent the group from taking full advantage of these opportunities; and they remain at a lower educational and economic level. The Negro situation is rather more complex than the gross simplification of having "started at the bottom and staying there." By some measures, the Puerto Ricans do worse in New York, and the Mexican Americans do worse in the South-west. One can indeed contend that the Negro is worst off of the major ethnic and racial groups in this country, but not that much worse off to explain by itself the special quality of despair and hysteria, and the tone of impending violence and doom that now dominates much Negro political discourse.

But of course we must add another factor to the equation: America's obligation as a nation to improve the position of Negroes is much greater than the obligation to groups that emigrated voluntarily. The Negro is aware of this obligation and responsibility, and so the inferiority of his position becomes far more grating than it would be in the case of ordinary immigrants.

The fact is that, regardless of the details of the actual economic and social position of the Negro, an increasingly large part of twenty-two million Negro Americans believes that Americans are "racists," insist on "keeping the Negro down," and will never allow equality, and that the only solution will be some form of separate political existence. One indicator as to how far we have moved is in the use of words. Consider, for example, "genocide." Last February, Stokely Carmichael spoke to a Negro audience in Oakland and felt he had to justify the use of "genocide" to describe the dangers facing Negroes:

> . . . we are not talking about politics tonight,
> we're not talking about economics tonight, we're
> talking about the survival of a race of people. . . .
> Many of us feel—many of our generation feel—that
> they are getting ready to commit genocide against
> us. Now many people say that's a horrible thing
> to say about anybody. But if it's a horrible thing to
> say, then we should do as Brother Malcolm said,
> we should examine history.

We have moved far in the course of a year. A leader of the
SCLC says "genocide" is a danger. James Baldwin (in the June 2
Book Review section of *The New York Times*) asserts "white America
appears to be seriously considering the possibilities of mass exter-
mination." By now even moderate leaders use the term genocide,
and feel they have to use it to appeal to young militants and to
show they are not "Uncle Toms." By now, of course, white men
who want to demonstrate their sympathy for Negroes will not demur
from the use of the term; thus, Eliot Fremont-Smith, reviewing John
Hersey's *The Algiers Motel Incident* in *The New York Times,* writes
that the book, "shows America to be deeply—and unknowingly to
most of its citizens—genocidal."

The public opinion polls report fantastically rapid changes
of attitude among Negro Americans. A Louis Harris poll conducted
before the Martin Luther King assassination reported on a measure
of "alienation," and concluded that the numbers of Negroes "alienated" had risen from 34% in 1966 to 56% in 1968. The items measuring alienation included: *"Few people really understand how it is
to live like I live"* (those agreeing rose from 32 to 66%); *"People
running the country don't really care what happens to people like
ourselves"* (those agreeing rose from 32 to 52%). The very same
poll reports that 73% of the respondents agreed there has been
"more racial progress" in recent years than there had been previously.

So the paradox exists in the very consciousness of Negro
Americans. They agree there has been more progress, but also
feel ignored, stepped upon, and remote from their society. (Whites
do too, but in much lesser degree.) The changes in these general
attitudes reported by the Harris poll are particularly striking because
they are the sort of general question measuring malaise that one
would not expect to vary much over time (*viz.,* "Are you happy?");
and yet they have changed rapidly. I speak of attitudes and the
use of words. More striking are the realities of action—the riots

since 1964, the general expectation of guerrilla warfare, the rise of the so-called Black Panthers in California and elsewhere and their amazing ability to seize the imagination of the ghetto youth with a programme calling for armed resistance to the police, community control of the ghetto, freeing of black prisoners, and the ultimate hope for some type of national, separate, political existence for blacks.

There are three positions now current as to what to do about this strange impasse: social improvement and increasing extremism. One is that we must put down extremism, strengthen the police, create riot control forces. A second is that we must increase the rate of material advance more swiftly—eventually it must lead to a harmonious nation. A third is that social improvement is no longer the issue—separate political power and existence for Negro Americans is the only reality that will satisfy.

I think the majority of white Americans reject the first alternative as any full response to the crisis, though certainly most believe the maintenance of civil order must be part of any response.

The second position is the one for which the Kerner Commission has written a brief in its report, and most liberal Americans are likely to accept it. It is almost the only thesis one can put forward if one's conviction is that, on the whole, American society has been a success, that a major sign of its success is that it has incorporated and will continue to incorporate many diverse groups, and that it can handle the complex and frightening problems of an advanced technological society rather better than the varied assortment of Communist authoritarian states or vague utopias that is the rhetorical hope of the New Left. And yet the liberal position—and we can take the Kerner Commission report as expressing it best—has one basic difficulty.

It is that we have *already* carried out and are carrying out social programmes at an ever-increasing scale without, as we have seen, any movement towards the reward of "a united and peaceful nation." Take the figures of the Kerner Commission itself:

> Federal expenditures for manpower development and training have increased from less than $60 million in 1963 to $1.6 billion in 1968. The President has proposed a further increase, $2.1 billion in 1969 . . . to provide work experience, training, and supportive services for 1.3 million men and women . . . [which happens to be more than twice the number of non-white unemployed].

Federal expenditures for education, training and related services have increased from $4.7 billion in fiscal 1964 to $12.3 billion in fiscal 1969.

Direct Federal expenditures for housing and community development have increased from $600 million in fiscal 1964 to nearly $3 billion in fiscal 1969.

There have been similarly heavy increases in health and welfare expenditures. All these figures are reported in order to criticise the build-up of expenditures as "not rapid enough" and to demand "far more money" in these and other areas. I am left with an uneasy feeling. If these rates of expansion reported by the Kerner Commission have taken place at the same time as the spread of urban riots and political extremism, is it not questionable whether further expansion will stem them? I am *for* the expansion of these programmes because they are the major means we have for achieving equality in occupations, education, housing, etc. But I do not think we can count on them to moderate attitudes—for political attitudes and development have a life of their own, and are not simple reflections of economic and social conditions.

There is no question in my mind that the demand for "Black Separatism" will not be easily moderated by new social programmes. Accordingly, we must face up to the demand for separatism in its own terms.

Here one must note that "separatism" seems to mean many different things. Some of them appear to me to be valuable and healthy, both for Negroes and for American society: the emphasis on positive identification with the group, "Black Power" in its sense of greater political impact and representation of Negroes; "Black Capitalism"; "Black history" and art. The chief difficulty presented by Black Separatism arises in the demands for territorial autonomy and "extra-territoriality." These have now been presented in many forms: a group of states to become a black nation; black enclaves in the cities, with certain rights and powers; special legal rights for blacks, as in the "Free Huey" demand and its argument that white judges and juries cannot try blacks (even though there are blacks among them). There is no question that American political leaders (and the great majority of the American people) will resist the demand for territorial autonomy and extra-territoriality. One war has been fought to preserve the Union, and the sense of what all Americans gain from a united nation, and what they might lose from a divided one, is strong enough to ensure that these demands will continue to be resisted. Nor is it clear that any substantial part of Negro Americans at present agrees with the Separatists. But their dynamism is frightening, and they are powerfully supported, in my view, not by the realities of the Negro condition and the hopes they offer of improving it, but by powerful ideologies. In particular, it is the new ideology that Negroes in America are "a Colonial People" and require freedom from colonial status.

If the demand for territorial independence succeeds in capturing the minds of Negro Americans, it will be because blacks and whites have not truly understood the relationship between the varying groups that make up American society. Many, in both groups, see the society as far more monolithic and homogeneous than it has ever been. I am afraid that whites will be moved to fight to retain something that has never existed in this country, and the blacks will fight because they have not been convinced of the enormous scope for group diversity the society provides.

Almost every ethnic and racial group that has settled in this country has been "nationalistic" and "separatist," and the laws have permitted a level of separatism for many groups that has not yet been quite reached by American Negroes. Many groups have harboured and supported with money (and sometimes with armed volunteers) nationalist leaders interested in freeing or revolutionising their homelands, even when this was a matter of great embarrassment to the U.S.A. Most groups have maintained schools in their own tongue. Most groups have tried desperately to maintain the original home language, religion, and ethnic customs among their children in America. There has been one limit set on the free development of ethnic and racial groups in this country—territorial autonomy. But short of that, subtle and complex adjustments were made to accommodate a wide variety of differences.

The history of the gross prejudice and discrimination which almost all immigrant and racial groups have faced is well known; but we tend to be less aware of these "American adjustments" to accommodate a mixed population of different ethnic and racial groups. Thus, we have developed a pattern of political recognition, through the parties, in which groups of any substantial number get represented, through appointive and elective office. This system has worked well, without any laws requiring quotas, or specifications of "how much" and "what kind." There has been a pattern of economic integration in which groups have developed bases of economic independence. (Undoubtedly the general freedom this country has given to economic enterprises has aided this development.) Unfortunately, the ability to create such an independent economic base is now considerably limited by, among other things, the host of state and social licensing and regulatory requirements, trade union requirements, federal tax and accounting procedures, all of which today make it much harder for the less literate and sophisticated to become successful in business. We have allowed full freedom to religious organisation, and under the protection of religious organisation a wide range of cultural, social, political activities is carried on. We have given freedom to the creation of independent schools. All this has occurred even though a young patchwork nation has had the difficult task of fashioning a single national identity.

Compared with most countries that have tried to create themselves out of a mixed population, there has been a certain genius in the American style of confronting this problem. The principle has been: no formal recognition of the ethnic and racial groups, but every informal recognition of their right and desire to self-development, assimilation or integration at their own chosen rate, to an independent economic base, independent social, religious, and political institutions, and political recognition as part of a united country. The principle has often been broken: laws have been erected against certain groups—most massively in the case of Negroes, but also in the case of American Indians and Orientals; and we have often restricted the free and spontaneous development of various groups through movements of "Americanisation" and forced patriotism. But the most massive and inhumane breaks in these principles have in the end been recognized as "un-American," and wrong: slavery for the Negroes; "separate but equal" facilities for Negroes; public discrimination against Negroes; separate schools for the Chinese; land laws restricting the right of purchase by Japanese; the forced relocation of the Japanese and their loss of property; the immigration laws establishing quotas for peoples and races; attempts of states to ban private schooling. All these have in the end been overcome by courts and legislatures, and the basic principle—no public recognition of race or ethnicity; every private consideration of its reality and meaningfulness—has, in the end, prevailed.

Undoubtedly, to argue that the Negroes, who stand at the very heart of American civilisation as a cruelly harmed people, can be (and, indeed, have been in large measure) incorporated into this pattern, will appear to many an act of Pollyanna-ish refusal to face up to evil in American society. Professor Robert Blauner (of the University of California at Berkeley) has argued forcefully that there are certain "colonised" peoples in the United States who do not fit the ethnic pattern I have described; and these are the Negroes, the American Indians, and the Mexican Americans. According to this thesis, the ethnic pattern that permitted a self-regulated rate of integration into American life prevailed only for the European immigrant groups; and to a much more modest degree, it prevails for the Chinese and Japanese. But there was a different pattern for those peoples who were conquered or brought here as slaves. They have been "colonised," made inferior to the "settlers" in every part of life (political, economic, social, cultural), deprived of their power and "manhood"; and for them only the colonial pattern of rebellion, resistance, and forceful overthrow of settler dominance is meaningful. Thus Frantz Fanon's passionate argument for the significance of violence against the settlers in recreating the colonised as a people (in his *Wretched of the Earth*) speaks to American Negroes as it speaks to the colonised everywhere.

If Professor Blauner is right, then all that remains for us "non-colonised," as settlers, is to figure out how, when the colonised are so scattered among the settlers, we may give them the independence that will make them whole—or, if we refuse, wait for them to take it, or destroy the Union in the effort.

But I think he is wrong, and for one basic reason: whatever the relevance of the "colonisation hypothesis" to the past—when the Negroes lived as agricultural workers in the South, the Mexican Americans in villages in the South-west, the American Indians on the reservation—it is scarcely relevant today when three-quarters of American Negroes have moved to cities to become not only workers and servants but skilled workers, foremen, civil servants, professionals, white-collar workers of all types; when (at a slower rate) the same thing is happening to Mexican Americans; and when even Indians can free themselves from any politically inferior status by giving up the reservation and moving to the city (as more and more are doing). These moves are voluntary—or if involuntary to some extent, no more so than the migration of many other groups escaping political persecution and economic misery. They lead to the creation of a voluntary community of self-help institutions. They lead to a largely self-regulated rate at which group cultural patterns are given up and new ones adopted. It is all quite comparable to what happened to the European immigrant groups. Statistics which show the wide range of outcomes that we find in all groups, whether European immigrant, racial immigrant, or the so-called "colonised," are strong evidence for the similarity.

Undoubtedly all these groups still face prejudice and discrimination; but this still does not make the "colonial" analogy fit. Prejudice and discrimination, it seems, are endemic wherever different groups socially interact. Are the Algerian workers of the slum settlements around Paris now "colonised"? Are the Spanish and Turkish immigrant workers of Europe "colonised"? Or are they not, rather, immigrant workers facing the prejudice and discrimination and inferior living conditions strangers so often do? Nor are prejudice and discrimination insuperable obstacles to economic advancement and political power. If we were to have to wait for "the end of prejudice and discrimination" before we could say the Negro was truly a part of American society, we would have to wait forever. The issue is: what is the *level* of prejudice and discrimination, how is it formulated in *harmful policies,* what *official assistance* does it get, and to what extent (on the other hand) *does the state act against its private manifestations.* If we apply these tests, I believe, we will find that the "colonial analogy" as applied to the American Negro is meaningless. For there has been a steady decline in all forms of expressed prejudice against Negroes, as indicated in public opinion polls and in everyday behavior, and there has been stronger and stronger state action, outside the South (and even in some parts of the South) against manifestations of prejudice. Even the recent riots (as far as we can tell from the evidence) have led to no increase in prejudice or white antagonism.

The "colonial pattern" makes sense if one of two conditions prevails: there is a *legal* inferiority of the colonised, in which the settlers are given greater rights and prerogatives; or, even if there is a *formal* equality, in fact only tiny proportions of the colonised can reach high status in society. But this is not true of the Negro Americans, nor will it be true shortly of the Mexican Americans, and, if they so choose, of American Indians. The fact is that instead of keeping these groups out of privileged status most public policy and the programmes of most large private U.S. institutions is to bring them in larger and larger numbers into privileged status. What else is the meaning of the work of the Federal civil service in continually upgrading minority employees, of the colleges in recruiting them beyond the numbers that could normally qualify, of the various corporation programmes for training minority group executives and franchise holders? The scale of some of this is much too small; but the point is that its aim is to speed up a process of incorporating these groups into the mixed American society, rather than slowing it down.

The issue of whether Negro Americans are "colonised" or not is not to be settled by arguments between professors: it will be settled by Negro Americans themselves. If they view themselves as colonised, as suffering unbearable repression, as prevented from leading that degree of national and separate existence that they wish within the present prevailing American pattern, then they will do everything to break that pattern; and it will be up to all Americans to decide whether the awful suffering of wars of national unity is to be preferred to the dangers of separatism. No one who has thought deeply about the American Civil War (or what is happening in Nigeria now) will be able to give a pat answer to this question.

The issue, I think, is not yet settled, despite the extravagance of Negro militant rhetoric. Three factors still argue against the victory of the "colonial analogy" among Negroes.

1. The substantial numbers of Negroes who *are* integrated into American society—the civil servants, the white-collar workers, the union members, the political party members, the elected and appointed officials. They are truly in a tragic situation, and no one can say whether they will choose to identify with those who insist on seeing them as "colonised," or whether they will argue for integration into American life, along the pattern that I have described.

2. The second is the possibility that moderate and available social change can still pacify the militants. While making large separatist demands, they would perhaps be satisfied with more jobs, better jobs, more Negro appointed and elected officials, better schools, better housing, a more integrated and respectful police force, and that degree of separate institutional identity and control which the American pattern can tolerate. Certainly we have done too little in all these areas; but we have done a good deal, and we must do more, hoping that in effect the separatists are not really as intransigent as they sound.

3. The enormous difficulty of any territorial solution to the demand for separatism, and the difficulty of devising any alternative.

But there are indeed factors which argue for the success of the "colonial analogy" and the victory of separatism.

One is the enormous impact on Negro experience of past and present experience in the South, where Negroes were held captive and colonised indeed, and where there still remains the most unrelenting and sophisticated resistance to Negro equality in whole states and in large sections of the population. The colonial imagery of the South has been transported to East and West and to the great cities which are largely free of colonialism. There it struggles against the immigrant analogy—and, on the whole, it is losing. They shout, "We are still slaves" and "We want freedom" in the North, where the issue is neither slavery nor freedom.

The second is our failure to adopt rapidly enough new approaches to achieving effective equality for the Negro. While the immigrant analogy is still, to my mind, in large measure valid, it is not fully valid. Negro business must be created, subsidised, sustained, advised; job programmes must become better and more meaningful; the colleges must learn new techniques for incorporating large numbers of minority students, and the urban schools must undergo a transformation (though its nature is hard to define) in becoming effective with minority students. But all this is enormously demanding, so demanding indeed that we may not succeed. Mayor Lindsay, speaking to businessmen in New York—and he was perhaps the dominant liberal member of the Kerner Commission—has described what businessmen must do to make the hard-core unemployed effective:

> You've got to literally adopt this kind of employee, be responsible for his total condition 24 hours a day, seven days a week. . . . Adopt their families, a piece of the block where they live, a chunk of the city and its future. Know where they live, their economic condition, how their children are, whether there's a police problem, what the neighbourhood pressures are. If it's a woman, you have to know whether there's a male in the house and what her problems are. . . .
>
> The businessman who does hire the hard-core unemployed is going to be confronted with absenteeism, poor working habits, deficiencies in reading and writing, negative attitudes. . . .

If this is truly what businessmen and perhaps teachers must do effectively to employ or educate a substantial part of the minority population, we may simply not have the required degree of compassion, commitment, and capacity to succeed.

The third is the inability of both black and white to comprehend the character of the American pattern of group incorporation which has already had so many successes. On the white side, there is widespread fear of Negro separatism and Negro power, and it is a fear which, as I have suggested, fails to understand that every group has gone through (and some have retained) a substantial degree of separatism, and all have demanded (and many have obtained) political representation in appointive and elective office, and control over pieces of the political action. As long as the nation does not succumb to a society of rigid compartments and fixed quotas and reserved seats, Americans can go some distance in meeting separatist demands. If suburban towns can have their own school systems and police forces, then, to my mind, there is no good reason why certain parts of the larger city should not have separate school systems and police forces. In any case, when the authority of teachers and the police have been destroyed—and they have been, in large measure, destroyed in the ghetto areas—there is no alternative to some pragmatic adjustment, to the creation of new social forms.

On the black side—and here blacks are joined of course by many whites, both liberal and progressive—there is an equal failure to comprehend the relationships of groups to the larger American society. There is a failure to understand that even while prejudice and discrimination exist, groups and individuals can achieve their ends and a satisfying and respected place in the American social structure. There is a failure to understand that groups vary in their cultural characteristics and in the area and character of their achievements, and that the owlish insistence on some total equality of representation is to deny the significance of special achievements and characteristics. There will come a time when the special gifts of Negro Americans may mean massive representation in politics, or in the arts, even if today it tends to mean over-representation only in such areas as professional sport. But the special character of American group life—its acceptance of individual merit and capacity and its calculated arrangements for group character and pride—should not be destroyed by a demand for fixed quotas and their incorporation into legal and semi-legal arrangements.

After all, I believe, there is a failure to understand, on the part of black militants and their too-complaisant white allies, that there *is* an American society with a tremendous power to incorporate and make part of itself new groups, to their advantage and not to the advantage of the larger society, and that this is not a *white* society. I find nothing so sad as hearing universities denounced as white racist enclaves, corporations denounced as white racist enterprises, the government denounced as a white racist establishment. A hundred years ago, it could have been easily said these were all "English institutions," and yet Germans and Irish became part of them. Fifty years ago it could have been said these were all "Christian institutions," and yet Jews became part of them. Today, it is contended that they are white institutions—and yet this too is not true. They will become and remain white institutions only if Negro Americans insist on some total separateness as a nation, only if they decide that the American pattern of group life cannot include them.

25
The
Negro Revolution:
Possible
or Impossible?

Lewis M. Killian

From May 17, 1954, until the March on Washington and the passage of the 1964 Civil Rights Act, the battle over segregation forcibly reminded the American people that race relations constituted their foremost domestic problem. Just as the end of this battle seemed to be at hand, it became evident that there existed a crisis that was far graver than the desegregation controversy had ever been.

Fantastic gains had been made in terms of judicial interpretation of the Constitution, of federal legislation, and of public acceptance of the "qualified" Negroes of the black bourgeoisie. The federal antipoverty program represented a broad attack on the plight of the poor, white as well as nonwhite, not originally envisioned as part of the war on inequality. With the death of the doctrine of separate but equal, the nation had a new, albeit incomplete, commitment to an equality of opportunity that was color blind.

INTEGRATION: A FADING GOAL

Now it appeared, however, that integration had lost its luster as a goal. In practice it had turned out to mean the token integration of a minority of qualified Negroes into what remained a white man's society. For the majority of Negro Americans, handicapped by generations of isolation from the mainstream of American culture, the mere relaxing of racial barriers could not mean "Freedom

Reprinted by permission from Lewis M. Killian, *The Impossible Revolution,* New York: Random House, 1968, pp. 147–176 and 185–187. © Copyright 1968 by Random House, Inc.

Now." In acknowledgment of this new facet of the Negro's problem, Whitney Young called for "a decade of dedicated special effort" to close the gap created by three hundred years of preferential treatment of white citizens. He said, "At this point when the scales of justice are so grossly unbalanced it is impossible to balance them by simply applying equal weight."[1] James Farmer, militant leader of CORE, soon to be replaced by the even more militant Floyd McKissick, expressed the same theme in stronger terms. He said of the impoverished Negro, "Offering him equal rights, even equal opportunity at this late date without giving him a special boost is the kind of cruel joke American individualism has played on the poor throughout history. And so CORE and the Movement of which we are part planned compensatory and remedial programs to provide the necessary boost."[2]

THE NEW CRISIS

The new crisis in race relations arose from this basic fact: an emergency program giving Negroes preferential treatment on the basis of their color, not just the mere cessation of crude color discrimination, was necessary to make equality meaningful for Negroes. Two years of experience with seemingly radical civil rights laws and with the much-vaunted War on Poverty revealed that both attempts fell far short of the kind of special effort that was needed. The near-rebellion of Negro leaders at the White House planning conference and the ghetto riots in the summers of 1965, 1966, and 1967 symbolized how far a decade of favorable court rulings, nonviolent demonstrations, and federal legislation had fallen short of satisfying the rising expectations of the Negro masses. It was evident that the Negro protest movement was at a critical juncture. To continue to pick away at segregation, the symbol of the Negro's inferior social and economic position, was not enough. An assault on the *de facto* inequality of the Negro masses in employment, housing, and education was now mandatory. The tactics of protest that had been effective in desegregating lunch counters and parks and in producing federal legislation were being brought into question.

A NEW "NEW DEAL"

First, there was a widespread fear even among militant Negro leaders that the limits of reform through federal civil rights laws had been reached. Effective enforcement of existing laws, a spirit of compliance on the local level, and broader social legislation were now needed. The failure of Congress to pass the 1966 civil rights bill suggested that this law-making body, too, felt that there were enough civil rights laws on the books. There was also an obvious fear among civil rights leaders that demonstrations could no longer be disciplined and nonviolent. The riots of the summers of 1965, 1966, and 1967 had revealed to Negro leaders how little control they had over the inhabitants of the ghettos. This apprehension led to another fear that continuation of the strategy of protest would alienate significant white support of the Negro movement and lead to a pervasive and clear-cut definition of the movement as revolutionary.

Bayard Rustin, whose credentials as a militant leader were impeccable, stated the case for a new strategy and new tactics in his famous article entitled "From Protest to Politics; the Future of the Civil Rights Movement." The strategy that Rustin suggested was radical, for he called for a shift from civil rights as a target to a program of "qualitative transformation of fundamental institutions, more or less rapidly, to the point where the social and economic structure which they comprised can no longer be said to be the same."[3] In amplification he called for "radical programs for full employment, abolition of slums, the reconstruction of our educational system, new definitions of work and leisure. . . . Adding up the cost of such programs we can only conclude that we are talking about a refashioning of our political economy."[4] He suggested that the civil rights movement had run its course and would have to be replaced by a broader social movement devoted to economic and political reform. There should be, in effect, a new New Deal and an enlargement of the Great Society to gargantuan proportions.

Rustin's proposal for bringing about these reforms was also reminiscent of the early days of Roosevelt's New Deal. Reflecting an optimism generated by the Democratic sweep in the elections of 1964 he said:

> The future of the Negro struggle depends on whether the contradictions of this society can be resolved by a coalition of progressive forces which becomes the effective political majority in the United States. I speak of the coalition which staged the March on Washington, passed the Civil Rights Act and laid the basis for the Johnson landslide: Negroes, trade unionists, liberals and religious groups.[5]

It was in the same vein that, a few months later, A. Philip Randolph called for a one hundred and eighty-five billion dollar

Freedom Budget to make possible full equality for Negroes. Randolph made it plain that he believed only a comprehensive, far-reaching federal program could accomplish the job. Both Rustin and Randolph emphasized the benefits that would accrue to the entire economy if Negro poverty were abolished and, along with it, the poverty of all deprived Americans.

Such a solution as Rustin and Randolph proposed would indeed provide an unprecedented model of peaceful social change as an alternative to revolution. The dream of the New Deal, revived as the vision of the Great Society, would become reality as poverty, poor housing, and inferior schools were abolished for all Americans. In the process of achieving this reality, race consciousness would also be abolished as ambitious, upwardly mobile whites and Negroes made common cause against the ancient, impersonal evils of poverty, disease, and ignorance. A utopian society would be created without the ordeal of either a class war or a race war, but through a marvel of social engineering.

GUNS OR BUTTER: A PROBLEM OF VALUES

Nowhere is there evidence, however, that the majority of the American electorate is disposed to pay the price for such a feat. That the price would be small as compared to the cost of Viet Nam or the space program does not change the fact that the American public is willing to pay for these latter ventures, but not for the former. The affluence of the majority of the population accounts in part for this phenomenon. In the words of two sociologists Sidney Wilhelm and Elwin Powell: "Our society prospers without a redistribution of income in favor of the lower brackets—despite liberal slogans. In the military system we have an impersonal, omnipotent consumer of tremendous proportions that, in effect, supplants a mass purchasing power that could have been placed in the Negro's hands."[6]

Economists and sociologists who take a pessimistic view of the crisis of automation predict that the problems of "uselessness" that now confront the Negro masses will eventually be recognized as a problem of whites also. Wilhelm and Powell comment, "For the Negro is merely a weathervane for the future. *His* experience will be a common one for many whites now deprived of some sort of usefulness; *his* frustrations will become those for many others the longer we hesitate to confront the meaning of human dignity in an automated society."[7]

The time in which the anxiety of the Negro is generalized to a large segment of potential political allies in white society has not yet arrived. The congressional and gubernatorial elections of November 1966, showed the existence of a backlash against the welfare programs of the Great Society, not a readiness to expand these programs. At a time when a radical program of social and economic reform was needed, the American people opted for moderation. Daniel Moynihan observed after these elections, "It appears that the nation may be in the process of reproducing the tragic events of the Reconstruction: giving to Negroes the forms of legal equality but withdrawing the economic and political resources which are the bases of social equality."[8]

In the meantime, the urgent needs and the intense dissatisfaction of the aroused Negro masses remained a present fact. The Negro Revolution had to continue in some fashion unless race relations were to enter a new era of accommodation. This would be an era in which the black bourgeoisie would enjoy the fruits of the civil rights movement while a larger body of "unqualified" Negroes remained segregated and deprived until the next renewal of the Negro's struggle for equality.

GRADUALISM REVISITED

In addition to the doubt of whether a radical program of political and economic reform would be supported by the white majority, there was the question of whether it would gain the support of Negroes themselves. Gradualism is an inherent feature of a program of building a viable political coalition and then reforming a society through social engineering. Maximizing voter registration, winning victories at the polls, and then translating votes into policy is a tedious, often discouraging task lacking the drama of a demonstration.[9] It is questionable whether Negroes could be mobilized for the long pull required to make them a decisive political power in the nation. Victories would not be quick and sure and setbacks, such as those encountered in the November elections of 1966, would be recurrent. Even if an effective progressive coalition could be forged, the task of reshaping the economic order could be accomplished neither easily nor quickly within the framework of the American political structure. The system of checks and balances, horizontal and vertical, that has always emasculated bold, comprehensive programs of social reform would still operate to frustrate the grand designs of the social planners and to disillusion Negroes who place their faith in such programs. Most important, the shift of the Negro's struggle from protest to politics and then to social engineering would offer little hope of providing that sense of identity that he is still struggling desperately to achieve. It may be argued that during the first decade of demonstrations it has been the struggle itself that has sustained Negroes, not the token victories they have achieved. To suspend the protest in the hope that more significant victories would thereby be achieved in a remote future would be to deprive Negroes of their chief source of pride in the present time.

NEGRO PRIDE AND THE NEW NATIONALISM

It is to this emergent pride that the revolutionary alternative offered by the new radicals, the advocates of Black Power, appeals. It is the same sort of appeal offered by an earlier generation of new radicals when, beginning in 1956, they led Negroes into the streets in demonstrations rather than wait on the result of the long, unsatisfying, legalistic strategy of the NAACP. Not a diminution of conflict and tension, but an intensification of the struggle has always been the answer of the radicals to the impasses the Negro Revolution has seemed to meet. But this latest version of Negro radicalism is the most revolutionary that has appeared. It is defined by white Americans and even by erstwhile radical Negro leaders as unrespectable and revolutionary. This definition is accepted as valid by the new radicals; they make no obeisances to the idols of national unity, legalism, and nonviolence. Instead of a strategy of coalition politics within the framework of a two party system, they propose the creation of a black political party. The suggestion has even been advanced that the black ghettos become separate cities within the metropolitan areas where they are located. Instead of the preparation of Negroes for integration into a prosperous and presumably expanding white economy, the creation of a parallel Negro economy and the expulsion of white capitalists from the ghettos has been recommended. Most notably, an appeal to the white man's fear rather than to his love or his guilt is the underlying theme of Black Power. This theme is couched in terms of self-defense, but included in it is a total rejection of the white man's law. Stokely Carmichael made clear his rejection of white America and of its laws when he said:

> We can't be expected any more to march and
> get our heads broken to say to you that you are
> nice guys. You are not nice guys. We have found
> you out. You are rotten through and through, and

that's what we are saying. And, Alexander the Great was really Alexander the Barbaric, and that's what we're going to start from.[10]

I've had so much law and order, I swear before God I want some chaos! I want some chaos so bad I can taste it on the tip of my lips, because all I see is law and order everywhere I go. Law and order: from Canton, Mississippi to Watts, Los Angeles, to Harlem, to Chicago—nothing but law and order.[11]

Carmichael and SNCC are not the only new radicals to put their foot upon the path of black nationalism. With the election of Floyd McKissick as its leader, traditionally nonviolent CORE assumed a posture that could scarcely be distinguished from that of SNCC. The words written by James Farmer shortly before he left the leadership of CORE presaged this decision to continue the struggle without dependence on white allies or white love. Farmer spoke of a new "mood ebony" in CORE and explained it on the basis of three reasons. First, he spoke of the pride that had developed among Negroes through the achievements of the civil rights movement, saying, "We learned that what was needed was not *invisibility* but a valid and legitimate *visibility*." Second, he spoke of the influence of the masses of black people who were attracted to the banner of CORE. He said, "The integration-which-would-end-in-assimilation has never been a prime goal of the Negro masses. . . . Garveyism remains latent in the Negro ghetto, as our new recruits taught us." Finally, and most significantly, he declared, "The present day black nationalist groups . . . and figures like the late Malcolm X have influenced us perceptibly."[12] Then he advanced the psychological justification for the new strategy of black nationalism, saying:

Like the nationalists, we must try to conquer the Negro sense of inferiority. We feel this will be possible only when it is legitimate to be a black man in this country. And here CORE has a unique contribution to make. *CORE knows that Negro identity will emerge only in the midst of purposive and realistic effort in America. The nationalists offer doctrine. We must offer program as well.*[13]

Farmer proposed that CORE stick to its "proven techniques of nonviolent direct action." While he had praise for the Deacons for Defense and Justice, he saw more danger than advantage in Malcolm X's bolder doctrine of violence. But McKissick, Carmichael,

Brown, and even more so the host of unheralded local Negro leaders who amass arsenals of small arms and Molotov cocktails in the ghettos, apparently do not share Farmer's fear of a race war.

The prospects for the success of the appeal of the new radicals in producing a large following and drastically changing the structure of American society must be considered from three perspectives. The first considers the sort of psychological appeal that the spirit of total war against white society might have, particularly for the younger generation of Negroes. The second considers the societal conditions that might accentuate Negro impatience and enhance the appeal of the black nationalists. The third perspective requires an examination of the program that may be dimly discerned in the Black Power movement.

THE APPEAL OF CONFLICT

Peaceful, secure men usually look at conflict, particularly violent conflict, from a strictly utilitarian standpoint. Unless they are pacifists, they view conflict as a necessary evil that must always be justified in terms of achieving some greater good. Thus it is assumed that the conflict in which rational men will engage will be directed at an enemy who is responsible for the conditions that the aggressors desire to have corrected and that victory will have some logical chance of changing these conditions. Conflict that seems to have no such chance is seen as the blind striking out of irrational, frustrated people who, in their desperation, think not of the consequences of their actions. This sort of conflict would seem to serve no function for the participants beyond a temporary release of tension.

It is this sort of thinking that leads to warnings that an intensification of the Negro's struggle for identity and equality will only serve to bring down the wrath of a powerful white community upon the heads of Negroes. There is another theory that holds that seemingly hopeless conflict has value both for the individuals who participate in it and for the group of which they are a part. The gains for the individual and the group are much greater than mere relief of tension. This doctrine holds that a prideful group identity must be achieved through the birth pangs of conflict. It has been enunciated by the Algerian revolutionist Frantz Fanon in his book *The Wretched of the Earth*.[14] Although the book is about the colonized people of the African continent, many similarities may be found between the plight of the Negro masses in America and that of the native peoples of Africa. Fanon argues that only by taking up arms against the European powers in a total and violent struggle can the peoples of the Third World achieve national identities, national cultures, and national pride. In the preface to Fanon's book, Jean Paul Sartre says:

> He shows clearly that this irrepressible violence is neither sound and fury, nor the resurrection of savage instincts, nor even the effect of resentment: it is man recreating himself. . . . The native cures himself of colonial neurosis by thrusting out the settler through force of arms. When his rage boils over, he rediscovers his lost innocence and he comes to know himself in that he himself creates his self. . . . The rebel's weapon is the proof of his humanity. For in the first days of the revolt you must kill: to shoot down a European is to kill two birds with one stone, to destroy an oppressor and the man he oppresses at the same time: there remains a dead man and a free man; the survivor, for the first time, feels a *national* soil under his foot.[15]

Fanon explains how in his view the struggle to achieve nationhood is an essential ingredient of group consciousness and group unity. He says:

> But it so happens that for the colonized people this violence, because it constitutes their only work, invests their characters with positive and creative qualities. The purpose of violence binds them together as a whole, since each individual forms a violent link in the great chain, a part of the great organism of violence which has surged upward in recognition of the settler's violence in the beginning. The groups recognize each other and the future nation is already indivisible. The armed struggle mobilizes the people; that is to say, it throws them in one way and in one direction.
> The mobilization of the masses, when it rises out of the war of liberation, introduces into each man's consciousness the ideas of a common cause, of a national destiny and of a collective history. In the same way the second phase, that of the building-up of the nation, is helped on by the existence of this cement which has been mixed with blood and anger. Thus we come to a full appreciation of the originality of the words used in these under-devel-

oped countries. During the colonial period the people are called upon to fight against oppression; after national liberation, they are called upon to fight against poverty, illiteracy, and under-development. The struggle, they say, goes on. The people realize that life is an unending contest.[16]

The new radicals of the Negro Revolution, in contrast to strategists such as Bayard Rustin and A. Philip Randolph, are following this philosophy in placing Black Power at the top of the agenda and the war on cultural deprivation at the bottom. They would no longer have Negro Americans come as suppliants seeking the crumbs from the white man's table, ever conscious of their own inferiority. Like Fanon, they argue that pride and a sense of peoplehood must be achieved first if the black man is to enjoy real equality in a society that heretofore has condemned him to inferiority simply on the basis of his blackness. Carmichael speaks of the need of Negro Americans to overcome their own feelings of inferiority when he says:

> Black people in this country have to move to a position of psychological equality and that is very, very important. And they can't do that with white people getting everything for them. They have to confront the white power structure themselves, so that means that white allies will have to be pushed aside; we can no longer have white people getting poverty money for you—you have to get it yourself so that you know black people can do those things on their own—so that they don't always need somebody white to do it for them.[17]

One of the charges most frequently thrown at Negro Americans is that having lost their native African culture in slavery they have developed no culture of their own of which they could be proud. The whole notion of cultural pluralism implies that within the framework of the white man's society Negroes should learn to develop and take pride in their own cultural forms. These should be more than pale, shoddy imitations of the white man's culture. Fanon addresses himself indirectly to this notion also. Speaking of the development of national cultures in the emergent nations of Africa, he says:

> A frequent mistake, and one which is moreover hardly justifiable, is to try to find cultural expressions

for and to give new values to native culture within the framework of colonial domination. This is why we arrive at a proposition which at first sight seems paradoxical: The fact that in a colonized country the most elementary, the most savage and the most undifferentiated nationalism is the most fervent and efficient means of defending national culture. . . . The nation is not only the condition of culture, its fruitfulness, its continuous renewal, and its deepening. It is also a necessity. It is the fight for national existence which sets culture moving and opens to it the doors of creation. Later on it is the nation which will insure the conditions and framework necessary to culture.[18]

By the same token, it may be argued that a meaningful and satisfying Negro culture can come into existence in a pluralistic American society only through an antecedent state of black nationalism. In turn, it is through the myth of Black Power that the new radicals are attempting to create this black nationalism.

This is the logic of Black Power as this philosophy might be seen through the eyes of one who views Negro Americans as a colonial people and who has lost all faith in the willingness of white America to grant him real equality. Certainly there are individual black leaders, some enjoying national notoriety, others known only within their own ghetto neighborhoods, who have accepted the major part of this philosophy. By their logic, Watts, Newark, and Detroit were not senseless tragedies of nonrealistic conflict but minor victories in the war by black Americans to achieve identity.

The next phase of the racial crisis will consist of a contest between such leaders and more moderate Negro leaders, such as Martin Luther King, Jr., for the allegiance of the activists within the Negro population. How big a following the new radicals can attract, both to a compact, organized hard core and to a diffuse reserve of adherents who will jump into the fray whenever violence breaks out, will depend upon changes in the social and economic context.

ECONOMIC FACTORS

One development that would increase the number of desperate Negroes who would be responsive to this doctrine of disillusionment would be a further deterioration of the economic situation of the Negro masses. Continued inflation combined with a lag in the wage scales of unorganized workers and in welfare stipends would have this effect. Even greater economic cramp would be produced, and more quickly, by an economic recession. Even in a period of unprecedented affluence for the society as a whole unemployment among Negroes, particularly young people, remains alarmingly high. For the ghetto youth for whom James Baldwin, LeRoi Jones, and Claude Brown attempt to speak, depression conditions already exist. Were a cutback in employment added to the effects of automation, the army of potential revolutionary fighters would be augmented rapidly. But in another depression it would not be communism, Buy Black campaigns, or the Double Duty Dollar that would beckon to Negroes; it would be Black Power.

One event that could lead to a drastic economic readjustment in the United States would be a return to a peace economy as a result of American disengagement in Viet Nam. Were a reduction in military spending followed quickly by a shift of federal funds to the Freedom Budget, the utopian dream of Rustin and Randolph might be realized and the Negro Revolution terminated peacefully. If this did not happen, however, the end of the Viet Nam war might set the stage for the most violent phase of the Negro Revolution.

THE WAR IN VIET NAM AND THE NEGRO REVOLUTION

Many students of revolution have emphasized the close relationship between the involvement of a nation in an external war and the occurrence of a revolution. Chalmers Johnson proposes the term "accelerator" to designate an occurrence that catalyzes or throws into relief "the already existing revolutionary level of dysfunctions." Accelerators "do not of themselves cause revolution; but when they do occur in a system already bearing the necessary level of dysfunction . . . they will provide the sufficient cause of the immediately following revolution."[19]

Johnson identifies defeat in a foreign war as one of the most potent accelerators, noting, "Defeat in war, as an accelerator, shatters the myth of sovereignty, exacts sacrifices—even the supreme sacrifice—from a society's members for an unpopular system, and completes the crippling of an already creaking system; most important, it opens the doors to revolution because of its effects on the army."[20]

It is difficult to speculate about the relationship between the Negro Revolution, which so few Americans recognize as a real revolution, and the Viet Nam war, which officially is not a war! Analysis of the potential relationship between these two rests upon the assumption that there *is* a revolutionary situation in the United States and that the nation *is* engaged in a war, one in which defeat is possible. The analysis is complicated further by the fact that the American army in the field in Viet Nam is the most thoroughly integrated force in United States history; yet it is fighting an enemy that is "colored" and, like the Negro masses in the ghettos, poor. The Negro leaders most disenchanted with the American society have been quick to point this out.

American withdrawal from Viet Nam, if followed by a final victory for Ho Chi Minh, would constitute a military defeat for the United States, even though the divisions returned intact. It would appear that the United States, although still on its feet, had conceded a technical knockout after challenging Asian communism. Belief in the invincibility of the white hope of the West would be shaken, not only among other nations and peoples but perhaps among Americans themselves, including Negro Americans. The lives lost in battle, including a disproportionate number of Negro lives, would appear to have been sacrificed in vain. To the most alienated Negroes, the altar on which these black soldiers would have been sacrificed would be the white American's vain belief in white supremacy in world affairs.

Chalmers Johnson argues that it is the crippling effect on the army itself, making it an inadequate instrument for defense of the status quo, that makes defeat in war important as an accelerator. There are no indications that the regular army that might be retained after a reduction of overseas commitments would become an active or even passive abettor of revolutionary violence. It is more likely that the armed forces would remain a bulwark against the *success* of a revolution. But the citizen soldiers, those members of the wartime armed forces who are rapidly demobilized at the conclusion of hostilities, could very well be the precipitant for violent revolution. It is significant that all ten of the founders of the Deacons for Defense and Justice were veterans of Korea or World War II.[21]

Negro veterans might find that they had exchanged the deprivations of the battlefield for the poverty and the indignities of the ghetto. But these would be the most battle-hardened, heroic group of Negroes who had ever fought for America simply because they had been given the greatest opportunity for combat and heroism. Trained, battle-tested, and embittered they could be the source of the guerrilla army that a Negro leader would need for the task of disrupting an American society from which he was totally alienated. Thus any end of massive United States military involvement in Viet

Nam, even one coming as a result of token victory, could serve as an accelerator for the Negro Revolution.

A BATTLE PLAN FOR REVOLUTION

But what if RAM (Revolutionary Action Movement) or a more violent version of SNCC did become a rallying point for such an army? By what conceivable tactics could the impoverished denizens of the slums attack the might of the civil police and the armed forces of a rich, powerful, white society?

In Los Angeles, Newark, Cleveland, Detroit, and other cities, ghetto residents have already shown how effectively they can defy the police in what were essentially spontaneous, unorganized uprisings. It is true that these uprisings have been brought under control by military forces. But that in so many cities the National Guard had to be employed to restore order is a tribute to the power of Negro violence. Every time the National Guard has been employed to put down a riot, their intervention represented a victory for the rioters over the civilian police, the normal guardians of social peace in an American city.

Although the urban riots of the 1960's have so far stopped with the destruction of millions of dollars worth of private property and an inordinate drain on municipal and state budgets for the restoration of order, at least one blueprint for more widespread social disruption exists. The author of this blueprint is Robert F. Williams, who has been described as the spiritual godfather of RAM and premier of the African-American government in exile.[22] It is impossible to know just how much of a domestic following Williams has had since his flight from a federal warrant in 1961 led him first to Cuba, and then to Red China. There is no question, however, that his tactical ideas for a violent internal struggle, a minority revolution which could succeed in powerful America, are known and quoted by Negro extremists within the country. His belief that a minority revolution has a chance of succeeding in the United States rests upon his analysis of the vulnerability of American society as it is presently constituted. He says:

> The American society is a highly industrialized complex. A highly industrialized and mechanized system is also a very sensitive one. The more machinery required to serve a community, the greater the incidence of mechanical breakdown.

The more dependent a community is on mechanization, the more important it is for the wheels of industry to perpetually turn smoothly. The American mind has been conditioned to think of great calamities, wars, and revolutionary upheavals as taking place on distant soil. Because of the vast upper and middle classes in the U.S.A. that have grown accustomed to comfortable living, the nation is not psychologically prepared for massive violence and a sudden disruption of the essential agencies of the affluent society. The soft society is highly susceptible to panic.[23]

To produce this mechanical breakdown and generate panic, Williams recommends urban guerrilla tactics reminiscent of the methods used in Budapest during the Hungarian uprising. His brief but detailed description of the weapons and tactics is worth repeating.

> The weapons of defense employed by Afro-American freedom fighters must consist of a poor man's arsenal. Gasoline fire bombs (Molotov cocktails), lye or acid bombs (made by injecting lye or acid in the metal end of light bulbs) can be used extensively. During the night hours such weapons thrown from rooftops will make the streets impossible for racist cops to patrol. Hand grenades, bazookas, light mortars, rocket launchers, machine guns, and ammunition can be bought clandestinely from service men anxious to make a fast dollar. Freedom fighters in military camps can be contacted to give instructions on use.
>
> Extensive sabotage is possible. Gas tanks on public vehicles can be choked up with sand. Sugar is also highly effective in gasoline lines. Long nails driven through boards attached with long ends are effective to slow the movement of traffic on congested roads at night. This can cause havoc on turnpikes. Derailing of trains causes panic. Explosive booby traps on police telephone boxes can be employed. High-powered sniper rifles are readily available. Armor piercing bullets will penetrate oil storage tanks from a distance. Phosphorous matches (kitchen matches) placed in airconditioning systems

will cause delayed explosions which will destroy expensive buildings. Flame throwers can be manufactured at home. Combat experienced ex-service men can easily solve that problem.[24]

Some of the weapons Williams recommends have already been used in urban riots. Small extremist groups in several American cities have already demonstrated their ability to collect weapons. The continued failure of Congress to pass an effective law controlling the possession and sale of small arms makes the creation of such weapons caches a continuing possibility. Ironically, the National Rifle Association has given as one of its grounds for opposition to such a law the need for citizens to possess arms to defend themselves against mob violence.[25]

THE NEED FOR LEADERSHIP

But the mere availability of weapons and individuals desperate enough to use them is not sufficient for launching a revolutionary war. There must be centralized leadership and organization, what Chalmers Johnson has called "a rebel infrastructure" or "autonomous government."[26] Williams concedes this in his explanation of how his own small-scale insurrection in Monroe, North Carolina, in 1957 ended in failure after two days of violence. He said:

The lesson of Monroe teaches that effective self-defense on the part of brutally oppressed and terrorized people requires massive organization with central coordination. External oppressive forces must not be allowed to relieve the besieged racist terrorists. The forces of the state must be kept under pressure in many places simultaneously. The white supremacy masses must be forced to retreat to their homes in order to give security to their individual families.[27]

There is no question that one reason Negro destructiveness has not reached greater heights is the absence of organization and central coordination. Negro leadership in the United States, much like the leadership of the native fascist movement of the late thirties, is fragmented. It consists of many individual stars who spend as much time competing with one another for eminence as they do in promoting their common cause.

The individual leader or the leadership group who might lead the Negro Revolution into a phase of mass insurrection is not yet discernible. Such a person would have to combine charisma with organizational ability. Had he lived, Malcolm X might have been the type of leader who, with his lieutenants, would have been the nucleus for the building of a revolutionary army. It remains to be seen whether SNCC or CORE will produce a charismatic leader who can effectively challenge Martin Luther King, Jr., in capturing the imagination of large numbers of Negroes. It is doubtful that SNCC will constitute an adequate organizational vehicle because of its self-conscious emphasis on internal democracy.

During the summer of 1967, against the background of the infernos of Newark and Detroit, Black Power advocates began a struggle to achieve coordination. In July a national conference on Black Power brought together in Newark not only the extremist groups, but some members of more conservative civil rights organizations. That there is a Black Power element even in the NAACP was demonstrated by an attempted revolt of a group of Young Turks at the 1967 national convention of the organization. Later in the summer, Black Power forces displayed at least temporary unity and strength in forcing concessions from white delegates of the New Left at the National Conference on New Politics in Chicago. Significantly, James Forman, who had been temporarily eclipsed by Carmichael and Brown as a SNCC leader, came to the forefront again in this convention. Among the other Negro leaders present were King and his lieutenant, Ralph Abernathy, veterans like Forman of the nonviolent, interracial phase of the Negro Revolution.

The spirit of Black Power first welled up out of the ghetto and was enunciated by latecomers to the Negro Revolution, to the dismay of these early leaders. If this spirit of desperation begins to inspire members of the black bourgeoisie, as it is slowly doing, the reservoir of capable leadership will be enlarged. Cool-headed, sophisticated strategists may become available to supplement the efforts of the reckless agitators who now dominate the Black Power forces. Then the Negro Revolution will develop the rebel infrastructure that it now lacks.

The emergence of yet a new strong man of the Negro Revolution depends, however, not just upon the existence of capable leaders. It is also contingent upon the unpredictable occurrence of a dramatic event that might thrust one individual into the limelight. Such an event might create a new hero of a new phase of the Negro Revolution, just as King was propelled into a position of leadership by the drama of the Montgomery protest.

Such a leader, yet unknown, may be waiting in the wings for the incident that will make him the rallying point for the now divided radical Negro leadership. How much of a following would gather around such a strong man depends upon situational factors, both domestic and international. Even as he was denouncing the philosophy of Black Power, Martin Luther King, Jr. described one of the circumstances that might cause large numbers of Negroes to turn away from his relatively moderate and nonviolent leadership. He declared, "The burden now shifts to the municipal, state, and federal authorities and all men in seats of power. If they continue to use our nonviolence as a cushion for complacency, the wrath of those suffering a long chain of abuses will rise. The consequence can well be unmanageable and persistent social disorder and moral disaster."[28]

The desperation of King's appeals for a continued adherence to the tactics of nonviolence seem to suggest that he fears that his own star is setting.* At the time his star was clearly rising, it was observed, "Negroes demand of protest leaders constant progress. The combination of long-standing discontent, and a new-found belief in the possibility of change produces a constant state of tension and aggressiveness in the Negro community."[29]

At this time certain situational factors giving the advantage to the more militant Negro leaders were identified. One was "the tendency of Negroes and white liberals to lionize the leader who displays aggressiveness and courage in defying the white power structure in his community." A second was, "the nationwide and even worldwide press coverage that such a leader is likely to receive, particularly if his tactics are met by illegal violence or police brutality." Then as now, it was observed that Negro leaders "realize that they must combat the suspicion among their followers that they have sold out to the white communitty and are permitting themselves to be used to preserve the status quo."[30] Martin Luther King, Jr., must today contend against the same situational forces that brought him to prominence as the greatest Negro leader since Booker T. Washington. The demands for ever greater militance and for constant proof of willingness to defy the white man continue to produce increasingly radical Negro leaders. Today King must defend himself against the charge that he is a modern-day Booker T. Washington whose leadership depends upon his acceptability to the white people. If the demand for militance produces Negro leaders even more militant than King, all omens indicate that

---

* *Editor's Note:* This selection was originally published prior to King's assassination.

such leaders will be advocates of violent, not nonviolent, resistance.

As has been pointed out, continued inflation or the occurrence of an economic recession could enhance the advantage that the new radicals already enjoy in appealing to the Negro masses. Even if American society continues to enjoy its precarious prosperity, such leaders will still have an advantage. Emergency action, not a business-as-usual approach, is required to reduce the frustration that is generated by the problems of race and poverty. It is just such a complacent, business-as-usual philosophy that Negro leaders, both moderate and radical, are already denouncing. The moderate leaders, such as Young, Wilkins, King, and Randolph, show even greater concern about the lack of responsiveness of the American body politic to the great needs than do the new radicals. They realize that they cannot maintain their tenuously held positions of leadership unless the Negro Revolution moves off dead center. The movement took a sudden, but nonviolent, spurt forward in 1960 when the sit-ins resolved the impasse created by the failure of the legal tactics of the NAACP to produce change at a greatly accelerated rate. The next spurt forward might well be in the direction of violence.

NEGRO AEMRICANS AND INTERNATIONAL RELATIONS

The faith of the new radical leaders and their followers in the desirability and feasibility of more aggressive, violent power tactics will be related also to world affairs. Many of these leaders see the Negro Revolution as part of the rise of the Third World. In the words of Harold Isaacs:

> Negroes accustomed always to feeling the big winds blowing against them now begin to feel the new sensation of having the wind at their backs. . . . Great and important things happening to millions of people all over the world affected what was happening to them and what happened to them had become important to everyone.[31]
> Frustrated Negroes are not the only ones, after all, who fear that Western white society is plunging towards some unimaginable hell, but Negroes in America do have their peculiarly equivocal status to resolve in their minds as they contemplate these prospects. Negroes of every estate have at one time or another exulted when some outside force

has dealt white America a blow, have seen the Japanese, the Russians, or the Afro-Asians at the U.N. as acting somehow for *us* against *them,* and at every crisis in our history for half a century they have had to steady themselves with reminders about which, after all, was which. The deep and abiding identification of Negroes with America that has been maintained despite these feelings has had to persist in the face of a society's deep and abiding refusal to identify itself with Negroes.[32]

Thus the relative strength, prestige, and popularity of the United States in reference to Red China, the Afro-Asian nations, the United Nations, the emerging nations of Africa and Southeast Asia, and the sometimes democratic, sometimes communistic, revolutionary parties of Latin America, will influence the extent to which Negro Americans are willing to give American society yet another chance to prove its willingness to count them in. Even if the United States can maintain its position of military might, *sans* popularity, Negro Americans would find it extremely difficult to maintain their identification with a white American fortress standing, like the Union of South Africa, in defiance of a world in which the colored two-thirds of the population play an increasingly influential role.

In 1967, a significant symptom of a possible weakening of Negro identification with what is perceived as an aggressive America appeared in the commitment of Martin Luther King, Jr., to the peace movement. Although his motives were different, King's move brought him closer to the anti-Establishment position of Stokely Carmichael. At the same time, it created a serious rift between King on the one hand, and Whitney Young and Roy Wilkins on the other, further dividing and weakening the moderate element of Negro leadership.

THE FAITH OF THE ANARCHIST

Barring an all-out war between Communist China and the United States, how could the most optimistic Negro revolutionaries, without prospect of outside aid, hope literally to overthrow the white man's rule? This is the question that logical, cautious men, not revolutionary leaders, might ask. Confident in the faith that, with organization and the tactics of urban guerrilla warfare, they could bring the American social system to a state of chaos, the revolutionary leaders leave to a later date consideration of what sort of social structure could be rebuilt from a disorganized America in which white supremacy had been proven untenable.

One of the major elements which Howard Elinson identifies in the new radical leadership of the Negro Revolution is the new anarchists who, he points out, play an important part in SNCC, and in the Congress of Racial Equality in some areas. The important thing to recognize about the new anarchists and the approach they represent is the *absence* of a program for societal reconstruction. As Elinson says, "The goals and principles of the new anarchists are extremely difficult to describe, partly because the movement is committed to an ideology of nonideology; they are prone to deny that they have any set program."[33] To the extent that a new generation of Negro revolutionary leadership accepts the philosophy of the new anarchists, their concern will be with tearing down the established order, not with devising a new order. The building of a new order would be left to the operation of their ideal of participatory democracy.

A RACE AGAINST TIME

The United States is engaged in a dangerous race against time. It is a race against the day that the majority of Negroes decide that the future must be better than the present that white America offers them. The new radicals among Negro leaders are playing an equally dangerous game, however. White America has not reacted to the social disruption and the threats of even greater violence by taking heroic measures to redress the grievances that every Negro leader points to as the basic cause of Negro protests. The demand for integration that dominated the movement for so many years has been met with an ingeniously engineered tokenism, so frustrating as to cause many Negro leaders to abandon integration as a value. The demand for relief of Negro poverty has been met by an antipoverty program that has become bogged down in the morass of patronage and power politics. This program now is threatened with retrenchment because of a popular demand to hold the line of federal expenditures while still maintaining the military efforts in Viet Nam. Hence, the warnings of continued and greater violence to come are likely to be fulfilled. The warning of de Tocqueville, voiced over a century ago, remains both timely and ominous:

If ever the free institutions of America are destroyed, that event may be attributed to the unlimited authority of the majority, which may at some future time urge the minorities to desperation, and oblige them to have recourse to physical force. Anarchy will then be the result, but it will have been brought about by despotism.[34]

There is every indication that the white electorate and its elected representatives will react to continued threats and to more violence in the streets not by a renewed effort to understand and alleviate the plight of underprivileged Negroes, but by reactionary measure to suppress these disorders. Given a choice between a massive freedom budget and a police state, the American electorate is more likely to choose the latter. The tide may have turned in the direction of a police state when, in the Eighty-Ninth Congress, the House of Representatives passed the so-called antiriot amendment to the civil rights bill while failing to pass the bill itself. Moynihan saw in the results of the elections of November, 1966, "a bruising declaration that the electorate is fed up to the teeth with demonstrations and riots. . . ."[35]

The simple truth, too often overlooked in optimistic analyses of the racial crisis in America, is that neither white nor black Americans are a breed of angels. They are not set aside from the people of other nations and other tribes by superior rationality or greater tenderness toward one another. Despite repeated exposés of the organization's utter perversion of Christianity and Americanism, white Americans have allowed the Ku Klux Klan to rise again and again to the point where it could terrorize whole communities. Less than twenty years ago, McCarthyism put the nation into battle against an enemy whose visibility was far less than that of the forthright, defiant black extremists of the present day. In the hard-core states of the Deep South, racist politicians still find it politically profitable to run on platforms proposing to turn back the clock of race relations, not just to stop further progress. In the city of Chicago, in the summer of 1966, white Americans responded to Martin Luther King's latest campaign of nonviolence by shouting "white power" and contributing to the war chest of the late George Lincoln Rockwell's American Nazi Party.

During the nonviolent phase of the Negro Revolution the majority of those white Americans who pride themselves on their Christian love have found it difficult to extend this love to Martin Luther King, Jr., and the middle-class Negro youth of the sit-ins and the picket lines. In the future, they will face the ultimate challenge to their capacity for Christ-like love as they are confronted by Negro leaders who talk of hate, not love, for the white man, and by the unlovely publicans and sinners of the Negro lower class. There is no assurance that the commitment of the majority of white Americans to democratic values and the forgiving spirit of Christ can stand the challenge of Black Power.

Nor is there assurance that Negro Americans will accept the verdict of logic that a Negro Revolution is, indeed, impossible in twentieth-century America. How much longer will they settle for whatever white Americans are willing to give them? From the lips of a traditional hero of white America, they have the battle cry, "Give me liberty or give me death!" They have their own heroes in Nat Turner, Denmark Vesey, and Harriet Tubman, and even in the street fighters of Detroit, Newark, and Watts. The new radical leaders can point to the failure of the conciliatory strategy of Booker T. Washington and Martin Luther King, Jr., to achieve the goal of freedom for Negroes. They can couch their own appeals in terms of a return to the strategy of power advocated by Frederick Douglass and W. E. B. DuBois. Even faced with the possibility of a fascist America dedicated to preventing Negroes from achieving their goals regardless of the cost to American democracy, they can harken to the yet unheeded appeal of Claude McKay, voiced in the thirties.[36]

> If we must die, let it not be like hogs,
> Hunted and penned in an inglorious spot,
> While round us bark the mad and hungry dogs,
> Making their mock at our accursed lot.
> If we must die, O let us nobly die,
> So that our precious blood may not be shed
> In vain; then even the monsters we defy
> Shall be constrained to honor us though dead!
> O Kinsman! We must meet the common foe!
> Though far outnumbered let us show us brave,
> And for their thousand blows deal one death blow!
> What though before us lies the open grave?
> Like men we'll face the murderous, cowardly pack,
> Pressed to the wall, dying, but fighting back!

Assessment of the countervailing power that the white Establishment could muster to oppose even the best organized revolution of Black Power makes the Negro Revolution seem indeed to be the Impossible Revolution. That such a revolution might be attempted in the face of overwhelming odds and without regard to the terrible consequences is not at all impossible.

Footnotes

1 Whitney Young, Jr., *To Be Equal* (New York: McGraw-Hill, 1964), p. 247.

2 James Farmer, *Freedom—When?* (New York: Random House, 1965), p. 170.

3 Bayard Rustin, "From Protest to Politics: The Future of the Civil Rights Movement," *Commentary* (February 1965), p. 28.

4 *Ibid.*

5 *Ibid.*, p. 27.

6 Sidney Wilhelm and Elwin Powell, "Who Needs the Negro?" *Trans-Action,* Vol. I (September–October, 1964), p. 6

7 *Ibid.*

8 Daniel P. Moynihan, "The President and the Negro: The Moment Lost," *Commentary* (February 1967), p. 31.

9 See Donald R. Matthews and James W. Prothro, *Negroes and the New Southern Politics* (New York: Harcourt, Brace & World, 1966).

10 Stokely Carmichael, "Black Power: The Widening Dialogue," *New South,* Vol. 21 (Summer 1966), p. 67.

11 *Ibid.*, p. 76.

12 Farmer, *op. cit.*, pp. 92–93.

13 *Ibid.*, p. 106.

14 Frantz Fanon, *The Wretched of the Earth,* Preface by Jean-Paul Sartre, translated from the French by Constance Farrington (New York: Grove Press, 1963), p. 10. Copyright © 1963 by Presence Africaine. Published by Grove Press, Inc. Quotations used by permission of the publisher.

15 *Ibid.*, pp. 18–19.

16 *Ibid.*, p. 73.

17 Carmichael, *op. cit.*, p. 66.

18 Fanon, *op. cit.*, pp. 196–97.

19 Chalmers Johnson, *Revolution and the Social System* (Stanford: The Hoover Institution on War, Revolution, and Peace, 1964), p. 12.

20 *Ibid.*, p. 14.

21 See Charles C. Moskos, Jr., "Racial Integration in the Armed Forces," *American Journal of Sociology,* Vol. 72 (September 1966), pp. 132–48.

22 See Russell Sackett, "Plotting a War on Whitey," *Life* (June 10, 1966), pp. 101–02.

23 Robert F. Williams, "For Effective Self Defense," in Francis L. Broderick and August Meier, eds., *Negro Protest Thought*

in the Twentieth Century (New York: Bobbs-Merrill, 1965), p. 329. Quoted by permission of the publisher.

[24] *Ibid.,* p. 331. Quoted by permission of the publisher.

[25] "Who Guards America's Homes?" editorial in *The American Rifleman* (May 1967), p. 16.

[26] Johnson, *op. cit.,* p. 62.

[27] Williams, *op. cit.,* p. 331. Quoted by permission of the publisher.

[28] Martin Luther King, Jr., "It is Not Enough to Condemn Black Power," advertisement in *The New York Times,* July 26, 1966.

[29] Lewis M. Killian, "Leadership in the Desegregation Crisis: An Institutional Analysis," in Muzafer Sherif, ed., *Intergroup Relations and Leadership* (New York: John Wiley and Sons, 1962), p. 159.

[30] *Ibid.,* pp. 160–61.

[31] Harold Isaacs, *The New World of Negro Americans* (New York: John Day, 1963), p. 50.

[32] *Ibid.,* p. 339.

[33] Howard Elinson, "Radicalism and the Negro Movement," in Raymond J. Murphy and Howard Elinson, eds., *Problems and Prospects of the Negro Movement* (Belmont, Calif.: Wadsworth, 1966), p. 361.

[34] Alexis de Tocqueville, *Democracy in America,* trans. Henry Reeve (New York: D. Appleton, 1899), Vol. 1, pp. 286–87.

[35] Moynihan, *op. cit.,* p. 31.

[36] "If We Must Die," in Claude McKay, *Selected Poems of Claude McKay* (New York: Bookman Associates, 1953). Permission to reprint granted by Twayne Publishers.

Selected Bibliography

The gravity of contemporary race relations has stimulated a great deal of scholarly interest in black studies; numerous works of varied quality have been published in recent years, and it appears that this outpouring will continue. No attempt has been made here to provide a comprehensive bibliography of the immense volume of material related to the topics dealt with in this reader. Instead, only those books have been listed which are, in the editor's view, of central importance to an understanding of the recent development of black politics and protest in the United States. For a more comprehensive bibliography, see Elizabeth W. Miller, *The Negro in America: A Bibliography,* Cambridge, Mass., Harvard University Press, 1966.

I. General

Frazier, E. Franklin, *The Negro in the United States,* rev. ed., New York, Macmillan, 1957.

Myrdal, Gunnar, *An American Dilemma: The Negro Problem and Modern Democracy,* New York, Harper & Row, 1944.

Parsons, Talcott, and Kenneth B. Clark (eds.), *The Negro American,* Boston, Houghton Mifflin, 1966.

Silberman, Charles E., *Crisis in Black and White,* New York, Random House, 1964.

II. Black History

Elkins, Stanley M., *Slavery: A Problem in American Institutional and Intellectual Life,* 2d ed., Chicago, University of Chicago Press, 1968.

Franklin, John Hope, *From Slavery to Freedom: A History of Negro Americans,* 3rd ed., New York, Knopf, 1967.

Jordan, Winthrop D., *White over Black: American Attitudes Toward the Negro, 1550–1812,* Chapel Hill, University of North Carolina Press, 1968.

Litwack, Leon F., *North of Slavery: The Negro in the Free States, 1790–1860,* Chicago, University of Chicago Press, 1961.

Meier, August, and Elliott M. Rudwick, *From Plantation to Ghetto: An Interpretive History of American Negroes,* New York, Hill and Wang, 1966.

Woodward, C. Vann, *The Strange Career of Jim Crow,* 2d ed., New York, Oxford, 1966.

III. The Ghetto

Brown, Claude, *Manchild in the Promised Land,* New York, Macmillan, 1965.

Clark, Kenneth B., *Dark Ghetto: Dilemmas of Social Power,* New York, Harper & Row, 1965.

Drake, St. Clair, and Horace R. Clayton, *Black Metropolis,* rev. ed., New York, Harper & Row, 1962.

Liebow, Elliott, *Tally's Corner: A Study of Negro Street-corner Men,* Boston, Little, Brown, 1966.

IV. The Development of Black Pride

Cleaver, Eldridge, *Soul on Ice,* New York, McGraw-Hill, 1968.

Grier, William H., and Price M. Cobbs, *Black Rage,* New York, Basic Books, 1968.

Kardiner, Abram, and Lionel Ovesey, *The Mark of Oppression: Explorations in the Personality of the American Negro,* New York, Norton, 1951.

Karon, Bertram P., *The Negro Personality: A Rigorous Investigation of the Effects of Culture,* New York, Springer, 1958.

Pettigrew, Thomas F., *A Profile of the Negro American,* Princeton, Van Nostrand, 1964.

V. Black Politics

Bailey, Harry A., Jr., (ed.), *Negro Politics in America,* Columbus, Merrill, 1967.

Donovan, John C., *The Politics of Poverty,* New York, Western Publishing, 1967.

Keech, William R., *The Impact of Negro Voting: The Role of the Vote in the Quest for Equality,* Chicago, Rand McNally, 1968.

Ladd, Everett Carl, Jr., *Negro Political Leadership in the South,* Ithaca, N.Y., Cornell University Press, 1966.

Matthews, Donald R., and James W. Prothro, *Negroes and the New Southern Politics,* New York, Harcourt, Brace & World, 1966.

Wilson, James Q., *Negro Politics: The Search for Leadership,* New York, Free Press, 1960.

VI. Black Protest

Broderick, Francis L., and August Meier (eds.), *Negro Protest Thought in the Twentieth Century,* Indianapolis, Bobbs-Merrill, 1965.

Burns, W. Haywood, *The Voices of Negro Protest in America,* New York, Oxford, 1963.

King, Martin Luther, Jr., *Stride Toward Freedom,* New York, Harper & Row, 1958.

King, Martin Luther, Jr., *Why We Can't Wait,* New York, Harper & Row, 1963.

Lewis, Anthony, and *The New York Times, Portrait of a Decade: The Second American Revolution,* New York, Random House, 1964.

Lincoln, C. Eric, *The Black Muslims in America,* Boston, Beacon Press, 1961.

Lomax, Louis E., *The Negro Revolt,* New York, Harper & Row, 1962.

Warren, Robert Penn, *Who Speaks for the Negro?* New York, Random House, 1965.

Zinn, Howard, *SNCC: The New Abolitionists,* Boston, Beacon Press, 1964.

VII. The Black Revolution

The Autobiography of Malcolm X, New York, Grove Press, 1965.

Barbour, Floyd B. (ed.), *The Black Power Revolt,* Boston, Porter Sargent, 1968.

Carmichael, Stokely, and Charles V. Hamilton, *Black Power: The Politics of Liberation in America,* New York, Random House, 1967.

Fanon, Frantz, *The Wretched of the Earth,* New York, Grove Press, 1963.

Killian, Lewis M., *The Impossible Revolution?* New York, Random House, 1968.

McEvoy, James, and Abraham Miller (eds.), *Black Power and Student Rebellion*, Belmont, Calif., Wadsworth, 1969.

Marine, Gene, *The Black Panthers,* New York, New American Library, 1969.

Masotti, Louis H., and Don R. Bowen (eds.), *Riots and Rebellion: Civil Violence in the Urban Community,* Beverly Hills, Calif., Sage, 1968.

Scheer, Robert (ed.), *Eldridge Cleaver: Post-Prison Writings and Speeches,* New York, Random House, 1969.